the
truth teller

the
truth teller

ANGELA
HUNT

WestBow
PRESS

A Division of Thomas Nelson Publishers
Since 1798

visit us at www.westbowpress.com

Published by WestBow Press, Nashville, Tennessee. All rights reserved. No part of
this book may be reproduced, stored in a retrieval system, or transmitted in any
form or by any other means—electronic, mechanical, photocopy, recording,
scanning, or any other—except for brief quotations in printed reviews, without
prior permission from the publisher.

WestBow Press books may be purchased in bulk for educational, business, fund-
raising, or sales promotional use. For information, please e-mail
SpecialMarkets@ThomasNelson.com.

Scripture quotations are taken from the Holy Bible, New Living Translation,
copyright © 1996. Used by permission of Tyndale House Publishers, Inc.,
Wheaton, Illinois 60189. All rights reserved.

Publisher's Note: This novel is a work of fiction. Names, characters, places, and inci-
dents are either products of the author's imagination or used fictitiously. All characters are fictional, and any similarity to people living or dead is purely coincidental.

Library of Congress Cataloging-in-Publication Data

Hunt, Angela Elwell, 1957–
   The truth teller / Angela Hunt.
     p. cm.
   ISBN 1-59554-047-4 (trade pbk.)
   1. Widows—Fiction. 2. Pregnant women—Fiction. 3. Genetic
engineering—Fiction. 4. Truthfulness and falsehood—Fiction. I. Title.
PS3558.U46747T78 2005
813'.54—dc22

2005025527

Printed in the United States of America
05 06 07 08 09 RRD 9 8 7 6 5 4 3 2 1

publisher's note

Dear Reader—

You hold in your hands a novel that was ahead of its time in many ways. *The Truth Teller* was first published in 1999 and brought readers into the world of genetic manipulations in a very personal way. Many of its themes and topics are more timely today than they were seven years ago.

Where most novels that deal with genetics get bogged down in clinical details, Angela Hunt always puts story first. So the core of this novel is a mother's love and how far a parent will go to protect her child.

Of course, Angela has long been praised for creating novels where readers know to "expect the unexpected"—and this novel is no exception. There are enough twists and turns here to keep you on the edge of your seat through the entire novel.

WestBow Press is proud to reintroduce this powerful novel to a new generation of fiction fans. Enjoy the story!

Publisher, WestBow Press

author's note

"Journeys," writes Lawrence Durrell, "like artists, are born and not made. A thousand differing circumstances contribute to them, few of them willed or determined by the will—whatever we may think."

Each of us begins our life journey as immature infants. We grow to an age of understanding; we grapple with God and man. As creations formed in the image of God, we exercise free will to deny, ignore, or accept Truth. And all the while, we follow a path God *knew* we would choose.

And as we walk, our life-paths cross others. This is the story of one path and those that intersected it.

The path of the Truth Teller.

"Make us choose the harder right instead of the easier wrong, and never to be contented with half truth when whole truth can be won. Endow us with courage that is born of loyalty to all that is noble and worthy, that scorns to compromise with vice and injustice and knows no fear when right and truth are in jeopardy."

—From the "Cadet Prayer" repeated every Sunday in chapel services at West Point

[BOOK ONE]

chapter 1

A crimson maple leaf swung from the sky and came to rest on the tip of Lara's best black shoes. She stared at the juxtaposition of ebony and red as the minister's voice droned beneath the whisper of an autumn wind: "Let not your heart be troubled; you believe in God, believe also in Me. In My Father's house are many mansions . . ."

She studied the hues of darkness and blood. Michael never painted in those colors. He preferred the bright oranges and pinks of a flaming sunset, the glowing greens and warm browns of wood and earth. Michael's paintings always shimmered with *life*.

The wind freshened, blowing the leaf from her shoe and rattling the brittle pages of the minister's prayer book. He continued, undisturbed: "Forasmuch as it has pleased Almighty God to take unto himself the soul of our dear brother Michael . . ."

Lara lifted her gaze, pleased that so many had followed from the church to the graveside. This little cemetery overlooked the park where she and Michael had enjoyed so many sunsets; she could even see the gabled roof of their town house from this sheltered hilltop. In the days ahead it might bring her comfort to know Michael was nearby . . .

But he wasn't, not really. She had seen his soul take flight; she had watched in wonder as his face, etched with lines of weariness and pain, brightened at the exhalation of that last breath. A shining look of joy and certainty filled his countenance as he stared at something she couldn't see, and the briefest smile lifted the corners of his mouth. Then, in an instant, his body relaxed. And he was gone.

Strange, how much grief felt like love. In the days since his death, her heart had been doing somersaults at the mention of his name, just as it

3

had in college when Michael looked her way. She walked around the apartment in a sort of love-struck daze, one ear cocked toward the telephone as if he might call. Yesterday her palms had grown moist when she found one of his scribbled grocery lists under the car seat. She tucked it into her purse, as thrilled with it as with the love note she'd once found tucked into her chemistry textbook.

Everyone said she was holding up well, and no one seemed surprised at her dry eyes. After all, she was a medical professional, and she had certainly known the end was coming. The one silver lining in the cloud of cancer was that it gave families time to say good-bye.

But how could she say good-bye when she was falling in love with her husband all over again?

She tore her eyes from the minister's little black book and let her gaze rove over the assembled guests. Michael's artsy friends from the local university were here, as well as most of her coworkers from the clinic. Connor O'Hara, their next-door neighbor, stood alone, his hands folded in respectful dignity. A handful of elderly people from church stood together in a knot, and a peevish little voice inside Lara wondered if they attended funerals out of pure and simple relief that it wasn't their time to go. Maybe it was a matter of plain common sense. If you were living in the twilight of your life, might as well check out your potential eternal neighbors. The funeral would give you something to talk about when you greeted the folks who lived in the heavenly mansion-next-door.

Hey, that was some sermon the preacher preached for you, Michael. Made me homesick for heaven just to hear him talk!

"I am the resurrection and the life. He who believes in Me, though he may die, he shall live. And whoever lives and believes in Me shall never die . . ."

A sharp sob broke into the minister's words, and Lara's gaze shifted to Michael's mother. Eva was sobbing into a wad of tissues, the brim of her hat betraying the trembling that rose from inside her. Something softened in Lara's heart. She took a side step toward her mother-in-law and felt Eva's iron frame sag a little as Lara's arm slipped around her shoulders.

". . . so in Christ all shall be made alive. Death is swallowed up in victory. O Death, where is your sting? Thanks be to God, who gives us the victory through our Lord Jesus Christ."

The minister paused, then stepped back, bowing his head. The service was done.

Lara squeezed Eva's shoulder, then released her and stepped forward to touch the burnished casket. A beautiful spray of long-stemmed roses, Eva's gift, covered the wooden surface, and Laura paused by the heart of the floral arrangement. She drew a breath to speak, but could not. Her knees felt as weak and trembly as they had the first time Michael kissed her.

Forsaking speech, she pulled the tiny pair of baby sneakers from her purse, set them in the midst of the roses, then took Eva's arm and led her away.

chapter 2

Lemuel Reis pressed his sweaty palms to the smooth leather of the satchel in his lap as the Lear jet taxied to the end of a pristine runway, then gently turned its sleek nose toward the steady lights of a terminal that rose from the darkness like a jeweled tiara. Flying always made Lemuel nervous, and the bumpy flight over the Octzaler Alps had sent panic rioting with him. He had made four trips to the lavatory in the past hour, but Devin didn't seem to have noticed.

Across the cabin, Devin Sloane was leaning forward—his aristocratic, sharply handsome face hovering near the window like a child's. "Fifty-three centuries," he murmured, probably more to himself than to Lemuel. "Thirty-three centuries before Christ. He lived before the great pyramids, before the Egyptians began to use papyrus, before the Bronze Age. Sumerian civilization was at its height when he walked the earth; King Memes the Fighter had yet to unite upper and lower Egypt. What could he have known, this man?"

"It's a pity his brain can't be dissected," Lemuel remarked, resisting a fresh wave of nausea as an image of desiccated brain matter rose before his eyes. "I hear the Austrians are quite vehement about protecting him even though—"

"His brain can wait." Devin turned to Lemuel, a look of implacable determination on his face. "It has waited fifty-three hundred years; it will wait until technology is able to assess its patterns and roadmap our friend's existence. When we are ready, we will plumb its depths and know all he knew. But now"—he turned toward the window again—"it's not his brain that interests me."

The lights aboard the jet flickered as the pilot's voice hissed over the intercom. "They are ready for you, Mr. Sloane. A car is waiting to take you into Innsbruck."

Devin stood, slipped into his cashmere overcoat, and grinned at Lemuel. "You look a little green," he said, adjusting the coat's collar. "Lift your thoughts above your stomach, my friend, and consider the possibilities. I'm taking you to meet a man greater than either of us."

Sloane swept down the aisle, pausing at the cockpit to speak to the pilot as Lemuel struggled into his coat. Why hadn't he made his parents happy and entered rabbinical school? He would have enjoyed a rabbi's life; the dissection of the *Talmud* and *Torah* seemed infinitely preferable to what awaited him in this place. But Devin Sloane's attention had been flattering, and the prospect of financial adventure positively tantalizing. And so after college he had ignored his father's advice and affiliated himself with a brilliant financier whose idea of adventure had landed them at this frostbitten airport.

"Lemuel! Bring the box under my seat. And be careful, will you? It's fragile."

"Coming." Leaving his forebodings behind, Lemuel pulled a brightly beribboned gift box from beneath Devin's chair and carefully slid it into his leather satchel. Pulling his coat over his still-queasy stomach, he glanced around to be certain he hadn't overlooked any detail, then hurried from the plane.

∞

The driver did not speak as he whisked them over the gleaming asphalt road. Since the jet had flown from Paris, Devin had asked that the car be reserved in a French-sounding name. His ruse had worked; the Austrian driver did not recognize Devin, nor did he feel inclined to make conversation with an unknown called Javier Raison.

Lemuel studied the clean-cut hairline that edged the driver's collar and wondered how the situation would change if the Austrian knew he was driving one of the world's few billionaires. Would he ask for something? A new house for his ailing mother, perhaps? A later model sedan?

Lemuel had heard others boldly ask for more and less, but this reticent fellow might be one of those contented men who would not ask for more than God had already given him.

His eyes met the chauffeur's in the rearview mirror for the flicker of a moment, then the driver shifted in his seat and focused his attention on the road. Lemuel tapped his fingertips on the satchel resting on his knees and looked out the window. Outside the car, civilization had replaced the forest. They were driving through the tourist district, a world of neon-coated sleaze.

The car stopped at a traffic signal and Lemuel studied the way the vehicle's reflection splintered on the wet road. Though the local time was just past midnight, music floated from a nightclub on the corner. Clusters of swaggering men and giggling women clogged the sidewalks.

Lemuel glanced at his companion. Devin's eyes were wide, his thoughts obviously a thousand miles away. He saw, he heard, but the sights and sounds of this place did not touch him.

The light changed; the car moved on through the city. After a few moments, they entered another stretch of forest and Lemuel relaxed, resting his head against the upholstery. The strobic play of oncoming headlights and the drawn-out sucking sounds of passing cars intensified his weariness, lulling him into a thin doze.

He woke when the car stopped outside a rigid concrete and glass building. In stiff lettering a sign proclaimed that they'd reached the University of Innsbruck's Cryogenics Laboratory.

Lemuel shook his head to clear the remaining cobwebs of sleep, then nodded his thanks to the driver, who had opened his door. By the time he reached the other side of the car, Devin stood on the sidewalk, his hands thrust behind his back. He looked around, appraising the building with a casual, proprietary air. "Well. Let's see if they've followed my orders," he said, not looking at Lemuel.

Devin strode toward the double glass doors, and Lemuel hurried to keep up, the heavy satchel nearly slipping from his gloved fingers. Inside the building, a pair of men in white lab coats flung the doors open as if they'd been waiting.

"Mr. Sloane, we are so glad you could visit." The first researcher, a graying man with the craggy look of an unfinished sculpture, thrust his hand toward Devin. "I am Dr. Hans Altbusser. We've been anxious to meet you. Before you so generously agreed to support our research, we were working with pitifully outdated equipment. We've been quite eager to exhibit the improvements—and the specimen himself, of course."

"I'm glad I could help." Devin shook the man's hand. "My impatience to see him has been outweighed only by my eagerness to meet you, Dr. Altbusser."

"Thank you." The man smiled, his brows flickering in the face of Devin's flattery. He released Devin's hand, then gestured to the man beside him. "I would be remiss if I did not introduce my colleague, Dr. Rupert Hirsch."

Hirsch was a younger, paler version of Altbusser, but his eagerness matched the older man's. Devin gave the second man a perfunctory handshake, then clasped his hands and nodded at the younger scientist. "I am delighted to meet you both. With me, of course, is my assistant, Lemuel Reis. We apologize, gentlemen, for the late hour, but we did not want to attract any media attention. We're most anxious, however, to see *Homo Tyrolensis.*"

Dr. Altbusser released a nervous laugh as he led the way through the functionally decorated lobby. "So you've heard what we're calling him. It only seemed natural, since he was found in the Tyrolean Octzaler Alps. In honor of the mountains, some of the locals are referring to him as Otzi."

Devin fell into step beside the doctor. "Naturally. Twentieth-century humans always seek to debase whatever is high and holy." His voice flattened out. "The American press has dubbed him the *Iceman.* Have you heard that?"

"*Ja,* the American papers reach even into our mountains." A polite smile flickered across the doctor's face. "But we have not had much time to read them. Our work, you see, keeps us busy."

"And the custody controversy?"

A muscle quivered at Altbusser's jaw. "You have heard of *that*?"

"How could I not?" Devin lifted his shoulder in an elegant shrug. "Last week all the Italian and Austrian papers published the results of the survey teams. The Iceman was discovered 101 yards inside Italian soil, so technically he should not be in Austria at all."

Sudden anger lit the doctor's eyes. "The Italians did not want him! When the hikers found him, they called police on both sides of the border. The Italian *carabinieri*, thinking the body was yet another climber caught unprepared for the cold, showed no interest. But the Austrian police went out the next afternoon. I myself spoke to Markus Pirpamer, the man who operates the nearest mountain shelter, and he said this body was nothing like the white, waxy, chewed-up corpses he usually recovers from the glacier. He knew it was unique, that it was unusual—"

Devin held up a restraining hand. "I applaud your righteous indignation, Dr. Altbusser, and I agree with your reasoning, though I disapprove of the rough way they handled the body. The Iceman is a treasure, yet your Austrian police nearly destroyed him."

Dr. Hirsch frowned at Devin. "But they did not. And what remains is still priceless, Mr. Sloane. You will not be disappointed."

They paused in a gleaming corridor before a locked steel door. Altbusser punched a code into a numeric keypad, the latch clicked, and then Hirsch held the door open while the others filed into the room.

"When *Homo Tyrolensis* first arrived here, he resembled a slab of meat that had been in the freezer too long," Altbusser said, walking toward a glass container upon a rolling table in the center of the room. "We took all possible measures to protect him. Filtered, sterilized air flows through this box. He is a cold mummy, not completely desiccated, so we dare not leave him out long enough for the ice crystals to thaw. After thirty minutes of examination we return him to his freezer chamber, which is maintained at a glacial temperature of twenty-one point two degrees Fahrenheit."

With the reverence he might have shown the Ark of the Covenant, Devin stepped toward the box. "The cryogenic chamber is monitored at all times?"

"The tank has six temperature sensors," Altbusser replied, following in Devin's wake, "connected to alarms and portable pagers. If the temperature should rise by even a single degree, one of our people would be alerted and the problem corrected within moments."

"How long has he been out?"

"Only ten minutes. Your pilot radioed from the airport. You have twenty minutes to examine him before the flesh will begin to thaw."

Standing alone near the door, Lemuel folded his arms and glanced around him. Aside from the Iceman's cryogenic coffin, the room appeared to be an ordinary laboratory. A pair of computer monitors blinked from a counter installed along the wall to Lemuel's right, while a series of stainless-steel doors lined the wall to his left. Styrofoam coffee cups, a newspaper, and stacks of green-striped computer printouts littered a long black table beside the tank.

The only item of interest in the laboratory was the glass-covered capsule, and the long, rectangular box dominated the room. Though Lemuel couldn't see inside the tank from where he stood, Devin was clearly enraptured with its contents. Lemuel leaned against the door frame and looked away, not trusting his queasy stomach enough to approach.

Reaching the box, Devin slowly lifted his arms, then spread his hands upon the glass. His face flushed. "Lemuel, you must see this," he commanded, his voice echoing in the lab's vast emptiness.

With an inward groan, Lemuel pulled himself off the wall, then set his satchel on the floor and joined Devin by the tank. A leathern body lay inside the sealed box, the chilliness of its flesh frosting the glass. After Dr. Altbusser produced a cotton cloth and wiped the exterior, through the clouded aperture Lemuel could see a shrunken body, one arm extended over its head, the other covered by a blanket of surgical gauze. The frozen man's eyes were open and vacant, his nose pressed flat, one lip bent upward in a snarl. The head was completely bald. Lemuel noted with some surprise that not even an eyelash remained.

"We found thick strands of wavy brown hair in the ice near the body," Altbusser was explaining, a ripple of excitement in his voice. "All of it was three and one half inches long, proving that men cut their hair prior to the Bronze Age. We had never suspected such a thing."

"His teeth are quite worn, and a broad gap separates the two upper middle incisors," Hirsch added. "The ice is responsible for the hair loss, the flattened nose and bent lip. You will notice that the shell of the left ear is also folded, leading us to believe that the Iceman fell asleep on his left side. He had to be totally exhausted not to notice that his ear was bent—"

"Nonsense," Devin interrupted. "If ice can flatten his nose, it can certainly bend his ear."

Altbusser cast his colleague a warning glance, then folded his hands and continued his narration. "In any case, our fellow obviously lay down to sleep in a ravine where he would be sheltered from the winds. But that night he froze to death, and snow covered the body long enough for wind to dehydrate the corpse. As the first snows of that winter hardened into ice, the glacier rose above him."

A tremor touched Devin's mouth as he returned his gaze to the corpse's face. "I can see pores in his skin! And his eyes—they are intact! The combination of wind and cold was sufficient to preserve even the eyes!"

"Yes." A tight smile overtook Altbusser's stern features. He lifted his elbow and leaned almost casually upon the edge of the tank. "Though he was ravaged by the excavators who had no idea what they had found, the specimen remains in astoundingly stable condition. Though the tank's sterile atmosphere cannot reverse cellular damage, it has demonstrated remarkable powers of preservation."

"The body alternately thawed and froze for several days and nights while the rescue effort was under way," Hirsch added. "Thirty men with picks and compressors worked to free him. Unfortunately, they tore the clothing from his body and ripped a sizable chunk of flesh from the left hip."

Devin's dark gaze flew up to meet Hirsch's. "You're joking."

Hirsch lifted a brow. "Afterward, we were horrified by the destruction, but six other corpses had been found in glaciers that summer. No one had any idea this was a Copper Age mummy."

Devin pressed his hand to the glass above the Iceman's face. "It doesn't matter. All I need for my work is a single cell. I never dreamed I'd be able to look upon an entire body."

"In keeping with your request," Altbusser gestured toward his assistant, "we have prepared this." From a compartment beneath the cluttered table, Hirsch withdrew a silver container the size of a child's jewelry box. With a poorly disguised frown, he handed the container to the doctor. Altbusser's spidery hands seemed to caress the metal box for an instant; then he offered it to Devin.

Devin's dark eyes inspected the row of dials above the latches. "The combination?"

"Nine, nineteen, ninety-one." Altbusser clasped his hands. "The date *Homo Tyrolensis* was discovered."

Devin lowered the box to the top of the tank, whirled the dials with his thumb, then lifted the lid. A stream of milky vapor poured from the opening.

Lemuel stepped forward and peered over Devin's shoulder. A small glass vial rested on a bed of dry ice inside the box. Within the vial Lemuel could see a square bit of leather not much larger than a postage stamp.

"It is a generous sample." Altbusser inclined his head in a deep gesture, emphasizing his double chin. "We will have a difficult time explaining the disappearance of such a large amount of flesh."

Satisfaction pursed Devin's mouth as he snapped the box shut. "No, you won't. The body is torn and mangled in several areas, so one other tear won't matter. This sample is of no great consequence, gentlemen, and you know it." His gaze turned again to the ancient body on the table, his eyes glowing with a sheen of purpose. "But it is worth every schilling of the money I shall deposit into your accounts."

Altbusser shifted uneasily. "You still have not told us, Mr. Sloane, what you intend to do with the sample."

"I will conduct research, Doctor," Devin answered. Taking charge with quiet assurance, he grasped the silver box's handle, then thrust it toward Lemuel.

As the cold metal came to rest in his hands, Lemuel felt an awful premonition brush lightly past him, stirring the air and lifting the hair at the back of his neck.

∞

While tourists and skiers partied in Innsbruck's nightclub district, the four men sat in a crowded lounge and debated over drinks. Lemuel kept glancing at his watch in a rather obvious gesture, but Devin seemed not to care that the hour was late and the jet still waited at the airport.

"How can you give credence to such a fantastic theory?" Altbusser exclaimed, his reserve and tact severely eroded by a succession of double vodkas. "Surely you can't believe that *Homo Tyrolensis* was a man more intelligent than you or me!"

"How do you explain his ax?" Devin countered.

Altbusser frowned. "His copper ax? It is unremarkable. Men had not yet learned how to blend copper and tin to make bronze."

"You are wrong. It is *quite* remarkable." Devin tapped a manicured fingernail against the base of his wineglass. "I've spoken to others on your team. I know that x-rays of the ax head show bubbles in the copper, proving it was cast, not chiseled. This man and his contemporaries knew how to make a furnace that could reach the melting temperature of copper—a precise 1,981 degrees." He leaned forward, his eyes glowing. "How many of your students could manage the same feat without modern tools?"

"Bah!" Altbusser waved Devin's supposition away. "Someone made a hot fire and got lucky."

Devin shook his head. "The Iceman was sophisticated. His ax was cast and hammered to a sharp edge in a manner that would be extremely difficult to replicate even with modern metallurgical knowledge. The ax head was fixed with millimeter precision into a yew haft shaped to provide our Iceman with mechanically ideal ratios of leverage. And what of his other goods? With him he carried a bag of fungus, a natural antibiotic; tools, glue, needles, live coals, ropes, and clothes. He had a wider variety of useful equipment on his person than the German hikers who found him."

"Mr. Sloane," Hirsch protested, smiling, "you cannot seriously suggest that the Iceman's mental capacities were greater than ours. Evolution dictates that we must grow stronger and more fit as the centuries progress."

Lemuel winced slightly, then lowered his gaze and tightened his grip on his coffee cup. Dr. Hirsch had wandered onto a volatile subject, one best left unexplored. Devin Sloane held strong views about the evolution of man, and Lemuel did not particularly want to follow his employer onto yet another philosophical battleground—especially not at 2:44 a.m.

Too late.

"And out of the ground the Lord God formed every beast of the field and every fowl of the air," Devin said, his voice calm and utterly reasonable, "and brought them unto Adam to see what he would call them. And whatsoever Adam called every living creature, that was the name thereof."

Altbusser blinked. "What on earth are you talking about?"

"The Bible, the Pentateuch." The corner of Devin's mouth dipped in a secretive smile. "Genesis, chapter two, verse nineteen. God brings every creature in the world to the first man, and Adam names them. *Every* creature, gentlemen." His long, slender fingers drummed the polished surface of the table. "Could you *recall* the name of every animal, or even every species? Yet Adam named them all."

Altbusser flushed. "Surely you aren't offering a creation myth as proof of your hypothesis? No rational scientist places his faith in myth, Mr. Sloane."

"Faith is irrelevant, Dr. Altbusser. My point is that oral traditions support the view that ancient man was wiser and more intelligent than his contemporary descendants. And for an age, at least, he was certainly longer-lived."

Unfazed by the skepticism in the scientists' eyes, Devin paused to sip from his drink. Lemuel took advantage of the silence to clear his throat and glance pointedly at his watch. "Devin, it's two forty-five and the jet is waiting—"

Devin put his drink down as if he hadn't heard a word Lemuel said. "If you prefer a more concrete example of ancient intelligence, consider the great pyramids of Egypt." His eyes sparkled with the love of debate as he looked at the bewildered Austrians. "The Egyptians accomplished their construction without wheels or computers. Could you and a research team design and build the pyramids or the hanging gardens of Babylon?"

Altbusser flashed him a look of disdain. "You can not possibly begin to compare—"

"The wisdom in Pepi's instructions to his son could not be improved upon by a contemporary psychotherapist, and yet Pepi wrote three thousand years before Christ," Devin continued. "At the same time, men began systematic astronomical observations in Egypt, Babylonia, India, and China. Five hundred years later the Egyptians were creating timeless lyric poetry lamenting the age-old quest for the meaning of life. They were also preserving their dead—so well that in 1985 Svante Paabo was able to extract and sequence DNA from a mummy twenty-five hundred years old."

"You have misled us, Mr. Sloane." Hirsch leaned forward, irritation struggling with patience on his pale face. "You led us to believe that you were a financier by trade and a philosopher by avocation, yet we see now that you fancy yourself a scientist. But science and philosophy do not mix; they are two separate disciplines." One of his dark brows drew downward in a frown. "In the face of contemporary technology and thought, you cannot seriously support the idea that ancient man was superior to contemporary humankind. If that were true, if we are *digressing*, we have no hope for the future."

Devin leaned back against the booth's upholstery and thrust his hands into his coat. "I would expect an educated twentieth-century man to respond as you have, Doctor. Pharaoh's wise men might have responded in the same way if someone had suggested that a wiser, more intelligent race might someday follow. But the idea that wiser men have preceded us is not hypothesis; it is the *truth*."

"Sir," Altbusser said, sputtering. "You are impertinent!"

"Perhaps," a thin smile twisted Devin's lips, "but the essence of science, doctors, is that a man may ask an impertinent question and be well on his way to a pertinent answer. You forget that evolutionary theory flies directly in the face of entropy, the second law of thermodynamics. Scientific law decrees that the overall disorder of most systems will increase. As individuals we age and our bodies break down; despite all our efforts, no one has yet been able to reverse the system of aging. We humans are also deteriorating as a species. According to the immutable laws of science, we must grow more disorganized; we must break down."

Altbusser's nostrils flared. "Your philosophy dooms the human race to extinction."

Devin gave the men a lazy smile. "Quite right—unless we overcome our human predisposition to illness and injury, to entropy itself."

"In time, perhaps that will be possible." Altbusser lifted his drink. "But not in your lifetime or mine, Mr. Sloane."

"Perhaps not." Lemuel felt his stomach tighten when a gleam lit Devin's eye. "But I'd like to think I can buy the human race another five thousand years. If my plan succeeds, gentleman, I may do just that. With the sample you have given me tonight, I plan to revitalize our genetic stock."

An awkward and embarrassed silence stretched across the table, and Lemuel lowered his head into his hand, desperately eager to be away. Devin didn't usually indulge in such Cinderella talk among mere acquaintances. The two researchers were shocked now, but by morning they would be laughing at the eccentric American billionaire over their coffee cups.

Altbusser shook the shadow of shock from his face, tossed back his drink, then dropped his glass to the polished table. "Now I know why they say you Americans are crazy," he said, showing his teeth in an expression of pained tolerance. "Mr. Sloane, obviously you are a charming, rich American who patronizes science the way others sponsor the arts." Contempt dripped from Altbusser's voice, and Lemuel wasn't sure if he heard the scientist or the liquor talking. "But you are not scientifically trained; you have not the faintest idea what you are talking about. These ideas of yours are idiotic, incomprehensible."

"If an idea can be framed in words, it can be comprehended." Devin's mouth curved in a confident smile. "You may disagree with me, Dr. Altbusser, but if you want to continue your work at my expense, you must humor me. I'm not asking for much."

"But now you have what you asked for." Altbusser's brows slanted in a frown. "You have had your look at *Homo Tyrolensis*, and you shall take with you one slice of the Iceman's flesh. And if the Italians hear that I have surrendered this biological material, I shall deny everything."

"There will be no need for denial." Devin smiled, but his smile held only a shadow of its former warmth.

Lemuel checked his watch again, then cleared his throat. "It's nearly three, Devin. The pilot is waiting."

"My assistant is right; we must go." Devin slid toward the edge of the booth, then paused and gave the scientists a benign smile. "It was a pleasure to debate with you, doctors. I'd invite you to visit me in order to continue this discussion, but I've a feeling you won't have time to do much traveling."

Lemuel tossed back the remaining dregs of his coffee, then picked up the silver box and his satchel, eager to be away.

∞

In a lingering silence, the Austrian scientists drove Lemuel and Devin to the airport. "Have the gift ready," Devin whispered as Lemuel opened the car door.

Fumbling in the cold, Lemuel pulled the box from the satchel and waited respectfully as Devin said his final good-byes to the inebriated Dr. Altbusser and his assistant.

"And there is this to thank you," Devin said, nodding toward the package in Lemuel's arms. Lemuel stepped forward and handed the wooden box to Dr. Altbusser as Devin continued: "A gift of appreciation for arranging this hasty rendezvous. I am certain you have sacrificed more than a few hours' sleep to meet with me tonight."

Smiling, Altbusser took the package and shook it slightly.

"Careful," Devin warned, thrusting his hands into the warmth of his overcoat. "I'd hate to discover that you cracked bottles of the best Italian vintage I could find. When you uncork your wine, gentlemen, raise a toast to your success and think of me."

Warmed by the unexpected gesture, the Austrians spewed forth a stream of gracious thanks; then Devin turned and walked briskly toward the plane. "Come, Lemuel," he called, hunching low into his coat. "This place is much too cold."

∞

"You should record our impressions of the Austrians," Devin said, shifting on the couch in order to face Lemuel. They were airborne, the jet surrounded by the emptiness of black velvet night. Devin kicked off his shoes and removed his suit coat, but despite the late hour, his attitude was far from relaxed. The specimen case rested on his lap, his fingers occasionally fluttering across its surface as though it were a musical instrument from which he was determined to wring music. A corresponding symphony of emotions played across Devin's handsome features, and Lemuel bit his lip, bidding farewell to his hopes for a few hours' rest.

"One moment," Lemuel murmured, struggling to keep resentment from his voice. He shrugged out of his own coat and hung it next to Devin's, then sat in the chair across from the sofa and balanced his satchel on his knees. In the act of pulling out his laptop, he spilled a folder of computer printouts, maps, and newspaper clippings, but Devin seemed oblivious to Lemuel's clumsiness. He folded his hands across the specimen box and stared at the ceiling, his mellow voice blending with the roar of the jet's engines.

Lemuel opened his laptop, punched the power on, then took a moment to fasten his seat belt, letting Devin ramble while the machine booted. Devin was describing the layout of the lab in general terms, so Lemuel let him talk, knowing he had taken more notice of the place than his employer had. Once Devin saw the tank, he had concentrated only on the Iceman.

When Lemuel was certain he would not be thrown from his seat if the jet slammed into another pocket of turbulence, he opened his word-processing program and began to record Devin's thoughts.

"I have in my possession," Devin said, his eyes closing as his voice softened to a dreamy tone, "DNA that Mother Earth herself protected from fifty-three centuries of environmental and mutational damage. *Homo Tyrolensis* lived in an age when people were strong. Their minds were quick and agile, not stagnant, atrophied, or chemically altered. Other men have tried to better the human race by looking forward, by taking what we are and making it better. I will change the world, I will change *humankind* by restoring what we were. The wisdom of Solomon, the strength of Hercules, the extrasensory perception of Greek gods and goddesses— they shall be ours again, for we were once better than we are now."

Devin fell silent and Lemuel stopped typing, knowing that his employer waited for his reaction. Too tired to play the devil's advocate at four a.m., he tapped the keyboard, bit the inside of his cheek, and waited for Devin to continue. The man's eyes had closed, but he wasn't asleep. His hand was uplifted, the index finger pointed at Lemuel as if to say, *Your turn.*

Lemuel took a breath and offered what he hoped was an inoffensive, yet challenging observation. "Dr. Altbusser did not have much to say in support of your theory," he said, tapping his fingertips against the lap-top's function keys. "And neither did Dr. Hirsch. Granted, they're not anthropologists, but they are well-versed in modern thought."

"Modern thought is nothing but ancient thought revisited," Devin answered, not opening his eyes. "And by his very success in inventing laborsaving devices, modern man has created an abyss of boredom and stupidity that only the privileged classes in earlier civilizations ever plumbed. The average blue-collar worker has more free time and expendable income than did the average man on the streets of ancient Rome, yet he is not a better man for it. He spends his evenings in front of his television, filling his mind with the moronic humor of whatever sleaze happens to be on that evening. Modern technology is supposed to serve us, but the average man serves technology. Our gadgets and gizmos have changed us from active to passive agents. Unless we restore our superiority they will eventually eliminate us altogether."

Devin's face settled into determined lines. "The Austrians think I am insane," he said, opening his eyes. "They forget that every great advance in science has issued from some audacity of imagination. I may be impertinent and audacious, but I am one of the few men bold enough to dream and to act." He smiled as if at a pleasant joke. "Soon they will remember me as a charming and rich American who had nothing better to do than improve humankind."

Lemuel let the idea resonate in the confined cabin; then he gestured toward the silver box in Devin's lap. "What arrangements should I make for the specimen?"

"As soon as we land in Washington"—Devin's gaze fell upon the container in an almost fond expression—"you will call Dr. Helmut Braun, of the University of Virginia's Cryogenics Lab. Dr. Braun does not know me well, but last month he received a $500,000 grant to expand and upgrade his genetics laboratory. He will be anxious to talk to me."

Nodding, Lemuel typed the name in his to-do list. Helmut Braun, whoever he was, was about to be handed a most unexpected responsibility.

∞

Leaning forward, Rupert Hirsch peered through the futile arch made by the wipers. Snow had begun to fall as he and Altbusser left the airport, and the distant lights of oncoming cars were barely distinguishable from the white flakes that fell like stars from the thick sky.

"Sloane is a madman," Altbusser said in German, thumping the package on his lap for emphasis. "A spoiled American lunatic. Nevertheless, if the Italians ever discover that we sold a sample of Otzi's flesh to Devin Sloane, the outcry will ruin us."

"He won't tell and the Italians will never know," Hirsch assured him, clinging to the steering wheel. A truck rumbled past, spraying slush over the front of the sedan. For a moment the world went black; then the wipers staggered across the windshield, and Hirsch sighed in relief.

He glanced at his colleague. "No one at the lab saw Sloane with us; no one will remember us at the bar. And I found his theory rather . . . interesting. Fantastic, but interesting."

"All I want to consider now is a nightcap and my bed," Altbusser growled. "It's four thirty. My wife will be frantic or angry, depending upon"—he picked up Devin's parting gift and gently shook it—"the quality of our friend's wine."

"I'm sure it's the best." Hirsch tilted his head to relieve the stiffness in his neck. "Sloane can afford anything."

"Why are we waiting?" Altbusser ripped the winding lengths of ribbon from the box. The wrapping came away easily and fell between the front seats in a tangled heap. Hirsch could see the words *The Vineyard of Ernesto Calabria* burned into the solid-looking wood. A tiny gold latch secured the lid.

"There had better be two bottles if you're taking one home to your wife," he muttered, returning his gaze to the road. He flinched as another truck blasted him with slush.

"Surely there are." Altbusser flipped the latch and lifted the lid. "The box is big enough—"

A high-pitched squeal pierced the darkness. Hirsch glanced over to see a look of sheer black fright on his companion's face; then he looked at the box. A small electronic device, hardly larger than a beeper, flashed a sequence of numerals at lightning speed.

A warning spasm of alarm erupted within him.

He looked at Altbusser.

Understood.

The squeal stopped.

A mighty flash of fire lit the night.

chapter 3

The leaves over Lara Godfrey's head whispered to themselves as she exhaled and allowed herself to relax. The park around her glowed with the golden green shades of early spring, and the quiet Friday afternoon held the promise of good weather for the weekend.

Lara leaned back against the solid bench and focused on a patch of shimmering silver water at the base of the hill. Since no one in town considered the pond significant enough to deserve a name, Michael had christened it himself. One afternoon while he and Lara sat on this bench at the end of a long day, in a fit of romantic fancy he named the pond Mirror Lake.

The memory, a safe one, blew through her like a warming breeze. "Mirror Lake?" Lara had protested, turning to him with a superior look. "If we're going to call that mosquito-breeding ground anything, let's just call it 'the pond.'"

"I like that mosquito-breeding ground," Michael answered, his strong arm curling around her shoulders. "It's beautiful, it's peaceful, and if you should look into it, you'd see your lovely face like a perfect mirror."

"It's a nuisance and if I looked into it, I'd see a bunch of minnows and weeds."

"You're such a pessimist, wife."

"No, husband, I'm a realist. One of us has to be."

The memory brought a wry, twisted smile to Lara's face. She had always been the realistic one, as matter-of-fact in her decorating as in her cooking, but that hadn't stopped Michael from hanging no fewer than a dozen water color representations of the pond throughout their apartment.

She crossed her arms, amazed that those innocent paintings had ever held the power to irritate her. Michael gave them useful, if unimaginative titles like "Mirror Lake in Summer's Heat Haze" and "Mirror Lake through Spring's Dogwoods," but Lara tended to think of them as "The Pond After Michael's Operation" and "The Pond After the First Chemotherapy." There was one sketch hanging over the kitchen sink that Michael called "Mirror Lake in Summer," but Lara would always know it as "The Last Pond He Painted."

A songbird perched on a branch somewhere in the oak behind the bench. Lara closed her eyes, listening to him practice his trills. A long sigh passed through her, a cascade of weariness that ended abruptly when footsteps crunched the pebbled path that pointed a curving finger through the park. Lara looked up and saw a young woman and her toddler coming up the path.

Not particularly wanting to be drawn into a conversation, Lara averted her eyes and studied the setting sun's reflection. The sky glowed with color, golds and pinks and reds. Though he was a good artist, Michael had never quite captured the glory of a sunset like this one . . .

"Do you mind if I leave this here?"

Lara's mouth twisted as she shifted her gaze. The young mother stood in front of her, one arm burdened with a huge canvas carryall, the other about to be pulled from its socket by a curly-haired boy.

"Help yourself."

The woman flashed a smile of thanks as she dropped the bag onto the bench; then she let the child lead her toward the playground. Ignoring the swings, the little boy broke free of his mother's grip and ran toward the faded plastic horses that rocked on rusted springs as thick as Lara's thigh. "Wait for me, Nicky!" the mother called.

Wait for me, Michael.

A flash of loneliness stabbed at Lara as the little boy's high, clear laugh rippled through the air. His mother had set him astride the hobby horse and was rocking him back and forth in an uneven rhythm.

Lara's eyes narrowed as she studied the corroded support springs. *The parks department ought to replace those things.* Rusting metal usually spelled "tetanus shot" for anyone unlucky enough to be cut, and tetanus was one of the more painful vaccinations. Lara had been required to have one when she entered medical school, and her arm had ached for a week.

"Mommy, ride more?" The little boy was begging now, his round face screwed up in a petulant frown. "Mommy, more! Ride more!"

"No, honey, Mommy's tired." The woman straightened, pressed her hand to her back for a moment, then lifted the boy from the rocking horse. "Let's get your truck, okay? Maybe you can play with your truck while Mommy rests."

Good. They were leaving, so Lara would be alone again—she groaned, remembering the woman's canvas bag. She had dealt with enough women at the clinic to know that mothers of preschoolers carried everything but their tax returns in those things.

Lara smoothed her face, hoping she could maintain an expression of polite interest until the woman and her son left the park. A half hour of sunset remained, and Lara wanted to enjoy the time in silence; she *needed* to be where she and Michael sat together so many times, just the two of them.

"Thanks for watching this." Lara nodded silently as the woman lifted the bag and rummaged through its contents. "Here, Nicholas." She pulled a shiny red truck from the bag. She led the boy to a patch of grass, then squatted beside him and ran the fist-sized truck over the ground. The low vrooming sound she made fluttered her lips and brought a smile to the boy's face. "Now you play for a minute so Mommy can catch her breath."

Lara lifted her gaze to the sunset as the woman stood and came her way. When she collapsed on the bench, exhaling heavily, Lara crossed her arms.

"He wears me out," the woman said simply, her hands falling limply into her lap. "We've been going since breakfast and we've got at least another half hour to kill before his daddy comes home." The corners of her mouth lifted in a weary smile. "Then my darling husband will have the nerve to ask if we did anything today."

The reply seemed to slip out the corner of Lara's mouth. "Well, you know what they say. We can't live *with* men—"

"And we can't live without them," the woman finished, laughing. She kept her gaze on her son and stiffened for a moment when the little boy lifted his head and looked toward the pond. "No, Nicky"—she leaned forward—"we can't go back to the water. Play with your truck."

The child hesitated, the mother's glance sharpened, and then the boy settled down again to play in the dirt.

"Bugs." The woman leaned back against the bench and clasped her hands around her middle. "He's fascinated with them, and that pond is crawling with insects."

"I know."

The woman's eyes flicked at the wedding band on Lara's left hand. "I see you're married. Got kids?"

Lara tried to smile, but the corners of her mouth only wobbled. "No time."

"You have to make time." Sighing, the woman rubbed her hands over the denim of her skirt. "I was a corporate lawyer, but I put the rat race aside when I heard the old biological clock winding down."

Lara looked toward the west, where a blaze of gold and coral contrasted exquisitely with the deepening azure of the sky. "Do you miss your job?"

"I thought I would, but so far I haven't had time to miss anything." Her eyes took in Lara's uniform. "Let me guess—do you work at the hospital?"

"The Women's Clinic at the University of Virginia Medical School." Lara relaxed her arms. "I'm a physician's assistant with Dr. Densen-Braun."

The mother arched her manicured brows. "Several of my friends go to her. I would have gone to her myself when I got pregnant, but that clinic isn't listed on my husband's insurance. I had Dr. Horvath as my OB."

"He's good"—Lara cracked a sardonic smile—"if you want to go to a man. Most of our patients say that men just don't understand women's problems. I have yet to find a man who understands exactly how debilitating a menstrual migraine can be."

"Or PMS! Oh, what I'd give for my husband to sympathize with my chocolate cravings!" The woman giggled so irrepressibly that Lara couldn't help chuckling herself. She had heard it a thousand times in the office—no one could understand a woman's problems like another woman. That sentiment was one reason the Women's Clinic employed two female OB/GYNs, one female physician's assistant, and a crew of female nurses and receptionists. The only man even remotely involved in the clinic's operation was Dr. Helmut Braun, Olivia's husband. As head of the university's genetics program and cryogenics lab, he visited the office about once a month to help Olivia consult with patients with fertility problems.

"Well, if you want to have a baby"—an exhausted smile crossed the woman's narrow face—"get pregnant while you're still young and energetic. Nicholas is two, and we're trying to have another right away. I want to space my kids close together so I can go back to work when they reach school age. After chasing a toddler all day, the office will feel like a vacation."

Lara took a deep breath, ready to explain her situation, then thought the better of it. She didn't even know this woman, and they'd probably never meet again. This stranger didn't want to hear about Lara's blighted hopes for a family.

She exhaled slowly, her eyes fixed upon the darling little boy. He had his mother's dark hair and brown eyes, but his round face must have come from his father.

"He is a beautiful child," she whispered, watching the boy toddle toward them with the truck in his hand. "You and your husband must feel very blessed."

"We do." The woman pulled the boy into her lap, then brushed a crust of orange mud from his jeans. "Are you ready to go, Nicky? Daddy will be home soon."

The little boy jabbered something in a tongue Lara couldn't understand, then stiffened his body and tried to slide out of her lap. "Oh no, it's time to go." With an expertise Lara envied, the woman stood, settled the flailing child on her hip, and adroitly deflected a blow from a pint-sized fist.

"Here." Lara lifted the canvas bag. "Looks like you have your hands full."

"He never wants to go home." The woman took the bag with a smile. "But it's time to call out the relief team." She slipped her arms through the canvas straps and took a step toward the parking lot, then hesitated and looked back at Lara. "You really ought to have that baby soon." Her brown eyes twinkled. "Mothering is hard work, but it's the best job you'll ever have."

Lara acknowledged the comment with a small smile, then turned her gaze back toward the lake. The sun was hovering over the water now, igniting the pond with fiery shades of copper and gold and bronze.

Michael would have loved it.

Lara tried to swallow the lump that lingered in her throat. That woman *had* a relief team, while Lara had none. Her husband's body lay at the crest of the next hill, in Charlottesville Memorial Cemetery. While his depleted body slept under earth greening with the promise of spring, his spirit rested in heaven. And Lara struggled to live without him.

But how wonderful to have a child, a perfect representation of two lovers who had become one. She and Michael had dreamed of the children they would have. One afternoon not long after their wedding he had impulsively picked up a box of disposable diapers and tossed it into their grocery buggy. Lara had protested, saying they couldn't afford to buy diapers they wouldn't use for years, but he had laughed and told her to have faith.

Michael had been a strong believer in hope—but then again, he was the original cockeyed optimist. His faith held strong even after the diagnosis of cancer. Before undergoing his first round of radiation, he went out and bought an adorable pair of baby sneakers, size zero, then made a deposit at the university's sperm bank. Lara protested that latter decision, too, seeing it as an admission of defeat, but Michael was resolute in his purpose.

"When we beat this cancer," he had said, holding her in the dark as she wept over those silly, useless sneakers, "we're going ahead with our plans. We're going to have our baby, and he or she will be extra special because we worked so hard to bring little Elvis or Merva into the world."

Lara choked on her sobs. "Elvis or Merva?"

"Yeah." He brushed a gentle kiss across her forehead. "Or whatever you want to name the kid. But remember that box of diapers, honey. We have to use them, 'cause I know how you hate to waste money."

She couldn't control her burst of laughter, and for a long time they lay in silence, their arms around each other, his lips occasionally touching hers like a whisper.

"You'll see, honey," he had murmured as she closed her eyes to sleep. "God wouldn't have given us these dreams if he didn't want us to make them come true."

Apparently, Lara thought, rising stiffly from the park bench, *God had other plans.*

∞

Not willing to face an empty kitchen and invent another meal for one, Lara drove to McDonalds and bought her fourth hamburger of the week. The shades of night had fully fallen by the time she pulled into the driveway of the tidy town house that had been her home for the last four years. Her neighbor's side of the building glowed with warm and welcoming light, but Lara's side wore a dark and furtive look.

She really ought to get one of those timers that turned lights on and off. Michael had always urged her to, but as long as he was around she never felt the need for a home security device. Now she spent so little time at home it hardly seemed worth the effort.

She grabbed the burger bag, her purse, and her diet soda, then stepped out of the car. She had just slammed the door with her hip when a stream of brightness flashed across the scrawny shrubs beside her sidewalk.

Her neighbor stood in a blaze of porch light, his front door open behind him. "Excuse me—Lara?"

Squinting, Lara peered in his direction. Connor O'Hara, to whom she'd spoken only half a dozen times in the six months since the funeral, stepped out onto his porch. She could barely see his face, backlit as he was, but she thought she detected a trace of concern in his voice.

She lifted her burger bag to block the light in her eyes. "Something wrong, Connor?"

"Not really." She heard the click of his door, then the sound of shoes lightly scuffing the concrete. As he moved across the lawn with nonchalant grace, Lara caught the glint of a white smile. "I just wondered if you knew your car was leaking oil. I noticed a stain on your driveway this morning after you left. I thought you wouldn't be likely to see it, since—"

You no longer have a husband to see to these things.

"—your car always covers the spot when you're home."

"Really?" Lara walked back to her car and set her food and purse on the hood.

"Um—I don't think you're going to be able to see anything without a flashlight."

Lara drew her breath through her teeth in exasperation. "I can look, can't I?"

"Be my guest." Ignoring the veiled laughter in his voice, she knelt on the driveway and peered beneath the engine. He was right; the space between her car and the concrete was as dark as the inside of a tire, the engine above even darker.

"I thought maybe I could see it dripping." She stood up and brushed her hands on her sweater, uncomfortably aware that the orb of porch light extended far enough that he might see the blush that burned her cheek. She dipped her chin, letting her shoulder-length hair fall forward. "Was it a bad stain? Is my engine going to overheat or something?"

"Probably not right away." Connor's longish black hair gleamed as he put his hands in his pockets. "But you ought to have someone check it. If you don't have a regular mechanic, I could look at the engine tomorrow—unless you have plans to go out."

Lara's embarrassment turned quickly to annoyance. Did he think her totally helpless? "No, really, I couldn't impose."

"It doesn't take any real effort to check the oil." He stepped forward and rested one elbow on the car's roof. In the dim light she could see him studying her, his eyes deep-set and gleaming. "I was planning to change my own oil tomorrow, so it'd be no trouble for me to pop the hood and take a look."

"Well"—Lara picked up her purse and burger bag—"that'd be nice of you, Connor."

"No big deal. Michael would want me to help."

She flinched, as startled as if Michael himself had suddenly material-ized in the space between them. Most of her friends avoided his name as if it were a curse, tiptoeing around her memories and her widowhood. But Connor O'Hara had never been a friend of hers—he was Michael's friend. And apparently a courageous one, if he dared to speak of the dearly departed in the widow's presence.

She broadened her smile. "I can't thank you enough." She hesitated in the empty silence, then pointed to her door. "I guess I'd better go inside before my fries get cold. There's nothing more unappetizing than a stone cold French fry."

"I know." He turned and led the way over the sidewalk, then stepped over her wimpy shrubbery and crossed the lawn toward his own porch. "If you need anything," he said, the grass making a wet slicking sound against his shoes as she turned her key in the lock, "don't hesitate to call. I'd be glad to help."

"Thanks, but I'm really fine." She waved and gave him a polite smile, then stepped into the darkness of her apartment. After closing the door, she reached for the lamp and turned the switch, then glanced around the spartan room to make certain nothing had been moved from its proper place.

She exhaled in quiet relief. The book on the sofa, the television guide, the afghan she'd been crocheting—everything was just as she'd left it this morning and the morning before that. Nothing of significance had changed since the October day when Michael died. The people from hospice had loaded up the hospital bed and the medicine trays; in time the sour medicinal scent had faded. But the place still seemed empty and lifeless. The house without Michael.

Lara crossed the living room in three long steps, then flicked the kitchen light switch and tossed her dinner bag onto the antique pub table. A scraggly philodendron, a funeral leftover, trailed across the oak surface, and Lara absently stuck her finger into the soil.

Dry again.

She filled a cup with water, poured half the liquid into the potted plant, then dashed the remainder into the sink. After setting the cup on a folded dish towel to drip dry, she pumped liquid soap onto her palm and began to scrub her hands with the neat, clipped edges of her fingernails, a habit she had picked up in medical school. As she scrubbed, her eyes moved to the window, seeing nothing but thick blackness outside and her own reflection, the picture of a nearly-thirty woman whose dreams were as arid and dry as the soil of that neglected houseplant.

She stared at her reflection, noticing for the first time that her hair had grown a full half inch past her shoulders. Michael had always liked her hair long, but Lara found that tending it took too much time. She had it cut to the level of her chin when he was first diagnosed, and in the three and a half years since she had only occasionally been able to find time for quick trims.

She slammed the water off and reached for a clean paper towel. Michael would have loved her hair now.

She tossed the wadded paper towel into her trash bin, then pulled out her chair and sat down. She paused to murmur a quick prayer of thanks before opening her hamburger bag. The meager meal wasn't much to be thankful for, but the habit was as natural as breathing.

Her thoughts drifted while she ate. She'd checked a newspaper at lunchtime; there weren't any movies she wanted to see on television or at the theater, but she'd sit through anything if she could persuade Eva to venture out on a Friday night. Lara hadn't talked to Michael's mother for more than a week, and it was about time they checked in with each other. Eva had been a widow for more than five years and wore the mantle of singleness more comfortably than Lara.

Lara swallowed a tasteless bite of hamburger bun, then reached for the cordless phone on the counter and pressed the speed dial. The phone rang twice; then Eva answered in her cultured voice. "Hello?"

"It's Lara. How are you?"

"Fine, darling." Warmth and concern echoed in the older woman's voice. "I was just thinking that perhaps you'd like to join me in London for Christmas again this year. That was fun last year, wasn't it? I know we've got a full seven months to plan, but if you'll have to take vacation time you might as well request it now."

"London again?" The idea sent an unexpected shiver up Lara's spine. December seemed so far away, but she had been dreading the idea of Christmas alone in this house.

"Thanks for thinking of me, Eva, but I was hoping you'd feel up to doing something tonight. We could see a movie and go out for dessert and coffee after—"

"I'm sorry, darling, but my women's club is holding our annual auction tonight. I'm the organizing chairwoman."

Lara bit her lip. "I'm sorry, I forgot. That's okay."

"Do you want to come to the auction? I could always use an extra pair of hands to keep track of the bidding lots."

Lara pushed her hair back and frowned at her half-eaten burger. The last thing she wanted to do was stand around counting boxes of bric-a-brac for a bunch of blue-blooded biddies. She loved Michael's mother, but Lara had been to enough of Eva's charity functions to know she didn't fit in with the stiff, starched ladies of the Charlottesville Women's Club.

"That's okay, Eva. I'm feeling a little tired. Maybe I'll just stay home and rest."

"How about lunch tomorrow? I'll be free after twelve."

"That would be nice. Shall I pick you up?"

"No, darling, let me play chauffeur. I'll be by after twelve, and we'll have a nice long visit. In the meantime, wish us well, will you? They're opening a new children's wing at the hospital, so we need to raise ten thousand dollars tonight."

"I'll say a prayer," Lara answered, meaning it.

After she hung up, she went into the living room, turned on the television, then sank onto the couch. She *was* tired; she felt hollow, drained, lifeless. Ignoring the steady drone of a sports announcer, she closed her eyes and kept her promise, asking God to bless the charity auction for the hospital and all those presently in the cancer unit.

She opened her eyes and glanced at the clock. Eight thirty. She had nowhere to go, nothing to do, no one but the Lord to talk to. And while she had grown used to conversations with the Almighty, tonight she would have enjoyed seeing a human face smiling at her from the love seat.

Turning sideways on the couch, she hugged her knees and rested her head on her arms, her restless gaze falling upon the wedding picture on the coffee table. Within that silver frame, some magic of chemicals and paper and light had clipped a small moment out of time, a memory that still had the power to wrench her heart.

Their first day as Mr. and Mrs. Michael Godfrey. How young they had been, and how optimistic! On that day five years ago they had promised to love and cherish until death parted them. Michael had placed the gold wedding band on her finger, and she wore it still. Lara had imagined that they would still be holding each other when they were wizened and gray.

Her thoughts filtered back to the afternoon and the woman in the park.

"I see you're married. Got kids?"

"No. No time."

They hadn't had time to begin a family. Michael had discovered the knot on his leg barely six months after their wedding day, and his health had slid steadily downhill after that.

"You really ought to have that baby soon. Mothering is hard work, but it's the best job you'll ever have."

Lara's heart twisted as she thought of the little boy at the park. She wanted a baby desperately, but Michael's illness had consumed every moment of every day and every ounce of her energy. As an artist, he had no medical insurance or steady income, so he had wisely insisted that she keep her job at the Women's Clinic. The moment she came home, she gave herself completely to Michael. She hadn't missed having a baby in those days; something inside her wanted to draw Michael into her arms and nurture and protect him. As his disease progressed, Lara's love evolved from the admiration a wife feels for her husband to the devotion a parent feels for a dependent child. And at the end, when Lara had to dress him, bathe him, and spoon soft, strained foods from his stubbled chin, she experienced the love that springs from giving to someone who can give nothing but a weak smile in return.

And so she had steeled her heart against the contagious joy of newly pregnant friends, perfected a polite smile when baby pictures and shower invitations were passed out at the office, and learned to offer appreciation for other women's children without exposing her heart.

But now . . . Why not have her baby now? Michael had made arrangements for the future . . . and perhaps this was the time. Lara was not yet thirty; her body was healthy and strong. Disease had stolen her husband, but perhaps God could yet make a way.

She lifted her head and chewed absently on her thumbnail. They had intended the small bedroom to be a nursery, and one afternoon not long after their marriage, Michael had painted the walls a cheerful yellow. When the hospice people moved the hospital bed into that room, Michael joked that the walls were so bright he couldn't sleep, but he put out a hand and smoothed the worry lines from Lara's forehead when she suggested repainting it.

"Leave it for the baby," he had said, his eyes melting into hers. "It's a happy color."

A happy color?

Lara closed her eyes, missing Michael's paint-spattered clothes, his absent expressions, the way he blew his nose during ragweed season in August.

She fell asleep on the couch, her arms hugging a square pillow that still smelled of her husband.

∞

Lara wouldn't have picked O'Briens for a Saturday lunch, but Eva had a passion for unabashed opulence and the means to indulge it. The tuxedoed waiter seated them in a round booth big enough for six, then produced oversized menus. Lara listened halfheartedly to his smooth spiel about the chef's specials, then sighed in relief when he moved away. She had been thinking of only one thing since she woke, and she needed to share her thoughts with someone she respected.

"Try the crab cakes, darling; they are a specialty of the house." Eva dropped her menu to the table, then laced her elegant fingers and studied Lara with a resolute expression on her perfectly painted face. "Now that we have that out of the way, I want you to tell me what's bothering you. I heard something in your voice last night, and I can see it in your eyes now. Do you have a problem at work? Is something wrong at the clinic?"

"No, nothing like that." Lara set her menu aside, too, idly regretting that Eva had recommended the crab cakes. Lara would have liked to try the broiled shrimp, but once Eva made a proclamation, no one dared argue the point.

"Tell me, then. I set this hour aside for you, and I want to hear about whatever has put those shadows in your eyes. You're still my daughter-in-law, and I'll always love you for being my darling Michael's wife. I'm listening. Talk to me, Lara."

Lara smiled her thanks at the busboy who brought glasses of water, then studied her hands and struggled to find the right words. Her thoughts had seemed so logical and right last night, but in the light of day they seemed a little fantastic. And for all her liberality and out-spokenness, Eva was a traditional woman. She might not think it a good idea for Lara to raise a baby alone.

Lara took a deep, quivering breath to still the leaping pulse beneath her ribs. "Eva"—she tucked a wayward strand of hair behind her ear—"I've been thinking. It's been six months since Michael died. Though I miss him terribly, I think I'm beginning to move through my grief. My pastor says I probably mourned quite a bit during the final stages of Michael's illness, and I believe he's right. I'm done with bargaining and anger and shock. I still feel a little depressed sometimes, but I think some of that comes from being lonely—which is understandable, considering that I'm by myself now."

She looked up and tried to read Eva's face. The older woman wore a blank, passive look, but her blue eyes flashed with speculation.

"What I'm trying to say is that I think I'm ready to put the hurt behind me. I want to move on."

"Good grief." Eva's outlined brows shot up to her hairline. "Don't tell me you're getting married again."

Lara sat back, stunned. "Married?" A ripple of mirth caught her by surprise. "Good heavens, how could I get married? I don't even *date*, Eva."

Eva's frozen expression seemed to melt in relief. "Of course, dear, I'm sorry, what a ludicrous idea. It was a stupid thing to say, really, and I don't know why it popped into my brain. Please continue. You were saying you want to move on. How? Do you want to take another job? Find another place to live?"

Lara shook her head. "No, the town house is fine. It's just that—well, Michael and I wanted a family. Michael wanted kids more than anything. He hoped that one of them might inherit his artistic ability."

"I know, dear." Eva's jeweled hand reached across the table and patted Lara's arm. "We all mourn what could have been. He was *so* talented, the world will never know what it lost when he left us."

"That's just it, he didn't *entirely* leave us." Lara's voice wavered. "Before Michael went in for his radiation treatments, he went to see Dr. Helmut Braun at the University's cryogenics lab."

"Helmut Braun? Isn't he related to—"

"Olivia Densen-Braun, my boss. He's a cryogenics researcher; she's an obstetrician-gynecologist. Anyway, Dr. Braun helps some of our patients with fertility problems, so Michael made an appointment with him."

A blush ran like a shadow over Eva's cheeks. "Really, Lara, should we talk about this? Some things ought to remain private between a husband and his wife."

Lara sighed. She'd hoped to have a frank and honest discussion, but if conversation about a routine medical procedure was going to embarrass Eva—well, she'd just have to blurt it out.

She fixed her blushing mother-in-law in a direct gaze. "I want to have Michael's baby. His sperm deposit is frozen at the cryogenics lab, and I think I'm ready to proceed with our plans. I'm not getting any younger"— her mouth curved in a smile—"and neither are the sperm. I'd like to ask Dr. Braun to inseminate me as soon as possible, but I thought I'd at least mention the idea to you. After all, you'll be the baby's grandmother."

Shock siphoned the blood from Eva's face. "What?" A sudden spasm knit her brows. "A *baby?* Lara Godfrey, have you lost your mind?"

Lara glanced up. The waiter, who had begun to approach, retreated. *Dear God, give me strength.*

Lara propped her arms on the table and leaned closer to her mother-in-law. "I've thought it through very carefully. In six months I'll be thirty, and I'll enter a higher risk age group. But if I get pregnant now, I'll have at least nine months to emotionally prepare for the baby. I'm also financially capable of handling the extra expense. The money from Michael's life insurance will allow me to take a few years out to be a stay-at-home mom, and I can work part-time once he or she is old enough for school."

"A baby," Eva repeated, a hair of irritation in her voice. She blinked, then shook her head in utter disbelief. "Lara, honey, I can understand if what you're feeling is a passing whim, but you've got to let it pass. Motherhood is no walk in the park, and *single* motherhood—well, I can only imagine how hard it must be. I was lucky; I had a husband. I don't know how I would have gotten through Michael's baseball games and high-school algebra without him."

"Lots of women are raising children alone." Lara tightened her hand around the stem of her water goblet. "I know it's not easy, and I know it's not the ideal situation. But I want to love a baby—*Michael's* baby. He wanted me to have his child. If the cancer hadn't gotten in the way we probably would have at least two kids by now."

Eva sat silent for a moment; then her eyes narrowed. "I know you plan your life around God," she said. "Have you stopped to consider that perhaps it was his will that you never got pregnant?"

Momentarily taken aback, Lara pressed her hand to her mouth. She had long suspected that Eva took pride in the way she tolerated Lara and Michael's "fanatic" religious views, but she had never directly referred to them or claimed to have any personal relationship with God herself. And yet now she was attempting to convince Lara that a baby was not God's will for her life—

Lara nearly laughed aloud.

"I'm not going to argue theology with you." Lara took a deep breath, remembering another conversation in which Eva had railed against heaven itself, claiming that a merciful God would never take a loving, talented son from his family before he had even lived thirty years. That night, scarcely a week before Michael's death, was the first and only occasion Lara heard Eva acknowledge that God could work in human lives. Before that night, Eva dismissed all of Michael's or Lara's comments about God with an uplifted brow and a saucy grin. "When I find that God can do better for me than I can do for myself," she had always said, "then I'll think about turning myself in."

Lara looked across the table at her mother-in-law, whose blue eyes glittered with raw hurt. "I've always believed," she began, "that God's will is found in doing what he's called us to do. If we make a wrong step, he'll either call us back or close a door."

Eva said nothing, but her chin quivered as she stared at Lara.

"Right now," Lara went on, her eyes filling in spite of her resolve, "I think the time is right for me to have the baby Michael and I always wanted. There's no shame in it. I'll be a woman having her husband's child, just like any other woman who bears a child after her husband's death. The only difference in my case is that I'll have a posthumous pregnancy—but it'll be Michael's baby and it's what he wanted."

She lowered her gaze, a little surprised that she had found the courage to speak so forcefully.

"So your mind is already made up? You're going ahead with this whether or not I approve?"

"If it's not God's will, then God will show me. Something will happen, or the insemination won't take, or the doctor will advise against it. But right now I feel strongly that this is something I want to do. Since you'll be my baby's grandmother, I thought you should know."

She paused, letting silence fill the space between them, and after a moment Eva folded her arms and lifted her chin.

"Is that all you wanted to say?"

"Yes. It is."

"Then I have something to say to you." Eva rested her arms on the table and leaned forward. "I've come to love you, Lara, so don't think I'm saying this out of spite." Her brow wrinkled, and something moved in her eyes. "You may think of me as some sort of social butterfly, but I know what loneliness is. I know how it feels to come home to an empty house, to sleep in an empty bed, to yearn for someone to talk to."

"It isn't just that," Lara protested.

Eva held up a hand. "Hear me out now." She took a deep breath. "Darling, if it's children you long for, why don't you volunteer at one of those day-care centers? There's a lovely one near your house. They are always looking for help with underprivileged children."

"I don't want someone else's children on a part-time basis." Lara heard a heavy dose of sarcasm in her voice, but she didn't care. "Surely you can understand that I want to love my own baby."

"Of course I can. It can't be easy for you, either, working with pregnant women all day." Eva fell silent; then her hand fluttered up to touch her perfectly coifed curls. "Let me be blunt, dear. If you're afraid that losing Michael means you'll lose his share of my estate, you needn't worry. You don't have to have a baby to be included in my will. As long as you remain Lara Godfrey, you'll share in the inheritance whether you have a baby or not. I've spoken to a lawyer, and after several contributions are made to my civic clubs, you'll be my only heir."

"You think this is about *money*?" Against her will, rage flushed Lara's face. "Eva, that's the last thing on earth I care about! I don't want your money; you can give it all to your clubs. I want a baby! I want to love a child; I want to care for him; I want to go to ball games and recitals and PTA meetings. I want to wipe runny noses and sing lullabies and buy those little paint boxes of watercolors. I want to love and give and see my baby grow strong and healthy." She gulped hard, hot tears slipping down her cheeks. "Don't you see? With Michael, it all got turned around. I want to set things *right*, I want to put things back the way they should be."

She picked up her napkin, shook the silverware out of it, then wiped the wetness from her cheeks, aware that Eva had lowered her gaze and leaned back in the booth, cold and still. Why had she ever thought Eva would understand? She was a polished sixty-year-old woman, decades past her childbearing years, focused more on her society work than on her past. She had raised a perfect, talented son, saw him married to a respectable girl, and faithfully reported every detail of the lovely ceremony to the society reporter for the *Charlottesville Herald*.

She had lost a husband and later, a son, but she managed to shove her grief aside while she went about her work for the Women's Club, the DAR, and all those other society organizations . . .

Lara stared, tongue-tied, when the blue eyes that lifted to meet hers shone with tears. "Are you certain"—Eva's voice dissolved to a thready whisper—"that you want to put yourself through the *pain*? It's not easy to love a child. Love and grief are not always evenly balanced."

Lara blinked in bewilderment. Why did Eva consider herself the expert on heartbreak? Franklin Godfrey had died of a sudden heart attack, but Michael had suffered in Lara's house and wept in her arms. He put on a brave front whenever Eva visited, but Lara had held him in the night while he moaned in pain. On other nights, Lara lay on the floor with a pillow and blanket, listening to Michael's rattling breath and praying he'd find the strength to draw another.

She opened her mouth, but her heart was squeezed so tight she could not draw breath to speak. Eva must have read her emotion in her eyes, because she reached out and caught Lara's arm.

"I can't say that I approve of your plan, but I see that you're determined. And I can't stop you. But at least promise me you'll have a few tests done."

"Tests?"

Eva nodded in conviction. "You would know more than I about the details of such things, but I know there are genetic tests available. Michael died of such an aggressive cancer—please have the specimen tested so you won't bring another tragedy upon our family." Her burning eyes held Lara still. "Promise me, darling, that you'll do everything you can to be sure the baby will be healthy. I don't want you to suffer again. I don't think either of us could bear another tragedy . . . like Michael's."

Lara exhaled slowly, realizing that Eva had at last made a sensible suggestion. She had a point—some cancers could be predicted from DNA tests, and Helmut Braun was more than qualified to perform genetic testing on the frozen material.

"All right." She squeezed Eva's hand. "I promise I'll have the specimen tested."

Eva acknowledged Lara's promise with a small softening of her eyes, and then she pulled her hand from Lara's grasp and picked up the menu.

"What did I recommend? Oh yes, the crab cakes." Her voice floated up from behind the slab of laminated cardstock. "You have to order them, darling; you won't be sorry. Trust me."

Lara leaned back against the cushioned booth, then fumbled for a tissue in her purse and wondered how Eva could behave as if nothing out of the ordinary had happened. Lara felt as though the world had shifted slightly on its axis. She had very nearly convinced herself to become a mother.

∞

Eva gave Lara a falsely cheerful wave, then backed out of the driveway, shoved the Jag into gear, and stomped on the gas pedal. Taking dull comfort in the roar of the engine, she slumped into the leather seat. It was only as the tension went out of her shoulders that she noticed it had been there.

One hand pounded the steering wheel as she negotiated the curving road. "Why can't she just move on?" Eva asked the air, her voice cracking under the weight of her pent-up emotions. "Why can't she see that she has to move forward and not look back?"

But even as one voice in Eva's brain railed against her daughter-in-law, another reminded her that Lara was still a young woman. Though her experience with Michael had been a thorough baptism of suffering, Lara had not come close to plumbing the depths of grief Eva had known.

She eased the Jag onto the interstate, then slanted the car from the right lane to the left, blowing past a slower driver. Life was too short to dawdle on the highway. Life was like water in a bathtub—once God pulled the plug, you could do nothing to stop it from flowing down the drain. Eva had tried. In the past she had cajoled and argued with doctors; she had, on one occasion, even slapped an arrogant intern who spoke to her in simple, two-syllable words as if she were an imbecile. The hospital staff learned not to push her, but her frantic shadowboxing could not intimidate Disease. He kept coming, opening the door wide for Death.

When Eva had spent the last of her energy, she waited and wept, saying little as Death approached with a steady, inexorable tread. And as he gathered her beloved child and took him away, she came to understand that death was part of life; grief was a bitter pill you swallowed and then tried to forget.

You never, ever *asked* for a second helping, though sometimes life forced one upon you. Michael's conception had been an accident, and if abortion had been legal, Eva would have opted for the procedure in a heartbeat. Instead she passed her pregnancy in a sea of anxiety that did not abate until Michael passed his tenth birthday, still a healthy, normal boy.

Her mind turned again to the conversation at lunch. Lara wanted a baby—Michael's baby. Eva could understand the longing for a child. She herself had desperately wanted to be a mother, and she knew the world was a difficult place for a woman denied children. During the twenty-one long months that she struggled to get pregnant that first time, Eva learned not to shop in department stores with large infant departments, not to attend baby showers, and not to linger over her friends' newborns. Fortunately, finally, the miracle happened, and Eva held her perfect son in her arms. The burning desire cooled to the steady flame of maternal happiness . . . until death rained cold grief upon her.

Lara, no doubt, burned with a desire every bit as passionate as Eva's own. Perhaps it was even greater, for today's young women thought nothing of raising babies without fathers. Lara, at least, had the decency to want her husband's child.

It ought to be a simple thing—a young woman wants a baby, so she and her husband conceive the child and nurture it together.

But Eva had never known life to be simple . . . or fair.

She eased onto the exit ramp, consoling herself with the thought that Lara had promised to investigate genetic testing. The results might be enough to quench her desire and help her lock the past away.

chapter 4

Eva's objections—and her bizarre accusation that Lara wanted to insure a stake in Eva's money—put Lara in a dark mood for the rest of the weekend. The Sunday morning church service, which usually lifted Lara's spirits to a peaceful plateau, did nothing to brighten her mood. For his text the minister read the Genesis story of Jacob and Rachel. Lara had just begun to relax in the love story when the pastor read Rachel's plea, "Give me children, or else I die!" Lara crumpled in the pew, certain that the minister had somehow read her mind.

"Rachel was not wrong to want a child," the minister explained, "but she was wrong to accuse her husband for not providing one. God is the creator of life, and he gave Rachel a son in the proper time."

Through the rest of the sermon, Lara held the preacher's words at arm's length, turned and twisted them, looked at them from above and below. Was she wrong to want a child? No. And her husband had done his part to provide one—though it was definitely a twenty-first-century means of provision. Would God give Lara a son in the proper time?

After church, she swam against the tide of fleeing members and managed to catch the pastor and his wife at the front of the auditorium. "Please, Pastor Jim," she said, imposing an iron control on her rambunctious emotions. "I need a moment. I know it's Sunday afternoon and you probably want to get to lunch somewhere—"

"We've got as long as you need," her pastor answered, taking his wife's hand. "Stephanie, if you'll get the kids, I'll have a moment or two with Lara."

The pastor's wife slipped away, and Jim led Lara to the front pew, where they both sat. Looking at her hands, Lara spilled out her thoughts.

Jim had stood with her and Michael through everything—the cancer, the chemotherapy, and the funeral. He had supported Michael's decision to freeze a sperm sample for possible future use.

"I feel really strange, talking about all this *here*." Lara spread her hands, indicating the pulpit and communion table only a few feet away. "But I've done nothing but think about this all weekend. I need to know—do you think a baby could be in God's will for me? Am I doing the right thing?"

Jim turned and rested one arm on the back of the pew, then folded his hands. "Lara, God is nothing if not relevant to contemporary life. He knows all about science and genetics, and he knows the desires of your heart. If you've really prayed about this thing, if you've sought wise counsel, and if all the doors remain open, I see no reason why you shouldn't proceed." His blue eyes flashed a gentle but firm warning. "Just remember that childrearing is a spiritual responsibility as well as a blessing. You'll not only have to be responsible for this baby's physical and emotional development, but his or her spiritual growth, too. And unless you marry again, you'll have to bear that responsibility alone. "

Lara glanced to the back of the auditorium, where Pastor Jim's wife was leading their five-year-old twin daughters down the aisle. "I know," she whispered, her heart aching at the lovely sight.

And on Sunday night, after two days of prayer, consideration, and debate, Lara found that her desire to have Michael's baby had not faded. If anything, it had grown stronger.

❦

A smudge of sun dappled through the rain-heavy cloud cover on Monday morning as Lara urged her sputtering Maxima to life. Connor had a point; the car probably did need a tune-up, but after her disastrous lunch with Eva, Lara had hidden herself away in the house, not even responding when Connor rang the doorbell late Saturday afternoon. She hadn't wanted to make polite conversation with Michael's friend; she certainly didn't want to stare at her car's guts and feign an interest in oil and engines.

She saw movement from the corner of her eye, and turned. In the twin driveway next door, Connor O'Hara was tenderly wiping the dew from his car, a vintage cherry-red Mustang convertible. The car had appeared only a month ago, replacing a battered nondescript sedan, and though Lara didn't know much about cars, she knew this one screamed Expensive. How he could afford such a thing on a reference librarian's salary, she couldn't guess.

Maybe he was playing the stock market. Maybe he read the *Wall Street Journal* every day and had gleaned some hot tips. If so, maybe he'd share the wealth and help her increase her little nest egg—just in time for the hatchling.

She really ought to apologize for not making herself available over the weekend, especially since he'd been kind enough to offer to check her oil.

Connor lifted his gaze as Lara revved the hiccupping engine, and as their eyes met he managed a hesitant wave. She answered with a quick swipe of her hand, then paused as he mouthed something she couldn't hear over the noise of the motor.

She rolled the window down and leaned out of the car. "What?"

Connor's ruggedly handsome face shifted into an embarrassed expression as he left the Mustang and walked toward her. "Sorry," he called, his brown eyes serious above his polite smile. "I don't want to slow you down. I just said I was sorry I missed you this weekend."

"It's my fault. My mother-in-law took me out for lunch, and I was so drained by the experience that I came home and took a nap." She lifted her left hand in a halfhearted wave, then shifted into reverse with her right. The engine began to hum on another note, and Connor halted in the grass.

His smile broadened. "Was it that bad?"

"It's all right. And I really appreciated your offer."

Lara gave him a final wave, then rolled down the driveway. She paused in the street and watched Connor walk back to his car with that easy noiseless tread that probably sprang from prowling around the university library all day. He probably was as nice as he seemed. Michael had really liked him, but then again, Michael liked almost everybody.

Sighing, she shifted the car into drive and tried to turn her thoughts toward the day ahead. Olivia had scheduled a full day in the office since Dr. Renee Stock, the other OB/GYN, was on call at the hospital. Unless an emergency arose, the day should be boringly routine: Pap smears, breast exams, and an endless stream of lectures on the importance of both. An entire morning and afternoon of watching women kick off their shoes, grimace, and step on the scales. Blessed normalcy, without time to think about personal dilemmas.

She drove too fast into a school zone, then cringed as the crossing guard wagged her finger in warning. Lara obediently braked hard, then bit her lip as the car crawled forward. She was running late because she'd spilled coffee on her uniform at the breakfast table. She was also feeling bloated and irritable, certain signs of PMS.

Another month without Michael, another month without a baby. Her body felt as empty as the bright nursery next to her bedroom.

When the traffic light ahead clicked from red to green, Lara pressed on the gas, hoping to make up for lost time. If Olivia came in early, Lara might be able to catch her before the place filled up with prying eyes and sharp ears.

∞

"You're thinking about *what?*" Dr. Olivia Densen-Braun stared over the rim of her coffee cup, her mask of professionalism shattering.

"Please, not so loud." Lara cut a glance to the doorway of Olivia's private office. The other staff members were milling about in the hallway, and she didn't want any of them to know what she was considering. If she decided not to opt for motherhood, she didn't want to endure a constant stream of comments on all she'd miss by never having a baby.

Olivia quirked her eyebrow. "Do you want to close the door?"

"That would only draw their attention." Lara sank to the love seat before Olivia's desk and clasped her cold hands. "Michael and I always planned to have a child. I've been thinking that maybe the time is right. "

"But surely you don't want a baby *now*." A flicker of unease stirred in the depths of Olivia's soft blue eyes. "It's too soon, hon."

"It's been six months. And it's not like the baby would come tomorrow. I'll have time to get ready, time to adjust." Lara felt her cheeks flush against the cool air in the small office.

Olivia eyed her with a critical squint. "I have no problem with artificial insemination. My concern centers on the fact that you'd be raising a child alone. Parenting is hard work, especially if you have a professional career. Helmut and I have never even *considered* having a child."

Lara sighed as the words rang in her ears. She'd heard a paraphrase of this from Eva. Didn't anyone think about the *joys* of parenting anymore?

"I've been considering it carefully and I know I want Michael's child. All I have left of him is a collection of old clothes, a few watercolors, and a bunch of baseball trophies. I need something more. I wanted a baby when Michael was alive, before the cancer. Now I'm twenty-nine, at the peak of my reproductive years, and I *still* want a baby. There's no social, moral, or ethical reason why I shouldn't have Michael's."

"I'm not questioning your right to have a baby"—Olivia lowered her coffee cup to her desk—"just your sanity. What about the expense—do you know they say it will cost more than six hundred seventy-nine thousand dollars to raise a child born today? You've got to think about college and schools, and those expensive gadgets all the kids want these days."

"I make a good living. And I'll make do the same way everyone else does—I'll shop at discount stores and try to get the kid a scholarship."

Olivia leaned back and crossed her arms in the posture she always assumed when she lectured pregnant teenagers. "Lara, are you sure you want to take on the responsibility of a baby? Children complicate things. You're young; you'll probably marry again. You might even fall in love with a nice guy with four kids of his own."

A reluctant grin tugged at Lara's mouth. "That'd be okay, I guess. Four kids, five kids—aren't they cheaper by the dozen?"

Olivia wasn't amused. "What about your career? If you take an extended maternity leave, I'll have to hire someone else to fill in for you. Of course I'll try to work things out when you want to come back, but

I can't guarantee you'll work as many hours. I don't know if we can keep two physician's assistants busy."

"You don't have to feel responsible for me. This is my own decision." Lara looked Olivia directly in the eye, her confidence spiraling upward. "Michael's life insurance money will provide enough for us to live on for the first few years. We had always planned to put away enough for me to take an extended leave when a baby came, but then Michael got sick and our savings dried up. There's money in my savings account again— but I never thought it would come the way it did."

A long, brittle silence fell between them as Olivia studied her desktop and searched for words. "Are you quite certain"—her eyes brimmed with concern—"that you aren't considering this just because you miss Michael? I don't mean to sound cold or heartless, Lara, but you've got to realize . . . having Michael's baby won't bring him back."

Lara forbade herself to tremble, then drew a deep breath. "I know Michael is gone," she answered, her voice firm, final. "And I'd like to have his baby. And if I decide to go ahead with my plans, I'd like you to be my doctor."

Olivia didn't protest again. Her blue eyes deepened with understanding. "We'll talk about that"—she uncrossed her arms—"after you make a final decision. Before you do, however, I'd suggest that you ask Helmut to run a complete genetic analysis on Michael's specimen."

Lara's mind whirled. "Michael's mother insisted on the same thing."

"Really? Good. One of Helmut's research teams is working on a project that tracks genetic predisposition to various cancers. I don't know all the details, but I do know they've isolated a gene that makes carriers susceptible to certain types of carcinomas. Since Michael died so young—"

"You think my baby could inherit the same kind of cancer Michael had?"

Olivia reached out to caress her coffee cup. "I'm not sure, hon. I just want you to take precautions. Michael's genetic history is at issue, as is the age of the frozen sperm. Some men with normal reproductive potential produce sperm that do not survive freezing. There is a great variation in survival among different specimens. Helmut can examine the cells for you, check out the genetic markers, and make certain that the sperm are still motile." Her voice softened. "I'd hate for you to risk all your hopes on a procedure that may not succeed."

"I think it will work." Lara's eyes drifted toward the framed picture of Olivia's cats, the only decorative item on her crowded desk. "I've been praying about it. And I have this feeling that God wants to grant the desire of my heart."

"And if he doesn't?" Olivia's voice wasn't much louder than a whisper, but the effect was as great as if she'd shouted in Lara's ear. "I know you're a religious person, so perhaps you should consider that fate ruled against you. Maybe this child was just never meant to be."

"I don't believe in fate." Lara gave Olivia a smile. "Not an unavoidable fate, anyway. God gives us free will. The challenge lies in making the right choices."

Olivia looked at Lara with a smile in her eyes. "Then I hope you make the right one."

chapter 5

"The complete genetic code for a new individual is present from the very moment of fertilization. The genome is what constitutes a human individual, not only in abstract philosophical terms, but also in a mechanical sense. The genome, a person's genetic makeup, controls a person's entire identity. Some would say it therefore controls his fate."

Lost in his subject, Dr. Helmut Braun reached up to brush a ticklish hair from his ear but caught the side of his glasses, nearly dislodging them. Sighing in exasperation, he pressed his index finger to the center of the frame to firmly entrench it upon his nose, then looked out on the sea of yawning students in the amphitheater. He turned, slapping his pointer over the image of a double helix on the wavering screen behind him, but the dull thwacking sound did little to rouse the young fools before him.

How much longer would he have to maintain this charade? Not a student in the group cared one whit about genetics. They were medical students, eager to slice into patients and collect fat fees for prolonging life; they endured his class like a penance to ease the guilt of their future prosperity. He had just given them the key to solving the mystery of human existence, yet not a single eye gleamed with appreciation.

Helmut lowered his gaze to the overhead projector, then picked up his pen and sketched a design of loosely connected circles. "The transfer of biologically necessary material in DNA directly links us with previous humans in an unbroken physical chain." He snapped the lid back onto the felt-tipped marker. "But the code of life is not immutable. The environment we modify also modifies us. We mutate, for good or ill, and the entire future of the world changes with us."

A door opened at the back of the darkened room and a slender form crossed the resulting rectangle of light, then vanished into the blackness of a back row. Another tardy student, no doubt, who hoped to sign his name to the attendance list and receive full credit for the lecture even though he had missed nearly the entire hour.

Helmut clenched his jaw and continued. "In recent centuries we have directly altered livestock and other naturally occurring organisms. Gene therapy of various inborn or acquired diseases is now emerging as a powerful technique to treat previously intractable diseases like cystic fibrosis, inborn immune deficiency, and AIDS. In some cases of an inherited genetic defect"—he lifted his eyes to see if anyone in his captive audience cared enough to take notes about something directly related to medical practice—"a permanent cure may be possible in the form of genetic replacement of a defective or missing gene at the gamete or embryonic level. Through genetic optimization, such enhancement could include features like protection from environmental carcinogens, immunological resistance to certain microbes, or the better metabolic utilization of food."

Someone waved down front, and Helmut squinted over the top of his reading glasses in surprise. The hand belonged to a young woman, pretty, and most likely concentrating on pediatrics or gynecology. Nearly all the young women these days were shifting to traditional women's specialties.

"Yes?"

"Are you saying that we could find and manufacture a 'skinny' gene? Something that would keep us all thin?"

"Yea-uh!" A masculine voice shouted from the back of the room. Light applause rippled through the darkness until Helmut removed his glasses and frowned.

"You have the idea," he replied, his voice heavy with sarcasm. "We could not only manufacture a 'skinny' gene, but also an intelligence gene, and a gene that would guarantee a child blue eyes. When we do, geneticists like me will make a fortune while doctors like you spend all day on your feet doing tummy tucks and liposuction for those not fortunate enough to have been designed from properly attractive genetic components."

A wave of laughter rose from the shadows at the back of the auditorium, and Helmut gathered his notes. "That is all for today," he said, not bothering to look up. "Tomorrow I shall discuss the Human Genome Project and its implications for society in the twenty-first century. You are dismissed."

The stilted atmosphere vanished in a flurry of sound as his students gathered their belongings and streamed toward the exit. Ignoring their chattering, Helmut flipped the switch on the overhead projector and shuffled his notes back into his briefcase. Five lectures per week was the price he paid for being allowed to conduct his research in the university's ultrascience lab. Though the sign on his office door proclaimed him a professor, he cared nothing for the students, nor they for him. A staff of research assistants and student aides kept the fresh-faced young doctors at bay, and Helmut discovered that preparing lectures was a wonderful way to consign his current projects to a mental back burner. Some of his most delightful insights had sprung from his subconscious while he was explaining genetic principles he could have recited in his sleep.

A man's voice called to him from the shadows. "Dr. Braun? May I have a word with you?"

Helmut stared toward the sound, then blinked when a slender young man stepped into the light. The fellow in the aisle wore a nicely tailored suit and a properly deferential expression, a far cry from the arrogant, blue-jeaned, bored doctors-in-training.

Helmut removed his glasses, then pulled a handkerchief from his pocket. "Do I know you?"

"No, sir, I have not yet had the pleasure of making your acquaintance. I am Lemuel Reis, administrative assistant to Devin Sloane."

Helmut frowned as he wiped the clouded lenses. Last month he had been astounded to receive a check from Devin Sloane for $500,000. Several of his colleagues had questioned why Sloane had singled him out, but Helmut had shrugged away their questions. "He lives nearby and he needs a tax deduction," he had said, relishing the texture of the check between his thumb and index finger. "Let's not question good fortune."

He had not hesitated to spend the man's money. Several pieces of specialized and expensive laboratory equipment had already been ordered, and Helmut had planned to write Sloane a thorough letter of thanks. He was grateful that a man of business would choose to reward a man of science, as long as the businessman took care of his business and left science to the scientists . . .

He slid his briefcase from the lectern and turned to face the young man. "I am afraid you'll have to tell Mr. Sloane that my schedule this afternoon is quite full. If he absolutely must speak to me, I will be happy to take his call during my office hours."

Reis smiled and shook his head slightly. "Sir, my employer has specified that this matter is urgent and for your ears alone."

Something in the man's voice struck Helmut as unusual—an air of respect or gravity. Or was that a hint of intimidation?

Helmut shifted his briefcase from one hand to the other and began to move toward the door. "I'm on my way to my car, young man. You have until we reach it to explain what could possibly be so urgent."

chapter 6

"So—what's the verdict, Doc?" The teenager on the examination table looked up at Lara through half-closed lids. "Was the home pregnancy test right?"

Lara laid the girl's file on the tray and leaned against the wall. "Yes. You are pregnant."

The girl closed her eyes. "Wouldn't you know I'd have lousy luck. My first time and here I am, pregnant by some guy I'll never see again."

"The father has a right to know." Lara picked up the chart again. Adrienne Mittroff, age fifteen, in the tenth grade at Charlottesville High School. Perfectly healthy—and six weeks pregnant.

Adrienne sat upright and pushed a strand of fine golden hair from her face. "The father? I don't even know his name. He was just some college student I met, and next month he'll be going back to wherever he came from. I wouldn't know how to find him if I tried."

Lara lowered her eyes, resisting a sudden urge to shake some sense into her patient. She and Olivia encountered pregnant teenagers nearly every day, but they never ceased to frustrate Lara. Some came to the office in tears; others walked in clutching a stick from a home pregnancy test kit. Many, Lara knew, left the Women's Clinic and drove straight to the nearest abortion provider.

"Adrienne, it's important that you realize you're carrying a new life within you." Lara folded her arms over the patient's chart and met the girl's bewildered gaze straight on. "Some people will try to tell you that the fetus is just a blob of tissue, but it's not; it's a tiny baby. If this pregnancy is a problem, we can refer you to several different groups that offer support services, including housing and adoption counseling."

"I'm going to keep it." Adrienne leaned back on her hands, and her gaze fell to the floor for an instant. "I always wanted something that'd be all mine."

Lara bit her lip. "A baby is not a *thing*, Adrienne. Your little boy or girl is a special person, and the baby deserves a loving home with parents who are prepared to sacrifice for him—"

She stiffened as her own words reverberated in her ears. *Parents?* She was planning to offer her own baby just one parent. But she was a medical professional, an adult, and a mature woman. She was certainly more qualified to parent than this naive fifteen-year-old.

Lara moved to the desk, then grabbed a notepad and began to write out the name of a local counseling center. "Adrienne, promise me that you'll see someone at this center. I applaud you for wanting to give your baby life, but there's a lot of work involved in raising a child."

"Not so as I can see." Adrienne slipped from the exam table and moved toward the curtained cubicle where she'd left her clothes. "My parents never did much with me. Anybody could do a better job than them."

Lara stood in dumb silence as the girl retreated behind the partition and began to dress. Where was the justice in life? This girl, this *child*, would give birth to a baby in less than nine months while Lara, an educated, responsible *adult*, had to practically beg permission and approval from everyone she knew before she could even *think* about having a baby.

"I'm going to write you a scrip for prenatal vitamins," she called, reaching for her prescription pad. "Be sure you have it filled and take the vitamins regularly. If you have no insurance or can't afford the vitamins, let me know, and I'll put you in touch with someone from social services."

"Okay," came the voice from behind the curtain. "Cool."

∞

The sun lay half-hidden behind the distant mountains by the time Lara pulled onto her street. She had stayed late to talk to Olivia about Adrienne Mittroff, and the conversation had confused Lara further. In the exam room, she had been a breath away from lecturing Adrienne about the importance of giving a baby a loving home with two parents, yet *her* child, if she chose to have it, would have only one. Of course she'd tell her baby about Michael and her child would always know he was loved and desperately wanted. And as strange as it felt to admit it, Olivia was right, she *might* marry again one day, so her child wouldn't be fatherless forever . . .

She pulled into her driveway, turned the key, and waited as the engine skipped and shuddered into stillness. The old Maxima definitely needed a tune-up, but she'd have to wait until Saturday to take it to a mechanic.

She gathered her purse and a few files she wanted to review, then slid out of the car and slammed the door with her hip. She hadn't gone two steps when a male voice shattered the stillness and made her jump.

"Good evening." Connor's head and shoulders appeared from behind the Mustang. He must have seen her startled reaction, for his mouth curved in an apologetic smile. "Sorry. Didn't mean to alarm you."

"It's okay." Lara managed a smile, then walked to her porch. While she opened her creaking mailbox, her thoughts turned again to her neighbor. Connor O'Hara seemed to be a nice guy, and he'd lived in the complex at least as long as she and Michael had. On many afternoons she had come home to find Michael and Connor on the couch, sipping Cokes and watching baseball, but Connor almost always dismissed himself when she started rattling pots and pans in the kitchen. He had definitely kept himself at arm's length, at least where she was concerned.

One afternoon, as Connor slipped out the door just after Lara had come in, she jokingly asked Michael if their neighbor was afraid of her. "No." He grinned as if she'd just told the world's funniest joke. "He's just jealous."

"Whatever of?"

"Me." Michael wagged his eyebrows, Groucho Marx-style. "He thinks you're beautiful and smart, and he's a little frustrated with the singles scene."

Lara felt herself flush at the compliment; then she shrugged it away. "He's a decent-looking guy. I can't see why he'd have any trouble finding someone to date."

Michael took another swig of his Coke, then waved his hand. "He dates, but it would take someone special to hold Connor's attention. He reads a lot and he's smart. Like *professionally* intelligent. He knows everything."

Lara laughed in spite of herself. "Nobody knows everything."

"Yeah, but Connor knows more than most. He's a walking, talking encyclopedia."

The memory faded as Lara looked across the lawn. Mr. Encyclopedia was sitting inside his car now, energetically polishing the dash. Maybe he wouldn't mind if she interrupted him. Maybe a man who knew everything could give her a bit of unbiased advice.

She dropped her mail and files by the door, then walked to the edge of her porch. "Connor?"

His dark head popped out of the car, and he paused to swipe at a leaf that had blown onto the windshield. "You need something?"

"Yes. Your opinion." She clung to the porch pole and stepped forward, the toes of her shoes hanging over the concrete edge. Both Eva and Olivia would say she was crazy for asking a mere acquaintance about such a private matter, but they hadn't exactly been able to give impartial advice. Olivia didn't want to lose a staff member, and Eva obviously didn't want to deal with a grandchild born over a year after her son's death. The blue-blooded guardians of Charlottesville society would have a grand time speculating about *that* scenario.

"You want my opinion?" Connor slipped through a gap in the hedge and came toward her, wiping his hands on a dingy rag as he approached. "Gee, that's different. All day long I hear requests for information, but no one wants to know what I think."

Lara tilted her head. "I thought you were a librarian."

"*Reference* librarian." He gave her a lopsided smile. "In the *I-gotta-have-an-answer-now* section of the university library."

Lara felt an unwelcome blush creep onto her cheeks. She'd known this guy for five years, and she had no idea what he did? "Sorry. I guess I thought you spent all day shelving books."

"It's okay." He gave her a look of faint amusement. "How can I help?"

"It's silly, really." Lara gripped the porch post with both hands. "In fact, I probably have no business asking you this, but I can't seem to get a straight answer from anyone else. I thought maybe you could offer an opinion, since we don't know each other well."

His dark brown eyes were soft. "I feel like I know you. Michael and I talked quite a bit—mostly at the end, when he would set up his easel out on the lawn. I used to come out and talk to him before I had to go to work."

For a moment Lara couldn't answer. Memories came crowding back like unwelcome guests—Michael hobbling in front of his easel after they amputated his leg, Michael sitting in front of his easel as the cancer gnawed away at his bones. She could imagine that Connor had been helpful even then, moving the easel, helping Michael carry his water-color box, perhaps even commenting as Michael mixed his colors and sponged his paper. And Michael, the world's most confident extrovert, had basked in Connor's attention, rambling about his work, his dreams, his wife.

"What do you want to know, Lara?"

Connor stood beside her porch now, waiting. Lara ran her hand through her hair as if the gesture could sweep the cobwebs of memory from her brain. "What do you think about single parenting? Michael and I always talked about a baby, and—well, he made arrangements. I can have his baby if I want to. But is it fair to bring a baby into the world when its father is dead?" Her gaze lifted to the western horizon, the sunset-and-pond landscape she and Michael had admired a thousand times. "I'll take some time off, so my career isn't the issue, but what if I get pregnant and decide this wasn't such a good idea? Or what if I find out I'm not cut out for motherhood after the baby's born? Maybe God kept me from getting pregnant while Michael was alive because he knew I wouldn't be a good mother. Or maybe it's not his will for me to raise a fatherless baby." She paused, grateful for the deepening dusk, when her eyes filled with tears. Maybe Connor wouldn't notice.

"I believe"—a strange, faintly eager note filled his voice—"you'd make a wonderful mother. I watched you with Michael, after he got sick. You were always patient and loving, even when I knew you'd been up half the night. You displayed gentleness, kindness, and love. What more could a baby need?"

Gathering her courage, she shifted her gaze to meet his. A wistful look had stolen into his expression. "I used to watch you two when you sat on the park bench over there, every night at sunset. I'll admit, sometimes I envied Michael for finding someone like you. And I think you have more than enough love to share with a child."

Lara swallowed hard. "What about not having a father? Am I being unfair to the baby?"

"I wouldn't advise every woman to go out and have a baby just because she wants one." Connor scuffed the toe of his sneakers into her bare flower bed. "But your situation is different. You had a husband; you can have his child. And doesn't God promise to be a father to the fatherless?"

Lara's brows lifted. He knew the Bible? "You reference librarians know a lot, don't you?"

Connor laughed softly. "Reference librarians know a little about lots of things. But I grew up in a minister's home. My father's still pastoring a church in Lynchburg."

The corner of Lara's mouth twisted. "You're lucky. My parents have been gone for years—they were killed in a car wreck while I was in college. They never even knew Michael. But I've still got Eva—Michael's mother. So my baby won't be totally alone in the world."

"Then I'll be praying that you make the right decision." Connor looked up and lifted his hand; for a moment she thought he intended to squeeze her arm. But he only wiped his palm on his shirt and gave her a bemused smile. "Bottom line, I think you'd be a wonderful mother."

∞

Lara turned on her bed and draped her hands over her head, trying to block the cuckoo clock's midnight warbling. It was no use. Though she felt achy and exhausted, her brain hummed with a million thoughts. Sleep would not come until she had dealt with them.

She flung off the quilts and left her bedroom, padding over the carpet to the small would-be nursery. The bright yellow walls seemed faded in the moonlight; the rainbow wallpaper border shimmered in shades of black and gray. The room seemed as empty as a tomb. The hospital bed had been taken away and all that remained of her dreams was a squeaky old dresser that had served her own childhood.

She crouched in the darkness and opened the bottom drawer, then felt for the silky fabric of her baby book. Finding it, she sank to the floor and pulled it onto her lap, then lifted the book into a stream of light from the streetlamp outside. *Lara Michelle Petersen,* her mother had lovingly inscribed with a fountain pen, *born October 14, 1970, weighed eight pounds, two ounces and was twenty-one inches long.* On another page, her mother had carefully listed every baby gift and the day it was acknowledged with a thank-you note . . . just as Lara had recorded every wedding gift and funeral bouquet.

She closed the baby book and hugged it to her chest. Why had she known so much sorrow? She had lost her parents and her husband in a relatively short time. The Bible said that to everything there was a season, a time to be born, a time to die, a time to kill and a time to heal, a time to cry and a time to laugh. There was a time to grieve and a time to dance—but Lara had endured more than a season of tears and sorrow. She wanted to laugh, to welcome a birth, to dance in joy.

Michael would approve of her pregnancy. Eva would eventually get over her initial disapproval, and Olivia would hire another physician's assistant until Lara wanted to come back to work. But was it the right thing to do?

Lara lifted her eyes to the ceiling, hoping to find an answer in the interplay of shadows and plaster swirls. "Please, Father, will you give me an answer?" she begged, searching her heart for the voice that had spoken to her on other occasions when she sought God's face. "I've asked everyone but you for an opinion, and I need your wisdom. I want this baby, Lord, but if it is not the right thing, show me. I know you can heal my broken emotions. But I can't help feeling that you've placed this desire in my heart, so let me know if it's right. Please, Lord, show me what to do."

She sat silently, her arms wrapped loosely around her bent knees, while the wind whistled outside and the branches of a dogwood brushed against the windows. After a moment, she obeyed a deep-seated impulse and pulled her Bible from the top of the dresser, then opened it to a passage in Proverbs.

Her gaze fell upon a verse that might well have been the only one on the page, for none of the others registered in her brain. Her voice trembled as she breathed in the words: "Hope deferred makes the heart sick, but when dreams come true, there is life and joy."

Hope deferred—she certainly knew about that. She had postponed her dreams of children; she had pushed aside life itself while Michael battled his cancer. After each treatment and surgery, they had treasured a hope that the cancer had been arrested, only to find that it hadn't. For some reason, God had deferred their hopes for years, allowing them to experience heart sickness, but—*when dreams come true.*

Not *if* dreams come true, but *when*! With pulse-pounding certainty, Lara knew she had discovered God's answer.

She lowered her Bible to the floor, then lifted her hands in the golden glow of the streetlamp. "Oh, God," she whispered, her throat clotting with emotions too deep to verbalize, "how good you are to me! Thank you, Father, for your goodness. Thank you for not forgetting me."

A profound and steadfast peace stole over her spirit. For the first time in days she felt truly calm. She pressed her hand over the lace of her nightgown and smiled at the grateful pounding of her heart.

Perhaps Eva was right. Motherhood might bring pain, but God had just promised that it would also bring life and joy. Eva would never understand Lara's conviction, but only because she had never waited on God or heard the clarity of his inaudible voice.

Lara laughed, the sound muffled against her hand as she pressed it over her lips. A baby. No matter what anyone said, she knew there would be a baby. Michael's baby.

She knew about the risks of love. Loving Michael—a carefree, unemployed, outgoing artist—had been a risk, too, but she had never regretted a single moment she spent loving him. Now she was ready to pass that love to their child.

The promised child of life and joy.

∞

The next afternoon, Lara caught herself glancing uneasily over her shoulder as she walked toward Olivia's office. The hallway was quiet now, the other staff members busy with their end of the day routines. The front doors had been locked promptly at four thirty, and Lara had made short work of dictating her notes for the transcriptionist. Her decision weighed on her mind, and she needed to speak to Olivia as soon as possible.

She cleared her throat, then leaned into the doorway. Olivia sat at her desk, and Dr. Helmut Braun, her husband and partner, sat in a chair at her right hand. Their heads, one silver and one blonde, were bent over a case file.

"Knock, knock." Lara deliberately kept her voice low. "If you have a moment, doctors, I'd like to speak to both of you."

"Thank goodness, an interruption." Olivia looked up from the chart and dropped her pencil onto the desk. "Sheesh, what a day." She rubbed her temples with her fingertips. "Remind me, Lara, never to schedule two initial visits in the same morning. Today I had two teenagers, both scared as cats in a dog pound. Don't mothers prepare their daughters for anything these days?"

"Drinking and driving, maybe," Lara answered, entering the office. "And AIDS." She nodded a hello to Dr. Braun, then perched on the edge of the love seat. "If this is a bad time, I could wait and speak to you later."

Olivia dropped her hands into her lap, then gave Lara a weary smile. "I can tell from the look in your eye that it can't wait. You've had that look all day."

"What look?"

"The look that tells me I'm about to lose the best physician's assistant I've ever had. Is this about the pregnancy you're considering?"

Lara saw the smile hidden in the corner of Olivia's mouth, then nodded in relief. "I'm not considering it anymore. I'm going to proceed." She pulled a slip of paper from her pocket and slid it across the desk. "If you really meant it when you said you thought the specimen should be checked for genetic abnormalities—"

"I meant it." Olivia picked up the registration form.

"—then there's the reference number, Michael's full name, and all the other pertinent information. His specimen is stored at the university's cryogenics lab." She turned to Dr. Braun, whose attention had returned to the case file on the desk. "In your area, sir."

Olivia tapped her nails upon the desk, then handed the paper to her husband. "You can take care of this for us, can't you?"

"What's this?" Helmut picked up the registration and studied it, his square jaw tensing. "Who is Michael Godfrey?"

"Lara's late husband." Olivia gentled her voice. "Surely you remember the funeral. The young man who died last October—"

"I remember." Dr. Braun looked up. "I am sorry for your loss."

"Thank you, sir. But I'm ready to stop thinking about my loss and start thinking about the future." Lara chose her words carefully in the hope that Dr. Braun would understand the significance of her request. "Michael's sperm deposit is all I have left of him. I haven't made this decision lightly."

"She's concerned about the age of the deposit," Olivia added, turning to her husband. "As well as the possibility of a cancer gene. Her husband died of bone cancer." Her gaze arched back to Lara. "If he finds a problem, you'll want to drop the idea, right?"

"No." Lara twisted her hands in her lap and looked at Dr. Braun. "If for some reason the specimen isn't ideal, I would appreciate anything you could do to help me have my husband's child. I know they've made tremendous advances in gene splicing. If there's a way to identify the gene and eliminate it, that's what I want to do."

Dr. Braun lifted his head like a cat scenting the breeze. "Interesting," he murmured, his gaze falling again upon Michael's registration slip. "Extremely intriguing. The Human Genome Project has discovered several genes that could play a role in the development of bone cancers—the other afternoon I was reading about two, EXT1 on chromosome eight and EXT2 on chromosome eleven. If those genes are present, it might be possible to remove them." Two deep worry lines appeared between his silver brows as he studied the registration. "Provided the DNA strand is still in good condition."

"Will you help, Helmut?" Olivia leaned her elbow on the desk, eyeing her husband with a critical squint. "She needs to know if you're willing to do this for her."

Dr. Braun pinned Lara in a long, silent scrutiny, then handed the registration slip back to her. "How badly do you want a baby, Ms. Godfrey? If I find EXT1 or EXT2, will you automatically consider another option? Artificial insemination by donor is an option, you know. Many women are opting to become mothers through AID."

Lara shook her head. "I want my husband's baby, not a stranger's. I'm not in love with the idea of being pregnant or being somebody's mother. I want to have Michael's baby. He always wanted kids—it was one of the few dreams we weren't able to make come true."

A thoughtful smile curved Olivia's mouth as she nudged her husband. "So what do you think? It might be a great research project for you, a sure way to get your name in the medical journals. Think of it as modern technology put to use on a human level."

"I would need to know"—Dr. Braun stared at Lara with an almost deadly concentration—"if Ms. Godfrey is truly committed. This might require a great deal of work, and if she cannot commit to see it through . . ."

Lara met the doctor's worried eyes without flinching. "I'm not a quitter, Dr. Braun, and I know how much work is involved. But I believe I was meant to have my husband's baby, so I will do whatever is necessary. There's only one thing that concerns me." Her gaze caught and held Olivia's. "The expense. I have some money put away, but I hadn't counted on an intensive laboratory procedure."

Helmut leaned back and clasped his hands around his ample middle. "We can find the money. One can almost always find grants for cancer research." He paused and looked at his wife. "You are happy about this?"

"Not really," Olivia answered, her voice dry, "but if a baby will make Lara happy, I'll get used to the idea."

The older man tapped his fingers on Olivia's desktop, his brows knitting as he stared at Lara. "If I find no sign of a suspicious gene, you can proceed with artificial insemination. However, AI would not be my method of choice if the DNA is flawed." He gave Olivia a bright-eyed glance, filled with shrewdness. "If we must manipulate the genetic strand, we ought to consider in vitro fertilization. It is a more tedious process, but ultimately more controllable. We can be certain that fertilization has occurred."

Olivia nodded. "IVF is the best way, Lara. We'll use drugs to stimulate your ovaries, then we'll fertilize several eggs with DNA-altered sperm. If we're fortunate, the fertilization will result in several embryos, one or two of which will be transferred into your uterus—"

Lara held up her hand. "We can't do it that way. Embryos are *babies* and I'm not going to leave them in cryogenic storage. No way. You can harvest several eggs and freeze them, but you can only fertilize one. If the fertilization fails, we can try later with another egg, but no baby of mine and Michael's is going to be flash-frozen forever."

Olivia gave Helmut a long warning look; then the researcher sighed. "All right. We'll use just one egg, but you have to realize that the odds for successful fertilization will drop considerably if we do."

"I'm not worried about the odds." Lara flashed Dr. Braun a quick smile. How could she explain the peace that had filled her heart? God had given her a special promise—not *if* the desire comes, but *when.* "I'll be the best patient you ever had, Doctor. I won't complain, and I'll take my meds on time. I'll do whatever you tell me to, because I'm certain this procedure will result in a healthy, happy baby."

"Will you wait a couple of months?" Olivia asked. "You probably need some time to get used to the idea of changes in your life."

"I have too much time on my hands now." Lara looked at the geneticist and lifted the registration slip. "I'm ready to begin whenever you are. Take Michael's information, have a look at the specimen, and tell me what you find. I'll be ready to proceed as soon as you say it's okay."

Dr. Braun paused for a long moment, his hands on his knees; then he took the paper from Lara's hand. "Well, ladies," he said, slipping the information into his pocket as he stood, "I am glad we have had this discussion. It could prove to be an interesting project."

Lara's heart sang as he turned to his wife. "Liv, go ahead and work up a calendar for Ms. Godfrey. You know the drill, fifty milligrams of clomiphene on the fifth day of the menstrual cycle for five days, then an ovarian sonogram. If she responds, we'll proceed with follicular aspiration." He tugged on the lapel of his lab coat and smiled at Lara. "While Liv takes care of you, I will thaw the specimen and take a look at what made your husband tick. Perhaps we will get lucky and find that he was quite an ordinary fellow."

Lara grinned. "I don't think anything about Michael was ordinary."

Helmut smiled, a rare sight, then nodded. "Excuse me, Ms. Godfrey, but I have a dinner appointment." He bent to kiss his wife's cheek. "I'll see you at home, but I'm certain I will be late."

Olivia murmured a farewell, then waited until Helmut had walked down the hall before looking at Lara again. "So." She leaned forward, her hands on the desk. "Have you thought it all out, counted the costs, so to speak?"

Lara forced dignity into her voice. "I have."

"Have you told Michael's mother that maybe, just maybe, she might soon be a grandmother?"

Lara looked away. "That news"—her cheeks flushed—"can wait until after I'm pregnant."

Olivia leaned back in her chair and grinned. "Coward."

"I know." Lara gave her friend a wry smile as she stood. "But you'd do the same thing in my shoes."

chapter 7

"I'm glad, Dr. Braun, that you agreed to fit me into your hectic schedule." Devin Sloane's lips parted in a dazzling display of straight, white teeth. "And I hope the chateaubriand is to your liking."

Helmut sliced the steak with his knife; a fork would have done the job. Great heaven, he hadn't had a meal like this in . . . why, he had *never* had a meal like this. He put another slice of beef into his mouth, savoring the texture and taste. He hadn't particularly wanted to meet with Sloane tonight; demanding benefactors were usually boring, bothersome pains-in-the-neck. But at least Sloane seemed to appreciate the value of Helmut's time.

Helmut swallowed, then sipped from his wineglass. "When your assistant mentioned the Iceman of the Alps, I could not resist the invitation." He sliced another bite of the luscious chateaubriand. "Curiosity, I confess, has caused me to fritter away more hours than anything else. But I suppose that is what makes a good researcher, no?"

"Indubitably." Devin Sloane lifted his glass and swirled the liquid. "I myself am a very curious man, Dr. Braun. Curiosity compelled me to go to Europe last weekend, and after my return curiosity demanded that I see you as soon as possible."

"Whatever for?"

Sloane smiled and set his glass on the table, then stared at Helmut with a look of implacable determination. "Because I want the same thing Lucifer promised Eve in the creation myth. Do you remember what it was? Fruit from the Tree of Knowledge."

Intrigued, Helmut lowered his knife and fork. "Isn't that what most intelligent men seek? We are all engaged in the pursuit of knowledge; we all yearn to know all a man can know."

"Yet we are limited by our very finiteness." Sloane's dark eyes sparkled like the wine. "Man's brain, as complex as it is, is restrained by certain biological factors. I'm well aware of the theory that genetic manipulation might be able to coax the brain cells into dividing one more time, thereby doubling its size—"

Following Sloane's thought, He___t cut in: "But the head would then be too large to squeeze throu___ __ __h canal."

"Exactly." Sloane's fist pounde_____ an emphatic thump. "The average man today possesse_____alf quart brain with ten billion nerve cells and ten times _____ells, but the average *intelligent* man uses only 10 percent of _____ften mistakenly referred to as his 'gray matter.'" His square jaw tensed visibly. "I'm willing to bet the average teenager uses only 2 percent."

"So what would you have science do?" Helmut frowned. "In particular, what would you have *me* do? I am a geneticist, Sloane. I am not a psychosurgeon or a neurologist."

"I am not pursuing those dead ends." Sloane lowered his voice and leaned closer. "Forget psychosurgery; ignore the quacks who are experimenting with electrical stimulation of the brain. I have no use for those who would have us pop a pill or meditate to biofeed our way to greater intelligence or mental health." Sloane leaned back, a feral light gleaming in the luminous depths of his eyes. "You, sir, are German. You should understand."

Helmut shrugged to hide his confusion. "*Ja*, I am German. But what has that to do—"

"Your forefathers." Sloane broke into an open, friendly smile. "Have you forgotten your own heritage? Your people were light-years ahead of other nations. They saw the dire necessity of improving human stock through eugenics. They knew that we humans have been inching down the genetic staircase and since World War II we have only accelerated our decline. Radiation, certain drugs, dyes, food additives, plastics, and other environmental agents are destroying the future of our race."

Struggling to mask his uneasiness, Helmut painted on a neutral smile. "The Nazis were defeated, Mr. Sloane. And Mengele's experiments horrified the world. You cannot be suggesting that we—"

"Mengele was an amateur. He had not one-tenth of the knowledge today's average schoolchild has available at his fingertips," Sloane answered in a low, composed voice. "And you are quite right to shudder at the thought of Mengele's horrific experiments. I am no Nazi, Dr. Braun. Hitler and his associates made the mistake of thinking *they* possessed superior genes. I am not so deluded. I know that my DNA, for instance, is not all it should be. As much as any man, I stand in the need of genetic improvement."

An easy smile played at the corner of the billionaire's mouth. "What's that old hymn? It's me, O Lord, standing in the need of prayer? I'd be the first to admit I'm as debased as my neighbor. While I'm healthy, reasonably well-bred, and of above-average intelligence, even I cannot escape the gradual genetic erosion that affected my parents and grandparents. Therefore even I am in need of a holy touch—and that's why I need your help."

A chill shock held Helmut in place. He lifted his hand to reach for his glass, then saw that his fingers trembled. He dropped his hand into his lap, then looked up and met Sloane's gaze. "I assume you have a plan."

"Of course I do." Sloane cupped his wineglass, then stared thoughtfully at the dark liquid. "My plan is threefold. The first phase involves the new pediatric hospital—a program I am underwriting, by the way. My public role is discreet, of course, but make no mistake, the program is completely under my direction. I've approved every doctor and specialist; I've even been consulted about the décor in the parents' waiting room."

Helmut forced himself to glance away, to slice another piece of beef. "I haven't much interest in pediatrics."

"Your talents are needed elsewhere. But the new Ethan Jefferson Pediatric Hospital for Genetic Research will concentrate exclusively on genetic illnesses—cystic fibrosis, certain cancers, sickle cell anemia, Tay-Sachs, and so on. Patients will be treated through gene therapy, and parents will be counseled so they don't reproduce again and compound the problem. In every consultation and publication we will proclaim that every child has a right to full educational opportunities, healthful nutrition, and a sound genetic heritage. Best of all, the hospital will be designed to aid the poor—all cases will be charity cases, and medical care will be given without cost to the patient."

With an effort, Helmut swallowed a slice of suddenly tasteless steak. "Gene therapy is an emerging science. Your success will be limited."

"Only in the first few years." Sloane's eyes glittered with restless passion. "Then, gene by gene, we will creep back up the genetic ladder. Using cell fusion, recombinant DNA, and germline therapy, we will improve the basis of the human race."

Helmut froze with his hands on his knife and fork. "Germline therapy?" His voice rasped. "But that procedure goes against the established protocols of genetic research."

"The standards are being pushed back even as we speak." Reflected light from the chandelier glimmered over Sloane's handsome face like beams of icy radiance. "The National Institutes of Health has been put on notice. Germline therapy is the logical next step—and it's the one I want you to take with me, Dr. Braun. It is the second phase of my plan, and I'm sure you can understand why it must remain a private matter."

Helmut lowered his utensils, then wiped his hands on his napkin, shaken by Sloane's hideous and alluring proposal. Germline therapy, which involved injecting a fertilized egg with an artificial human chromosome carrying specially designed DNA, had not yet been approved by the National Institutes of Health. When the NIH approved gene therapy in 1987, doctors promised they would never alter any patient's egg or sperm.

But germline therapy would be a gigantic step forward in genetic research. A doctor would not have to insinuate the new gene into millions of cells in order to cure a patient's diseased organ. One single cell—a fertilized egg—would result in a disease-resistant human being.

Times were changing rapidly . . . and the thought of being in the front wave of research was tantalizing.

"My work at the children's hospital will be slow and laborious," Sloane said, watching Helmut through half-closed eyelids. "But through germ-line therapy I have an opportunity to take a giant step forward. With one procedure, I believe I can bring mankind to the brink of perfection."

"How?" His mind spinning in a new direction, Helmut croaked the question. "You are talking about cataloging and carefully evaluating up to 100,000 different genes, not to mention the thousands of nucleotides in a single gene. I would rather be asked to find one particular snowflake in a blizzard than to do what you are suggesting. It's impossible."

A wry but indulgent gleam appeared in Sloane's eye. "It would be impossible if we were working from contemporary DNA. But, my friend, I have already found the key to perfection, and I have it safely locked away in a vault. The future fell into my possession last weekend when I visited the fabled Iceman of the Alps."

A hundred bits of the evening's conversation collided in Helmut's head like bits of glass in a kaleidoscope. The Iceman, intelligence, genetics, germline therapy—

He lifted his hand to his chin and regarded his host with somber curiosity. "You're talking about the Iceman's DNA."

Sloane cast Helmut a bright look of eagerness. "I *knew* you'd understand. I have searched throughout the world, Dr. Braun, and I believe you are the man who can help me restore mankind's potential. The rewards for your work on this project will be greater than you can imagine, both financially and professionally. The money I have granted thus far is a mere pittance, I am prepared to spend far more. And when our project is completed, your name will be lauded across the entire world, honored throughout the millennium to come. Mankind will be all he was designed to be; he will use 80, possibly even *90* percent of his brain. Have you any idea how such a project could change the future of mankind?"

Helmut began to wonder just what Sloane wanted of him. "What, exactly, does this project involve?"

Sloane lifted a warning finger. "I am saying no more—yet." He sank back in his chair and folded his hands. "I cannot share the complete details of my intended experiment until I hear more from you, Dr. Braun. If we are to venture together on this road to the future, we must be of one mind and one determination, wedded in intent and purpose."

Helmut lifted his hands. "What could you possibly want to know about me? My work is a matter of public record. I've been working to isolate genetic markers for cancer and other diseases—"

"I know about your current work; I have at least a half million dollar stake in the outcome," Sloane interrupted smoothly. "What I want to know is if you are willing to leave all that behind for the second phase of my research project."

Despite his initial misgivings, Helmut felt his excitement rise. "If the project has to do with germline testing, I will make the time. What are assistants for, if not to leave me free for critical work?"

"Well said." Sloane's eyes darkened. "What about your wife, Dr. Braun? This research might require a great deal of your time . . . and all your discretion."

Helmut shrugged. "Olivia and I are married to our careers as well as each other. After twenty years of marriage, Mr. Sloane, I can assure you that my wife understands the demands of my work. Her own patients keep her busy at all hours of the day and night. She operates a very successful obstetrical practice."

"Amazing." Sloane's face creased into a sudden smile. "There is one other concern, Doctor, and a crucial question only you can answer. The experiment will make it necessary to involve at least one other person in a terribly important role."

"Another researcher?"

"A subject. Someone who must not be *fully aware* of the experiment's implications. Can you, Doctor Braun, participate in my project under such a condition?"

Helmut felt his mouth go dry. He had chosen to work in the field of genetics precisely because there were few living, breathing humans involved in his research work. Olivia handled the occasions that called for a brilliant bedside manner because he had the social graces of an ox.

Yet, with rewards so great . . .

From some place deep inside he summoned an ounce of courage. "Will the subject be harmed or altered in any way?"

Sloane shook his head. "Absolutely not. Our test subject will not even be aware of the experiment. Partially informed, of course. But not completely." He must have sensed Helmut's reticence, for he continued: "May I take the liberty of reminding you of Hippocrates' thoughts? Though we remember him as the medical ethicist who told physicians to 'do no harm,' Hippocrates also admonished physicians to perform their duties calmly and adroitly, *concealing most things from the patient*. He told his students to give necessary orders with cheerfulness and sincerity, turning the patient's attention away from what is being done to him while revealing nothing of his future or present condition."

Sloane's dark eyes moved into Helmut's. "Can I count on you to agree with Hippocrates?"

"You are absolutely certain the subject will not be harmed?"

"Completely."

Helmut pressed his lips together as a persistent memory niggled for his attention. If he accepted, his research partners could continue his present projects, but he would be able to devote only the barest amount of time to Lara Godfrey's case. Though he had made her a promise, which mattered more—helping only one woman, or charting the course of mankind's future?

He shifted in his chair. "You spoke of a three-phase plan, but we have only discussed two."

"Phase one is public, phase two is private, and phase three is confidential." A secretive smile softened Sloane's mouth. "Please, doctor, be patient with me. All will be revealed in good time."

Helmut tilted his head, considering. The man certainly had a right to his little secrets, and he'd already given Helmut more than enough to consider. Though he wasn't certain the Iceman's DNA would prove to be of any great worth, he would have a tremendous edge over other researchers if he began working with germline therapy now.

He lifted his wineglass. "Mr. Sloane, I would be delighted to participate in the second phase of your program. I will devote my utmost concentration to your project."

Honest appreciation shone from Sloane's dark eyes. "Let us drink to our work, then, and to the child who is to come."

Helmut clinked his glass against Sloane's. "The child?"

"The fruit of the tree of knowledge," Sloane answered. "The son of *Homo Tyrolensis,* the most perfectly preserved human genetic specimen in existence."

chapter 8

The tiny red light on Lemuel Reis's tape recorder glowed like a demonic eye as the microcassette inside whirred, catching all of Devin Sloane's commands, requests, and observations. "Send a check for one thousand to Bill Masters at the university for his search fee," Devin said, tossing a note into the trash can at the side of his desk. "And write five letters to the women whose names he sent. Polite replies to all, thanks for their interest, but they aren't appropriate—or something discreet. Be tactful, but don't say anything to imply I gave them any serious consideration. We wouldn't want to invite a breach of contract suit."

"Were none of them suitable?" Lemuel asked, thinking of the five files Masters had delivered the day before. Each had contained a dossier on a beautiful, intelligent university student. All five were young and healthy; all had IQs of over one hundred twenty . . .

"None." Devin's gaze flitted over the folders on his desk with impassive coldness. "I don't know what Masters was thinking. The first one, this Stephanie Maple, didn't even bother to respond to the question about her favorite comedy. I'll not have my child carried by some humorless female with the soul of a microchip. Nicole Haley's mother died of breast cancer, a genetic risk, and Andrea Belknap is at least ten pounds underweight. I can't risk everything on an anorexic beauty queen. Janet Redfield's family is living below the poverty level—"

"Surely you don't think poverty is genetic," Lemuel interrupted, lifting a brow.

"No." Devin's eyes darkened dangerously. "But if the girl is not money-hungry, her mother or father will be; count on it. These women

76

are applying to be the surrogate mother to *my* child, and intuition tells me Janet Redfield is thinking mostly of dollar signs."

Lemuel's eyes darted toward the last folder on Devin's desk. "There was one other."

"Ah, Glazier Thomas." Devin picked up the file and flipped it open. From where he sat Lemuel could see the photograph paper-clipped to the folder—Glazier Thomas was a lovely blonde with green eyes. "Twenty-three years old, IQ of one twenty-two, psychology major, good health, stable parents, no obvious poverty or physical defects."

"So why not interview Miss Thomas? If she is willing to participate in the experiment—"

"No religious affiliation." Devin abruptly snapped the folder shut and tossed it onto the pile with the others. "No spiritual concerns whatsoever. A woman with vast emotional, physical, and social resources, but nothing else. And my child, Lemuel, will be a spiritual person. Our ancient ancestors knew how to embrace the mystery of creation, how to feel its vast power within the depths of their souls, how to plumb its riches and majesty. But people like Glazier Thomas scarcely take the time to look up and consider the stars, much less the power behind them."

He smiled, but with a distracted inward look, as though imagining something only he could understand. "My child will be different," he whispered, swiveling his chair. He leaned forward, flicked the louvers of the shutters over the massive window behind his desk, then stared out over the emptiness of his perfectly manicured lawn. After a long moment, he turned to Lemuel and shoved the folders across the desk. "Polite rejection letters to each. Thanks but no thanks, the sort of thing you do so well."

Lemuel gathered the files and stacked them on his lap. "So what should I do now? If none of the university students are acceptable, will you broaden your search?"

"I'll find the woman on my own," Devin answered, standing. He moved to the wide window again and looked out across the silent lawn. "Pay Masters his thousand dollars, but do not accept any more of his calls. We're finished with him. But write another check to Helmut Braun; I'll deliver it myself."

"Another five hundred thousand?"

"One million." Conviction edged Devin's mellow voice. "For that kind of money, Dr. Braun will help me find the woman I want."

chapter 9

The university's cryogenic and genetics lab was housed in a nondescript brick building, its interior cut down the center by a single corridor. No one sat behind the receptionist's desk when Lara arrived on a Wednesday afternoon, and Lara moved past it without stopping. She didn't have an appointment and would feel foolish trying to explain her reason for visiting Dr. Braun.

Better to just drop in and act as though this were a casual visit. Helmut Braun hadn't visited the Women's Clinic since her meeting with him three weeks before, and she wanted to be certain he was still committed to helping her. She had spent the last eight days on hormonal medications, and this morning's ultrasound had indicated that the follicles of her ovaries were enlarged. Olivia was ready to proceed with the injection to cause the final ripening of the eggs; retrieval would have to occur soon afterward. Though the harvested eggs, or oocytes, could survive freezing indefinitely, Lara didn't want to waste time. She needed to know if Dr. Braun had begun the genetic screening of the DNA from Michael's specimen.

The first door on her left bore Dr. Braun's name, and Lara paused to peer through the window. Bright fluorescent light gave the laboratory a slightly blue look, and along the wall an array of stainless steel tanks shimmered beneath the overhead lights. A freestanding chalkboard, scribbled with numbers and symbols, stood against one wall; stacks of files and bound documents cluttered the tables. Suspended from the ceiling like a work of art, a winding double helix spiraled slowly above the heads of two young men working at computers along the far wall. In the corner of the room stood another door—undoubtedly the entrance to Dr. Braun's private office.

Lara pulled the lab door open and walked toward the office, then jumped when a voice broke the quiet.

"You looking for Braun?" One of the students had turned in his seat. He looked at her through a fringe of brown bangs, an inexplicable, lazy smile sweeping over his face.

"Yes," she answered, her face burning under the frank approval in his eyes.

"Back there." The boy jerked his thumb toward the inner door, then draped his arm over the back of his chair, watching her as she walked by. Lara groaned inwardly. College men—she'd almost forgotten that the average model came equipped with an overactive libido.

She straightened and kept walking, reassured by the sight of Olivia's husband through the door's rectangular window. Dr. Braun sat at his desk, a frustrated expression on his face. He waved his hand as if he were trying to explain something to the dark-haired man seated in the chair before him.

Momentarily embarrassed, Lara paused at the edge of the nearest lab table. She had hoped to catch Dr. Braun on his lunch hour. She wanted her visit to be a casual reminder, not an irritating nudge to action, but if she had caught him at a busy time he was certain to be annoyed.

"You can have a seat, if you want."

Lara glanced over her shoulder and saw that both students were hunched over their chairs, grinning at her like gargoyles. *Good grief, didn't women ever come into the genetics lab?*

"Thanks." After giving them a fleeting smile, she pulled out a wooden stool and perched on it while she pretended to study the scrawled chalkboard on the wall. Couldn't Braun hurry? She had not changed her mind about her decision, but in the last three weeks a host of doubts, fears, and questions had plagued her peace. She still believed God wanted to give her Michael's child, but so many things could go wrong. Were Michael's sperm still viable? Were they healthy? And if they did carry a gene that might indicate cancer, would Braun be able to eradicate it?

Inside the office, the doctor stood and moved toward the door while the dark-haired visitor remained seated. Lara slid from her stool as the door opened. If Dr. Braun were stepping out to grab a bite to eat, she might be able to walk with him to the snack machines or to the cafeteria . . .

She cleared her throat and stepped forward. "Dr. Braun?"

He blinked at her, surprised. "Ms. Godfrey?"

"Hi. I just wanted to stop by and let you know that Olivia did an ultrasound this morning. The time is ripe—if you'll pardon my pun." She looked down as blood began to pound in her temples. "I just wondered if you have had a chance to examine that specimen."

The doctor's mouth took on an unpleasant twist. "You should probably call me later—I seem to have misplaced the registration information. But you will have to excuse me now; I have to run a brief errand."

Lara stepped back. "Please, don't let me stop you. I know I should have called for an appointment, but I was in the area and thought I'd just stop by."

He gestured toward the lab door. "I have to run to a colleague's office. You can call me with that information later."

"Okay." Embarrassed by the overeagerness that had brought her to the lab, Lara gave him a tentative smile. "I'm sorry. I'm probably being presumptuous."

"You are not the first to intrude," Braun mumbled, moving toward the door. "No one ever thinks I am busy. Nobody ever calls. They just come and ask and expect me to provide . . ."

The door closed behind him, muffling his voice. Mortified beyond belief, Lara looked away so the two gargoyles wouldn't see the heat stealing into her face. Where in the world had Olivia found that man? He might be a genius, but he seemed so different from his wife. How could two such opposite people fall in love?

"He's quite a character, isn't he?"

Startled by a new voice, she turned and cringed when she realized that Dr. Braun's visitor had moved into the doorway. The man was startlingly attractive and familiar, probably forty-five, with dark hair, deep eyes, and classically handsome features. He wore an exquisite suit, elegant and subtly dramatic, and leaned against the door frame with languid, slimly muscled grace. His appreciative eye traveled from her sneakers to her forehead; then his gaze caught and held hers. "I'm sorry, but I couldn't help overhearing. You work with the absentminded professor's wife? Dr. Olivia Densen-Braun?"

"Yes." Lara found it impossible not to return his disarming smile. "I'm a physician's assistant in her clinic."

Casually, he folded his arms. "You look rather young for such an important job."

She laughed. "Thanks, but I'm older than I look." She locked her hands behind her back and rocked slightly on her heels, wondering how to extricate herself from the conversation. If this man was trying to charm her, he deserved an A for effort, but she wasn't in the market for a Prince Charming.

"You're intelligent too," he said, his dark eyes holding her in a vaguely appraising glance. "It shows in your face, Miss—"

"Mrs.—Mrs. Godfrey." She lowered her gaze as tears welled in her eyes. "Lara Godfrey."

"I'm sorry." The man's voice deepened in concern. "I didn't mean to intrude."

"It's okay." She crossed one arm across her chest and suddenly felt as awkward as a schoolgirl before the captain of the football team. "My husband passed away a few months ago. I'm afraid I'm not used to—well, sometimes I don't know who I am anymore. If it weren't for friends and God-given strength—" She bit her lip, aware that she was talking too much. This stranger didn't want to hear about her personal problems.

"You have my sincere condolences." After a brief moment, the man extended his hand. "Devin Sloane. I'm pleased to meet you, Mrs. Godfrey."

She stared up at him, surprised that his name struck a chord in her memory. She might know the name, but she had never seen this striking face, at least not at close range. She would have remembered it.

She took his hand. "Nice to meet you, Mr. Sloane."

"I know a little about what you're feeling." He released her hand and returned his own to his pocket. "My wife and teenage son were killed in an automobile accident two years ago." He shifted his gaze to the nondescript floor tiles. "Life has not been the same, but I have moved on. You must not give up hope."

"I haven't." She lifted her chin, finding a strange comfort in his words. If she didn't believe that life could and should go on, she wouldn't have come to see Dr. Braun. "I believe God has a plan for my future," she answered, "and I'm determined to move forward."

"That's the spirit." Sloane's smile widened; then he looked at his watch. "Excuse me, but I have to make a phone call. Why don't you wait for the good doctor in my place? I'll finish with him later."

"I didn't mean to interrupt," Lara protested, looking toward the door for some sign of Dr. Braun.

"It's a pleasure to forfeit to you," Devin Sloane called, moving toward the exit. "Take your time, Ms. Godfrey. I can always find Braun when I need him." At the doorway, he glanced at the two wide-eyed students for a brief second, then gave her a cordial smile. "I wish you the best, Lara Godfrey. I am quite certain you deserve it."

She nodded her thanks and watched, mystified, as he stepped into the hall and moved out of sight.

"Wow!" One of the students turned wide eyes upon her. "*The* Devin Sloane spoke to you!"

Lara chewed on the inside of her lip. She hated feeling out of touch, but who in the world was Devin Sloane and why were these students so impressed by him?

"Um," she stepped closer to the computers, "what's so unusual about finding Devin Sloane here?"

"Nothing," the second student answered, scrubbing his curly hair with his knuckles, "if your lab caters to *billionaires*."

Lara gaped at the doorway through which Sloane had departed. So *that's* how she knew the name! Sloane was a famous financier and philanthropist. Though the man was rumored to be as powerful as Bill Gates, he was of far more interest to the locals since he'd built a mansion on a hundred acres of rolling hills outside Charlottesville. She had never paid much attention to either the financial or the society sections of the paper, but perhaps she ought to start reading them.

She glanced at her watch. "I've got to get back to the office," she said, not caring whether the students heard her or not. "I'll call the doctor later."

"Come back to see us," one of the students called as the door closed behind her.

∞

The next morning, Devin slammed his hands on Braun's desk and leaned toward the bewildered doctor. "Lara Godfrey—tell me why she came to see you yesterday."

"Lara?" Braun's round face went red. "Why—it is nothing. She needed an analysis of her husband's sperm in preparation for IVF."

"The dead husband?"

Braun nodded. "Deceased only six months, but the sample is three years old. I have not yet completed the genetic screening, but the sperm shows fair motility." His faint smile held a touch of sadness. "I had planned to spend quite a bit of time on her case, perhaps even publish my results if I succeed in eradicating a cancer indicator. But I do not see how I'll be able to work on her case and yours too." He stopped and lifted his hand. "But of course I will concentrate on your project. I only began the screening for her last night because my wife insisted. Olivia is performing the follicular aspiration this morning, and we will freeze the oocytes early this afternoon."

Still staring down at the doctor, Devin straightened and rested his hands on his belt. "She wants a baby?"

"Of course."

His mind racing, Devin sank back into the utilitarian chair across from Braun's desk. "Any genetic risk in her medical history?"

Braun made a face. "I shouldn't think so. She's a strong woman and a good PA. My wife adores her. She would have no problem carrying a child. She is concerned, though, because her husband died of a rare bone cancer."

"What did your preliminary tests reveal? Is her husband's DNA defective?"

Braun pressed his lips together. "I should not be talking about this. It is a private matter concerning Ms. Godfrey."

Devin leaned across the desk and grasped the doctor's plump wrist. "I am funding your research, Doctor, so whatever happens in this lab is of extreme personal concern to me. And Lara Godfrey is not your patient; she is your wife's. So tell me, Braun—is her husband's sperm defective? What did you tell her?"

Braun sighed heavily and tented his hands. "I have not told her anything yet. The tests are not complete. There are so many things we ought to look for—markers for Huntington's disease, cystic fibrosis, Tay-Sachs, hemophilia A, fragile X syndrome, Duchenne muscular dystrophy, Lesch-Nyhan syndrome, Down syndrome . . ."

Devin gave the doctor a black look. "What *have* you found?"

Braun exhaled. "I found the first thing I looked for—EXT1 on chromosome eight, and EXT2 on chromosome eleven. The presence of these genes does not mean that a child *will* develop cancer, but he certainly could."

"Have you told her this?"

"Yes. I spoke to her about an hour ago."

"And her reaction?"

"Guarded." The doctor looked away. "She is an idealistic sort, and she wants this baby desperately. I think she would have proceeded with AI even without genetic testing, but Olivia insisted upon the tests."

Braun looked down at his desk and absently straightened a stack of papers. His countenance fell, taking on the withered look of an empty balloon. "I do not know how to tell her. She is counting on me to eradicate the EXT1 and EXT2, but I have not had time to do the research—especially not the way she wants it carried out. Lara is religious; she will give me permission to fertilize only one harvested egg; the others must remain frozen." He sighed as his gaze wandered to the phone. "I will have to call her this afternoon."

"Don't call her." Devin smiled, his mind curling itself around the sweet possibility Braun had just presented. He propped his foot on the edge of the doctor's desk. "Let's suppose," he said, eyeing the doctor carefully, "you could assure Lara Godfrey that the questionable genes had been eradicated."

Braun lifted a brow but said nothing.

Barely able to control his eagerness, Devin leaned forward. "You will use the husband's sperm, but his flawed DNA will be overruled by artificial human chromosomes carrying the Iceman's genes. Like a string of perfect living pearls, the genes will infiltrate the fertilized egg and copy themselves into every cell of the fetus's body, thus guaranteeing that even the *child's* descendents will spring from *Homo Tyrolensis.*"

The doctor's mouth opened. "Use Lara as the germline test subject?"

Devin dropped his foot and grasped the edge of the desk. "She is the perfect candidate. She's bright, independent, healthy, careful, medically knowledgeable, and there's no husband to complicate the situation. With both you and your wife involved, we will have her under nearly constant observation. If anything goes wrong, you'll be the first to know. The situation is inconceivably perfect."

Braun's broad face twisted in shock. "It is impossible; Olivia would never permit it. Lara herself would not agree; she wants her husband's child."

"Legally, it will be her husband's child, conceived with his sperm sample. And no one but you and I need know about the germline test." Flush with the idea, Devin grinned and tented his hands. "Get Mrs. Godfrey's signed permission to manipulate the DNA strand in her husband's sperm, and you're legally covered in case the truth ever comes out. But it won't, Helmut, because I won't allow it. She will conceive the child, she will be thrilled to carry it, and the purest example of DNA on the planet will once again be gifted with life! The biological son of *Homo Tyrolensis* will be born on the cusp of a new millennium! Don't you see the possibilities?"

The doctor's brows slanted downward. "What about the child? After it is born, what then? How can you explain why the child does not look like her husband? What if it is born with big feet, or a hairy back—"

"Good grief, Doctor, we're not talking about a Neanderthal. We're talking about a superman in the most spiritual sense of the word, the complete opposite of modern human beings. I do not know what qualities he will possess, but I am certain he will be extraordinary."

Warming to his subject, Devin rested his elbows on Braun's desk and focused his gaze on the doctor's granite face. "Have you seen the latest parade of tortured individuals featured on the television news? We are plagued, Doctor, by humans who can't conceive an original thought above marrying their mother's boyfriend or abusing their own offspring. We are hunted by serial killers who expend their best energies devising ways to destroy innocent lives. We are entrenched in a social system in which the top 20 percent of our population controls 94 percent of wealth and income. Don't you see that our society is mirroring conditions in midtwentieth-century Germany? If mankind is not improved, our 'tough love' programs like Norplant for welfare mothers and 'three strikes and you're out' will relegate our undesirables to prisons, selective breeding and yes, even controlled euthanasia. *Homo Tyrolensis* is our answer! He will be our salvation! And once he lives, his DNA will provide the foundation for a new generation of superior humans."

"But what about the woman?" Braun's brow creased. "Half of the child's genetic stock will come from an eroded twentieth-century female. How can you avoid human frailty if you use a contemporary woman as the mother?"

"He will need her." Devin closed his eyes. "Her body, her genes, will contain the immunities and biological codes he will need to survive in our world. His strength will be made perfect in her weakness, and hers in his. They will complement each other; they must!"

The doctor clamped his jaw tight and stared into his own thoughts. Realizing that he had hit upon a sore spot, Devin picked up a pencil from the doctor's desk. "You told me once that you hoped for a type of immortality," he said, twirling the pencil between his hands. "If you help me in this, you will go down in history as the man who saved the human race from self-extinction. But we must hurry. I want to achieve pregnancy as soon as possible."

"And Lara Godfrey?" A faint thread of hysteria lined Braun's voice. "What will become of her after the child is born?"

"I will take care of everything," Devin answered, his eyes glued to the pencil. "I never do anything without a contingency plan. Ideally, we will take the child from her at delivery. If by some fluke of fate she refuses to surrender her maternal rights, we will present her with legal documents attesting to the fact that she has been hired as a surrogate to carry my child."

Sloane looked up, noted the fearful grimace on Braun's face, and continued. "You said she wanted her husband's baby—well, the child won't actually be her husband's. Later, two or three months after the delivery, you will proceed with your plan to fertilize another of her eggs with her husband's sperm. You will have your cancer research project, she will have the child she so desperately wants . . . but I will have the son of *Homo Tyrolensis*."

Braun's nose quivered beneath his glasses. "Are you certain she will not be . . . physically harmed?"

Devin lowered the pencil and gave the doctor a slow smile. "You have my word upon it."

chapter 10

Her thoughts whirling in a crazy mixture of hope and fear, Lara thrust her head into Olivia's office. "Any word from the good Dr. Braun?"

"Honey, these things take time." Olivia's eyes were gentle as she glanced up. "Gene splicing is a complicated process, and this is a particularly interesting challenge. Helmut has worked late every night this week."

"I feel guilty asking so much of him." Lara came into the office and perched on the padded arm of the love seat. "Having a baby ought to be simple."

"Nothing worthwhile is ever easy." Olivia glanced back down at the chart on her desk, and Lara felt another stab of guilt for interrupting her boss. She had not been the ideal employee over the last week; twice Olivia had to remind her to pull prescription refill requests from the answering machine. Her thoughts kept drifting toward Helmut's lab, where her egg and Michael's sperm waited to begin a baby.

Last week she had been disturbed but not shaken by the news that Dr. Braun had found the suspicious EXT1 and EXT2 in Michael's DNA. Confident that he could eradicate the genes, she pushed his report to the back of her mind and allowed Olivia to proceed with the follicular aspiration. The procedure, performed under a local anesthetic and sedation, wasn't painful, but Lara hoped she wouldn't have to repeat it. "Make sure you take enough," she had murmured in a sleepy voice as Olivia studied the ultrasound screen and guided the harvesting needle into one of Lara's ovaries. "I don't like being the patient."

After the sedative wore off, Lara drove her freshly harvested oocytes over to the cryogenics lab. With a businesslike nod, Dr. Braun took the biological material from her and placed it into a storage tank, then shoved a folder of forms in her direction. Lara skimmed the first one—an informed consent document stating that she realized the eggs/sperm/embryos might not survive cryopreservation—and signed it. Another form granted Dr. Braun permission to manipulate the DNA in semen sample #88-GOD3947398, and yet another stated that Lara's participation in the procedure had not been coerced in any way. She signed both documents. A fourth paper caught her attention—according to the statement, the Muriel Foundation had agreed to subsidize all costs of her care, including all laboratory expenses, medications, prenatal exams, hospital expenses, and genetics research—for *two* pregnancies.

"Dr. Braun—" She hesitated as he frowned up at her. "What is the Muriel Foundation? And why are they paying for two pregnancies?"

"I told you I could find a grant." Braun waved his hand as if the matter were inconsequential. "And you might want another baby someday, no? Do not look a gift horse in the mouth, Ms. Godfrey."

Lara signed the statement. He had done so much for her, how could she complain? The Muriel Foundation was probably one of those private organizations that funded cancer research. She ought to be grateful that Dr. Braun had thought ahead. She was so fixated on this particular pregnancy that she could scarcely think one month into the future, let alone several years.

She signed paper after paper, more routine consents and disclaimers, then paused at the last page in the folder. The entire top portion was blank.

"What's this?" She waved the page before his eyes and made an attempt at humor. "A blank check?"

Dr. Braun clamped his jaw tight. "What is that? It is legal stuff and nonsense."

"Well—" Lara hesitated, her mind whirling at his dry response. "It's a blank page. Is it important?"

"Of course it is." Braun pressed his glasses to the eyepiece of his microscope and fussed with the magnification control. "Sign it; leave it; I will fill it in later if I need it. How can I know what I will need permission to do until I know what I will have to do? The lawyers, the red tape—you know how foolish it all is. But everything is important."

"Whatever you say." Lara signed her name at the bottom of the page and added the date. Braun was probably right. She would hate to have him stop work at some crucial juncture because she hadn't signed the proper consent form. Recent developments in malpractice and privacy law had made it impossible to even begin treating a patient without a dozen consent forms signed in triplicate.

After signing all the documents, Lara returned them to the folder and stood. The doctor was still peering through an electron microscope, occasionally lifting his head and making notes on a notepad. She wanted to ask if he was examining part of Michael's DNA, but he wore a concentrated look, an expression guaranteed to insure privacy. Lara left the lab and drove back to the Women's Clinic, praying that the doctor would have good success in his work.

Though modern medical science had worked wonders for many of her patients, Lara found it difficult to adjust to the idea that her baby would be conceived in a laboratory miles away from home. The conception would still result from an act of love, but in vitro fertilization was a far cry from the route to conception God had designed.

This new life would begin in a laboratory petri dish, under the dispassionate gazes of Dr. Braun, his research assistants, a few students, perhaps a janitor or two. But Lara didn't care. Once the embryo had grown to the sixteen-cell blastocyst stage, it would be implanted in her womb where her warmth, her food, and her blood would shelter and feed the growing baby.

If only Braun would call with good news.

"Your attention is wandering again." The sound of Olivia's voice snapped Lara back to reality. The doctor was studying her, one corner of her mouth lifting in a wry smile. "Keep busy, Lara, and the time will pass quickly. And don't waste time feeling guilty. Helmut loves a challenge. He'll probably write a paper on your case and earn all kinds of kudos."

Lara lowered her chin to the stack of files she hugged against her chest. "If this works, I may name my kid after him."

Olivia rolled her eyes in disbelief. "Please. A simple thank you will do."

Lara dropped the files to her side, then rapped lightly on the edge of

Olivia's desk. "You'll call me if you hear from him? The minute you know something?"

"I promise." Olivia waved her away, then picked up her recorder. She opened a file and began to dictate her notes, her voice droning in Lara's ears as she walked out. "Kay McMiller, healthy, well-nourished thirty-eight-year-old, presents with abdominal pain and episodic spotting . . ."

∞

Straddling a lab stool, Helmut Braun leaned back and pulled the surgical mask from his face. Blowing out his cheeks, he glanced at the clock—eleven fifty-five p.m. He had spent hours bent over this microscope, yet he was no closer to a solution than he had been a week ago.

His assistants had all gone home at the usual hour, and now silence lay over the lab like the pall at a funeral. The tense lines on his face relaxed as an irreverent thought struck—a funeral was what they'd be planning for *him* if Sloane learned that the first fertilized egg had failed to divide after being injected with the Iceman's DNA.

Yesterday morning he had put egg and sperm together for the first time. Twelve hours passed without the sperm penetrating the barrier around the egg, then Helmut resorted to ICSI techniques. Using a specially designed microscope, tiny needles, and micromanipulation equipment, he held the mature egg with a specialized holding pipette, then vacuumed the sperm into a delicate, sharp, hollow needle. Holding his breath, he gingerly inserted the needle through the zona and into the egg, then injected the modified sperm into the cytoplasm. He immediately followed this injection with another—the artificial chromosome carrying the Iceman's DNA.

He waited twenty-four hours, preparing another artificial chromosome in case this test should fail, and a moment ago he had checked the egg under the microscope. He had hoped to see two cells, a divided egg, but the oocyte had lost viability. The cell beneath his eye was as dead as stone.

Disappointment struck him like a blow in the stomach. He stood and stepped away from the microscope, swallowing several times to choke back his dismay. He would have to bring another precious egg from the cryogenic tank, and there were not many more to lose.

Pacing, he swiped his hands through his thinning hair and idly wondered why he hadn't followed his brother's lead and gone into the military. Kurt was a leading officer in the German army; he and his family lived in a modern Berlin apartment. Kurt played a key role in the changing face of Germany, while Helmut, the brightest Braun son, toiled in obscurity, searching for *the* experiment, *the* breakthrough that would catapult his name into the scientific journals and onto the front page of the *New York Times*. Twice he had been close to announcing a major discovery, once in his study of hematopoiesis and again in his work in the development of mammalian transducing vectors, but in both studies colleagues with better-funded programs had beaten him to publication.

Yet now, in the autumn of his life, Fate had smiled upon him. Destiny had sent Devin Sloane, who offered unique genetic material and an opportunity to establish his reputation. Helmut wasn't blind to Sloane's wide-eyed fanaticism, but the corruption of Michael Godfrey's DNA actually supported Sloane's theory about the deterioration of the human race. Helmut could not help but believe that this experiment might actually benefit Lara Godfrey. In return for her role in the procedure, she would receive free medical care and the best genetic work the university could offer.

His watch chimed, reminding him of the hour. Midnight. By all rights he should be home with his wife, but he could not relax yet. Olivia had mentioned that Lara Godfrey walked around the office in a tense daze, and Sloane would soon want to know what progress he had made. Unless Helmut accomplished something within the week, the billionaire would not be happy . . . and might be tempted to offer his money and this opportunity to some other geneticist.

Helmut looked around at the lab, his eyes falling upon the small canister that contained the remainder of Michael Godfrey's deposit. He would have to think of an answer very soon.

chapter 11

"Now you know," Olivia handed Lara a gown, "this first implantation attempt may not work. The success rate for typical IVF is only 18 percent, and women who have it are more prone to miscarriage—"

"I know the statistics." Lara took the gown and slipped behind the modesty curtain. Her fingers trembled as she slipped out of her lab coat and uniform, her mind still reeling with the news she had received only a few moments ago.

According to Dr. Braun, fertilization had occurred on Friday, May fifteenth. Now, five days later, the fertilized egg had reached the blastocyst stage and was ready to be transferred to Lara's uterus. If all went well, it would implant itself in the lining and within three or four days she would know if she could carry this child.

She shivered as she slipped her arms into the thin gown. She'd been preparing her body with hormones and medications; there was no medical reason for the procedure not to work. Still, it felt strange to know that her baby had begun in a laboratory, not in her womb. The child had begun this adventure without her, and his start would invalidate all the usual rules about due dates and forty-week pregnancies. All she wanted was an ordinary, happy baby, but her pregnancy had already proven itself exceptional.

It's all in your hands, God; I'll try to trust what you're doing. And I know when the desire comes, it will be a tree of life and joy.

Pushing her nervousness aside, she pulled the edges of the gown together and tried to tie a bow with the strings at her neck. Her trembling fingers wouldn't cooperate; the bow tangled into a knot.

Lara gave up and stepped out from behind the curtain, holding the gown closed at her waist. "Is the good Dr. Braun here yet?"

"He's on his way with the embryo." Olivia's eyes were soft with compassion. "Do you want him to do the procedure?"

"I'd rather you did it."

Lara stepped onto the footstool, then lowered herself to the exam table and rocked gently from side to side, ripping her legs free from the sticky paper. She'd taken a low dose of Seconal at the nurses' station, and the drug was beginning to make the furniture look fuzzy. The embryo transfer procedure was supposed to be nearly painless; she only needed to relax.

As if she could.

"Lie down," Olivia ordered, unfolding a paper drape. She spread it over Lara's legs and stomach, then pulled the door open. "Let me go see if Helmut's here."

Lara lay flat on her back, her legs dangling over the end of the exam table, her hands folded loosely over her stomach. She loved being a physician's assistant; she hated being a patient. She had explored every nook and cranny of this exam room over the years, but she could count on one hand the times she had lain on this table.

Her eyes grazed the ceiling. One of the nurses had plastered the ceiling tiles with pictures of Mel Gibson, Brad Pitt, Denzel Washington, and Franklin Sinatra. "Something for everyone," Lara murmured, closing her heavy eyelids.

She couldn't tell how long she lay there, but finally the door opened again. Olivia entered, followed by Gaynel Sheridan, one of the office nurses. Gaynel grinned as she wheeled in the ultrasound monitor.

"Guess who?" Gaynel sang out. As Lara rose up on her elbows, Olivia held up a small vial. "We got it. Now you relax and let us work our magic."

Lara pressed her hand over her mouth, afraid she would break out in hysterical laughter or tears. What if it worked? What if it didn't? At the moment, she didn't feel up to considering either option.

Obediently, she lay back down and closed her eyes, knowing that

Olivia would insert a very fine tube into her uterus, then transfer the embryo. A simple, painless, and unpredictable procedure.

Everything was up to God.

∞

Lara moved through the next three days in a fog, trying, not very successfully, to concentrate on her work. She saw patients, listened to complaints, drew blood, wrote prescriptions. But every time a pregnant woman came in and they listened to the rhythmic, swooshing sounds of an unborn baby's heartbeat, Lara's hand flew to her own flat stomach. She couldn't help but wonder—*me, too?*

On Friday morning, in the privacy of her own bathroom, she opened a home pregnancy test. She thrust the stick into the urine sample and closed her eyes, almost afraid to see the result. The fertilized egg had either dissolved harmlessly into her system or nestled into the rich uterine lining. The baby was either not meant to be or it was now warming itself with her blood, taking in the nutrients she'd been imparting, growing as her child.

She opened her eyes and caught her breath. A plus sign. Positive. Pregnant.

She sank to the closed toilet seat and pressed her hand over her mouth. *Michael, we're parents.*

God had kept his promise. She hadn't misunderstood. She would have a baby; part of Michael would live with her for years to come. One of his dreams had been to produce work that would last, and their child would be the best work of his life. Modern medicine had failed in the battle against Michael's cancer, but it had worked a miracle in providing Michael's child.

Caught up in the first wave of joy she'd felt in months, Lara threw back her head and laughed. She dressed quickly; threw a healthy banana, apple, and turkey sandwich into a lunch bag; then hurried out to her car. As she unlocked the door, she saw Connor sitting on his front porch, the newspaper covering his face.

"Hey, Connor," Lara called, not caring who heard.

The paper lowered; his brown eyes peered at her. "Something wrong?"

"Something's right!" Lara opened the car door and tossed her lunch bag inside. Leaning on the window, she grinned at her neighbor. "I'm pregnant!"

His brown eyes widened as his arms crunched the paper in his lap. "Is this good news?"

"It's the best. The plan worked—I'm going to have Michael's baby."

He stood and moved to the edge of his porch. The smile he gave her seemed genuine. "I'm happy for you. If you need any help, just let me know."

"Thanks."

Lara got into the car and turned the key, feeling her heart beat in time with the pounding engine. Olivia would be thrilled, and Dr. Helmut would be pleased. Olivia, however, would probably caution Lara not to share the news with too many people until after she'd successfully passed the first three months. The first trimester of any first pregnancy is risky, she'd warn. Especially in an IVF case.

But Lara wasn't worried. She was carrying the child of her heart, the one God had promised to give her.

chapter 12

"Okay, Lara. You can open your eyes!"

Lara obeyed, then grinned. During the afternoon the nurses had somehow found time to decorate the break room with pink and blue streamers and balloons. A huge sheet cake sat in the center of the table, a smiling baby's face painted on it in soft flesh tones. Lara stood speechless in the doorway, amazed that the others had managed to do all this without attracting her attention.

"We knew you wanted to share your happiness," Olivia explained, her brows rising in obvious pleasure. "And we've never needed an excuse to throw a party."

"And there's this to mark the occasion." Gaynel, the chief nurse, came forward with a button that read, *I'm PG2*. As she pinned it to the collar of Lara's lab coat, she met Lara's gaze and smiled. "We're so happy for you," she said, her blue eyes darkening with emotion. "You've been through so much; you deserve a little happiness."

"Aw, you guys . . ." Lara balled her hands into fists, fighting back tears. She shouldn't have been surprised, for the clinic staff was a tight-knit group, but she had wondered if her coworkers would approve of her decision. "I can't tell you how much you all mean to me," she finally said, her eyes moving from one woman to the next. Her gaze came to rest upon Olivia, who stood beside her. "It's good to know that you are all supportive. Michael would have appreciated what you've done, and—well, I appreciate your friendship."

A half-dozen feminine voices rose in a chorus of support. Gaynel gave Lara a brief hug; then Olivia squeezed her shoulder. "We are behind you, Lara," she said, her eyes brimming with tenderness. "If you need anything, you only have to ask."

Lara thumbed a tear from her cheek. "You've already done too much. None of this would be possible if Dr. Braun hadn't agreed to help me."

"Helmut thrives on challenges." Olivia accepted the slice of cake Sharon Swensen placed in her hand, then passed it to Lara. "Eat up. I'm counting calories, but you're going to need some extra energy." She side-stepped past Carol Bartlett, the transcriptionist, and waved. "Have a great time. I need to finish going over my charts, then get to the hospital. Ann McClain is in the first stage of labor."

"Thanks, Olivia."

Amid the happy chatter of her friends and the dull monotone of the corner television, Lara moved toward the table, then grabbed a plastic fork from a box. "Glad to see you all went all out for me," she said, holding the plastic fork in front of Gaynel's eyes. She gave the nurse a teasing smile as she sank into a chair. "What, no silverplate?"

"We didn't think a woman whose car is littered with McDonalds bags would mind plastic forks," Gaynel answered, completely unruffled. She perched on the end of the table and rested her feet on an empty chair. "Eat quick, girls; we've still got to close up the office."

"The office can wait." Sharon stretched out her legs as she leaned back in her chair. "I've been on my feet all day." She glanced around, then pointed with her fork to a tabloid newspaper tucked behind the coffeemaker. "Hand me that *National Enquirer*, will you, Rita? I haven't had my weekly fix of lifestyles of the rich and infamous."

Lara struggled to swallow a mouthful of the sticky-sweet icing, then made a face. "Don't tell me you read that stuff. Don't you know it's only gossip?"

"If it wasn't true, they wouldn't print it." Sharon caught the newspaper as Rita tossed it across the room. "They'd get sued if they lied."

"They *do* get sued." Gaynel emphasized the point with her fork, pointing it at Sharon. "About every other week some celebrity sues the *Reporter* for millions. I read about *that* in the regular newspaper."

"True or not, there's no harm in it." Sharon opened the tabloid. "Look—here's a story about a pregnant alien abductee." She shivered. "Can you imagine?"

"That stuff is nonsense." Gaynel waved another forkful of cake in Sharon's direction. "Tell her, Lara. Tell her no sane woman is going to come through our door and say she's carrying an alien's baby."

Lara sliced off another bite of cake and grinned. "I have heard some pretty strange things. I know at least a dozen patients who've conceived after their husband's vasectomy."

Gaynel opened her mouth, about to respond, but Sharon interrupted with a squeal. "Look at this!" Straightening in her chair, Sharon began to read aloud: "Billionaire Devin Sloane, part-time New York resident and escort to some of the world's most beautiful and wealthy women, was spotted in Macy's shopping for nursery essentials. When pressed for an explanation, the handsome billionaire admitted that the babe-in-waiting is his own, due to arrive in late winter."

"That's no surprise," Rita mumbled around a mouthful of cake. She paused to swallow, then continued. "I have a friend at the university who told me that some rich guy was quietly advertising for a healthy, intelligent surrogate a few weeks back." She lifted a brow. "I guess he found one."

Carol jerked her head up. "Around here? How exciting!"

"Sloane lives only about ten miles out of town," Rita pointed out. "If he found a girl at the university, she could very well be one of our patients."

Carol pressed her hands together. "Read on, Sharon. What does it say?"

Sharon snapped the paper and kept reading. "'I am delighted that I am soon going to become a father,' Sloane told our investigative reporter, 'but I do not wish to divulge the name of the surrogate mother. We have a private arrangement and I wish it to remain confidential.' Before leaving with an armful of goodies, Sloane added that he has no plans to marry."

Sharon looked up, her eyes glowing. "What I wouldn't give to be that woman!"

"Surely you're not serious." Gaynel's voice dripped with sarcasm. "This sounds a little too weird, if you ask me. Surrogate arrangements almost always end in trouble or a trial. It's not natural. I've never met a woman who could hand a baby over with no thought or concern for it."

"I have." Lara spoke quietly, but her voice echoed in the room. She turned and met Gaynel's gaze. "Not every woman has a highly developed maternal instinct. I've met women who left their babies on doorsteps, who auctioned them off to the highest bidder, who let their boyfriends abuse them to the point of death. You can't assume every biological mother will be a good parent. Sometimes I wonder if I will."

"You're going to be a great mother." Gaynel draped her arm over Lara's shoulder. "If you're worried, well, you just put those thoughts out of your mind. I remember being scared to death when I first got pregnant. I didn't know a thing about being a mother. The thought of being responsible for a child petrified me."

Lara patted Gaynel's hand, wondering how the nurse had managed to read her mind. "Thanks. I guess it's natural to feel a little apprehensive. I'm not worried about the pregnancy part, just about—well, things like telling my mother-in-law. Eva wasn't at all supportive when I mentioned having Michael's child."

"She'll change her mind once she knows it's a done deal." Rita's curls bobbed as she nodded. "Just wait until you show her that first sonogram picture. Or make a tape of the baby's heartbeat and play it for her. That'll make her come around."

Gaynel glanced at her watch, then tossed her paper plate into the corner trash can. "Come on, Sharon, we've got to get back to work." She stepped forward and tugged on the corner of the tabloid, pulling the paper from the other nurse's hands. "Come back to earth, honey. We can't have you mooning over some rich guy when there is work to be done. I've got to get home and cook dinner."

"He's so handsome," Sharon groaned, draping herself over her plastic chair in a melodramatic pose. She pressed the back of her wrist to her forehead and sighed. "All those good looks and money, too! Life is not fair! Why couldn't I have met him before I met Bill?"

Lara stared thoughtfully at the black-and-white photograph. "You know"—she bent to pick the paper up from the floor—"I met Devin Sloane a few days ago. At Dr. Braun's lab."

Sharon's eyes flew open as she pulled herself upright. "You're kidding, right? Or are you just trying to bedevil my poor broken heart?"

"No, I'm sure. At the time I thought his name sounded familiar, but I didn't think much about it because I had other things on my mind."

Sharon placed her hands over her heart and looked at Lara with a glint of wonder in her eyes. "Is he as dreamy in real life as he is in his pictures?"

Gaynel pointed toward the corner television. "He was featured on the 'Celebrity Minute' on the twelve o'clock news. I saw the whole thing 'cause Olivia asked me to tape a news report about the new children's hospital."

Sharon's eyes widened. "Please tell me you still have the tape!"

"Sure I do." Gaynel moved to the VCR, then punched the power on. "Hang on a second, and I'll find it."

Lara watched as Gaynel pressed the rewind button and a grainy panorama of the hospital filled the television screen. "Devin Sloane was at the hospital for the ribbon cutting ceremony," Gaynel said, her eyes alert and trained on the screen. "A reporter caught him as he was getting into his limo."

Rita grabbed the remote and jacked up the volume as Gaynel pressed *play*. The twelve o'clock news report's "Celebrity Minute" logo flashed across a black-and-white photo of Devin Sloane in a tuxedo; then a blonde reporter's head filled the lower corner of the screen.

"Devin Sloane, billionaire companion to Hollywood stars and local philanthropist, has admitted that he expects to join the ranks of other celebrities who have fathered children late in life," the reporter said, a video of Sloane rolling across the screen. "Like Jack Nicholson, Warren Beatty, and Donald Trump, the handsome entrepreneur has fallen under the beguiling spell of booties and baby rattles. His spokesman reports that Mr. Sloane expects to be diapering a wee one sometime in early February."

"February!" Sharon grinned at Lara. "Isn't that when you're due? If you see him again, you'll have to talk about babies."

The reporter's next words were drowned out by a wave of reproachful shushing; then the room fell silent.

"Sloane has remained silent about the mother of this affluent babe-to-be," the anchorwoman continued, "citing the need for confidentiality in what is reported to be a surrogate arrangement." The reporter tilted her head and gave the camera a saucy smile. "Is it truly a surrogate arrangement, Mr. Sloane? Or will we hear the pealing of wedding bells in your future?"

"He's awfully sure of himself, isn't he?" Gaynel said, her gaze glued to the television screen. Devin Sloane, appearing cool and utterly natural, was working his way through a crowd outside the hospital with smiles and handshakes. No woman clung to his arm, Lara noticed, though more than a few flashed eager smiles in his direction.

"If you were worth two billion dollars, you'd be confident too," Sharon said.

Lara shook her head, scarcely able to believe she'd spoken to the billionaire. She should have recognized Sloane that afternoon, but she'd been so concerned about Michael's genetic screening that she had scarcely given any thought to the men loitering in Braun's lab—and what business would a wealthy financier have with Dr. Braun?

She dismissed the question. The two probably played golf together or something.

Lara stood, picked up a napkin, and wiped a smear of icing from the lapel of her lab coat. "Thanks again, ladies. This was fun." She tossed the napkin in the trash can, then winked at Sharon. "If you find out who Sloane's lucky woman is, let me know. Maybe we can work out a deal to share maternity clothes."

⚬⚬⚬

For the next few weeks, Lara felt like a medical textbook come to life. She could recite the early symptoms of pregnancy in her sleep—light cramping, nausea, breast tenderness, and an enervating exhaustion—but when those sensations rose in her own body, she wanted to crow for joy.

The Women's Clinic did not usually schedule OB patients for an exam until after their second missed menstrual period, but Olivia welcomed

Lara to the exam table a month after the fertilization date, as thrilled with the pregnancy as Lara herself.

"Helmut is ecstatic," Olivia remarked as she made her notes on Lara's file. "He is quite proud—almost amazed—that the first implantation took hold. He's already begun work on the paper he wants to publish about your case, but he's being very secretive about it." She laughed. "He probably thinks I'm going to correct his grammar or something."

Lying on the exam table, Lara turned to look at Olivia. "Isn't anyone else doing similar work? I thought gene splicing had come a long way."

"In farm animals, perhaps," Olivia answered, "but though gene therapy is a common treatment these days, Helmut doesn't know of anyone who has succeeded in reshaping a child's genes before conception." She clicked her pen, then slipped it into the pocket of her coat. "He wants to know how you're doing at every stage of the pregnancy. So"—she shot Lara a piercing glance—"if you have no objections, I'd like to allow him access to your file. You'll have to sign a consent form."

"I'm so grateful to him." Lara folded her hands across her belly. "Of course, he can see anything he'd like. I'll sign the release."

Olivia nodded. "I'll tell Carol to forward your file to his office after she enters changes on your record. He can examine it over the computer network." She gave Lara's chart one final glance, then snapped the folder shut. "I appreciate your openness, but I'm asking Carol to forward only your patient number, not your name. I don't think you want Helmut's students poring over your weight and measurements week after week, do you?"

Lara laughed. "So, Doc, how do I look?"

Olivia's professional expression softened into a smile. "You're beautiful. You're healthy. Your heart and lungs sound great, and the clinical pelvimetry indicates that you'll have a disgracefully easy birth. According to our calculations, you'll deliver a healthy baby right around February fourth, plus or minus two weeks."

She leaned against the counter and crossed her arms over the chart. "Now, do you want to hear the standard speech, or will you let me save my breath?"

"I have it memorized." Lara pushed herself up into a sitting position. "I can continue to do the things I did before pregnancy, including climbing mountains, water-skiing, and riding horses—as long as I regularly did those things before I became pregnant. I should not, however, jog long distances or at a fast pace after the first four months. I should exercise to keep my weight down, but moderately, and remember that labor is a physical event, so I'd better stay in shape."

"Diet?" Olivia prompted.

"A balanced diet is crucial." Lara grinned. "And a two-pound weight gain per monthly visit is all you'll allow without fussing at me."

"Absolutely right." Olivia pulled herself off the counter and took a step forward. "And the baby, Doctor Godfrey—how big is the little daredevil now?"

Lara felt a curious tingling shock. She knew the answer, but until that instant had never applied the fact to herself. "An inch long," she said, sliding her palm over her belly. "Little Morgan or Megan is an entire inch long by now."

Olivia patted Lara on the shoulder, then moved toward the door. "Very good, Doctor Godfrey. Now get back to work." Her eyes twinkled as she paused in the doorway. "Just because we're thrilled for you doesn't mean we don't want you around."

chapter 13

The early weeks of Lara's pregnancy passed without incident, and she breathed a sigh of relief as she entered her fifth month. No pregnancy could be guaranteed, of course, but the risks of losing a baby fell considerably after the twentieth week of gestation. Once October second came and went, Lara walked with a firmer step, more confident than ever. This was the child of promise, and God wasn't going to fail her. Not this time.

Her latest ultrasound confirmed that she was carrying a healthy baby boy. On Monday morning, October fifth, she stood in the shower and watched the water stream over her changing body. Now she could clearly see the top of her uterus at the level of her navel. Her baby, little Michael, was between eight and ten inches long, half the height he should be at birth. He weighed at least half a pound. Hair had begun to grow on his head, and he could make tiny facial expressions as he floated in the sea of amniotic fluid. His heart and brain were functioning. He could hear and recognize her voice, his eyes could open and see light through her skin, and he was sensible enough to be bored by the repetitive rhythm of her exercise bike. Only this morning, as she mindlessly endured her half hour on the bike, a faint fluttering caught her attention. Her legs froze, her hand flew to her abdomen, then her momentary fear vanished. She laughed when she realized Michael Junior had just made his opinions known.

"Swimming around, are you?" She smoothed the mounded flesh beneath her nightgown. "Trying to stay in shape too?"

At work that morning she listened to her patients with an extra ounce of understanding and dashed away tears on more than one occasion. Birth was such a miracle; why hadn't she realized the enormity of it before this? God had designed such a miraculous way to bring life into the world, and women were so honored to be the chosen vessels!

At lunch she forfeited the conversation of the other nurses and went outside to eat her sandwich and fruit. The clinic sat next to the sprawling campus of the University of Virginia Medical School, and several benches had been planted along the sidewalk for the students' use. Lara sat on one and unwrapped her lunch bag, then pulled out her sandwich and took a ravenous bite.

The October wind was chilly, but a bright afternoon sun warmed the sidewalk where she sat. A visibly pregnant woman waddled toward the clinic, her hand pressed to the small of her back, and Lara gave her a "me too" smile as she finished her sandwich and tossed the plastic wrapping back into her lunch bag.

A group of students walked by, leaving a trail of laughter along the sidewalk. Lara sat silently, enjoying the warmth of the sun on her face. The day and the setting reminded her of Michael, and for a brief moment she felt the pang of missing him and a sharp qualm of guilt.

She had been so wrapped up in the baby that she had scarcely thought of Michael in the past few days. Though he was the only reason she had even considered having the baby, still, for a moment her lower lip trembled, as if his spirit had risen in the wind and accused her of unfaithfulness.

"I wish you could be here." She whispered the words as the wind blew a quartet of fallen maple leaves into a minicyclone. "And though I have been concentrating on the baby, Michael Junior will never replace you."

After work she stopped at the grocery instead of McDonalds, filling her buggy with milk, bananas, apples, and eggs. On an impulse, she picked up a box of newborn-sized disposable diapers and tossed them into the buggy too. Might as well get another box—the box of diapers Michael bought so long ago was gathering dust in the closet. This package could keep it company.

A brilliant autumn-orange sun hovered just above the horizon when she pulled into her driveway. She opened the car door and swung her legs out, aware of her increasing weight, then heard a cheery voice.

"Well, hello there!"

She looked up as she got out. Dressed in a warm and fuzzy sweater, Connor sat on his porch. She waved and opened the back door to bring out her groceries, then heard the sound of his sneakers whispering through the grass.

"Let me help you with that."

She turned; he blocked her path. With no other recourse, she gave him a polite smile and the first grocery bag.

"I was about to worry," he said, taking the bag with one hand. He held out his other arm, allowing Lara to loop a couple of grocery bags over it. "You're late today."

"Just a grocery run." She spoke in a light tone and avoided his eyes. Connor had become a part of her life in the last few weeks, and she still wasn't certain how she felt about him. He was a terrific neighbor and a handsome and attentive man, but therein, as Olivia would say, lay the problem. He was a *man*. Lara had not developed a close friendship with any man since Michael, and she wasn't sure where she should draw the boundaries with Connor. Fortunately, he had never pressed her, only offering his help when she obviously needed it.

A hint of mischief lined his smile. "Diapers already?"

"A wise scout is always prepared." Lara pulled the last bag from the backseat. "It'll be easier on the budget if I plan ahead. If I get a box every time I go to the grocery, I won't feel the expense when the baby comes."

Connor took a step toward the house, then turned and looked at her through narrowed eyes. "This is a new look for you too."

He had noticed the maternity smock. Lara made a face, then laughed and closed the car door. "I am officially growing out of my clothes, so I guess it's time to invest in a few tents. I was hoping to find some time to go shopping this week, but things have been so busy at the office . . ."

Her voice trailed away as a gold Jaguar slowed and pulled into the driveway. The tinted window powered down; then Eva's blonde head appeared. "Lara, darling! I've brought my pictures from Europe to show you! You'll never believe it—I met Prince Albert!"

Keeping her back to the Jag, Lara lowered her eyes and exhaled slowly. Eva had left for London at the end of July, before Lara found the courage to tell her about the baby. She had hoped to face Eva armed with ultra-sound photos and a perfect genetic scorecard from Dr. Braun, but this assault had caught her completely by surprise.

Still—she had known this confrontation would come. And it *would* be a confrontation, for Eva had been clear about her feelings. Most people gave Eva's feelings great weight.

"This isn't good, is it?" Connor regarded her with a speculative gaze, his eyes dark and gentle. "Perhaps I should go. Why don't I set your groceries on the porch and come back later to help you put them away?"

Lara flinched as she heard the slam of the Jag's door, then the grinding of high heels on concrete. "Lara, darling, aren't you glad to see me?"

Lara hung the last grocery bag on Connor's arm, then patted his hand, taking support from his strong frame. It was now or never. Tossing her hair across her shoulders, she straightened her posture, smoothed her maternity smock, and turned to face Eva.

Her mother-in-law's smiling countenance sagged like a plastic doll tossed into a fire. Lara heard a little gasp; then the yard fell silent but for the applause of the trembling oak leaves.

"Hello, Eva. I didn't know you were home."

Eva's look of horrified disapproval evolved into an expression of offended determination. She clasped her hands at her waist and set her mouth in a firm line, her blue eyes glittering like chips of ice. "You've been busy, I see. Aren't you going to introduce me?"

Lara bit her lip as she realized what Eva had to be thinking. A visibly pregnant woman and a handsome man unloading one car . . .

She forced a smile to her cold lips. "Eva, this is my next-door neighbor, Connor O'Hara." She tilted her head toward her mother-in-law. "Connor, this is Michael's mother, Eva Godfrey."

"Nice to meet you." Connor nodded pleasantly and stepped forward as if he would shake Eva's hand, but she only stared at him, her flush deepening to a shade as crimson as the flaming sky. When Eva didn't respond, Connor turned to Lara. "I'll leave these bags on your front porch."

"Thanks."

As he walked away, Lara fished her keys from her purse, then smiled at Eva. "Would you like to come in and tell me about your trip?"

"It seems I missed out on a lot while I was away." Eva spoke in a measured, cool voice. "Am I to assume you're as pregnant as you appear to be?"

"Correct," Lara answered, walking toward the porch. When she did not hear the sound of footsteps behind her, she turned again. "I'm carrying Michael's child and due in February." She lifted a brow, pretending a careless indifference she was far from feeling. "Anything else you'd like to know?"

Eva's shoulders rose and fell in a dramatic sigh. "Did you at least have the genetic testing done?"

Lara nodded, glad she could answer truthfully. "The geneticist did find and eradicate two genes associated with cancer. So I kept my word." She softened her voice as she met Eva's hard gaze. "Eva, I'd love to stand here and chat, but my ice cream is melting. Won't you come inside so we can talk?"

"I think not." Eva glanced at her watch, then gave Lara a tight smile. "I was on my way to a Women's Club social and I'm already late. I just wanted to see how—to say hello."

"I'm absolutely fine." Surrendering to the heavy pull of her purse, Lara let it slide to the first porch step. "And so is the baby. It's a boy, Eva. I think I'm going to call him Michael."

Lara saw a suggestion of movement beneath that smooth face, as though a hidden spring wanted to break through a layer of ice, but couldn't. Eva nodded gravely, then turned and moved back to the car.

Standing on the porch, Lara watched her mother-in-law drive away. Eva had certainly been shocked, disapproving, and probably even hurt that Lara hadn't called to share the news. But she would come around eventually. What grandmother could resist being a part of her grandchild's life?

Eva's rapid departure was due to shock . . . and perhaps the stunning revelation that someone could actually proceed without her blessing and permission.

Gulping back the uncharitable thought, Lara turned and stepped into the house.

◇◇◇

She had just finished assembling a giant tuna-salad sandwich when someone rapped on the door. Hoping that Eva had returned so they could exchange apologies, Lara hurried through the living room, then peered through the peephole. Connor stood on the porch, a bouquet of bright yellow mums in his hand.

She leaned her forehead against the door and paused. What was he thinking? She didn't want to accept flowers from a man she hardly knew, especially a man who lived next door. If he got the wrong idea, the situation could become difficult, and how could she avoid a man she couldn't help but see nearly every day? If she encouraged him, he might wait for her to come home at night; he might begin to intrude. She might find herself a prisoner in her own house, avoiding him at all costs . . .

She pressed her palm to the door and took a wincing little breath. What was *she* thinking? Connor O'Hara had been nothing but helpful and kind. His little expressions of thoughtfulness had brightened many a gloomy day, and even Eva would approve his manners. He was attentive, considerate, and more intuitive than any man she had ever known. Not even Michael would have realized all Lara was feeling in the moment Eva pulled into the drive, and yet Connor had immediately sensed her anxiety.

She closed her eyes, realizing that she wouldn't hesitate to open the door if he were unattractive and merely protective. If he were seventy years old, eighteen and pimple-faced, or even thirty and obnoxiously boring, she would accept his friendship without a second thought. If he were the *woman* who lived next door, she would probably have run to his house every afternoon after work to sit and talk over coffee. She had kept Connor at arm's length precisely because he *was* attractive, interesting, and kind. Because deep inside she recognized his masculinity and his strength . . . and was a little frightened by it.

He rapped again, gently. Lara lifted her head and pasted on a smile, then opened the door.

"I thought you could use some cheering up." With a sheepish grin, Connor offered the flowers. "I hope you won't think I'm prying into places where I have no business being, but I saw the look on her face . . . and on yours. I know I made things awkward."

Lara waved his apology—and the bouquet—away. "That's really not necessary, Connor. You didn't do anything wrong. The last thing I want to do is get you involved in a family squabble."

His eyes clouded, and Lara immediately regretted her words. Was she making something out of nothing? He had no designs on her; he'd be a fool to fall for a pregnant woman. His concern probably stemmed from his friendship with Michael; he felt obligated to help her for Michael's sake. That's why he brought chrysanthemums, not roses. This was a friendly gift, offered from a simple and forthright heart.

"Thanks, Connor." She accepted the flowers and gave the petals a perfunctory sniff.

"Um—I don't think those flowers smell. At least they don't smell good."

She laughed. "You're right."

She hesitated a moment, wondering if he expected to be invited in, but Connor thrust his hands in his pockets and took a half step back. "I'll be going now." He glanced toward his own door. "I just wanted to be sure you were okay. You looked a little less than happy to see your mother-in-law."

Lara bit back the words of explanation. He wouldn't appreciate being burdened by her history.

"Thanks again for the flowers." She closed the door a few inches. "That was really thoughtful."

He nodded, then turned and moved away in the gathering gloom.

∞

Connor rubbed his hand hard through his hair as he followed the sidewalk to his own porch, then slipped into the house and let the screen door close behind him with a sharp bang. What a fool he was! He had recognized the look in her eyes when she saw the flowers, and it wasn't happiness. The gesture had frightened her; *he* had frightened her, when he had only meant to reassure her that everything would be okay.

He strode to the sofa in the living room and stretched out on it, then propped his feet on the padded armrest. Things would be different if Michael were still alive. Lara wouldn't see Connor as a threat, and he'd be able to help her without worrying about what people like Eva Godfrey might think. Then again, if Michael were alive, Lara wouldn't see Connor at all. Her eyes, her life, would be filled with Michael.

He brought his hand to his forehead and absently brushed away the hair that had fallen into his eyes. How would it feel to be the center of Lara Godfrey's universe? To bring a smile to her lips and light a flame in those blue eyes? He reached for a sofa pillow and cradled it against his chest, unable to stop himself from fantasizing. He'd give anything— his baseball card collection, even his car—for one moment of knowing that she admired him . . . and needed him.

She'll never need you, bucko. She's a postfeminist, capable woman, creatively competent and completely confident.

Yeah, maybe. But she had asked his opinion about whether or not she would make a good mother, and that meant she needed someone to talk to. Even a woman as bright as Lara Godfrey needed friends.

He picked up the remote and powered up the small television in the corner, then nestled his head against the pillows and clicked through the stations. The newscaster on channel 4 wore her hair a bit like Lara, and he paused to mentally superimpose his neighbor's oval face over the newscaster's square countenance.

He had never allowed himself to think much of Lara while Michael was alive. Of course he had noticed her—a man would have to be blind, deaf, and ignorant not to notice Lara Godfrey. But in the mornings and Saturday afternoons he and Michael spent together, Michael struck Connor as a free spirit, an extrovert who would talk to trees if no one else would listen. Lara was more reserved, more in control of her thoughts and actions. If Michael's personality was rumpled cotton, Lara's was crisp linen.

And yet he couldn't help feeling drawn to her now. Michael had asked him to keep an eye on Lara should anything ever happen to him, and Lara had never seemed to need much help. But she had opened her heart enough to ask what he thought of her plan to become a mother—and Connor had been impressed by the independent and determined spirit her question revealed. He knew she had thought long and hard about whether or not to have this baby. In proceeding with her plan, she had resisted prevailing public opinion, opposition from an opinionated mother-in-law, and a kind employer who would rather not lose a valued employee. Her decision seemed all the more heroic when he considered that those three areas encompassed most of Lara's daily life.

Yet in recent months he had discovered another aspect of Lara Godfrey—an aspect she kept hidden from the rest of the world.

Connor felt his cheeks warm as he recalled the nights he lay awake listening to the muffled sound of Lara's prayers. Only one wall separated the master bedrooms of the two townhomes, and sometimes he could hear her voice through the walls. On weekends when televisions and radios blared, he heard nothing, but several times he woke in the darkness of the night and felt his heart twist at the broken sound of weeping. The first time it had happened, only about two months after Michael's death, Connor rose to his knees and pressed his hands to the wall above his headboard. In his mind's eye he saw Lara curled beneath her covers, weeping into her pillow on the opposite side of the plaster and drywall. Then he heard her prayers—heartfelt cries to God for peace, for strength, for understanding. Though at the funeral and in public Lara cloaked her countenance with a sad smile, in the silence of the night Connor realized that Lara's peace was as thin as tracing paper.

She had not suffered through a midnight prayer vigil since becoming pregnant, and Connor hoped the baby would heal her heartsickness. As a mother, she would look forward instead of backward; she would turn her thoughts from death to life.

A loud knock startled him. He automatically turned off the television, then stood and moved toward the door. He found himself gaping at the sight of Lara on his porch, a plastic grocery bag dangling from her arm and a manila envelope in her hand.

She gave him a hesitant smile. "I thought you could use some cheering up."

He shifted his weight. "Excuse me?"

"I was terribly rude to you."

"No, you weren't. Is something wrong?"

She sighed heavily. "Connor, you're always asking me that. I'm fine, it's just—well, I've never had any male friends or brothers, so you'll have to forgive me if I don't quite know how to approach you. But I was thinking, and"—an almost hopeful glint filled her eyes—"I was hoping we could have dinner together. It's nothing fancy—I brought spaghetti noodles and sauce. If you've got a pot and water, I think we could be in business."

Connor stared for another moment, then stepped back and held the door open. "I might be able to find the makings of a salad."

"That's the spirit. Oh, and I found this propped against your door."

He took the envelope and felt a tide of warmth creep from his throat when he recognized the return address.

"Are you leading a double life?" A smile lit her eyes, but she spoke slowly, as if feeling her way. "I'm sorry, but I couldn't help noticing the address. It's not everyone who gets letters from the FBI."

"It's no big deal." Connor tossed the envelope on the table by the door. "Just a little job I have on the side."

"Secret agent?"

"Nothing so glamorous. I'm a reader—like the character in that Robert Redford movie, *Three Days of the Condor*. Only I don't work for the CIA. And nobody's out to kill me."

She looked down, the fringe of her lashes casting shadows on her cheeks. "That's good."

Connor stood in the doorway, his mind as blank as an empty page, then abruptly realized he was blocking her way. "Excuse me. Come on in—if you still want to make that spaghetti dinner. I promise I'm not one of the nation's ten most wanted."

"I didn't think you were." Smiling, she stepped into the living room and looked around with wide eyes. "Mirror opposites, aren't we?"

"I wouldn't say that."

Featherlike laugh lines crinkled around her eyes. "I meant the apartments. My living room is on the right; yours is on the left."

Rattled by his earlier thoughts, he felt himself flushing. "It's easier to build adjoining homes that way. When the kitchens and bathrooms meet in the middle, you can run all the pipes through the same wall."

"I suppose you're right." She hesitated, then pointed around the corner. "Shall we go into the kitchen? I'd like to see yours. Something tells me you're a better housekeeper than I am."

"I don't know about that," Connor answered, leading the way. "I'm neat by nature, but I'm sure my kitchen counters never met a bacteria they didn't like. If I'm healthy, it's because I've been around enough germs to establish a strong resistance."

He flipped on the light switch and stared at his clean counters as if he had never seen them before. The kitchen seemed bare—despite the coffeemaker and the row of blue ceramic canisters his mother had forced him to take from home, anyone could tell this was a bachelor's apartment. His kitchen definitely lacked atmosphere. No matter. His kitchen would be lit by her smile tonight.

"You need a pot." He moved around the husky oak table and squatted at a cabinet, then pulled out a ceramic pot. "How about this one?"

"That'll be great." She took it and moved toward the sink, then laughed as she filled the pot with water. "This feels weird."

Being with me? he wanted to ask. Instead he said, "Being here?"

"In opposite world. Having the stove on my left instead of my right."

"I can imagine." Feeling out of place and useless, he slipped his hands into his pockets. "I could run to the grocery for a head of lettuce if you really want a salad. I'm afraid I only have a couple of cucumbers and some limp celery in the fridge—"

"Don't go to any trouble. This will be fine. I'm limited to canned sauce and prepackaged noodles." She glanced over her shoulder as she moved the pot to the stove. "Goodness, I forgot to ask. Have you already eaten?"

He had snacked on a sandwich and a bag of potato chips, but he wouldn't spoil this night by saying so. "Dinner? No. And spaghetti is great; I love it."

She gave him a pleased smile, then turned on the stove.

∞

Halfway through dinner, Lara realized that good conversation could make even mediocre spaghetti seem delicious. Connor had the rare gift of making a guest feel right at home, and he listened attentively as she rambled about her work, her patients, the office staff, even about the baby. Before the wall clock struck nine, she had also told him the entire story of her relationship with Eva, including a detailed accounting of Eva's opposition to Lara's pregnancy.

"Maybe," he said, his face displaying an uncanny awareness, "Eva thinks Michael is somehow being cheated. Not only was he deprived of his life, so to speak, but if there's a child, he is also deprived of his right to be a father."

Lara rested her chin on her hand, considering the thought. She had never seen the situation from that perspective.

"I thought I was *giving* him that right." Lara frowned. "We had talked about it—not specifically that I should have the baby if he died, of course, because until the end Michael refused to admit that he might not make it. But he desperately wanted to have a child. He wanted to pass on his artistic gifts."

"Is his mother an artist?"

Lara snorted softly. "Eva? Not hardly. But his dad could have been. Mr. Godfrey had a great eye, but he went into architecture instead of art. His family was more concerned about his profitability than his artistic soul."

When Connor rubbed his hand across his face, Lara could hear the faint rasp of his evening stubble. "I take it Mr. Godfrey made money."

"A ton of it. Eva is set for life. And you know, the thing that hurt me most was the fact that she thinks I'm having this child to stake my claim in the Godfrey family fortune. I could care less about their money. I don't need it. I may never be rich, but physician assistants make a good wage."

"Michael always said you were good at your job." Connor shifted in his chair and stretched his long legs beside the table. "He used to joke that he was a kept man because your salary paid most of the bills—"

"He didn't!"

"Yeah, he did. But I know he really appreciated the freedom you gave him to pursue his dreams. He loved and supported you. And I know he'd support your decision to have this baby. Michael once told me he believed you could succeed at anything."

A sudden lump rose in Lara's throat. She had no idea Michael had shared so much of their lives with Connor.

"Well"—Connor stood and reached for her plate—"since you did the cooking—"

"The warming up." Pushing the words over the thickness in her throat, she stood too.

"Whatever. I'll handle cleanup duty."

"I want to help."

She reached for the bowl of leftover spaghetti, but Connor caught her hand. "You've had a long day and you're tired. Why don't you prop up your feet in the living room and let me do this?"

She froze as her senses leapt to life at his touch. No man but Michael had touched her in ages.

Keeping her eyes downcast, she exhaled slowly, grateful that her long sleeves hid the goose bumps on her arms. "There's not much to do, Connor," she said, her voice sounding strange and stifled in her ears. "Let me help."

Without another word, Connor released her hand and carried their plates toward the sink. While he scraped the dishes under running water, Lara stared at the spaghetti bowl and tried to force her brain to function. What did she need? Plastic wrap. Good grief, she was behaving like a bedazzled fifth grader who had just discovered that boys didn't have cooties after all.

She moved to the pantry and opened the door. Rows of cereal boxes lined the top shelf. Bags of potato chips, soft drink cans, peanut butter, soups, and baked beans filled the rest of the space. A bathroom scale sat on the floor; a pair of snow boots and a shovel leaned against the wall.

This was definitely a man's kitchen. She was just about to ask for direction when she saw the rectangular shape of a box under a stack of brown paper lunch bags. She pulled it out, not caring whether it was foil, plastic wrap, or waxed paper—anything would do.

"Did you find the foil?" Michael called over his shoulder.

"Yes." She waved the box at his back, then moved to the table and ripped off a long sheet. She pressed the foil around the spaghetti bowl, more than a little unnerved by the sight of Connor's broad shoulders at the sink. The sight, the sound of running water, and the mingled scents of food and dish soap awakened the memory of nights she'd spent with Michael. Her own kitchen had filled with the sound of laughter as they compared the events of their day. Michael had always insisted on washing the dishes, leaving her free to put things away and wipe the table . . . just like this.

She slid the leftover spaghetti into the refrigerator, then stepped away and clung to the back of a chair as the baby fluttered within her. "I'm sorry, Connor, but I'm feeling a little woozy. I should probably go home."

Connor turned to her, his face lined with concern. "Why don't you lie down on the sofa? Please, rest in the living room until you feel better. I don't want you tripping up the porch steps."

"I'm fine, really."

"I insist. You need to get off your feet."

She couldn't argue that point. Pressing her hand to the small of her back, she moved toward the living room and dully wondered if she even had the energy to drag herself back to an empty apartment. Connor didn't follow her, but kept working in the kitchen, so Lara sank onto the sofa, then obeyed his urging and propped her feet on a frayed footstool.

She closed her eyes and pressed the back of her hand to her forehead. It felt so good to rest. So good to let someone take care of her for a change. She spent eight hours a day looking after other people; how nice to sit down and know that someone else would take care of little things like cleaning up and wiping the stove.

A profound but peaceful weariness settled on her like a blanket. Her bones and body fell into torpor even as her brain hummed and her eyes flickered from right to left, studying Connor O'Hara's living room.

The couch was leather and of good quality, but worn to saddlebag softness. The television sat on an antique trunk in a corner, and a computer workstation occupied the wall across from the sofa. A collection of small photo frames cluttered the end table at Lara's right, and she propped herself up on one elbow to peer at the pictures: a gray-haired couple, an attractive young woman in a cap and gown, a little crew-cut boy with a mongrel pup in his arms.

Lara sank back to the couch, absorbing these bits and pieces of Connor's life. The gray-haired couple had to be his parents; the resemblance was unmistakable. The little boy could have been Connor himself, and the young woman—who was she? A sister or a sweetheart?

She closed her eyes. He wore no wedding ring; so she doubted he had ever married. She could ask . . . but such a personal question would bring her to the threshold of a different level of friendship.

She wasn't ready.

She closed her eyes and allowed her mind to drift into a fuzzy haze populated by images of the little boy and the smiling young woman. When the world sharpened again, a hall clock was chiming the hour.

Awareness hit her like a punch in the stomach. She had to go home.

As she lifted her head, the world shifted dizzily, then righted itself. Connor sat at the desk across from the sofa, his gaze intent upon a computer screen. At the creaking of the leather sofa, he turned and gave her a look of concern. "Feeling better?"

Her mouth dipped in a wry grin. "I knew pregnant women tired easily, but I never thought I'd fall asleep in the middle of someone else's living room." She swung her feet to the floor. "I'm sorry, Connor. I know it's rude to eat and run, so it must be even ruder to eat and crash on someone's sofa."

The warmth of his laughter sent a shiver down her spine. "It's okay. I needed to get some work done, anyway. That's the best part of my job—I'm actually paid to stay abreast of what's happening on the Internet."

She leaned forward, her elbows on her knees. "What job is that? Your work for the library or the FBI?"

He froze at the keyboard, a betraying flush brightening his face.

"Sorry," she whispered. "Didn't mean to pry. If it's one of those deals where you'll have to kill me after you explain, forget I asked."

"It's nothing like that." The glow of his smile warmed her across the room. "The FBI would probably prefer that I not give interviews, but there's no harm in telling you what I do."

"So—you read books and surf the Internet? Michael said you knew everything."

"Nobody knows everything." He clicked on an Internet link, then leaned back as the screen flickered. "But yeah"—he grinned—"I read books and surf the Web. Since agents can't be expected to keep tabs on professional bad guys *and* current issues, I help them out by providing background information. I summarize every book I read and submit a report to my contact at the Bureau. Every once in a while they give me a special topic and ask me to keep tabs on it for a few months. I'm not supposed to talk about those assignments."

She gazed at the screen. "What are you looking up now?"

"Everything. Anything." His fingers curled over the keyboard. "Ask me something and let me astound you."

Leaning back, she crossed her legs at the ankle and smiled. "Okay, I'll bite. What can you tell me about this building? Michael had a crazy idea that our landlady isn't a real person, but a fictitious name created by a Japanese conglomerate or something."

Connor laughed and turned back to the computer. "Easy enough."

He typed a Web address, and a moment later the words *Charlottesville Property Appraiser* filled the monitor's screen. "Now I type in our address," he said, his fingers moving lightly over the keys. He clicked the enter key, and an aerial map appeared on the monitor. Lara shifted her weight onto the footstool to better look over Connor's shoulder. Every vital fact about their town house had been recorded—the legal description of the property, followed by dimensions of the rooms, the condition of the building, and the total square footage.

Connor pointed at a box in the corner of the screen. "Owner of said town house is Mrs. Amelia Duncan, 2284 Lincoln Lane, Charlottesville."

"Imagine that." Lara parked her chin in her hand. "Amelia Duncan is a real person after all. So why does she have us send our rent checks to a post office box instead of a street address?"

"She probably uses the post office box for business." Connor kept typing. "She might even have an accountant who handles her rental properties." He tossed a resigned smile over his shoulder. "Amelia Duncan might not even know our names."

"What else can we find out about her?" Lara lifted a brow. "I'm curious. Every time I have a problem, I call the maintenance supervisor. For years I thought he was Mr. Duncan, but the last time he was here, I called him by that name and he laughed."

Connor went to another Web page, typed in the names "Amelia Duncan" and "Charlottesville," then flicked the enter key. A moment later a long list appeared on the screen.

Lara let out a long, low whistle. "Our landlady gets around, doesn't she? Do you think there's a picture? I'd love to know what she looks like."

"Here's a recent article from the *Charlottesville Herald*." Connor moved his cursor over one of the highlighted entries, then clicked the mouse. The screen flickered, then filled with a column of text and a black-and-white photograph of several people at a gala. A petite lady with silver hair stood in line with several tuxedo-clad gentlemen.

Connor read the caption: "Mrs. Amelia Duncan receives the Muriel Award from the Greater Virginia Philanthropy Society. Attending dignitaries included Charlottesville Mayor James Albert, Dr. Martin Allan—"

Lara gasped in recognition. "Wait! I know two of those men." She rose from the footstool and stepped closer, resting one hand on Connor's shoulder while she pointed at the screen. "That man is Helmut Braun, my boss's husband, and that"—she pointed to a dark-haired, handsome gentleman—"isn't that Devin Sloane?"

Connor kept reading. "—Thomas Morgan, Mrs. Amelia Duncan, Dr. Helmut Braun, and Dr. Devin Sloane."

"*Dr.* Devin Sloane?" Frowning, Lara sank back to the footstool and rested her chin on her fingertips. "I thought he was a stock-market investor or something."

In a flash, Connor moved back to the search screen. His nimble fingers typed in "Devin Sloane + doctorate," and within ten seconds the screen had filled with references.

He clicked on another entry. "This ought to explain it."

Lara found herself staring at another news report and photograph. This one showed a younger Devin Sloane in a graduation cap and gown, a brilliant smile on his chiseled face. A woman and boy stood by his side, the woman thin-faced and unsmiling, the boy frozen in an attitude of belligerence.

"Devin Sloane, entrepreneur and financial consultant," Connor read, "receives an honorary doctorate of philosophy from Harvard University. Sloane has been largely responsible for directing the university's endowment fund, which realized unprecedented gains last year."

"Is that Sloan's wife and son?"

Connor leaned forward, skimming the article. "Yeah. The article says his wife, Muriel, and son Ethan were on hand to congratulate him, but I think this was before the accident."

"Accident?"

"Fatal collision in 1995, I think. The wife and kid were coming home from Wintergreen, and the car skidded off the highway. The police weren't sure, but it looked like the boy was driving."

"How awful."

"It was. The kid was only fourteen—he shouldn't have been driving at all. There was a lot of talk afterward about how the mother had spoiled him. Apparently she gave him everything but limits."

Lara compared the photograph to her memory. "I met Sloane a few months ago. In Dr. Braun's office."

"Really?" Connor clicked on another link. "What was he like?"

"Nice. Quite charming. He looked classy, but nothing about him suggested he was a billionaire." She paused as a surge of adrenaline moved through her bloodstream. Something was on the tip of her tongue—and then it was gone. Something important. Something familiar.

"What were we just talking about?"

Connor looked at her. "Devin Sloane?"

"Before that."

"His kid? The accident?"

"His wife." She closed her eyes and tried to summon the thought that had been lost or pushed aside. "What was her name?"

Connor tapped at the computer and pulled up the photo. "Muriel."

"And what was the award Amelia Duncan received?"

Connor sighed in satisfaction when the first photograph reappeared. "The Muriel Award. Sloane must have named the award after his wife."

Lara nodded, grateful that the pieces fit. "I knew that name sounded familiar." She watched Connor scroll through the text a moment more, then smothered a yawn. "Connor, I'm running out of steam. I've got to go home."

He twisted in his seat. "Are you sure you're okay? If you're still woozy—"

"I'm tired. I think I can manage to walk from your door to mine."

He stood as she did, then walked her to the door. She stepped out onto the porch and shivered in the sudden chilliness, then turned to face him. "Thanks for letting me in. And thanks for the company."

"It was a nice surprise." His mouth twitched with amusement and Lara smiled, grateful that he probably considered her a hormonal pregnant woman and therefore exempt from all rational rules of behavior.

"Good night, then." She padded softly across the lawn, ignoring the sidewalk, then used the key in her pocket to let herself in.

Let Connor think her temporarily insane. He might be right—she didn't quite understand why she had sought out his company.

Hooray for hormonal madness.

chapter 14

"Lemuel, would you come in, please?"

Devin Sloane released the intercom button and let his hand drop to his lap, then stared out his window. It was a cold day but a bright one, the sun casting a white glow over the dusting of snow on the grounds. His curving drive sliced through the white like a black snake, cutting a wide swath from the road to his front door. Along the drive and on the tall iron fence bordering the county road, his groundskeeper had hung thick evergreen garlands studded with tiny white lights. In an hour or two, as dusk fell, the locals would begin their nightly drive-bys, slowing to gawk at the extravagant display. Yes sir, they'd say, Devin Sloane was a community man, eager to do his part to keep Albemarle County beautiful.

Giving himself a stern mental shake, Devin turned away from the window and bent over the letter on his desk. After skimming it, he pulled out his fountain pen and signed the correspondence with a thick flourish. Business brought him far less pleasure these days than dreaming of the future, and too often he found himself staring into space. Lara Godfrey was doing well. The latest reports from Braun indicated that the baby weighed a healthy four pounds and measured fifteen inches.

He had made a good choice. Lara Godfrey was an excellent breeder and the baby was developing beautifully.

And would be born in less than six weeks.

Devin shoved the letter aside and drummed his fingers on the desk. Though all the world seemed atwitter with the news that he expected a son, he had disciplined himself to proceed with business as usual. He had leaked the baby's sex to a reporter from CNN; within twenty-four hours the news had been featured on *Entertainment Tonight* and *Nightline*. Barbara Walters—whose request for an interview Devin had turned down—had promptly done a segment for *20/20*: *Do Single Men Make Good Parents?* The resounding answer seemed to be yes. Opinion polls and newspaper editorials from around the nation supported his fatherhood, a far cry from the outbursts that had arisen when he announced his arrangement with a surrogate mother. In the last few months, while reporters and photographers vainly searched for the invisible woman, the surrogacy issue had quietly disappeared. But it would certainly rise again.

Devin pulled his organizer from his pocket. The media would launch a full-scale assault once he took custody of the child. If a surrogate situation *had* existed, the mother most certainly would be found.

With every passing day, Devin grew more grateful for Lara Godfrey. Destiny had handed him a perfect opportunity, and he would do all he could to preserve her anonymity. For a few weeks he had toyed with the idea of creating a role for her in the child's life—after all, the boy would need a mother as well as a father—but the risks were too great. The great spiritual strength that had attracted him to Lara Godfrey would work against him if she knew the truth about her son's conception. She would not be bought off; she might make serious trouble. Devin had the feeling that half his fortune would not be enough to assuage her affronted moral sensibilities.

The carved mahogany doors opened and Lemuel's dark head appeared. "Sorry, sir," he called, panting his way into the room. "I was on the telephone with a news agency from Paris. They'd like an interview, of course."

"Denied." Devin's gaze fell upon the gold-framed photograph on the edge of his desk, the obligatory portrait of his loved ones. His wife appeared in the picture much as she had in life—cool, elegant, lovely. His son, on the other hand, had been nothing like the angelic cherub in the photo. Ethan Jefferson Sloane had grown from a charming baby into a degraded product of his times.

Lemuel dropped into the chair before Devin's desk. "I also had a call from the president of the American Eugenics Society. He'd like you to say a few words at the organization's banquet next spring."

"I've changed my mind; I'm not going." Devin shifted his gaze to his assistant. "I made those arrangements before the child; I'll not leave him so soon after the birth. You may as well go through my calendar and cancel any engagements where I would be away more than two days."

"For how long, sir?

"Indefinitely. I'll not be away more than two nights." Irresistibly, the family photo drew his gaze again. "I'll not make the same mistakes this time."

"But what about the financial conference in Washington? That's a three-day seminar, May fourth through the sixth—"

"Schedule nothing from mid-January through the following December. No traveling at all. If anyone cares to know my opinion, they can visit me here." He folded his hands and regarded his assistant with somber curiosity. "You didn't know my son very well, did you?"

Lemuel's narrow face twisted into a human question mark. "Sir?"

"Ethan. Did you know him well?"

"Not really." Lemuel cleared his throat. "Occasionally he'd come up and say a word or two while waiting to see you—"

Devin stared past the photo into his own thoughts. "You didn't miss much. He was a typical American teenager, spoiled, audacious, and arrogant. He carried a C average in a private school that cared more about catering to him than challenging him. He thought of me as a living money tree, and his mother as his defender. When I tried to discipline him, she rushed to his defense; when I tried to rebuke him, she sent him out of the room lest his tender psyche be damaged."

He focused on his wife's brown eyes. "It was fitting that they died together. Appropriate that his recklessness killed them. She allowed him to drink; she let him drive; she let him take that corner too fast. And though I mourned them both, now I see the irony in their deaths. They died as they lived, mother and son together. And that is why my second son must live with me, not with the woman who will give birth to him."

The corners of Lemuel's mouth were tight with distress, his eyes slightly shiny. "Sir—how do you know Lara Godfrey will not want to have some say in how the boy is reared? If she is as strong a woman as you say—"

"It's part of the surrogate contract. She has agreed to bear my child and surrender him at birth. In exchange, I will pay for her medical care and the laboratory expenses she will incur during the conception of her next child."

A sense of unease crept into Devin's mood as he studied his assistant. Lemuel knew about his plans for the Iceman, and he handled the Godfrey file almost daily. What he did *not* know was that the surrogate contract had been copied onto a blank form with Ms. Godfrey's signature and the woman had no idea she carried the hope of the future in her womb. Though Lemuel was a consummate professional, discreet and loyal, the entire truth was a rare treasure—too valuable to share.

Devin's mouth curved in a mirthless smile. "It's best that you not worry about Ms. Godfrey. I have promised to protect her, and I will do so to the best of my ability—just as I will protect my son."

Lemuel looked down at his hands as a blush burned the contours of his cheekbones. "Of course, sir."

Devin tented his hands. "We are only six weeks away from the child's birth, so we must double-check our preparations. Follow up on that decorator who's redesigning the west wing—I want the nursery ready in two weeks, in case the baby comes early. Make sure the contractor cuts a door from the nursery to the nanny's room—and call Mr. Thackery in London and check on the progress of his search. I want a properly trained English nanny here within three weeks." He snapped his fingers as a thought suddenly surfaced. "And remove every television from that wing. My son will not be weaned on Sesame Street."

Lemuel made a few notes, then looked up. "Contractor, nanny, televisions—anything else?"

"Prentice Technologies in Alexandria—they are designing my son's subdermal identification chip. Have it hand-delivered to Dr. Braun for insertion immediately after the birth."

Lemuel stared. "An ID chip? I'm sorry, but this is the first I've heard of it."

The corner of Devin's mouth lifted in a dry smile. "It's not something I'd like broadcast to the world, but there's no denying its importance.

My son will be unique, and I'll not lose him to terrorist kidnappers. If by some chance someone manages to foil the security system and the perimeter defenses, I want to be able to track the boy."

"Of course, sir." Lemuel jotted down the name, then glanced up again.

"One more thing." Devin pulled a business card from his coat pocket and flipped it across the desk. "Call this woman and invite her to the house for lunch as soon as possible."

Lemuel smiled as he read the card. "A social call?"

"Strictly business. Nadine Harrington is a private investigator, and I want to employ her full-time for a few months. If she asks the reason for the invitation, be as honest as you need to be about our surrogate situation." He chuckled. "If you lie, she'll discover the truth sooner or later, so play straight with her."

"What if she asks about the subject of the investigation?"

"That question"—Devin closed his eyes—"will have to wait until our luncheon."

∞

To his dismay, Lemuel discovered that Nadine Harrington, of the Harrington Group in Washington, D.C., was not exactly hungry for work. Her secretary flatly refused his telephone requests for an appointment, so on the sixteenth of December he flew from Charlottesville to Washington to meet the woman in person. At the agency's circular reception desk he boldly stated his name and his mission, then spent two hours cooling his heels in the lobby.

The Harrington Group's headquarters was nothing like the seedy private eye's office of Lemuel's imagination. There was no dark hallway, no sultry secretary at the telephone, no chain-smoking thug loitering outside. By ten a.m. on Wednesday morning, the Harrington Group's office echoed with a busy chorus of telephones and fax machines. After passing through the brass-and-glass reception area, Lemuel found himself surrounded by a sea of cubicles where smartly dressed men and women attended an array of computers, printers, and cell phones.

Nadine Harrington's office lay at the rear of the building. Her secretary, a clean-cut fellow with a polished veneer, escorted Lemuel through the maze with a vaguely sympathetic smile. For an instant he felt like Daniel venturing in to face the lions, but then he passed through the double doors and saw Ms. Harrington, blonde and beautiful, sitting behind her desk. The woman who rose to shake his hand seemed more *finished* than fierce.

"Mr. Reis," Nadine Harrington gestured toward an empty seat, "why must you pursue me so doggedly? I've told you, I'm not interested in traveling to Charlottesville for lunch with Devin Sloane." She lowered herself into her chair, then looked at him and arched her brow. "It seems to me that men of Mr. Sloane's stature have the freedom to travel anywhere they want. If he wants to see me, why doesn't he come to Washington?"

"Mr. Sloane is involved in a crucial project at the moment and doesn't want to leave the area." Lemuel colored his voice in neutral shades. "He apologizes for any inconvenience a trip might cause you."

"Why me?" Ms. Harrington asked smoothly, with no expression on her face. "Surely there are excellent investigators in Charlottesville or even Richmond—"

"What Mr. Sloane has in mind is more complex than the usual background check on an employee." Lemuel leaned forward, resting one elbow on the arm of his chair. "I would add that my employer does not give up easily, Ms. Harrington. You're the best, he wants you, and he'll pay handsomely for the privilege. He has authorized me to offer you this"—he pulled the check from his inner jacket pocket and laid it on the desk before her—"and to tell you that his private jet is waiting at the airport. I will escort you to Charlottesville myself."

Her mouth quirked with disbelief. "You want me to leave *now*?"

Lemuel nodded.

"Well"—the lady toyed with a gold pen—"for sheer chutzpah, I'll have to admit no one has ever come close to your boss." She picked up the check; then her eyes met Lemuel's. "Twenty-five thousand? Is this a retainer?"

"It is payment for your time if you agree to come with me." Lemuel searched her eyes for some sign of acquiescence. "If you don't care to take on Mr. Sloane's project after you've heard about it, we ask only that you respect his privacy and not share any confidential information. Mr. Sloane's jet will return you to Washington, and you are free to keep the check."

"You still haven't answered my question." Though her mouth stayed curved in a polite smile, the wariness in her eyes froze into a blue as cold as ice. "I'm good, yes, but so are others. So why did your boss send you to fetch me?"

Lemuel looked at his hands as something in his soul shriveled.

"May I be honest?"

"I wish you would."

"Then to be frank, Ms. Harrington, I think Mr. Sloane chose you because you have a son. Mr. Sloane's case concerns the child a surrogate is carrying for him. I'm sorry, but I'm not authorized to say anything more at this time."

Nadine Harrington gave Lemuel a look hot enough to sear his eyebrows, then transferred her gaze to the check in her hand. For a long moment she sat silently, idly tapping the check on the desk.

Finally she picked up the phone. "Stuart," she said, her eyes meeting Lemuel's at last, "cancel all my appointments for today; I'll be leaving for Charlottesville within the hour. Leave my messages on the desk; I should be back to return calls this evening. Thanks."

Lemuel cleared his throat. "I should warn you, Ms. Harrington—if you agree to take the job, you may not be back this afternoon."

Ms. Harrington dropped the receiver back into the cradle and gave Lemuel a flat smile. "Please don't think the sight of money tempts me, Mr. Reis; it doesn't. But I have to admit your boss's request is intriguing. And he is right." Her voice softened. "I do have a son."

Lemuel uncrossed his legs and stood, ready to be on his way. Grateful to have accomplished his goal, he spoke the first words that crossed his mind: "Do you need to make arrangements for your son if you do not return this evening?"

"Mr. Reis," Ms. Harrington answered, standing, "a judge made those decisions long ago. I haven't seen my son in six years."

∞

Nadine Harrington sat across from Devin Sloane and struggled to maintain an inscrutable expression as he related the most incredible story she had ever heard. Through the science of artificial insemination, he explained, he had impregnated a young medical professional in Charlottesville. The woman had signed a surrogacy contract, she had accepted free medical care and genetic testing, and she would continue to receive free medical care if she wished to conceive another child to raise as her own. According to the terms of the agreement, the baby, a boy, was to be placed in Sloane's custody immediately after the expected February birth.

"The arrangement is specific and clearly defined," Sloane told Nadine, his eyes shining darkly above his coffee cup, "and my lawyer, Madison Jarvis, has assured me that the contract is as airtight as a surrogate arrangement can be."

"But you're not entirely confident of his assurances." Nadine smiled, reading the worried lines above his brows. "Or we would not be having this conversation."

Sloane lifted a finger. "Touché, Ms. Harrington, you have hit the nail precisely on the head. Surrogate arrangements are not exactly common, and this will be a high-profile case. I have done my best to ensure that the surrogate will not cause trouble, but she lost her husband a few months ago, and lately I have begun to worry that grief might . . . disturb her sense of reality. She seemed perfectly stable at the time of the insemination, but I do not trust human nature."

Nadine took a moment to spoon sugar into her coffee. A butler had removed their luncheon plates; she and Sloane were now alone in the dining room. "So what do you want from me, Mr. Sloane?"

The billionaire didn't hesitate. "First"—one finger tapped the elegant linen tablecloth—"I'd like you to covertly discover all you can about this woman in case she decides against surrendering the child. I do not want a public custody hearing, nor do I want to part with the child I have begotten. He is mine, I have worked hard to bring him into the world, and I cannot—I *will* not—take the slightest risk regarding his welfare."

"You have already taken a risk." Nadine dropped her teaspoon onto the saucer. "The moment you went public with the news, you opened yourself up to conjecture. *People* magazine has already begun to speculate about the mother's identity—in the last issue I saw a list of the top ten contenders."

Sloane waved his hand. "I don't care about idle gossip." He hesitated, his dark gaze falling on the unusual table centerpiece, a sterling silver sculpture consisting of six concentric moveable rings. He idly stroked the largest ring. "Have you ever considered that relationships are like circles within circles?" He cocked an eyebrow in her direction. "The world, Ms. Harrington, is like this outer circle. Let people talk; I don't care. The people I care about"—his finger moved over the rings until it caressed the inner circle—"are here, safe and secure."

"If I am to move from an outer ring to an inner one"—Nadine brought her own hand to the sculpture and pointedly let her finger travel from the largest ring to the smallest—"we should begin with you calling me Nadine. Unless you want to advertise the fact that we are business associates, it would be better if we are on a first-name basis."

His smile brought an immediate softening to his features. "A good idea, Nadine. And in keeping with your suggestion, I will invite you to an inner circle. The world knows that I have hired a surrogate mother, but you will join the few who know her name. But"—the amused look abruptly left his eyes—"no one else must know who this woman is. You must not tell your people why she is under investigation, and you must never breach our confidentiality agreement. Only four people can know her identity: Dr. Braun, my assistant, myself, and you."

"You've miscounted." Nadine lifted a brow. "You forgot to include the woman herself."

Inclining his head in a distracted nod, Sloane returned her smile. "Of course. Five."

Nadine leaned back and mentally ran through a list of basic considerations. "You have the proper documents, of course. She signed a surrogacy agreement, the pregnancy has been monitored by a doctor—"

"Certainly, but paperwork is a weak weapon against a mother's tears." Sloane's eyes flashed as his hand fell upon the table with a dull thump.

"I've seen how the courts favor birth mothers, so I don't want to give this woman a chance to grow attached to the child. I want physical custody from the moment of birth. I want it known from the beginning that the child is mine."

Nadine looked away as her heart rate quickened. Sloane couldn't know everything about her past, could he? Surely he would never have contacted her agency if he knew she had lost a son on a courtroom battlefield. She sipped her coffee, burying her expression in her coffee cup, until she was certain her eyes were as veiled as the pain in her heart. "Not all courts favor birth mothers," she said, her voice flat.

"True." Sloane's eyes warmed slightly, and the hint of a sympathetic smile betrayed his knowledge of her thoughts. "Let me put you at ease, Nadine. I know about your divorce and your ex-husband's charges against you. And I am certain they were false."

Were they? Nadine lowered her gaze lest Sloane look into her eyes and read the secrets there. He had discovered the facts, but he wouldn't have had to dig far. Her divorce was a matter of public record, the judge's ruling available at the Washington courthouse for a photocopying charge of $2.00 per page. She was an unfit mother, the court had declared, unable to properly nurture a child. The judge had believed every story her ex-husband told him.

And she had lost her son.

She lifted her chin and stared at the man who seemed intent upon resurrecting her pain. "I am surprised you would call me, Mr. Sloane, knowing what you do about my past. How do you know I won't feel compassion for this woman?"

"I know you were an alcoholic, but you've been sober five years." Sloane's brown eyes darkened as he held her gaze. "I know you are a chain smoker, you walk three miles every morning, and you have an aversion to red meat. You grew up in Missouri, you took speech lessons to rid yourself of a midwestern twang, and you keep a one-hundred-dollar bill, the first you ever earned, taped to the back of a picture hanging on your office wall." A bright mockery invaded his stare. "Need I go on?"

She shook her head. "Someone has been thorough. If you're capable of finding out so much, why do you need me?"

Sloane smiled. "That was nothing, a mere collection of details Lemuel pulled from a talkative receptionist in your office. I need more than details." He leaned forward and spoke with a delicate ferocity that underlined his words. "I am the one who initiated this child's birth. I provided the genetic material that gave him life. I have dreamed of him and yearned for him, and I can give him every advantage."

"This woman might love the child too."

"But he will be better off with me—just as your son is better off with your ex-husband." Sloane's sharp smile softened. "Lemuel also learned that you have not attempted to see your son in six years. I have to believe you know what is best for him—and I admire all you have sacrificed for his benefit."

Exhaling slowly, Nadine studied the edge of her coffee cup. Sloane was thorough; she'd grant him that. His wily assistant had done far more than sit in the two hours she kept him waiting, but he had not been able to plumb the depths of her heart. No one knew the secrets residing there.

She shifted her gaze to the window. The afternoon seemed to sleep under a clouded molasses-colored sky; it was a lousy day for flying. She might as well take the case and nose around Charlottesville for a few hours. Sloane was a high-powered mover with high-voltage friends; some people would take the job for nothing. In a month, after she'd been well paid, she might receive a furtive phone call from Donald Trump or Julia Roberts or some other celebrity parent in need. Best of all, Sloane had already set a new precedent in her fee schedule—twenty-five thousand for a lunch conference wasn't exactly peanuts.

Turning toward Sloane, she assumed all the professionalism she could muster. "Give me the background."

Sloane lifted his coffee cup. "I salute you, Nadine. You will not regret this decision." He took a sip, then leaned back and clasped his hands on his knee. "I will give you copies of all the paperwork I have, including documents from the lab and affidavits signed by Dr. Helmut Braun, the supervising geneticist. I am not expecting trouble, but I want to be prepared if something goes amiss."

Nadine pulled a notepad from her briefcase. "What can you tell me about the surrogate?"

Sloane tugged on the knot of his tie. "Her name is Lara Michelle Godfrey; birth date, October 14, 1970. A widow. Lives at 3948 Maple Leaf Court. Husband was Michael James Godfrey; eighteen months ago he died from bone cancer. No children prior to this pregnancy. She is a physician's assistant at the Women's Medical Clinic affiliated with the University of Virginia Medical College. Her social security number is on the paperwork from Dr. Braun's lab."

Nadine jotted down the particulars. "Anything else?"

"You tell me."

She snorted softly. "Have your assistant assemble a file with the pertinent documents. And if it's all the same to you, I think I'd like to take a hotel room and spend a few hours getting to know our subject. I should be able to return to Washington tomorrow, where we'll do the background search."

Sloane watched her with shrewdness. "How will you proceed?"

"To begin, I'll have my office track her Social Security number and pull her credit report. Simple Internet searches can bring up all sorts of organizational memberships, news items, and the like." Nadine slipped her notepad and pen back into her briefcase. "There are other avenues, not entirely legal but extremely effective, that will tell us anything else we want to know—her credit balances, employment history, unusual bank deposits, that sort of thing. By this time tomorrow, the guys in my office will know more about that lady than her own mother—but they won't know about her connection to you, of course. We do background checks all the time; this one will be like a hundred others."

"Lemuel could do most of those things. What will you do that he can't?"

Nadine lifted the napkin from her lap and placed it on the table. "If you can have your assistant provide me with a car, I think I'll visit the Women's Medical Clinic."

Sloane's expression tightened. "As an investigator?"

Her mouth twisted. "As a patient."

As he lifted his coffee cup, Sloane's smile matched her own. "To your success, Nadine—and to the hope that we won't need your hours of preparation."

Nadine lifted her own cup and touched it to Sloane's. "To your son," she countered. "Life, joy, and happiness to you both."

∞

From the back of the limo Sloane provided, Nadine pulled out her cell phone, activated the scrambling program that prevented eavesdropping, called her office. After telling her secretary that she wouldn't be back for the rest of the day, she asked to be put through to Joe Costello.

"Joe"—she smiled when the connection was made—"I need you to come down here to Charlottesville."

"Charlotte-who?"

"Charlottesville, Virginia. It's a lovely town; you'll like it. Anyway, we've a subject here who will require the works. Devices in the house, maybe one or two outside in the shrubs, and in her car—I'll fax you the license number. Do the usual routine—weeklong surveillance, note arrival and departure times, and configure any likely escape routes."

"Whadda we got this time? An escaped felon?"

"Nothing so spectacular. Just write up the usual and put it in a file, okay? Pack plenty; you'll be here at least a week. But the scenery's gorgeous, and I promise you'll be home for Christmas."

She heard an exasperated sigh, then, "Okay, Nadine. I'm packin'."

"And Joe?"

"Yeah?"

"Find out who worked the reception desk this morning."

"Cecelia's been out front all day. I just talked to her about an hour ago."

"Fine." Nadine ran her hand over her hair and began to yank out the hairpins that held her smooth chignon in place. "Tell her she's fired."

chapter 15

Lara stepped into the break room and leaned over a chair, stretching her back and shoulder blades. She had felt listless all day, and the baby must have sensed her mood. He kicked more than usual, landing one particularly effective jab at her kidneys in the middle of a consultation with a new patient. Lara had to excuse herself and visit the ladies' room—not a particularly auspicious way to establish the professional/patient relationship.

She glanced up and sighed when she read the clock on the wall. Four o'clock. She could go home in another half hour unless an emergency arose.

Gaynel walked by, a chart in her hand. She smiled when she saw Lara. "New patient in room two."

"OB case?"

"Migraine headache."

Lara pressed her hand to her back and straightened, then girded herself with resolve. Just one more patient, maybe two, then she and Junior could go home and collapse on the couch. Maybe Connor would stop by with something to eat, or maybe he'd suggest going out to grab a bite . . .

No. She'd rather eat peanut butter and jelly than go out again.

She moved to the exam room, then lifted the chart from the receptacle on the door. The new patient was Natasha Hendricks, age forty-one, presenting with throbbing at the left temple, extreme nausea, and photosensitivity. BP was 130 over 90; high/normal, but so much depended upon the severity of the migraine . . .

Lara gathered the energy for a professional smile, then opened the door. "Ms. Hendricks?" She extended her hand to the woman sitting on the exam table. "I'm Lara Godfrey, the clinic's physician's assistant."

"I wanted to see a doctor." The woman frowned and swiped a hand through her shoulder-length blonde hair. "I've already spoken to the nurse."

"I'm qualified to do everything the doctor does except surgery." Lara leaned against the wall and folded her arms, ready to do battle but thoroughly tired of the struggle. Most women accepted her without complaint, but once in a while she encountered this kind of prejudice against PAs . . .

Apparently Ms. Hendricks was in no mood to argue. "Whatever." She pressed her hand to her left temple and spoke in the slow accent common to northern Virginians. "I don't care who helps me as long as somebody does. My head is killing me."

Lara peeled herself off the wall and took a pen from her lab coat pocket. "When did the headache begin?"

The woman winced. "I woke up with it this morning."

"Would you describe it as a constant or pulsing pain?"

"Throbbing. I'm dying here."

"Nausea?"

"Some."

Lara made a note on the chart. "Do you have these headaches often?"

"Nearly every month, right before my period. My family doctor tells me to take aspirin with caffeine, but I'm away from home right now."

"Does the aspirin usually work?"

"Not really. I go to bed and try to sleep it off, but I can't do that now. I need to feel better in a hurry."

Lara checked the chart for a home address and found none. "That's odd. The nurse didn't finish filling in the chart."

Ms. Hendricks closed her eyes. "Can we worry about the file later? I need something for the pain."

Lara pressed her lips together and studied her patient. There were no tests to confirm migraine, but the woman exhibited all the classic signs. And the pain, Lara knew, could be debilitating.

"Ms. Hendricks, have you ever taken sumatriptan succinate? The brand name is Imitrex."

The woman shook her head. "It doesn't sound familiar."

"The nasal spray works quickly in most cases, but one of our nurses will have to monitor your blood pressure for at least an hour after you take it for the first time. We want to be certain there are no adverse effects."

The woman opened one blue eye and squinted at Lara. "Are you insane?"

Lara sighed. The full moon must be approaching.

"There are other drugs, but they don't work as well. If you want immediate relief, I'd go with the Imitrex. I could give you an injection of Demerol, but it tends to make people drowsy."

The woman's brows pulled into an affronted frown. "No shots."

Rapidly running out of options, Lara scratched her head. "I could give you a dose of ergotamine. It won't work as well or as quickly, but you should feel better before too long." She cut a look from her patient to her watch. "It's four fifteen. I can give you a sample now and write you a prescription if you'd like to have it filled tomorrow."

"That would be great." The woman gave her temple one last circular massage, then lowered her hand and gazed at Lara through watery eyes. "You're very kind."

"Thanks." Lara moved to the counter and buzzed the intercom. "Gaynel, could you bring in a single dose of ergotamine with caffeine? And a cup of water."

"So you're a physician's assistant." More talkative now, Ms. Hendricks tilted her head and held Lara in a long and interested search. "This is a first for me. I usually see a general practitioner in my hometown."

"That reminds me." Lara sank to the stool, then opened the chart and poised her pen over the space for the home address. "The nurse failed to finish your chart. Can I have your address, please?"

"20473 Logan Lane, Falls Church, Virginia." The woman's eyes closed as she began to massage her left temple again. "My physician's name is Jarred Smith."

Lara jotted down the information, then glanced at her watch again. Gaynel was dragging her heels, but it was nearly time to go home. Lara's buzz had probably interrupted a late-breaking gossip session in the break room.

"What brings you to town?" Lara asked, trying to be polite.

Ms. Hendricks smiled. "Business. I breed quarter horses and I'm supposed to hold a seminar tonight." She cracked a wry smile. "Some job I'll do, feeling like this." Her eyes narrowed as she lowered her gaze toward Lara's abdomen. "Speaking of breeding, you're pregnant, right? I know some folks would say it's rude to ask, but it's a perfectly natural thing, whether it's horses or people. I thought you might be pregnant, but sometimes you can't be too sure what's going on under a loose-fitting top."

Lara smiled. She'd answered a thousand questions about her pregnancy, many from women a lot less tactful than Ms. Hendricks. "Yes, I'm in my thirty-third week. It's a boy."

"I'm sure you're happy."

Lara looked up and gave the woman a smile. "I'm thrilled."

The woman's fingers drummed distractedly on her crossed knee. "I imagine your husband is just about to bust his buttons. Every man wants a son."

Lara's gaze fell to the wedding band on her left hand. She had thought about taking it off, but since becoming pregnant she'd decided to continue wearing it. The ring stopped a lot of questions she didn't want to answer.

"My husband . . . well, I'm sure he's thrilled too," Lara answered, her voice quiet. "We always wanted a child, boy or girl. It really didn't matter."

Her patient's gaze softened. "Honey, is something wrong? Don't think you can fool me. I know pain when I see it, 'cause I've worn that look myself."

Lara looked up, surprised again by the unpredictable woman. "I'm fine. Really."

Ms. Hendrick's fingertips flew to her lips. "Don't tell me—your husband's divorced you."

Against her will, Lara's chin trembled. "He's deceased."

"I'm so sorry." Sympathy dripped from Ms. Hendricks's voice as her eyes blazed with earnestness. "Honey, I know exactly what you're feeling.

I lost my husband two years ago, and for the longest time I didn't care about anything. If it weren't for my babies, I wouldn't have even been able to get out of bed."

Lara glanced at the woman's chart. "You have small children?"

Ms. Hendricks snorted with the half-choked mirth of a woman in pain. "I meant my equine babies, my horses. I had to get up and take care of them, so that's how I got through the grief. Apparently you're getting through pretty well. You've got your job and you've got your baby."

"Yes." Lara's hand fell to her rounded tummy. "I've got a lot, really."

A staccato rap broke the silence, then Gaynel came in with the medication and a glass of water. While her patient took the pill and the cup, Lara pointed to the chart. "Gaynel, Ms. Hendricks's chart was incomplete. Who was the admitting nurse?"

Twin stains of scarlet appeared on Gaynel's cheeks. "I got all the information I could. She, um, wasn't in a cooperative mood."

"Don't you blame the nurse for my reluctance to chat," Ms. Hendricks said, again massaging her temple. "I'm afraid I wasn't in much of a mood for conversation when I came in. Your nurse tried to get me to write down all my particulars, but I can't stand the thought of answering questions when it feels like someone is trying to gouge out my eyeball from the inside."

Lara sighed and looked back to Gaynel, knowing the nurse would not appreciate what she was about to ask. "I'd like you to monitor Ms. Hendricks for half an hour, just to be sure the ergotamine helps. If it doesn't—"

"I'm not sticking around." The woman slid off the exam table, then slipped her stockinged feet into a pair of discarded pumps. "I feel much better. I'm not about to keep you all here just to watch me."

"I'd really like to monitor you," Lara protested. "If the ergotamine doesn't ease your symptoms in half an hour, we should consider another approach—"

"Thank you, dear, but no." The woman picked up her purse, then smoothed her skirt and gave Lara a sincere smile. "I like you, Doc. If you're ever in Falls Church, look me up and let's have lunch. I could tell you some of my battle stories, honey, and maybe they'd help you cope. The first year is the hardest 'cause some things get easier with time. But you're lucky to have a baby to take your mind off things."

Lara shifted uneasily beneath the woman's piercing gaze. "I'd feel better if you'd stay and let us watch you for a while."

"Can't stay." The woman moved briskly out into the hall, then looked right and left until Gaynel pointed to the check-out desk. "Thank you, dear," she called, moving toward the receptionist like a yacht in full sail. "I'll recommend you."

By four thirty, Lara had moved to the records desk. She was in the midst of dictating a report for Natasha Hendricks's file when Gaynel peered at her from around the corner. "Guess what I found in exam room two?"

Lara snapped off the Dictaphone. "What?"

Gaynel thrust her fist toward Lara and opened her fingers. One thick brown pill, emblazoned with the letter C, sat in the center of her palm— Cafergot, a brand name for ergotamine tartrate.

Lara picked up the tablet and ran her thumbnail over the initial. "Natasha Hendricks didn't swallow it?"

"I thought she did." Gaynel leaned against the doorframe. "She did a good job of faking it."

Lara crinkled her brow. "Why would a woman only pretend to take the medicine that would make her headache go away?"

Gaynel shrugged. "Maybe she's mental and only wanted attention."

Lara stared at the pill, thinking. "Could anyone else have dropped this?"

Gaynel shook her head. "The room was swept clean last night, and that woman was the only migraine patient we saw all day."

Lara's thoughts moved from the improbable to the incredible. "Maybe she tossed it in her mouth and missed. Maybe she was too embarrassed to tell us she dropped it."

"She didn't complain, though," Gaynel added, "and she paid the bill in cash; I checked. She paid ninety bucks without attempting to file an insurance claim."

Lara leaned back in her chair and stared at the pill in her palm. The world was full of eccentrics, and she'd seen her fair share. Once she spent an hour interviewing a patient who claimed to be in labor with a full-term pregnancy, only to discover through ultrasound that the woman's womb was empty—she had enlarged her belly by swallowing air. Another pregnant patient had come in with stomach pain that resulted from ingesting more than a dozen watch batteries. In a world of such possibilities, one woman's aversion to needles and unfamiliar medication didn't seem terribly strange.

Lara dropped the tablet back into Gaynel's hand. "Flush it. We'll probably never see her again."

"She was kind of nice." Gaynel sighed wistfully. "I love those country blue-bloods. They sound so cultured."

"They do, don't they?" Lara tilted her head, trying to remember where she'd heard a similar accent, but at that moment Sharon walked around the corner. "Excuse me, ladies, but have you checked the time? It's five o'clock and my husband's Christmas party begins in two hours."

"We're finishing up." Lara glanced down at Natasha Hendricks's chart one last time, then shook her head and placed it in the "to be filed" bin. Just one more adventure in a day, one more crazy story to share with Connor. If she was lucky, he'd have a few funny library stories to tell too.

She pushed herself up from her chair, slipped her stethoscope from around her neck, and waddled slowly down the hall.

∞

Nadine Harrington smoothed her hair into a clasp, then pulled a small notebook from her purse. The limo moved at a stately pace through the street, and Nadine was grateful for the darkened windows. Tomorrow she'd tell Sloane to find a rental car or truck for Costello's use. This vehicle was far too conspicuous in a midsized town like Charlottesville.

She bit her lip and sorted through her thoughts, measuring one impression of Lara Godfrey against another. The young woman was professional and competent, no doubt about it. A marked camaraderie existed between the women in the clinic; Nadine had noted the exchange of smiles and lots of friendly comments between the nurses, the receptionist, and Lara Godfrey, PA. At work, at least, Sloane's surrogate seemed to have a firm grip on reality.

That reality seemed to shift, however, when she talked about the child in her womb. "I'm thrilled," she'd said when Nadine asked how she felt, and she consistently referred to the child as "my baby." And Sloane was right—the woman still struggled with grief over the dead husband. Nadine had seen the quivering chin and the hint of tears in Lara Godfrey's eyes. Most alarming was the woman's contention that her dead husband was thrilled about the child too. How could she know such a thing? Was she in denial about his death?

Subject does not refer to surrogate arrangement, she wrote. *Is this discretion or denial?*

She brought her pen to her lips and held it there, like a cigarette, as she remembered Sloane's probing eyes across the lunch table. "Lemuel also learned that that you have not attempted to see your son in six years," he'd said. "I have to believe you know what is best for him—and I admire all you have sacrificed for his benefit."

What she had *sacrificed*? You couldn't sacrifice what you never had to give.

Weary of that train of thought, she tossed her pen and notebook onto the upholstery, then dug through her handbag for her cigarettes. She found them, shook out a slender stick, and pressed it to the limo's cigarette lighter. Trembling, she brought the cigarette to her lips and inhaled deeply, then crossed one arm over her body and stared out the window as Christmas lights and festooned houses slid by beyond the swirling smoky haze.

chapter 16

Lara pulled into her driveway and shut off the car, then wearily rested her head on the rim of the steering wheel. Because the office would be closed on December 24 and 25, a wave of anxious patients had flooded the clinic in a preholiday rush. In addition to handling the usual number of routine patient visits, she had reassured a dozen very expectant women that a doctor would be on call in case of an emergency and encouraged eight weight loss program patients to remain on their diets through the holidays.

Now she wanted nothing more than to sit in the complete relaxation of utter weariness, but the car was chilly and Junior needed warmth. Taking a deep breath, she pulled the fur collar of her coat high about her throat, then ducked her head and hurried into the house. A cold front had settled over the area, and Lara didn't think her tired body had energy enough to even shiver.

Inside the living room, she dropped her purse into a chair and walked straight to her comfortable chintz sofa. Without ceremony or grace, she dropped onto the soft cushions, too tired to slip off her shoes. The stillness of the house wrapped around her, comforting in its silence. "Forgive me, Junior," she whispered, rubbing her belly as she rolled onto her side, "but I'm too tired to cook. If Uncle Connor doesn't pop over, you can gobble up a few fat cells. I'll feed you when I find the energy to get up."

She drowsed on the edge of sleep for what could have been ten minutes or an hour, then woke to the sound of someone pounding on the window. She scanned the dark space between her gingham curtains, then recognized the shadowed profile. Connor stood outside and, thank the Lord, he was carrying something.

"Lord, please let it be edible." Strengthened by the thought of food, she rolled off the couch and shuffled to the door, then turned on the porch light.

"Hi." A flush darkened Connor's face as he waved a spatula in her direction. "I didn't mean to scare you, but I saw your car in the driveway."

Lara closed her eyes as the delicious scent of sizzling beef reached her nostrils. "Are you *grilling*? In this weather?"

She opened her eyes in time to see the flash of his grin, dazzling against his flushed skin. "The grocery had steaks on sale and they come two in a package. Doesn't wintertime grilling make more sense than cooking out in the heat of the summer?"

Falling under the spell of his impish smile, she grinned back at him. He had been feeding her for weeks, and she had decided to enjoy it. She tried to reciprocate by making his lunch on the weekends, but Connor made a far better host than guest. Even when she cooked, he insisted on giving her a hand in the kitchen.

She propped her hands on her ever-expanding tummy. "You sure there's enough for me and Junior?"

"There's plenty, and I threw some potatoes into the oven. They'll be ready in ten minutes, if you want to come over."

"Okay. Ten minutes." She stepped back through the doorway.

"Wait—Lara?"

"Hmm?"

"I don't want to alarm you, but have you noticed a white truck parked across the street? It's been around almost all week."

Lara covered her mouth with her hand as she yawned. "No, Connor, I haven't noticed a white truck. I haven't noticed much of anything."

The laughing light had left his eyes; they flickered now with an intensity Lara had never seen. "You sure you didn't see a kind of a utility truck earlier today? With a dark-haired guy inside?"

"Probably something to do with the park."

"It's not a typical city truck. I know what those look like."

Lara leaned on the door. "Let me go, Connor; I want to change into something floppy and fuzzy. I'll be over in ten minutes."

"Okay." He saluted her with the spatula, then stalked off into the night.

∞

"Merry Christmas, Mr. Sloane."

The greeting came from Nadine Harrington, and Devin stood as Lemuel escorted the striking private investigator into his office. She wore a cranberry-colored suit adorned at the lapel with a gold Christmas wreath, a simple concession to mark the holiday two days away. He had not seen or heard from her in a week, but she moved across the carpet with the confident walk of a woman who brings good news.

Nadine kept her intelligent gaze on him as she shook the hand he offered, then sank gracefully into the chair Lemuel indicated with an outstretched hand. While she pulled her briefcase onto her lap, Devin looked at Lemuel and nodded toward the adjacent chair. Understanding, the assistant sat down, ready to absorb impressions and take notes.

Nadine wasted no time in coming to the point. "I've completed the background work and established an alias should I need to contact your surrogate directly." She pulled a file from her briefcase and handed it to Lemuel. "Your child's biological mother rents one half of a town house; she is friendly with the next-door neighbor; she is also quite attached to her coworkers at the Women's Medical Center. She attends services every Sunday at Charlottesville Community Church on Spruce Street, but she does not linger or socialize with many members. She has eighty thousand dollars in her savings account, a little over two hundred in checking as of last Friday, and two credit cards, both of which she pays off every month. Her parents are deceased and she has no siblings. All in all, Mr. Sloane, I'd say you picked a good candidate, a woman with few attachments."

Watching her, Devin saw something that almost seemed like cynicism enter her eyes. "Lara Godfrey is what I would call a good girl—in fact, I'm a little surprised she'd agree to act as a surrogate mother. She has no crucial need for money, no obvious vices, no outstanding debts, no enemies to speak of. The only quality I can see that would motivate her to be a surrogate is altruism."

Devin shrugged. "She is a medical professional, so she obviously cares about helping others." He smiled. "Surely that is reason enough for a good girl."

"She may be a saint for all I know, but I'd still handle her carefully." Nadine's brows flickered a little. "She is still grieving for her late husband. It's possible she sees this child as an extension of her husband—in fact, I strongly suspect that she does. My advice to you, Mr. Sloane, is to accept delivery of your child as soon as possible and treat this woman with kindness and compassion. Send her on a vacation to Tahiti and present her with a picture of the child every year. If you keep her happy, you should have nothing to fear from her."

Devin leaned back, at once impressed and suspicious. "How do you know this?"

Nadine crossed one long leg over the other. "I posed as a patient and went to the clinic. As we chatted, I asked her about her pregnancy. Her answers led me to believe that she is either very good at covering her feelings or she is terribly attached to this child."

"I thought you were joking when you mentioned going to the clinic." He laughed. "Nadine Harrington, you are either the most resourceful or the most foolish private investigator I have ever met."

"Last week you said I was the best." Despite the flush of color on her cheekbones, her tone was as cool as ice water. "Consider this, Mr. Sloane—I have met your subject. We have made a cordial acquaintance. I have established a cover story, an alias, and a medical condition of chronic migraine—which, by the way, no medical instrument can verify. I do not live in the area, so we are not likely to meet on the street. And later, if necessary, I can go back to that clinic and learn more about my favorite physician's assistant, Lara Godfrey."

Devin looked at Lemuel in amused wonder. "She *is* the best."

Nadine ignored the compliment and pulled another folder from her briefcase, this one thicker than the first. "These are transcribed recordings of her telephone conversations for the last week. We also transcribed her conversations in the house, but I'm afraid you won't find much useful information in these pages. There's one interesting phone call to Lara's mother-in-law, Eva Godfrey. Apparently they are not on good terms."

Devin reached for the folder and riffled through the pages. A meddling mother-in-law was the last thing he needed. "What was the nature of the call?"

"Lara called Mrs. Godfrey and invited her to dinner on Christmas Eve. Mrs. Godfrey declined, saying that she was leaving for London on the twenty-fourth. Lara seemed to take the news with good grace, but she cried for half an hour after disconnecting the call."

Devin closed his eyes, grateful that his own parents were deceased. Life was far less complicated without that sort of interference and pressure. "Any other calls? Any friends to whom she might turn?"

"All of her friendships are work related but one. Lara is quite friendly with the man living next door. His name is Connor O'Hara, he's a research librarian at the university, and he lives alone. We did discover one interesting fact about him—last year he applied for a loan in order to buy a vintage Ford Mustang convertible. On the loan papers he listed additional income of $35,000 from the Federal Bureau of Investigation."

A large measure of Devin's enthusiasm immediately evaporated. "What did this guy do for the FBI?"

Her expression stilled and grew serious. "We're not exactly sure—yet. I'm guessing it's probably something academic."

Devin gritted his teeth. "How serious is Mrs. Godfrey's relationship with this man?"

For the first time, the flicker of a smile crossed Nadine's face. "It's friendly, but not what you'd expect from two attractive young adults. Mr. O'Hara seems to have adopted Lara Godfrey in almost a familial relationship. They often eat dinner together, with Mr. O'Hara furnishing the meals. I believe he feels responsible for her."

"So if she needed help—"

"My money's on the librarian. She'd run to him first. He's convenient, he's supportive, and he's a man. The good news, of course, is that he lives next door." Her mouth curved in a wry smile. "If she decides to run, she won't go far."

Devin pressed the palms of his hands together, then tapped his fingertips against his lips. "Anything else of interest on the tapes?"

"One peculiar thing." Nadine's polished face was smooth with secrets. She smiled, obviously enjoying the upper hand. "Something I didn't expect from a competent, modern woman. I hope it won't bother you or influence your son."

Devin paused, imagining all sorts of perverted practices, then lowered his gaze to meet hers. "What in the devil are you talking about?"

Derision and sympathy mingled in Nadine's expression. "Lara Godfrey prays. Aloud. Spontaneously, I think."

Devin stared wordlessly, waiting for further explanation.

"At first we thought she was just talking to herself—you'd be surprised how many people engage in the habit. But then we heard clear requests and a pattern—she was definitely praying."

"To God."

"Yes, and in Jesus' name." The phrase brought another flush to Nadine Harrington's cheeks. "She prays for protection through the day, for the baby's health, for wisdom in her work. She prays for people in her office and even for the estranged mother-in-law. Sometimes she sings as she prays—rather repetitive songs about God's goodness, his faithfulness, and so on. I don't know how you feel about religion, but this raises a red flag for me. Religious people can be . . . erratic."

"You think so?"

"Does September 11 ring any bells with you?"

He shook his head. "Lara Godfrey is not a suicidal terrorist."

"Perhaps not, but she definitely looks to a higher authority for answers. In my opinion, this is the single most worrisome aspect of her character."

Devin bit his lip as delight pulsed through his veins. He couldn't have chosen a better mother for the Iceman's child if he'd held open auditions in a convent. This woman was *genuinely* spiritual. Her sensitivity, combined with the Iceman's genetic purity, would surely create one of the most numinous beings the world had ever known. Jesus Christ, Buddha, Mohammed—they had been great teachers, but *this* child would be greater than any of them.

Wrapped in a warm bunting of confidence, he settled back in his chair and grinned at Lemuel. Hiring Nadine had been a wise decision. This was the kind of necessary information Helmut Braun couldn't provide, and it was worth every penny if it helped insure the child's safe delivery.

Devin nodded to Lemuel, who pulled a check from his pocket and handed it to Nadine. She accepted it, read the amount, and for the briefest instant a flash of pleasure shone in her eyes.

"My dear Nadine," Devin said, gesturing to Lemuel, "will you join me in a cup of Christmas tea? I'd like to discuss keeping you on retainer, just in case your services are needed again."

She smiled as she slipped the check into her briefcase. "Mr. Sloane, I would be delighted."

chapter 17

On the afternoon of December twenty-fourth Lara sat on her sofa and watched as fat wet flakes of snow fell from a soft gray sky. Bing Crosby crooned "White Christmas" on the radio, unperturbed when Lara's cuckoo clock interrupted with four strident chirps.

Four o'clock and all was . . . quiet. Too quiet.

Tamping her rising melancholy, Lara pulled herself off the couch and wandered to the hall closet where she and Michael had stashed their single box of Christmas ornaments. Michael always bought a live Christmas tree from the Boy Scouts, but this year Lara hadn't found the time or the energy to haul a six-foot tree back to the house. Still, it didn't feel like Christmas without some sort of holiday decorations around the place.

She opened the cardboard box, sneezed as a cloud of dust tickled her nostrils, then pulled out something she'd wrapped in a faded dish towel. The towel fell away, revealing a crystal ball in which a sea of snowflakes swirled around the image of a miniature Victorian house—a painted lady, they were called, perfectly ornamented in a rainbow of colors and artistic detail.

Lara shook the ball, then set it on the coffee table, watching in silence as the snowflakes sifted down.

Michael had bought the crystal ball for her the first year they were married. She complained that he spent far too much on the knickknack, but he had pushed aside her protests, promising that the ornament would become more precious over the years.

He had no idea how soon it would mean so much.

The old feelings of grief surfaced into Lara's consciousness; like a powerful undertow they pulled her into the deep well of memory and heartache.

She had thought that this Christmas would be easier than last. Last year, supported by a wave of public sympathy, she had numbly sailed through a series of December holiday rituals. In a frenzy of eagerness, the girls at the office had invited Lara to their family gatherings, their church activities, even their family dinners. As Christmas approached, Eva whisked Lara off to London, where together they spent a bittersweet Christmas in Eva's flat across from the Royal Mews.

Eva, however, had not offered to console Lara this year. Though earlier in the month she had left a beautifully wrapped gift on Lara's front porch (deposited during work hours, Lara suspected, to avoid a face-to-face confrontation), she had made no effort to visit or call.

Didn't she care about her grandson?

Lara tapped the glass globe with her fingernail, disturbing a pair of snowflakes on the dainty Victorian shingles. Eva had been opposed to Lara's pregnancy and upset to find Connor at the house, but the child was Michael's, and Lara had kept her promise to do the genetic screening for cancer. So why wasn't Eva being more supportive?

"Oh, God." Lara closed her eyes and swallowed the cold despair in her throat. "You were lonely too. Can you help me now?"

Her tears were flowing in earnest when she heard Connor's familiar syncopated knock. She dashed the wetness from her eyes, then moved to the front door.

Connor stood outside, wearing only a thin sweater, jeans, and socks. He rubbed his hands over his arms, then gave her an abashed smile. "Hi."

An unexpected warmth surged through Lara. "What on earth are you doing out here without shoes?"

"I'm inviting you over." He shivered dramatically. "And you'd better hurry and come, or I'm going to freeze."

She dropped her lashes to hide her hurts. "Connor, I don't really feel like—"

"Please come." A pleading note filled his voice, and something in her melted at the sound of it. Her son might one day speak to her in that same sad-puppy whine, and she'd crack just as easily.

"All right. Let me find my shoes."

"Hurry. I'll wait."

She closed the door, then searched the living room, muttering while she bent from the knees and struggled to see beneath the sofa. How like a man to plan something at the last minute. Connor was always doing things without warning her in advance. He seemed to assume she needed coddling and attention—

What she needed was someone who could bend over.

She saw the backs of her leather loafers beneath a wing chair, then stepped back and timidly sent her questing toes into the darkness under the chair. Connor must have known she'd have the day off. He must have guessed she'd be lonely and depressed.

Wasn't she?

Surely she had every right to indulge in a crying jag. Last year she had been too numb and too overwhelmed by London to cry, but this year she intended to weep loud and long. Next year she'd concentrate on the baby.

She heard thumps from the front door; friendly Connor was growing impatient.

"I'm coming," she yelled crossly, finally slipping her feet into her loafers. She moved forward, then stopped to pick up a knitted throw from the couch. After flinging it over her shoulders, she opened the door.

Connor threw back his head and laughed. "You look like one of the refugees from *Fiddler on the Roof.*"

Her cheeks burned with resentment. "It's my day off. I didn't see any point in putting on makeup or doing my hair."

His laughter stopped as suddenly as if he had flipped a switch. "Lara, you look beautiful; you always do. I was kidding." His hand fell upon her shoulder and pulled her forward. "Come on, let me help you keep Christmas the way it ought to be kept."

"Connor—" Lara hesitated, her feet as heavy as her confused heart. Maybe this wasn't such a good idea.

"Come on." His arm slipped around her shoulders, as comforting as a brother's . . . or a husband's. She closed the door behind her and let herself be led over the sidewalk to Connor's side of the town house.

He paused on the threshold of his apartment. "Merry Christmas," he whispered before flinging the door open.

Lara blinked in surprise. A broad Douglas fir stood in the farthest corner of the living room, aglow in tiny blue and white lights. Shiny silver baby rattles dangled from fragrant branches while an assortment of blue and white booties shivered slightly in the breath of the furnace. A single baby bottle rested upside down at the top of the tree, a silver star-shaped cookie cutter glued to its side.

Stepping into the room, Lara felt a warm glow flow through her. "Connor, it's wonderful. How creative! I would never have thought of it."

He closed the door and came to stand beside her, his hands in his pockets. "It wasn't all my doing—my fellow librarians came up with most of the ideas. But I enjoyed putting it all together." The Christmas lights glimmered in his eyes as he looked down and gave her a shy smile. "Anyone else who saw it would think I've lost my mind."

Lara stroked the soft satin of a blue bootie—a perfect little shoe for a perfect little foot. "I think this is the sweetest thing anyone has ever done for me." She turned and squeezed Connor's arm. "Thank you. I was just thinking that this was going to be the most miserable Christmas of my life—"

Her voice broke and Connor pulled away, probably embarrassed. "I put a chicken in the oven," he called, moving toward the kitchen. "I don't know if it'll be any good; it's my first attempt at making Christmas dinner. But there's a pumpkin pie in the fridge with whipped cream and I bought a heat-and-serve sweet potato casserole. Hard to mess up heat-and-serve . . ."

Lara sank to the ottoman and gazed up into the tree's branches. Connor had sprinkled a few traditional ornaments among the baby baubles, but the man's inventory of Christmas decorations was even lower than hers.

"I've got a box of ornaments in my living room," she called. "Want me to bring them over? We can fill in some of the gaps in this tree."

When he didn't answer, she turned toward the kitchen and saw him leaning against the door frame, his arms folded, his eyes intent upon her. "That'd be nice," he said, his voice thick. "Why don't you get the ornaments while I put this makeshift dinner in the oven?"

Lara leaned forward, ready to rock herself upward, but in a flash Connor was at her side, helping her up from the low ottoman. "I'll be right back," she promised, lumbering toward the door.

One corner of his mouth turned up as one dark eye glinted over his shoulder. "I'm counting on it."

∞

When they had entirely dispersed Lara's store of snowmen, glass globes, and tiny nativity scenes over the tree's aromatic expanse, she wrapped her fuzzy throw around her shoulders and stretched out on the couch. Connor sat on the floor and fussed with a string of lights that refused to stay lit. As Barbra Streisand's Christmas album poured from the stereo speakers, Lara lost herself in the strains of "The Best Gift," then remembered the package she had hidden under the sofa when she returned with the ornaments.

"That reminds me, I have a little something for you," she said, struggling to sit up. "It's not much, but I thought you might enjoy it."

On her one and only shopping expedition, she had resisted the idea of getting Connor a gift—not because she didn't want to, but because she didn't want *him* to feel obligated. If she gave him a Christmas present and he hadn't intended to give her one, he'd feel like he had to go out and get something for her. But if she *didn't* give him a gift while she gave presents to everyone at the office, she'd feel like she had deliberately ignored one of her best friends. The truth hit her as she moved automatically toward the men's department in a sprawling store—Connor had become a closer friend than Gaynel or Sharon or even Olivia. And wasn't Christmas meant for showing friends how much you appreciated them?

Now she pulled the rectangular package from beneath the sofa and set it on the ottoman.

"Lara," Connor's eyes softened. "You didn't have to get me a gift. I have everything I need . . . and in your friendship, I've found everything I want."

She lowered her gaze, embarrassed by his graciousness. He'd probably insist that she return this gift and use the money for the baby, but her grateful heart wanted him to accept it. "Please, Connor, open it." She nudged the shirt-sized package toward him. "I hope you like it, because I bought it on sale, and I can't take it back. For better or worse, it's yours."

He hesitated only an instant, then pushed the tangled lights from his lap and lifted the box. In a burst of childlike enthusiasm he ripped off the paper, then lifted the lid. Inside lay a brilliant red cashmere sweater that would positively glow against his dark hair.

He smiled up at her with gratitude in his eyes. "Thank you. Now the kids at the library will think I really am Mr. Rogers."

She wadded up a sheet of the torn wrapping paper and threw it at him. He ducked, then stood. "I've got something for you too," he said, moving toward the spare bedroom.

He was gone only a moment, then he sat on the ottoman and extended his hand. Lara's heart sank when she saw the small jeweler's box. Surely he didn't intend to propose . . . did he? She never knew what was stirring in the depths of Connor's fertile mind, but she wasn't ready to marry again.

"Connor, I can't—"

"You can accept this. Trust me."

She unwrapped the box with timid fingers, then lifted the lid. The object inside was a ring, but it wasn't an engagement diamond. A delicate gold band decorated with pink roses and green leaves lay on a velvet cushion.

"Black Hills gold," Connor explained in a soft voice, his eyes probing her face. "It's a family favorite. My sister has several pieces she really likes."

Lara lifted the ring from the box, then slipped it onto her right hand, finding it a perfect fit for her fourth finger. "I love it."

Connor tugged at his sleeve. "You can have it sized if you'd like. The jeweler said a lot of women like to wear them as pinky rings."

"I like this one just the way it is." She held out her hand and examined the ring, then gave him a reproachful look. "But I can't help feeling guilty. You should be with your family at Christmas, not stuck here with me."

Connor planted an elbow on his knee, then rested his chin on his fist. "My folks went up to be with my sister and her husband in North Pole, Alaska. Not exactly the kind of place I'd like to spend Christmas. Besides, I'm working on a special project."

"For the university or the feds?"

His grin broadened. "Let's just say it's an interesting assignment, okay? I was glad to get it, because it meant I'd have to stay home and spend Christmas with you."

Lara felt her reserve thaw in a rush of gratitude. Impulsively, she crooked her index finger at him. "Come here."

Connor leaned forward, a question in his eyes. "Is something wrong?"

She reached out and caught his collar, then pulled him closer and planted a swift kiss upon his smooth cheek. For a moment he froze, his eyes shuttered by his thick lashes, then he pulled away, a blush burning the back of his neck as he bent to pick up the string of lights.

Lara felt a sharp stab of regret. She shouldn't have kissed him. She had crossed some line and brought him closer than he wanted to be.

They sat in embarrassed silence for a moment, then Lara cleared her throat and gestured toward the stereo. "Do you mind if we give Barbra a rest? There might be something good on TV."

"Fine with me."

Lara turned off the stereo, then picked up the television remote and surfed through the channels until she found a program featuring a local church choir. She leaned into the sofa cushions, watching the tree's lights twinkle in time to the music, as Connor continued to mutter over the tangled string. From the television, a group of children sang a sweet rendition of "Mary, Did You Know?"

"When do you think he knew?" Connor asked.

Lara turned. "When did who know what?"

"Jesus. He was born an infant, but he was God incarnate, so when did he realize he was the Son of God? Do you think he always knew, or was it something that came to him in a flash of understanding?"

Lara propped her head up on her arm. "I never thought about it. But we know that Jesus knew a lot, if not everything, by the time he was twelve. Remember when Mary and Joseph left him in Jerusalem? They found him teaching the priests in the Temple. He said he had to be about his father's business—and he wasn't referring to Joseph."

Connor pulled the string of lights—untangled now—through his fingers, checking each bulb. "That makes sense, I guess. But do you think he knew then that he was born to die?"

Lara considered the question. Her imagination conjured up the image of a little boy who stared at his playmates with somber eyes, realizing that they would live long and marry and bear children, while he was destined to die on a Roman cross . . .

How could any child live like that?

She swallowed the lump that had risen in her throat and reached for the reassuring mound of her belly. "I don't know," she said, her fingers caressing her womb, "but I believe that God, in his mercy, allowed Jesus a measure of grace. I'm sure he knew what he was able to bear and when he was able to bear it. After all, if God promises not to give us more than we can handle, surely he would shelter his own son."

Connor dropped his hands into his lap. "But Jesus could handle anything."

"Jesus the Savior, yes." Lara pillowed her head on her bent arm. "But Jesus the child? We don't know much about his childhood, and I don't think we *can* know what those years were like. We know he was God; we know he was man; we know he never sinned. Maybe that's all we're meant to know . . . for now."

Connor absorbed her comment in silence, then picked up his lights again. "I read an interesting article about your friend Devin Sloane the other day."

"He's not my friend."

Connor shrugged. "You know him better than I do. Anyway, a few weeks ago Sloane gave a speech at a global unity seminar. He basically said that all the world's problems spring from corruption."

"Sloane believes in sin?"

Connor snorted. "Not hardly. His definition of corruption includes genetic, environmental, and social pollution. In his speech he quoted Joshua Lederberg, a Nobel laureate, who estimates that 80 percent of our genetic mutation rate comes from controllable environmental factors. Sloane claims that because we are all slowly degrading, prehistoric man is closer to the man God created than we are."

"Sloane believes in *God*?"

"I don't know if he believes in a personal God. But several times he referred to 'the Creator'."

"Isn't that interesting?" Lara's eyes closed as her stomach rumbled. Junior was growing restless, and she was hungry. "Connor, how long until dinner?"

"I don't know." A worried note entered his voice. "I put the chicken into the oven an hour ago. It ought to be done, but it certainly didn't look ready the last time I checked."

Lara's eyes flew open. "A chicken? A whole chicken?"

"Yes."

"Did you defrost it first?"

His features blanched. "Defrost it?"

She sighed and pulled her knees closer to her body, as comfortable and warm as the baby in her womb. "Wake me when it's cooked," she said, not bothering to hide her yawn. "In about an hour, I'd guess."

And while the children sang in the background, Lara surrendered to the sweet allure of sleep.

chapter 18

Standing like an ancient Pharaoh amid the treasures of his kingdom, Devin Sloane swirled the champagne in his class and smiled at Dr. Helmut Braun. "I'm sorry your wife couldn't make the party, Doctor. Some great emergency, no doubt?"

Helmut felt an alarming quake in his serenity, but managed to crack a smile. "She was on call at the hospital"—he inclined his head—"and one of her patients went into labor at five p.m. But of course she sent her regrets. She was looking forward to this occasion."

"Please give her my regards." Devin lifted his glass, then downed the remaining liquid in a stiff, practiced gesture. "Lemuel," he called, handing the empty goblet to a passing waiter, "see that everyone is properly escorted into the dining room, will you? I'd like to take Dr. Braun on a quick tour of the renovated west wing."

From across the hallway Sloane's assistant nodded, but Helmut thought the man's eyes narrowed as he acknowledged his employer.

"This way, Doctor." Devin pointed toward a carpeted hallway. "I want to show you my latest project. The construction is nearly complete."

He led Helmut through a magnificent paneled hallway, then up a wide staircase carpeted with a rich oriental rug. The stairs opened onto a landing that led to a group of rooms quite removed from the rest of the grand house. From a gilded perch high on the wall, a security camera tracked their movements, and a soft beep sounded when they rounded a corner.

"Don't mind that." Devin waved his hand at a glass panel set into the wall. "We've just tripped the security beam. No one enters or leaves this part of the house without alerting a security guard."

Helmut felt everything go silent within him.

"This will be Adam's wing," Devin continued, a note of affection lining his voice. "His nursery, his nanny's room, his playroom, his computer center. Everything is here, and everything is nearly ready."

"Adam, you said?"

A glow rose in Sloane's face, as if the name had switched on a light inside him. "It's fitting, don't you think? Adam was the first, the most perfect man. My Adam will be as close to perfection as we of the twenty-first century can possibly come. In this contained environment, I intend to keep him unsullied from the world."

Helmut stepped forward and peered through the first doorway. Blue walls and white lace curtains framed the tidy bedroom. A narrow, maidenly bed stood against the far wall.

"For the nanny." Devin answered Helmut's unspoken question. "I've already hired a girl from an English agency. She's working for the royal family now, but she'll depart London the moment I send for her."

Helmut thrust his hands behind his back and continued down the hall. The right side of the hallway seemed to be reserved for the nanny's use; the interconnected rooms on the left were for the child. The first room, outfitted with a crib, bassinet, and rocking chair, was obviously a nursery. A doorway in the south wall led into a carpeted playroom, which connected to a third room. This room remained unfinished; the drywall had been taped but not plastered or painted.

Devin gestured toward the empty space. "This will be his computer room, of course. He will be trained on the keyboard before he is even able to speak."

"What if—" Helmut paused, taking time to consider his words. "What if the child does not show an aptitude for the computer?"

Devin's dark brows shot up. "My dear Dr. Braun, you disappoint me. I suspect that he will display an aptitude for a great many things." Sloane rubbed his hands like a starving gourmet eyeing a French feast. "My son will have gifts we can only dream of."

Helmut's shoes crunched a lump of dried spackle as he turned and pretended to admire the taped walls.

"My Adam will have the best of everything from the time he is born."
Devin stood directly behind Helmut, yet his voice echoed as if it came
from far away. "Purified air is pumped through these vents; purified
water flows through every faucet. Film on the windows prevents the passage of harmful UV rays; shields on every monitor will protect Adam
from even miniscule amounts of radiation. He will never take an un-
tested drug; he will never eat food with additives. Not a single strand of
chemically dyed fabric will be allowed in his presence."

A thunderbolt jagged through Helmut, a realization that sent the
blood sliding through his veins like cold needles. "Do you intend to
keep the child imprisoned in this place?"

Devin's expression clouded. "Doctor, you astound me. This is no
prison! It is a fortress of protection against the environmental causes of
genetic degradation." His eyes filled with contempt. "I am not a typical
parent; I have power to protect. Nothing bad can touch him here. His
genes will remain undefiled."

Helmut knew he ought to keep silent, but he couldn't stop himself.
"You say the boy will not be a prisoner, but will he be free to walk on
the lawn? Go to the zoo? Have a friend come over to play?"

Fury lurked beneath the smile Devin gave in answer. "Think back to
your creation myths, Doctor, for they contain germs of truth. The creator
always establishes a garden, a zone of security and contentment, a place
where evil cannot intrude. As long as the creation is happy and in love
with the creator, he does not desire the evils that exist outside his Eden."

"But man has free will," Helmut pointed out. "Even children are
driven to exercise their strength of will."

The fury was fading from Devin's face, but his brown eyes remained
narrow and bright. "My son will not be one of those spoiled little brats
you see on the street, Doctor. He is unique. I never plumbed the depths
of love until I tapped into the love a creator feels for his creation."

Shaking his head, Helmut turned to survey the rooms again. "You
certainly seem to have thought of everything."

"I would never have succeeded in business if I had not learned to
prepare for every contingency." Devin stepped forward, intersecting

Helmut's gaze. "Our secret is quite safe. So safe, in fact, that I must tell you this: I am too eager to wait."

Helmut barked a laugh. "Waiting is not negotiable. Every father waits."

"For the birth, Doctor, I know I must be patient. But I cannot be separated from my child another week." Sloane reached out and plucked a strand of lint from the lapel of Helmut's jacket. "I want to be near my Adam. I want him to know my voice."

Another spasm of alarm shook Helmut. He turned and strode toward the stairs. "*Nein.* Absolutely not. Too risky."

"I know we must proceed with the utmost discretion," Devin continued. "But contact is possible, Dr. Braun, and would not be difficult to arrange. I am an associate of yours, and you are a partner in your wife's clinic. No one would think it strange if I accompanied you to the clinic—say, once a week."

Restless and irritable, Helmut stopped in midstride. "I'm already forwarding you a copy of her file!" His rough whisper echoed in the empty hallway. "If I am discovered, how can I explain *that*?"

Devin's face twisted in a conspiratorial grin. "Quite easily. I'm funding a hospital for children with genetically transmitted diseases. It's only natural that I would be interested in the results of your genetic testing. I'd do anything to ease the pain of my suffering little ones."

Helmut pushed at the narrow hank of hair that had fallen onto his damp forehead. "My wife would find your presence odd. You've never been to the Women's Clinic, and you've no rational reason to develop an interest."

"Only a few visits; no one will think anything about it." Devin thrust his hands behind his back and rocked slightly on his heels, his eyes glowing with a savage inner fire. The charming host had completely disappeared, his handsome and elegant veneer peeled back to reveal the ruthlessness underneath. "You owe me this, Helmut. And you must remember—thus far I've restrained myself to a remarkable degree. I've provided everything you asked for and required nothing of you but a few computer reports."

Helmut shifted and looked away, abruptly regretting his decision to attend this Christmas Eve party. This adversarial assault was unconscionable and Devin's desire to ogle Lara Godfrey obscene. But what choice did he have?

Slowly, he turned to meet Sloane's gaze. "You will guard your tongue while you are at the clinic?"

"I will be the soul of discretion."

Helmut jerked his head in a sharp nod. "Call me next week and we'll set up the first visit."

"Lovely." Sloane grinned and reassumed the mask of a charming host. "Now, let us get back to the dinner. After tasting my chef's offering, Dr. Braun, you will be ever so grateful you celebrated Christmas with me."

Swallowing his dignity, Helmut turned away from the surveillance camera and followed.

∞

On Monday morning, December twenty-eighth, Lara was startled by the robust sound of men's voices in the clinic hallway. She recognized Helmut Braun's heavy accent immediately, but though the other voice seemed familiar, she couldn't place it.

After finishing with her patient, she exited the exam room, turned the corner, and nearly bumped into Gaynel, who was trembling in the hall. "He's here," Gaynel whispered, frantically pointing toward the break room.

"Who?"

"Devin Sloane. He's sitting at our table." She brought her fingertips to her lips. "Ohmigoodness! I think he's drinking from *my* coffee mug!"

Amused by the girl's enthusiasm, Lara smiled. "What happened, Gaynel? Did you ask Santa to bring him for Christmas?"

Olivia stepped out of an exam room and caught Lara's eye. From the look on her boss's face, Lara knew she wasn't thrilled with the presence of her husband's guest.

"Mr. Sloane has financed one of Helmut's genetic projects," Olivia said, her voice low as she dropped a chart on the counter. "Helmut apparently thinks it necessary to show him off."

Lara bit back a giggle. Olivia often said Helmut could behave like a child, so perhaps this was an example of immature behavior. But it wasn't every day that a billionaire appeared in their break room.

"Should I go in?" Lara asked Gaynel as Olivia moved away. "I'll probably act like a fool. He won't remember meeting me, and if I remind him, I'll make *him* feel like an idiot."

"Stop babbling and go say hello." Gaynel slipped behind Lara and gave her a gentle shove. "He's only a man. Just ignore the fact that he's the *most* handsome, rich, intelligent, cultured man we've ever had in our building."

Lara hesitated for a moment, then smoothed her lab coat. She would just casually walk in and head toward the refrigerator, where she had stashed a carton of orange juice. If Sloane remembered meeting her, she'd let him mention it. If not, she'd pass quickly through the room and act as if his visit were no big deal.

Gathering her courage, she walked down the hall and turned the corner. Her cool resolve vanished like a puff of smoke when she saw Dr. Braun and Devin Sloane relaxing at the break table like two men on vacation. Dr. Braun had a newspaper spread before him; Devin Sloane was reading Sharon's copy of the *National Enquirer*. Both men were sipping from coffee mugs.

Helmut reddened like a kid caught with his hand in the cookie jar when Lara entered the room. "Hello," he said, his voice tight. "Are we in your way? We are just camping out until Olivia is free for lunch."

Devin Sloane lowered the *Enquirer*, then stood. "Perhaps Ms. Godfrey would like to join us." The warmth of his smile echoed in his voice. "A pleasure to see you again, Ms. Godfrey."

"I don't believe it," Lara whispered, meeting the smile and the hand he offered. She felt a blush burn her cheekbones as his hand gripped hers. "I didn't think you'd remember me."

"I never forget a lovely face." He released her hand but stood beside the table, his face a study in grave politeness. "So—would you like to join us for lunch?"

"She has patients," Helmut protested. "It is not fair to spring an invitation on a busy woman."

"I'm certain Ms. Godfrey is more than able to handle her caseload." Sloane spoke in a cultured rumble that was both powerful and gentle. "Won't you join us?"

Lara smiled as she moved to the refrigerator. "Thank you for the invitation, but I've already promised to have lunch with Gaynel and Sharon." She glanced back at Dr. Braun. "They're planning to throw me an office baby shower, so the least I can do is let them tell me what I'm going to need."

"Ah, yes." As Sloane's gaze fell on her swollen stomach, Lara noticed that Sloane seemed to be one of those rare men who could look at a pregnant woman's belly without pulling away in a rictus of embarrassment.

"Congratulations." Sloane met her gaze. "When will the blessed event occur?"

"Sometime around February fourth." Lara opened the fridge and took out her orange juice, then remembered her manners. "Let me return the congratulations, Mr. Sloane. I understand you are expecting a baby too."

His dark eyes filled with fierce sparkling. "Thank you for remembering. My son is also due in a few weeks."

"You must be very happy."

"I am over the moon." He lowered himself back into his chair. "Nothing I have ever accomplished will compare to holding that child in my arms."

Lara lifted a brow. She'd met pleased, nervous, and agitated expectant fathers, but she'd never met anyone who seemed to embrace fatherhood quite as expansively as Sloane.

Carol leaned around the corner and cast a bright smile at the visitor. "Lara, there's a call for you," she said, not even looking in Lara's direction. "Good morning, Mr. Sloane."

Sloane's smile was polite and noncommittal.

Carol stepped into the room, then placed her hands behind her back and leaned against the door frame, blocking Lara's way. "I hope you'll pardon my curiosity, but we're all dying to know who your child's mother is. You've been linked with everyone from actresses to heiresses, and most of us think that surrogate story is only a smoke screen."

"Actually"—Sloane's voice came out hoarse, as if forced through a tight throat—"the surrogate story is true, and I'm not at liberty to say who the mother is."

Carol swallowed hard, her face going as scarlet as a ruptured artery. "I'm sorry. I didn't mean to intrude." She glanced at Lara, whose own cheeks felt as if they'd been seared by a candle flame. Sloane would think they were all a bunch of gossips.

Sloane picked up his coffee mug and smiled over the rim. "Don't worry, I'm not offended. After all, we're all sophisticated professionals, and we understand how the world works. Science has brought us a long way in the last two decades."

Lara smiled as her hand fell upon her rounded stomach. Sloane was right. Without the miracle of modern science, she wouldn't be carrying her own beloved baby.

"It's very nice to see you again, Mr. Sloane." She moved toward the hall, but paused in the doorway. "And thank you for the invitation to lunch, but as you can see, it's a busy morning."

Sloane waved at her. "Perhaps another time."

A thrill shot through her as she moved toward the telephone. He sounded as if he actually meant it.

January passed in a continuous loop of restless days and uncomfortable nights. Lara gave up her sneakers for a pair of hideous slip-on canvas shoes—for their traction over snow and ice and because she could no longer tie her tennis shoes. Her workday wardrobe shrank to four colorful smocks, three pairs of elastic maternity pants, one tent dress for church, and two voluminous nightgowns. Lately her dreams consisted solely of beach scenes in which she stretched flat on the sand, belly down, while a cherubic baby made sand castles at her side and a sea gull pinwheeled overhead.

"I'm ready to be 'un-pregnant' again," she told Connor one night as they munched Kentucky Fried Chicken on TV trays in her living room. "I'm ready to walk and not waddle, wear jeans instead of tents, and sleep on my stomach. Having this little shelf"—she patted the mound of baby suspended over her lap—"has been convenient, but I'm ready to move on. I hope Junior comes early."

"Got your suitcase packed?"

"All the essentials are in a bag by the front door."

The tip of Connor's nose brightened. "Um—if the time comes when you're home, can I drive you to the hospital?"

Lara leaned over and squeezed his shoulder. "I was going to ask you. Thanks for offering."

Evenings with Connor were the brightest spots of the day, for working at the clinic completely wiped her out. After a few hours on her feet, Lara felt the baby pressing upon her pelvis, and resting in a chair did nothing to relieve the pressure. Olivia graciously allowed her to take short breaks, one in the morning and another in the afternoon, so Lara took advantage of the time to stretch out on the love seat in Olivia's office. In a reclining position, no matter how cramped, the baby floated up out of the pelvic cavity, and Lara could close her eyes for a few minutes of blessed relief.

In the last four weeks she had experienced nearly every symptom known to her third trimester patients—leg cramps, insomnia, nausea, heartburn, exhaustion, and lightening. This last sensation was something she had found hard to imagine—the baby literally dropped in her womb, shifting from beneath her ribs toward her pelvis. Often she felt as though the baby was poking or elbowing her in tender areas. It took every ounce of concentration to focus on work and not stare in bewilderment at her swollen body and the active actor behind the veil of flesh.

Because she had experienced an uncomplicated pregnancy, she expected a healthy baby. Olivia projected a birth weight of at least eight pounds, a figure that made Lara wince. The noisy and strong heartbeat squirted happily through the fetoscope, and Lara's blood pressure remained low and steady.

Her heart rate, however, did occasionally rise when Devin Sloane appeared in the office. He seemed to show up about once a week, always in Dr. Braun's company. Gaynel thought the financier had a crush on Olivia, for the threesome always ate lunch together on Sloane's visiting days. The billionaire often extended an invitation to Lara, but she continued to decline. From the frustrated look in Helmut Braun's eyes, she intuited that he would not approve of a mere physician's assistant dining with two doctors and a billionaire.

More disconcerting than Dr. Braun's tacit disapproval, however, was the creeping uneasiness she felt whenever Sloane appeared. She couldn't put her finger on the reason for her wariness and finally attributed it to a simple unwillingness to embarrass herself in front of a celebrity. He never said anything improper; he never complained or questioned; he never seemed to do anything. So why *was* he visiting so often?

When she tried to get an answer from Gaynel, the nurse stared at Lara with rounded eyes. "Are you complaining? He's a perfect gentleman!"

"I didn't say he wasn't—I only wondered why he's coming around so much."

Gaynel shrugged. "You're experiencing pregnancy paranoia. Maybe he makes you nervous because he's famous."

"I think," Sharon piped up, lowering the latest *Enquirer*, "he comes here because he enjoys looking at you, Lara."

Lara blinked. "At me?"

Sharon nodded. "Think about it. You're pregnant, and he's expecting too. Since he's hired a surrogate, he probably has little contact with the woman. Watching you, gauging your progress, is almost like being with his baby before it's born." She furrowed her brow and brought a finger to her lips. "Wonder if I could sell *that* story to the *Enquirer*?"

"You do and I'll never speak to you again." Lara eased her bulk into one of the plastic break room chairs, then propped her feet upon an empty seat. "That's crazy."

The other nurses had agreed with Lara and laughed off Sharon's suggestion. Yet sometimes as Lara drifted in that strange netherworld between wakefulness and sleep, Devin Sloane's piercing eyes seemed to shine through the gloom and focus on her unborn child.

∞

On Friday morning, January twenty-ninth, Lara went to the office, prepared an exam room, and told Gaynel to alert Olivia as soon as the doctor arrived.

Gaynel frowned as she studied the appointment list. "Who's the patient?"

"I am."

Inside the exam room, Lara slipped into a gown and climbed onto the table, breathing deeply as she counted twinges and waited for Olivia to arrive. *Please, Lord, help her to be on time for once!*

When the doctor finally came through the door, Lara wiped wetness from her eyes and gave Olivia an apologetic smile. "I've been having twinges for two days. I think I began real labor this morning."

Olivia nodded in her no-nonsense way. "Let's have a look and see if the cervix is dilating."

Lara lifted her feet into the stirrups, then stared at the ceiling and folded one arm behind her head. If this *was* labor, Connor would be disappointed that he missed driving her to the hospital. Any of the girls would be thrilled to play chauffeur.

"I skipped breakfast this morning," she added helpfully as Olivia sat on her stool and scooted closer. "Just in case this is it."

Olivia murmured a noncommittal response, then slapped her hands on her slacks and pushed back. "You should have eaten," she said, her eyes sympathetic. "Those 'twinges' you're feeling are Braxton-Hicks contractions. The cervix isn't thinning. I'm sure you're ready, but Junior isn't. Not yet."

Struggling to disguise her disappointment, Lara pushed herself into an upright position. "Guess now I'll be more sympathetic to our overeager patients. I was certain this was the real thing."

"The baby will come, hon. In his own sweet time."

Lara slipped from the exam table and shuffled behind the curtain where she'd left her clothes, then grimaced when she saw the piled heap in the chair. She was rapidly growing sick of maternity pants and smocks.

"If you're not feeling well enough to work, you could go home." Olivia's voice floated over the curtained alcove. "We could spare you."

"No, thanks. Braxton-Hicks can come and go for a week, right? I'll follow my own advice and try to grin and bear it."

"That's a good girl." Olivia's voice softened. "Feel free to use my office at any time. Just give a shout if you're feeling tired and I'll step in to cover your patients."

"Thanks, Liv." Lara pushed the sliding curtain aside, then rolled up the sleeves of her smock. "If you could just slide my shoes toward my feet . . ."

Grinning, Olivia picked up the shoes and dropped them into the void beneath Lara's belly. "It won't be much longer," Olivia said, probably trying to lighten the load. "The baby has dropped. He certainly *looks* ready."

"Any time is fine with me." Lara slipped into her shoes, then picked up her chart from the desk. "Want me to hand this in?"

"That'd be great, I didn't write much." Liv glanced at her watch, then opened the door and gave Lara a final smile. "Chin up, honey. It will be over before you know it."

Lara lifted her chart and studied Liv's neat schoolgirl handwriting. *1–29: Patient presents with Braxton-Hicks contractions, but cervix is not dilated. Baby's head in good position.*

Lara felt the corner of her mouth lift in a lopsided smile. As long as the baby was ready to go, labor could begin at any time.

She flipped back through the chart, reviewing her pregnancy through a series of notes and methodical measurements. Olivia had made meticulous observations, and Lara wasn't surprised when she discovered a sticky note attached to a page at the back of the file. "Forward case notes under patient's ID number to UVA cryo lab." The handwriting was Olivia's, and Lara dimly remembered giving permission for Olivia to share her case information with Dr. Braun. He, after all, had provided the means through which Junior came to be. If his techniques for gene splicing helped other couples conceive children without the threat of cancer, Lara would be grateful.

She stood in the hallway, her thumbnail clicking against the edge of the file. What was Dr. Braun doing with her data?

She checked her watch—she had over half an hour before her first patient would arrive. Time enough to follow the computer trail and see if Dr. Braun had made any notes on his copy of her file. She might find references to a paper he planned to author on the subject. She hadn't asked Olivia about her husband's plans, but even now other women could be benefiting from the trail she had helped blaze.

She jotted down her patient number on a prescription pad, then stepped down the hall and dropped her file in the transcriptionist's "in" basket. She switched on the lights and stared at the empty computer room. Carol, the transcriptionist, wouldn't be in for another hour.

After lowering herself into a rolling chair that groaned under her weight, Lara powered up the hibernating computer. With two keystrokes, she exited the clinic's records program and clicked on the link that connected her to the university's medical registry. A blinking cursor came up in the field labeled "patient number," so Lara typed her number in, then snapped the enter key. A moment later her file came up: a long list of dates and notes, an almost verbatim account of Olivia's observations.

One anomaly caught Lara's eye. In a box marked "Send CC to", five other departments were indicated by code numbers. The first, Lara knew, was the billing department. The second, she strongly suspected, was Dr. Braun's cryogenics lab. She also recognized numbers for the patient records department and hospital obstetrics, but what other department could possibly be interested in her medical records?

She highlighted the unfamiliar department code, copied it, then moved to a search window and pasted the number into the search field. After a moment, an error message appeared on the screen:

Classified File
Password?

Lara leaned back and chewed her thumbnail. What department would *classify* her records? Individual patient files were confidential, of course, but there was no need to protect a file identified only by a number. This security measure was highly irregular, particularly in a teaching hospital where the process of education depended upon physicians' and students' access to general medical records.

Lara stared at the blinking cursor, then typed in her patient number and pressed the enter key. The same annoying message appeared.

Classified File
Password?

What password? She couldn't even begin to guess without knowing which department owned this registry. She rocked back in her chair and absently imagined several scenarios. Perhaps some professor wanted information about single mothers, or perhaps Dr. Braun had found a partner to help with his research. But any professor could get anonymous information from patient records, and if Braun had a research partner, there would be no need for a separate department number. Any partner of Braun's could use his computer network . . .

She snorted softly. Dr. Braun didn't really need a computer in his lab; heaven knew he used *this* computer often enough. No, the only reason Braun might establish a separate department number would be if he wanted to share information with someone outside the university network. With a separate number, someone off campus could enter the system through the Internet and access the file . . . with a password.

She bit on her thumb, remembering how Dr. Braun often sat in this same chair, its sharp squeak cutting through the ghostly clatter of the keyboard. On many an afternoon she had seen him here, catching up on case notes while Olivia finished her dictation. Liv often said that Helmut preferred working at her office so they could ride home together . . .

Helmut should know the password. And he had been working at this computer yesterday.

With great difficulty, Lara pushed herself up and out of the chair, then trudged to the intake area. Gaynel was taking a patient's blood pressure, so Lara waited until she had finished before speaking. "Excuse me, Gaynel—remember that computer program we installed to save data in case of power failure? What's it called?"

"Last Chance." Gaynel pulled the stethoscope from her ears, then unwrapped the pressure cuff on her patient's arm. She gave Lara a curious glance. "Did the computer crash?"

"No—I was only curious." Lara turned and waddled toward the records room. She only had a few minutes before she would have to go to work. The woman with Gaynel might even be one of Lara's patients.

Back at the computer, Lara exited the university's registry program, then went into the operating system and opened the window that allowed her to scroll through the program folders. She highlighted the folder beside LCHANCE.exe, then held her breath as another window opened. She skimmed the instructions, then selected the option for "save all keystrokes in a text file." Within ten seconds, another message informed her that the program had executed. Lara opened the text file in Notepad, then stared at a fluid stream of notations about patients and their prognoses.

Gaynel tapped on the open door. "Got a patient waiting in exam one for you," she called, her voice bright and cheery. "Do you need help getting out of that chair?"

"Not yet." Lara returned Gaynel's smile, then returned her attention to the computer screen. She didn't have time to scroll through pages of gobbledygook in search of one lousy word she might not even recognize, but she wouldn't have access to the computer once the transcriptionist arrived. After an instant of indecision, she pressed the button for "print," then leaned back and sighed as the printer began to spit out the text.

These pages wouldn't be the most interesting reading material she could peruse during her midmorning break, but they might offer some clue.

chapter 19

Lara finished with her last morning patient at 11:56, completed her notes on the chart, then dropped it into the transcriptionist's basket. From the break room she could hear the chirpy chatter of the nurses' voices, but she had no appetite. Turning her back on the other women, she retrieved the long computer printout from the supply closet shelf where she'd stashed it earlier.

Olivia was at the hospital with a patient in the final stage of labor, so her office was empty and quiet. Lara sat on the love seat and leaned back on the pillows, sighing with relief as her bones melted into the thick cushions. She enjoyed the momentary release of pressure on her spine, then lifted the stack of printed sheets. Her eyes skimmed over the entries— patient numbers, billing and diagnosis codes, physicians' notes, a thousand shortcut phrases only a physician or nurse would understand. She flipped through page after page; then her eyes skimmed notes about chromosomes and plasmids and organelles—words from a geneticist's lexicon.

She backed up and reread the last page, running her finger along the text. There! Amid the notes she recognized her patient number, followed by last week's weight, blood pressure, and measurements. The entry ended with the notes Olivia had made after last week's examination.

Lara turned the page. Carol would have entered these notes from Lara's file; and Dr. Braun could have accessed them from his own lab. But if he had wanted to send her records to a password-protected file, he'd have to enter the password, then her case number . . . and perhaps he had done so from one of the Women's Clinic computers.

She continued skimming through the pages, searching again for her patient number, and felt a sudden surge of joy when she found it. No notes followed this entry, no measurements or numbers. Only one word: ICEMAN.

Lara sat up, her blood pulsing with adrenaline. *Iceman?* If it was a password, it certainly fit Dr. Braun—after all, he did oversee the freezers in the cryogenics lab. But his office wouldn't need a password to access her file; the term ICEMAN had to mean something else.

The answer would lie in the computer. Gripping the printout in trembling fingers, she slipped out of Olivia's office and walked the long way around the office suite, avoiding the open doorway where the staff relaxed over lunch. The records office was dark, for Carol was eating with the nurses. Lara flipped on the light, slipped into the transcriptionist's chair, and typed in her patient number. When her chart came up, she tabbed through the fields, then clicked on the department number she hadn't recognized.

Classified File
Password?

She bit her lower lip and typed I-C-E-M-A-N. She clicked the enter key and held her breath.

The screen went black, then opened into another registry—a directory in which hers appeared to be the only record.

Patient Name: Lara Godfrey, Patient Number: GODL49383-92
Birth date: 10-14-70
Blood Type: 0 neg   Donor Blood Type: B+
Follicular aspiration: 5-07-98
Conception date: 5-15-98   Conception Method: IVF AID
Embryo Transfer Procedure: 5-18-98, blastocyst stage
Pregnancy: Positive, 5-22-98   Due: 2-04-99
Instructions ——-BEGIN PGP MESSAGE——-
MessageID: 6NOMhIDpqZvAiq3pykwy6zVz2fynZ+Sw
qANQR1DBwU4Dj1QWb23RM4kQB/9cknhNCZB25fxb4mONT0jFxU3QxR
qEFT4H5C1o

mTvWlWXeKJXlnzcBhSPz/gl2gPtIyGBSaUPG77YFXGtDgSsewfniP+Xh+sz
/Tw87
rZOxua3aibCcFzVd2naO8/X5RC4y3pEDmMHXZfgk5CxOfAwgC8vDENHIE
qMqS5FW
/lJ6qsbWo/riXBLQ5AT5BlOlt3ZxUmUfOUO0BIht543acU1SE2alWu4hOo
zAee/8
sMQ1ALF86m4jEVx4n152MJLo6qfiUGEuTxoOwoHf9iEV/VDCI7oQa0GaE
YOWiw9K
eivu81lcUojNm+d1E3zMLHnvVNlLxfhokJs00c/SvMOVmlS3CACFhRfqPEr
zUQPm
/6Jxx/ty/abeU2wA2lScbXBqdPuEFsoIKZRi2bMnq8QKpS+pQAzlNto
X9nqQwwPyauoH70g7e1a3toOu+k5WprzDASZTrOMYrD6teYOMbcW+FBK
CRlZOipS
ScCODHOX2Jx13JJUdzldlIb76JFQjm3ynyp/Zpf1Bg/v5WMZfLqjPLzeMIr
C8kkJ
7kdNlJ4WBGgtty8sxEOFbAjoeTirxBzPMm92TijD5ZdUuNCdQwk8s41QMs
uXl5oL
+MuohFhuzcdcpkLt00q0JCpxDylNwNGUyk4lMGXRHK3u+5E=
=/0Uy
———-END PGP MESSAGE———-

Lara stared wordlessly at the screen, questions bubbling up by the dozens.

∞

Helmut answered his phone on the fifth ring, then heard Olivia's exasperated voice on the line. "Honestly, Helmut, can't anyone in your lab stop whatever they're doing long enough to pick up the phone? This is the third time I've tried to reach you."

"Sorry." Helmut flicked a dark string from his lab coat, then frowned at the microscope he'd been forced to abandon. "What is so urgent?"

"I've got a first-time mother who's taking longer than expected, and I'm afraid I'm going to have to do a cesarean. I'll be tied up here all afternoon, so I won't feel like going out tonight. Would you mind calling George and Beverly to cancel our dinner plans?"

"No problem." Helmut tapped his calendar, grateful for an excuse to cancel. One of the hardest things about being married to a bright and beautiful woman was having to endure her social life.

His gaze moved toward the window as another thought crossed his mind. "How are things at the office? Will Dr. Stock and Lara be able to handle anything that comes up while you're out?"

"That's a potential problem." A worried note entered Olivia's voice. "Lara was experiencing Braxton-Hicks contractions this morning, and she's convinced the baby's going to come soon. Dr. Stock is on call for emergency patients, so Lara may have her hands full this afternoon."

"Are you certain it was false labor?"

Olivia laughed. "She was only two centimeters dilated and zero percent effaced."

"Well, then, I feel sorry for the girl. Most women would spend the day in bed, but she will have to handle your office in a most uncomfortable condition."

"The others will help her."

Helmut flinched as a shrill beep cut across the phone line.

"Sorry, that'll be the charge nurse. Talk to you later." Olivia hung up.

Helmut replaced the phone, then studied his calendar, his hands drumming on his desk. Though Lara Godfrey's pregnancy could go another week, these things were unpredictable. If she was experiencing contractions, the time was certainly near. The child could be induced now with no risk.

With a shiver of vivid recollection, Sloane's dark, covetous eyes rose up before him. His visits to the Women's Clinic had grown more suspicious and more difficult for Helmut to endure. The billionaire gazed at Lara Godfrey's belly with such frank longing that Helmut wondered why none of the nurses remarked upon it.

Why not end the suspense now? The baby was ready and Sloane would come running the instant Helmut called. What better time to take care of the situation than while Olivia was tied up at the hospital?

Helmut pushed his rolling chair toward the computer, entered the university registry, and typed in the code number for the secure directory Sloane had established. He entered the password, then settled back for the file to open. It contained special instructions he was to follow when Lara began to deliver . . .

He froze as an error message flashed on the screen.

Access denied. File in use, Department 30582, The Women's Medical Center.

A thrill of fear shot through him. No one at the clinic knew about the directory. Even if someone had noticed it, they shouldn't have been able to access it.

But apparently someone had.

Helmut shot out of his chair with such force that it slammed against the wall. In a hoarse voice, he told his assistant he would be out for the entire afternoon.

∞

In the quiet records office, Lara's mind spun with bewilderment as she studied the computer screen. After the rows of computer gibberish, every single item of Lara's medical history had been recorded. Lara saw details of her weight, blood pressure, the results of the fetal nonstress tests, and a listing of every complaint she had ever mentioned. The latest entry was dated January twenty-fifth, last Monday.

She leaned back and crossed her arms, then glanced up at the shelf where Carol kept patient files. The "in" basket had been emptied of all files but the one Lara had deposited before lunch, so the transcriptionist had already entered the notes from this morning's exam into Lara's official record. Whoever was forwarding the information hadn't brought the file up to date . . . yet.

She stared at the screen, disturbed by the invasion of her privacy. Her *name* was entered in this registry, not just her patient number. She'd have to ask Olivia what department owned this file; then she would write an outraged letter to whomever was in charge.

Another contraction, a sharp one, caught her by surprise. Lara drew a deep breath and closed her eyes against the pain. *Something* was happening within her womb, and she'd be surprised if she wasn't fully dilated by the end of the day. She'd ask Olivia to take another look when she returned from the hospital. It certainly *felt* like Junior wanted to be born today . . .

She pressed her hand to the small of her back and massaged gently, urging the pain away. She lifted her right hand, about to exit the strange directory, when her gaze fell upon the entry for "conception method." IVF AID? The chart should have said IVF AIH, artificial insemination by *husband*. Even though Michael was no longer living, the official record should have affirmed their marital relationship.

Had to be a typo, but she leaned forward to study the record more carefully. Her blood chilled when she saw the note beside "donor blood type." Someone had recorded B positive, but Michael had been O positive. One did not walk away from three years of nursing a cancer patient without knowing his blood type.

She frowned, disturbed at what could potentially be a crucial error. Someone got careless, either in transcribing Michael's information or in determining the blood type from his specimen.

But . . . what if it wasn't a mistake? Nothing about this file seemed haphazard or careless. On the contrary, someone had taken great pains to insure that this information would remain protected and hidden, even from her.

Father God, what does this mean?

She pressed her hand to her mouth as horror snaked down her backbone and coiled in her belly. Helmut's lab was a *research facility* . . .

She bent as a sudden wave of nausea assaulted her. Braun was a respected scientist, but researchers had been known to take shortcuts. Just last year, Olivia told Lara about a California physician who fathered more than twenty children at his IVF clinic. The parents were completely unaware of his deception until routine blood tests raised questions and issues the doctor had hoped to bury forever.

Dr. Braun had told her that removing the defective cancer genes would be difficult. Was it possible . . . did he use a stranger's sperm rather than admit defeat?

She clung to her chair as a larger realization bloomed in her chest. If Braun *had* deceived her, would he have told her the truth? Not likely. She would have borne her child and loved him. She would never have questioned Braun's generosity unless she discovered that her baby had B positive blood . . .

But why would the doctor trick her? She had made her feelings clear when he raised the question of conception by donor. She didn't want just *any* baby; she wanted her husband's child.

She shivered and ran her hands over her arms. If the worst were true—if Braun had used donor semen—who had fathered this baby? She thought of the two libidinous lab assistants she'd met the day she went to visit Dr. Braun's lab and the countless young medical students who lounged on the university lawns during the warm days of spring and autumn. Any one of those young men could be the father of the child that now stretched in her belly.

She took a deep breath and forced herself to settle down. These feelings sprang from raging hormones; she was in the grip of paranoia. Dr. Braun hadn't tricked her; he couldn't. This had to be a clerical error. *Father God, please let it be a simple mistake . . .*

"Everything okay, Lara?"

Lara jumped at the sound of Gaynel's voice. The nurse stood in the doorway, a patient chart in her hand and a frown on her face. "You don't look too good."

"Where's Carol?" Lara's voice sounded strangled in her own ears. "I think I've found a mistake on a patient chart."

Reading the seriousness in Lara's eyes, Gaynel gestured toward the break room. "I'll get her."

Carol appeared a moment later, a half-eaten sandwich in her hand. "What's wrong?"

Lara pointed at the computer monitor. "This says my pregnancy was IVF AID, not AIH. And it says the donor blood type is B positive, but

Michael was O positive. This chart is filled with mistakes . . . and what *is* all this gobbledygook?"

Carol took another bite of her sandwich, then leaned forward. After scrolling through the chart, she swallowed hard. "Gee, Lara, I've never seen a file with that kind of gibberish." She frowned. "How'd you find this?"

"I followed the department codes." Lara focused on the computer screen and tried to ignore the nauseating smell of Carol's tuna sandwich. "I know this isn't one of our department codes, so I thought it might have something to do with Helmut . . ."

Carol shrugged. "Why don't you ask Dr. Braun about it? He'll be in later this afternoon. Maybe he hit the wrong button and messed something up."

Suddenly anxious to be rid of the transcriptionist, Lara gave her a smile. "Sorry for disturbing your lunch."

When Carol had gone, Lara picked up the phone and dialed the library, then gritted her teeth against another contraction. After pounding her way through the automated answering system, a woman's sharp voice answered. "Reference."

"Connor O'Hara, please."

"I'm sorry, but Mr. O'Hara is assisting another patron. May I help you?"

Lara considered waiting, then pressed on. "I need to know about something called PGP. I think it has to do with computers."

"Oh my." The woman let out a cackling laugh. "Then you'll *have* to talk to Mr. O'Hara; that's his area of expertise. I'll put you on hold."

Lara tapped her nails on the keyboard, irritated by the clash of the canned music in her ear and the easy listening schmaltz oozing through the office speakers. To take her mind off the music, she scrolled to the top of the file and stared again at the rows of computer characters listed under "instructions." Instructions for what?

Finally she heard Connor's voice. "May I help you?"

She could have wept with relief. "Connor, it's Lara."

His voice roughened. "Is it time?"

"Not yet, but soon." The baby kicked, and Lara pressed gently upon her stomach, willing Junior to keep still. "Connor, do you know about something called PGP? I think it's a computer program."

"Pretty Good Privacy. It encrypts computer files."

"Why would someone use it in a patient file?"

"There's only one reason to use PGP—to keep material secret." She could almost see him frowning. "You say you found this in a patient file?"

"I found it in *my* file—a copy of my file in a password-protected directory, that is. But a section of the file has been encrypted with PGP, and I can't read a word of it."

Silence reigned for a moment, then Connor lowered his voice. "PGP can only be unencrypted with a key, usually available on the Internet. But you'd have to know the sender's and the receiver's names, along with their passwords. It's a tough program to crack. Practically unbeatable."

Lara clutched the phone as panic began to riot inside her. "Connor, I've got to know what it says. There's other information here, but it's all wrong. This file says my baby was conceived from a donor insemination, not from a husband. And Michael's blood type is wrong. At first I thought it was a clerical error, but two mistakes is too much—"

Connor must have heard the sound of tears in her voice. "Calm down, hon," he said, his voice a soothing balm. "Make a backup copy of the file and bring it home tonight. We'll look at it and see what we can figure out."

She sniffed and wiped her nose on a tissue from her pocket. "I also have a computer printout that might help. We installed a backup program that records keystrokes—that's how I found the password that got me into this file in the first place."

"Atta girl." He paused. "Are you sure you're okay? Do you want me to come get you?"

"I'm fine. I'll see you later." She thanked him and hung up, then rummaged through Carol's cluttered drawers for a spare floppy disk. Maybe, if Junior didn't decide to interrupt tonight, she and Connor would solve the puzzle.

She had just pulled a diskette from a bottom drawer when a shadow fell over the computer workstation. "Good afternoon, Lara," Dr. Braun said, a firmness in his voice that verged on the threatening. "Carol tells me you have a question about your file."

Slowly, Lara looked up. Braun stood in the doorway, blocking her escape. He smiled at her, but a shadow lay behind his eyes. A quick flicker of some emotion—fear?—moved across his granite face.

"Yes. I did." Uncertain whether to confront him or continue investigating on her own, Lara froze in a paroxysm of indecision. Her uneasiness grew when the man came forward to stand behind her, one hand dropping to her shoulder as he bent and peered at the computer monitor.

"Ah." He nodded and pressed his lips together, but the pressure on her shoulder increased slightly. "You have found the foundation file."

With an effort, she pulled out of his grasp and swiveled the chair to face him. "What foundation would that be?"

The geneticist backed away and leaned against a cabinet on the opposite wall. Folding his hands, he looked at her with a genial, almost paternal expression. "Surely you've heard about the Muriel Foundation. A wealthy donor has contributed over one million dollars to eradicate cancer through genetics, and yours is our first case. All of your expenses—for the genetic testing, the cryopreservation, lab tests, even your obstetrical care—are being underwritten by the Muriel Foundation. If your baby is born without any trace of Michael's defective genes, we will know our work has been successful."

Suddenly ashamed, Lara crumpled in her chair. "If that's true"—she groped for words—"then why the secrecy? Why did you give them my personal information? And there are mistakes on the file, Dr. Braun. Michael's blood type wasn't B positive and the procedure was insemination by husband, not donor."

Braun stepped closer and peered at the file over her head. "The form is basic information, Lara, intended to be more of a service to the foundation than a medical chart. You do not have to worry about anyone giving you or your baby the wrong blood."

"That's—ohhhh." Lara clamped her mouth shut and groaned as a hard contraction gripped her insides. She hunched forward, cradling her abdomen, and from the corner of her eye she saw Braun's face shift into an expression of worried concern.

"How far apart are the contractions?"

"Five to eight minutes." She panted to catch her breath. "I'm okay; that one caught me by surprise."

Braun frowned. "Why don't you go into Olivia's office and rest?"

"Not yet." She grasped the edge of the computer table, then pulled her chair forward until she faced the desk. She picked up the floppy she'd dropped when he came into the room. "If this file is nothing special, you won't mind if I make a copy."

"I would advise against that." His voice, so friendly a moment before, had gone sharp. With a grace that belied his size, he stepped forward and caught her hand, then pried the diskette from her grasp. "Our generous philanthropist is quite concerned about privacy."

Lara managed a choking laugh. "It's my file, my medical history. I'm the one who should be concerned."

An inner alarm blared when Braun's hand tightened around hers. Wincing, she met his gaze. "What have you done, Doctor? Did you use a donor's sperm in place of Michael's? Have you altered my file to hide the truth from this foundation?"

"Is that what you think?"

"I don't know what to think!" She wrenched her hand free and blazed up at him, wishing she was less pregnant so she could stand and glare at him eye-to-eye. "I think you failed in your attempt to repair Michael's DNA strand. So you threw out his specimen and brought in another one. Then you had to change my chart because if this baby has B positive blood, your donor will know Michael was not the father!"

Braun's face flushed. "Lara, you are delusional. You do not know what you are talking about."

"I'm right, aren't I?" She lowered her voice, her feeling of uneasiness growing into a deeper and more immediate fear. "You have given me some other man's child." Blood pounded thickly in her ears as she glared up at him. "Dr. Braun, how could you? You knew I wanted Michael's baby!"

"Lara, you are upset. I am going to have Gaynel bring something to calm you."

With a superhuman effort, Lara pushed herself out of the chair. "You're not going to give me anything. I'm going straight to the hospital authorities."

"You are going to sit back down." Dr. Braun's hands clamped onto her shoulders and pushed her into the chair even as he called for a nurse.

Anxiety swelled like a balloon in Lara's chest, expanding nearly to the breaking point. She slapped uselessly at Braun's arms, trying to drive him away, while the sounds of her struggle retreated to background noise. The room spun for a moment, but she clung to consciousness, knowing she could not lose control.

When the room had righted itself, she opened her eyes to see Gaynel, Sharon, Rita, and Carol clustered in the doorway.

"Seconal," Dr. Braun ordered, his hands like iron on Lara's trembling shoulders. "One hundred milligrams. And hurry!"

The nurse's face crinkled. "Seconal?"

Braun shot her a cold look. "Are you questioning me?"

"No, sir." Gaynel pushed past Sharon and hurried to the dispensary while the others stood helplessly in the hallway. "Sharon," Lara choked, "help me. He gave me some other man's baby, and now he's trying to cover it up."

Sharon stared at Dr. Braun, her face a mask of alarm.

"Paranoia and fear, an unusual but not totally unexpected symptom of approaching labor," Braun said, his hands sliding down to hold Lara's wrists. "Especially among women with an inadequate support system."

"Look at my chart!" Lara commanded, struggling to free herself. "It's all there, on the computer." Sharon and Rita turned to the monitor, then looked back at Lara with pity in their eyes. She frowned, confused, until she leaned forward and saw that the computer had shifted to its screen-saver mode, displaying only a series of flying stars.

Dear Lord, they think I'm crazy. Help me, Father.

She had to calm down. She had to think. What else could she do? She was pregnant and about to deliver a child. She had to play by the rules.

When it was all over, she would find a way to expose Braun's treachery. After the baby was born, she'd have a DNA test performed. If the kid wasn't Michael's, she would sue Braun for all he was worth.

This baby was a mistake.

She panted, bracing herself against the pain, until Gaynel appeared in the doorway with a paper cup and a pair of white pills.

"One hundred milligrams of Seconal, Doctor." The nurse cast a worried glance at Lara. "Is she in labor? Should I page Olivia at the hospital?"

"Olivia is in surgery," Helmut answered, still holding Lara's wrists. He twisted slightly and looked at her. "Will you take this? We want you to calm down. After you're relaxed"—his eyes narrowed—"we'll talk."

Lara eyed the pills in Gaynel's hand. One hundred milligrams was the maximum dosage advisable, particularly for a patient in the early stages of labor.

She shook her head. "No, sedative will slow the baby's respiratory system."

"The baby will be fine; we'll counteract the sedative once we get you to the hospital. Please, Lara, be a good girl and take your meds."

She closed her eyes. If she refused, he might order an injection of something stronger. If she took the Seconal, Braun might believe she had begun to settle down.

She opened her mouth and held the tablets on her tongue until Gaynel offered the cup of water. Dr. Braun lifted his hand from her wrist, and Lara hesitated as she took the cup. She could dash the water into Braun's face and run toward the door, but she'd be lucky if she got two steps away from the chair before he caught her.

She swallowed the pills, then tossed the empty cup over her shoulder.

"All gone?" Braun asked.

She opened her mouth in answer.

"Good." Braun gestured toward the other women. "If you ladies will give us a few moments alone, I believe I can reason with Ms. Godfrey. Call her afternoon appointments and reschedule them; it looks like Lara is closer to labor than we thought."

He waited until the women retreated, then he pulled up a chair and sat facing Lara. The silence between them lengthened, increasing her apprehension, until he gave her a look that was compassionate, troubled, and still. "I did not want to hurt you."

Lara closed her eyes as the room swayed again. "What did you do?"

"I did what I was told."

She clung to reality and prayed she would not betray her agitation. "Is this my husband's child?"

Dr. Braun sighed heavily, then glanced away. "I suppose the time for truth has come. No, Lara, strictly speaking, the fetus is not your husband's. I know you did not want a stranger's child, so let it go. I will help you have another baby, a better baby. The gene splicing did not go as well as I had planned, so—" He shrugged wearily. "I listened to someone else."

She brought her hand to her mouth. For nine months she had sheltered, nourished, and loved a baby that was not Michael's.

A whirlwind of emotions swirled inside her—grief for the child who should have been, anger at Braun's deception, and overwhelming despair—

"How could you?" she cried, choking on sorrow and rage. "How could you betray me like this?"

Braun's face crumpled. "I had no other choice. I cannot expect you to understand, but I ask that you forgive me. I was under such pressure—"

"What sort of pressure could make you lie to me? What could be so important that you would deceive—" She gasped and clenched the chair's armrests as another contraction caught her.

Braun's face went pale. "Please, Lara, try to relax. In a moment I will get my car and take you to the hospital. By this time tomorrow it will be over and you can begin again. We will make you another baby; then you will understand."

She looked at him through a blur of pain and tears. "How could I ever understand this?"

"You will understand tomorrow, and you will be glad to be rid of the fetus." His broad hands clenched. "The thing you carry is not the child of an ordinary man. It is spawn from the ancient Iceman."

Lara stared as a tide of gooseflesh rippled up each arm and raced across her shoulders. What was Braun talking about? Who—what—was the Iceman?

"I don't understand," she said, her voice breaking.

"The caveman, the frozen man found in the Alps. We used his DNA, his genetics—"

"No." She shook her head. "Such things aren't possible. You wouldn't do this to me; Olivia wouldn't *let* you do this to me."

He muttered something in German, then rolled his chair to the computer. While Lara kneaded her forehead with trembling fingers, Braun fretted at the keyboard and reopened Lara's file. With swift, sure strokes Braun highlighted the encrypted text; then a dialog box appeared. Braun pasted the material from Lara's file into the box and punched another key.

Lara leaned forward, forgetting the pressure within her womb as the string of computer code condensed and rearranged itself into a simple message:

When labor begins, call 804-555-2937, cell phone 804-555-8374. Escort patient to hospital; proceed with delivery under nitrous oxide. Other instructions concerning ID chip implantation will follow.

Without even glancing at her, the doctor straightened and picked up the telephone. He glanced back at the screen and punched in the first number, then snapped off the computer's power supply. Only then did he look at Lara.

She watched him, her body numb while her brain tried to make sense of the words she'd seen on the computer. *Proceed with nitrous oxide?* She wanted an almost-natural childbirth, and Olivia knew it. But if the fruit of her womb was some *thing* . . . maybe that's why the code mentioned an ID chip. Good grief, maybe the creature inside her belly wasn't even human . . .

Wait, of course it was. She'd seen Junior's picture on the sonogram; she'd heard his heartbeat on the fetoscope. She had already furnished his nursery with stuffed dinosaurs and toy trucks and two dozen baby rattles from Connor's Christmas tree. But Braun wanted her to get rid of this fetus, to start over again. Which could only mean that she was never meant to have this baby, never meant to bear Michael's child . . .

Dear God in heaven, what have you allowed?

She tried to focus on Braun, but his square face now seemed to float before her eyes. That was the Seconal beginning to take effect. She'd be groggy soon, completely at Braun's mercy unless she found a way to escape.

The doctor whispered a few words into the phone, grunted, then hung up. "We are going in my car, and Olivia is already at the hospital," he said, his voice soft and soothing as he turned to Lara. "Do not be alarmed. This is for the best."

Escape!

She accepted Braun's help as she pushed herself up out of the chair. "I have to use the restroom," she whispered, taking an unsteady step. "Please."

The doctor strode to the door, threw it open, and called for a nurse. Gaynel stepped out from exam room one, her brown eyes snapping. "Is she okay?"

With a tight grip on Lara's arm, Braun led her into the hallway. "Please take her to the restroom. She's a little unsteady, and I don't want her to fall."

Lara lowered her head and allowed Gaynel to take her hand.

"Stay with her," Braun called, a warning note in his voice. "We don't want her to hurt herself."

Lara shuffled toward the restroom, reaching for the wall with her free hand. Braun wanted her woozy and weak now; he wanted her out cold during the birth. Why? Because someone pressured him, and Braun had planted a freak in her womb. Who was responsible? And what did they want with the life that swam in her belly and kept her awake at night?

She looked up and met Gaynel's compassionate gaze. "It's not Michael's baby."

"Of course it is, honey," the nurse said, guiding Lara into the restroom. "The Seconal has confused you, that's all."

"No." Lara stood placidly beside the commode as Gaynel helped her slip out of her lab coat. "Dr. Braun made this baby, and it's not normal. It's a science experiment. And he wants me to have nitrous oxide. It's all on the computer." She brought her finger to her lips, then widened her eyes. "Do you think they want to dissect it?"

"Of course not, sweetie." Gaynel stepped back and braced her hands on her hips. "Do you need some help with those clothes, or can you manage?"

Lara blinked. She hated to hurt a friend, but the Seconal was numbing her brain, and time was slipping away. Braun was probably outside, bringing the car around to the front of the building. The other nurses would be clustered around the front desk, wondering what had happened . . .

Lara gave Gaynel a droopy, drunken smile. "Before I go to the hospital, I think I need help . . . with my shoe. It's untied, isn't it?"

"Let me check." As the nurse bent, Lara reached for the aluminum basin on the back of the toilet. Her fingers caught the cold, curved edge and she pulled it forward, then lifted it with both hands and slammed it down on Gaynel's head.

"Hey!" Gaynel yelled, bringing her hand to her head as she glared up at Lara. "What's the big idea?"

Driven by desperation, Lara pushed the nurse, knocking her backward. Gaynel's head struck the edge of the sink with a dull thud; then the nurse folded into a heap, her eyes closed, her hand stretched toward Lara.

"Dear God, don't let her be dead."

Breathing heavily, Lara slid down the wall and stretched out her hand to search for a pulse in Gaynel's neck. There—steady and strong. Grasping the last shreds of her strength, Lara pulled herself up, then stepped over Gaynel's sprawled form and opened the door. After pressing the lock button, she pulled the door shut, then lurched toward the security of Olivia's darkened office. The doctor's private entrance opened directly into the parking lot, only a few feet from the highway where taxicabs routinely disgorged passengers too sick to drive.

The frigid wind bit into Lara's flesh as she stepped into the cold sunshine, and she blinked as the world spun around her. The taxi stand stood less than one hundred yards away. Lara staggered toward it, trying to ignore the cacophony around her. Cars whizzed by with long, whooshing sounds, someone honked, and one man called to another man, who answered in a high, whining voice . . .

But no one called her name. Yet.

"Lady, are you okay?"

The question came from somewhere behind her. Lara ignored it and walked on, waving a hand over her shoulder as if all was well with her world. Some part of her brain registered the fact that she had run without her purse, her money, or any sort of identification, but if she could only get home . . .

A yellow taxi pulled up to the curb in a sunshiny blur. An elderly man in a black overcoat slid out of the backseat and bent through the passenger window, counting bills out of his wallet. Lara quickened her pace, hearing her own increasingly quick breaths, knowing that her blood pressure was rising as her contractions intensified.

The old man straightened and turned away; the driver's head protruded from his window as he scanned the street and prepared to pull away.

"Wait!" Lara yelled, waving now in earnest. She commanded her legs to walk faster, but they seemed set upon their wooden, irregular pace. "Wait, please!"

The driver glanced right and left, then pulled away from the curb. "Wait!" Lara called again, her voice breaking. "Please, come back!"

The taxi pulled to the far right lane, then did a U-turn. Lara closed her eyes, afraid he was answering a radio call, but in another moment the car braked at the curb,

"Lady, you need a cab?"

With her remaining strength Lara yanked the door open and crawled into the backseat.

The driver grimaced and covered his eyes, then opened his fingers and peered at her as if she were a bomb that might explode at any moment. "Good grief, lady, you look like you should be driving *to* the hospital, not away from it."

"Take me home," she said, struggling to close the door. "Three-nine-four-eight Maple Leaf Court. And please hurry."

"Sure thing."

She felt the cab shift into drive, saw the hospital slide away. Then, surrendering to the heavy pull of the sedative, she slipped sideways onto the seat, her arms flung out and away from the baby she could no longer think of as hers.

∞

The wings of shadowy foreboding brushed Helmut's spirit as he stood in the hallway and watched the nurse pound on the restroom door.

"Lara! Gaynel!" Sharon thumped the door with her hand, then stopped as someone murmured, "I'm coming."

Gaynel opened the door, her fingertips gently probing a red knot in the center of her forehead. "She's gone." Gaynel winced as though speaking caused her pain. "I was helping her with her clothes, and she hit me with a basin. Next thing I knew, I was on the floor and Lara was gone."

Helmut crossed his arms, then made a fist and rested his chin upon it. Lara Godfrey was frightened, and she knew the baby wasn't her husband's. She was traveling under the influence of enough Seconal to knock a grown man off his feet, so where would she go? Driving was out of the question, so she was either on foot, or moving in a bus, a taxi, or a friend's car . . .

His thoughts fluttered anxiously away from Lara Godfrey's transportation problems. Sloane would *kill* him if she disappeared with the child. He would have to stress that one of the nurses had let the woman slip away.

"Page Olivia," he snapped, not caring which nurse leapt to obey. "Tell her that Lara is anxious and may be headed toward the hospital maternity ward."

Sharon ran toward the office, but Gaynel remained in the hall. "Are you going to look for her?" the nurse asked, rubbing the knot on her head. "If not, I could get in my car and go—"

"You do that." Helmut moved toward the records office. "I have to make a call."

The transcriptionist had rebooted the computer and was preparing to work on the afternoon patients' charts, but she vacated her chair the moment Helmut entered the office. He dismissed her with an abrupt gesture, then typed in Lara Godfrey's patient number. Within a few keystrokes he had arrived back at the password-protected directory.

He typed in the password, then softly cursed his own carelessness. He didn't know how Lara had managed to open the directory, but obviously she had.

He accessed the file, decrypted the encoded instructions again, then picked up the phone and punched in the number for Sloane's cell phone. The billionaire had been ecstatic to hear that Lara was near delivery. Without a doubt he was now hurrying to the hospital.

Sloane answered on the first ring. He listened to Helmut's report without comment, then told Helmut to go to his lab.

"I made plans for this contingency," Sloane said, his voice flat and cool. "We'll find her. Don't worry; just go to your lab and wait. Say nothing to your wife."

Helmut nodded slowly, then disconnected the call.

chapter 20

Unnerved by Lara's phone call, Connor left work early and went home, hoping she'd call again. He had just slipped out of his coat and checked the answering machine when the frantic pounding began. Smothering his annoyance, he opened the door and prepared to give the meddlesome neighborhood kids a stern rebuke. But there were no freckle-faced kids on his porch, only a wizened little man who would have looked more at home on a racehorse than behind the wheel of the big yellow cab in the driveway.

"I hope you can help me, buddy." The cabby's dark eyes looked up at Connor from beneath the brim of a Redskins cap. "I got a pregnant lady in the cab drunk as a skunk. She says she lives here."

A spasm of panic shot across Connor's body. Pushing the man aside, he moved toward the cab in long strides. He saw a form on the backseat, a mass of blonde hair, and a bright yellow circle—that silly "I'm PG2" button Lara insisted on wearing even now.

The taxi driver hurried along behind him, his short legs working like pistons. "I didn't do anything to her, honest. She gets into my cab, tells me the address, then passes out. I tell you, I don't know what the world's coming to, with women in her condition drinking—"

"She's not drunk." Connor jerked the door open, then leaned in and reached for her hand. "Lara?" He gently chafed her wrist. "Honey, can you wake up?"

Her eyelids fluttered, then flew open. "Connor. Something wrong."

"I told you." The cabby's thin voice came from behind Connor's shoulder. "Drunker than a fish."

Connor whirled on the little man. "Listen"—he brought his finger dangerously close to the tip of the man's nose—"if you say that again, I'm likely to send you flying across this lawn. Now, help me get her out of there, will you? She's sick."

The cabdriver shut up, then eased his shoulder beneath Lara's as Connor pulled her from the taxi. Together they walked her to the house, then Connor helped her lie down on the couch. She mumbled something about the baby and Dr. Braun, but he shushed her back to sleep.

"That's fifteen dollars from the hospital," the cabby said, extending his hand. "And something for the extra effort would be appreciated."

Connor blew a fallen strand of hair from his forehead, then pulled his wallet from his jeans. "I tell you what"—he counted out the cash— "I'll pay you fifty if you promise to forget about bringing this woman here. If anyone calls, if anyone follows up, you haven't seen any pregnant woman, you understand?"

The cabby's eyes narrowed, but his hand closed around the cash. "It's your business, man. Whatever you say."

"Thanks." Connor let the man out, then stood at the window until the cab drove away. Satisfied that no one had followed, Connor drew the curtains, then switched on the lamp and turned to Lara. Her face was slack, but her eyes opened when he knelt and lifted her hand.

"Braun gave me Seconal," she said, her voice heavy and thick. She blinked in an effort to hold her eyes open. "Said I was crazy. But I found the file, Connor, and I confronted him." Her eyes filled with tears and her chin wobbled. "He said it wasn't Michael's baby. It's an experiment for some foundation."

Connor clung to her hand, wondering how severely the drug had affected her. "What's that again?"

She focused, her eyes gleaming black and dangerous in the lamp light. "It's the Iceman's baby, Connor, not Michael's. Whatever the Iceman is."

She stiffened and held her breath for a long moment, then gave him a tearful smile. "I hope you're good at following directions. I think I'm going to have this thing tonight."

Connor shook his head, more than a little alarmed at her rambling. "Then I should get you to the hospital—"

Her grip tightened on his arm. "No! They'll be waiting. The file—Braun decoded it while I watched. The instructions told him to call some number and give me nitrous oxide. They want me out cold when it's born." A look of intense, clear light poured from her eyes. "What if they want me dead?"

He laid his finger atop her lips. His touch seemed to relax her, though her words had made his blood run cold. He waited until her eyes closed, then he stood and moved to the easy chair across from the couch. Sinking into its depths, he rubbed his hand over his face and watched her sleep.

What was he involved in here? He had heard that pregnant women could be nervous and excitable, but Lara had always been calm and levelheaded. He'd never known her to drink anything stronger than root beer, so she was under the influence of something other than alcohol.

He felt his heart soften as he studied her. Some people would call him foolish for losing his heart to a pregnant widow. He competed against a charming ghost for her affection; he competed against a demanding job for her time. Soon, very soon, he would compete against a helpless infant for her love.

It wasn't a fair fight; the odds were stacked against him. But anything worth having was certainly worth fighting for.

Lara Godfrey was neither his wife nor his responsibility, yet she only had to look at him and he melted. If she felt safe in his house, he'd do everything in his power to keep her here, even if it meant battling unseen dragons and larger-than-life foes. If Lara believed herself in danger, he would believe it too.

The phone rang, but Connor did not move from his chair. After the third ring the answering machine clicked on, and he heard a woman's voice, high and reedy with anxiety. "Mr. O'Hara, this is Gaynel Sheridan from the Women's Clinic. We are concerned about Lara Godfrey, who left the clinic about two o'clock. Her car's still here in the parking lot, but if you see her, will you please call us? Thanks very much."

Connor rubbed his brow. Lara had mentioned Gaynel; as far as he knew, they were friends. But he would not call anyone or do anything until he had a chance to talk to Lara.

Fifteen minutes passed; then he heard a car pull into Lara's driveway. A moment later he heard voices and muffled pounding from her town house. He sat still, wondering if someone would knock on his door.

His sense of unease gelled when someone did. He didn't move when the doorbell rang, and he only clenched his fist when he knocked. Lara stirred at the sound, and Connor tensed, afraid she would cry out, but she never even opened her eyes. When the intrusive knocking ceased, Connor moved to the door and squinted through the peephole. Two men were walking away, one man dark-haired and dressed in an expensive wool coat, the other heavy and solid with thinning silver hair. Only when the better-dressed man turned to enter the car on the curb did Connor recognize him—Devin Sloane.

Connor pressed his hands to the door, feeling as though his breath had been cut off. What would bring an eccentric billionaire to Lara's door?

Connor moved to the computer in his living room, then punched on the power.

∞

Lara began to stir at four thirty and was fully lucid by five. Connor made coffee and urged her to sip it, but she protested that caffeine would only intensify her contractions. "No doubt about it," she muttered, clutching her belly as she panted through another pain, "it's coming tonight. This isn't Braxton-Hicks."

Connor sank to the ottoman near the couch. "Then we'll get you to the hospital."

She shook her head with a vehemence that surprised him. "No. We can't go there; even Olivia may be in on it."

"In on what, Lara?"

"I don't know, but I'm not a raving lunatic. I know what I saw in the file, and I remember every word Dr. Braun told me. He admitted the baby isn't Michael's. He tried to tell me something about a foundation to cure cancer, and he kept saying I'd understand later." Her eyes filled with distress. "I don't understand everything, Connor, but I know this isn't the truth teller   201

Michael's baby. Braun said they took DNA from an Iceman, but I have no idea what he was talking about. And there was a phone number—Braun called someone right before he tried to take me to the hospital. I think they want to take the baby—Braun said I wouldn't want it."

Trying to soothe her, Connor placed his hand on her arm. "Of course you will. Every woman wants her baby."

Her brow wrinkled. "No, not all women. I know it's terrible, but I *don't* want it. I don't want some *thing*, I want my husband's baby!" A glaze seemed to come down over her swimming eyes as she rocked on the couch. "What will I do? I don't think anyone can help me."

Connor blew out his cheeks. "Lara"—he tightened his grip on her arm—"I did some research while you were asleep. I think I found the Iceman."

Her expression didn't change for a moment; then the words fell into place. Curiosity fired her eyes. "Who is he?"

"He's no one, not anymore." Connor rubbed his hand over his face and leaned closer. "In at least a dozen reports, I found stories about a Copper Age traveler frozen in the Italian Alps. The body was discovered in 1991, and experts believe the corpse is at least 5,300 years old. The remarkable thing is that the body remains in excellent condition."

He sat silently, watching as her mind raced. "His DNA," she whispered, her hand clutching Connor's. "They extracted his genetic code."

Connor shrugged. "It's possible. But there's more to the story. Last April, two Austrian scientists entrusted with the care of the Iceman were murdered in a mysterious explosion. The police investigated reports that they had worked late that evening in order to meet a wealthy Frenchman with an inordinate interest in the Iceman."

Lara frowned, not seeing the connection, and Connor placed his hand over hers. "Lara, why would Devin Sloane come to your apartment?"

The curious light vanished from her eyes. "Devin Sloane was here?"

Connor nodded. "While you were sleeping, he and another man knocked on your door and mine before driving away. I recognized Sloane almost immediately. The other man was older, with silver hair and glasses."

Lara stared at the floor, her face stiff with fear. "Dr. Braun and Devin Sloane. Devin Sloane is supposed to have a baby this month—and he was always coming by the office with Dr. Braun." She lifted her head, her face going pale as her eyes widened. "Heaven help us—*I'm* the surrogate. Sloane wants to take my baby and use it somehow. I asked him once about his child's mother, but he would only say she was a surrogate."

Connor took a deep breath as a dozen different emotions collided in his chest. "Lara—do you remember me telling you that sometimes the FBI assigns me to special projects? I shouldn't tell you this, but six months ago they asked me to read anything and everything I could about Devin Sloane. They knew I'd be in a good position for the assignment because he lives here in Charlottesville—I'd have access to local news reports, that sort of thing."

A tremor touched her lips. "Does the FBI suspect him of something criminal?"

Connor ran his hand through his hair. "I don't know what they suspect. But they're interested in anyone who's throwing money at genetic research. The FBI has become curious about Sloane's operation ever since he opened that pediatric hospital and began accepting patients from out of state."

"But they have nothing on him. I mean—surely you didn't discover anything criminal about him in the paper."

"Not in the paper." He paused, burdened with a terrible knowledge and hesitant to share it. "Maybe it'd be better if I showed you."

"Showed me what?"

Connor slid a sheet of paper from his printer tray. "I had just finished downloading a story about the Iceman when I remembered to check my e-mail. I left work early today and thought something might have come up."

Pausing, he gazed at her speculatively. Her mouth was grim and her expression serious, but there was no trace of hysteria or panic in her eyes.

"Anyway"—he glanced back down at the paper—"I found this message. It came to me at the library, and Ethel forwarded it to my personal mailbox. I read it, but it's really for you."

With quivering fingers, she took the paper, then leaned back on the sofa and began to read aloud.

Dear Mr. O'Hara: You're probably wondering how I found your name, but that is not important. What is important is your close friendship with Lara Godfrey and her contractual obligation to my employer, Devin Sloane.

Lara lowered the paper and frowned. "What contractual obligation?"
"Read on."
With one hand resting on her belly, Lara continued to read.

Though Ms. Godfrey signed an ordinary surrogate contract with Mr. Sloane, I'm afraid she is unaware of certain aspects of her situation. Though Mr. Sloane has made no secret of the fact that he expects a son, he has concealed one particularly relevant truth—the son he expects is not biologically related to him. Through a grant provided by the Muriel Foundation, Dr. Braun has created an embryo from 5,300-year-old DNA—found in genetic material discovered several years ago in the Italian Alps.

Lara gave Connor a quick, denying glance. "This is science fiction. I never signed a contract with Sloane, not for anything."
Connor dropped his gaze and waited for her to continue. The thoughtful message had not impressed him as the ravings of a madman.
Lara continued reading, her voice ragged with fury.

I would not be contacting you now, but since this afternoon it has become clear that your friend, Lara Godfrey, has had second thoughts about surrendering the child. I would most certainly be in grave danger if my employer discovers that I have contacted you, but I feel compelled to issue a warning. First—know that you and Mrs. Godfrey are under surveillance. Second—do not underestimate Mr. Sloane's commitment to this child. He has great resources and he will not hesitate to employ them.

You might wonder why I would contact you, Mr. O'Hara. My reason is simple: my religious traditions compel me to believe that all children, no matter how they are conceived, mirror the Divine Image. Children should not be brokered like commercial goods. If Mrs. Godfrey wishes to keep her child, I wish her well. But I thought she should be aware of the entire truth. A *little* truth can be a dangerous thing.

Lara dropped the paper to her lap. For a moment her eyes and expression closed, as if she were mentally retreating to some safe place; then her lashes fluttered upward and her gaze locked on Connor's. "The letter is signed by 'a friend.' How can we trust this guy if he won't even give us his name?"

Connor shrugged. "Employees like this usually have a talent for remaining in the background. I hope this one is on a fast jet out of town."

Lara's jaw clenched. "Nice of him to have an attack of conscience now. Why didn't he say something before this?"

"Apparently he believed you were a willing party to Sloane's surrogate arrangement." Connor straightened as he rose to the man's defense. "And he has to be at least a little intimidated. Sloane has a lot of power."

"And he used it to buy a baby . . . and to use me." Her voice broke in a horrible, heart-rending sob. Tears rolled down her face, hot spurts of loss and fury. "I can't *believe* this is happening, Connor. How could God allow it to happen? First he takes Michael; then he brings a man like Sloane into my life—"

"You can't blame God for men like Devin Sloane."

"I certainly can't blame myself. I thought I was doing the right thing. I tried to keep everyone happy. I did the genetic screening for Eva; I went to Braun for Olivia; I arranged the pregnancy for Michael." She peered woefully at him through tear-spangled lashes. "Why is this happening to me?"

Connor took her hand again. "The important thing now is the baby."

"The *thing*, you mean." She swallowed hard and let out a bitter laugh. "It makes sense. Sloane gave Braun a ton of money, so Braun owes him something. When Braun told me he worked on Michael's DNA to replace a cancer-prone gene, he killed Michael all over again. My husband disappeared the moment he injected the Iceman's DNA into that cell."

Connor roughly gripped her hand. "Stop, Lara; maybe it's not true. Have you any idea how crazy that sounds? I'm not even sure such a thing is possible."

Lara regarded him with bitter amusement. "Of course it is. That's what Braun has been working on for years. It's beautifully simple. Devin Sloane somehow got a piece of the caveman, and he paid Braun to extract the DNA. You told me yourself that Sloane believes our genetic material has been corrupted." She laughed again. "Don't you see? Sloane wants to rejuvenate mankind. He'll take this baby and chop him up into little pieces, then sell off the DNA to the highest bidder. Why stop with one child when you could replicate the procedure with thousands?"

Searching anxiously for the meaning behind her words, Connor bent his head to look into her eyes. "Lara, you can't believe that. Everything we've heard indicates that Sloane intends to raise the child as his son."

Her face twisted in a small grimace, as if he'd struck her. "Whose side are you on?"

"On yours, of course. I want what's best for you and the baby. When we figure out what happened, we'll bring them all to justice."

"I don't think we can." She pressed both hands over her eyes. "It's all so clear now, Connor—they want the child for reproduction. Braun knew I wouldn't want it once I knew the truth. But I don't think he was supposed to tell me. The instructions on the computer said I was to have nitrous oxide. Somehow—I don't know how—Dr. Braun was going to take my baby and give it to Sloane." She broke off and gritted her teeth, the muscles in her neck straining.

Connor felt his adrenaline level rise. "Are you okay? Should I call the paramedics?"

"No." The word came from behind her clenched teeth. "My water just broke. It's going to be soon, Connor, and I'll need your help."

Connor leaned back, the words barely registering on his brain. He had wanted to be by her side during labor, to help in any way he could, but his vision of service had not involved private acts, exposure to prolonged periods of pain, or blood.

"It'll be okay." She panted three times, then slowly rolled herself off the wet couch. "I'll explain everything to you as we go along."

He sat motionless, watching her trudge across the room like an old woman. "Lara, you're not serious about this, are you? I could call 911 and they could take you to a different hospital—"

"I'm not going to any hospital. They'd find me."

"Then where are you going?"

"To the bathroom." She cast an annoyed look over her shoulder. "I suggest you take down your shower curtain and lay it over a bed, then put a clean sheet over that. Have a blanket ready, and something we can use for a hemostat—paper clips or garbage ties, if you can find them. We'll need scissors and alcohol and some clean towels. A bulb syringe, if you have one. If not, a turkey baster might do."

Connor stood. "Should I boil water?"

"Not unless you want to make soup."

With one hand pressed to her back, Lara moved down the hall into a stripe of shadow. Driven by the sharp spur of dismay, Connor hurried to the kitchen and began opening drawers. He clawed through an assortment of gadgets, mindlessly searching for anything useful; then from out of nowhere came the realization that the woman he loved had never needed him more.

Some dim recess of his mind not occupied with complete panic remembered that he needed scissors, garbage bag ties, and a turkey baster.

"Dear God"—he lifted his eyes to the ceiling—"if ever you helped a helpless man, tonight's the night."

∞

Biting her lip, Lara bore down with every ounce of her strength. "Oh, God, please!"

Five hours had passed since she moved to Connor's guest room. Her little fledgling contractions had matured and sprouted wings. This particular pain eased, and Lara leaned back on her elbows and breathed a hoarse prayer for relief. This was not at all what she had planned. She was supposed to be in a nice, clean hospital; she was supposed to have an epidural to kill the pain. She was supposed to be delivering her husband's baby in an act of love, but the more she considered the origin of the thing in her womb, the more she hated it.

Throughout her labor, Connor prowled the house like a pent-up cougar, pacing back and forth in the hall. His pitiful array of instruments lay on a TV tray near the bed, and he had stacked a mountain of clean towels next to the door. He'd done everything she asked—he put Mozart on the CD player, propped pillows behind her back, and sponged her sweaty brow with a cool washcloth—but it was obvious from his expression that the man would rather be barefoot in the Gobi desert than imprisoned with her.

For imprisoned they were. At least twice during the early hours of the night, Connor held up a quieting hand and darted into the darkened living room to squint out at the street. A car had appeared on the curb across the road, he told Lara, and once he had seen the telltale gleam of a flashlight as someone checked Lara's apartment windows. Someone was watching the house, and Connor was more willing to deal with intruders than with the coming baby. He locked all the doors, pulled a baseball bat from a hall closet, and assured Lara that no harm would come to her.

At that moment, Lara had little appreciation for Connor's masculine vigilance. She hissed through another contraction, then panted and glared up at him.

"I'm going to sue," she said, gathering her strength for another onslaught of pain. "I'm going to sue Devin Sloane for every cent he's got, and Helmut Braun too. I'm going to press criminal charges, and I'm going to make them suffer. I'm going to—" She was about to say *take this baby where they'll never get their hands on it*, but she couldn't bring herself to feel anything for the creature emerging in the midst of such despair. What was it? It wasn't Michael Junior. It wouldn't have Michael's hair, or his eyes, or his artistic gift. The child might be part of her, but the other part was alien.

A scream clawed in her throat, but she imprisoned it behind clenched teeth. "Connor," she screeched when the pain had passed, "kneel on the floor. It's time."

He looked at her, his face absolutely blank with shock, but he fell to his knees at the foot of the bed and waited. His expression shifted into a bewildered and abashed look, and Lara let her head fall back, satisfied that he wouldn't be so embarrassed that he dropped the child. At least he had stopped blushing.

"Wow," Connor said, his voice tight and tense, "something's happening. I can see *a lot* of the head. What do I do?"

Lara braced herself against the mountain of pillows at her back. "I'm going to push," she said, wrapping her fingers in the sweaty sheets beneath her hands. "And the head is going to slide forward. I need you to put your hand against the top of the head and prevent it from popping out. You've got to *ease* it out, face down, so the mucus can drain from the mouth and nose."

"Mucus."

"Right." She bit her lip, resisting the urge to add, *if it's human.* Of course it was human. She'd felt it kick and hiccup, watched it swim in the amniotic fluid, heard its rapid, strong heartbeat. She had adored the child until she learned the truth about its parentage, and some elemental part of her still yearned to see that baby face.

But it wasn't the son of her marriage. It might well be a hunched, hairy, low-browed creature from the Copper Age. And even though her body had borne the stress and pain of labor, her brain had remained detached, coaching herself and Connor through the ordeal as though she were overseeing a routine delivery in the hospital's birthing center.

But it was her baby.

Or was it?

She bore down through another contraction, then nearly strangled on her own breath as Connor held up his hand. "Listen!"

She heard it then, a hard pounding at the front door. "Connor O'Hara!" a man shouted. "Police!"

Lara felt a fresh scream rise in her throat, then choked it off. Connor turned as if he would stand and go to the door, but she kicked at his shoulder with her bare foot. "Don't you dare leave me." She glared at him through tears of rage and pain. "It's them."

Connor met her gaze, then knelt again in his position. "I won't leave."

Lara gathered her strength as the urge to push grew stronger. "Are you ready? I think this is it."

"Go ahead, lady; I'm with you."

Calling upon muscles she didn't know she possessed, Lara pushed a new life into the world.

⨒

Awash in a strange sense of déjà vu, Connor held up his hands and heard his father's voice through a veil of memory: *Hands up, Con! Catch this one!* It wasn't a softball coming his way now, but the pulsing, wet head of a baby. He watched, spellbound by all sorts of streaming sensations, as the infant slid into the world on a warm, wet tide.

The sounds of Lara's groaning and the voices outside faded into oblivion. Connor heard only the rushing of his own blood in his ears; felt only the small, slippery child in his hands. He felt too clumsy, too inexpert, to handle anything this fragile, but the tiny head was nestled against his palm. He stared at the perfectly formed face and the tiny fingers trembling in the slight breath of the heater.

His eyes took in every detail—the pulsing umbilical cord, the strong, pink legs, the neat row of stumpy toes, the dimple in the fleshy knees. He didn't know what Lara had expected, but the baby in his grasp was completely beautiful. He inhaled deeply, then realized he was weeping at the miracle of it all.

The child turned his head toward the light, but made no sound.

Following the instructions Lara had given him, Connor reached for the turkey baster. The thing felt ridiculously huge in his hand, but he did his best to lightly suction the baby's mouth and nose. The child flinched at the intrusive action, then lifted his tiny fists as if to protest this humiliation.

"The baby," Lara gasped, falling back on the pillows, "might cough or cry, and that's okay."

Connor brought the infant closer to the warmth of his sweater, then carefully freed one hand so he could reach for a towel. He wrapped the towel around the baby and batted away a gnat of worry. The child remained silent, but he looked so perfect . . .

"What's wrong?" Alarm filled Lara's voice. "He should be making noise. Did you suction his mouth and nose?"

"Yes." A cold sweat prickled on Connor's jaws; he could feel his heart pounding. Those tiny lips were now tinged with blue; the child was not breathing.

"Put him on the bed," Lara instructed, her words coming out fast and panicked. "Open his mouth and breathe in it. Quickly. A puff of air."

Connor obeyed, but still the child remained silent. "Nothing." Connor could feel each thump of his heart like a blow to the chest. "I'm sorry, but there's nothing."

"There's got to be something!" Lara leaned forward, pulling her weight over the mussed sheets, until she crouched by the baby's side. "Come on, little guy." She placed her hands on the infant's cheeks, then lowered her mouth over his mouth and nose. She inflated her cheeks for one instant, then blew a quick, forceful breath into the baby's airways.

The child stiffened and gasped, then turned his head and protested with a bloodcurdling cry.

Limp with exhaustion, Connor leaned against the wall. Lara curled around the child and wept in quiet relief.

Connor smiled, realizing that the sound of a baby's cry was the sweetest music on earth; then he remembered the men outside. Leaving Lara and the little one, he stepped into the living room and lifted the edge of the curtain. The street outside was empty . . . for the moment.

When he returned, Lara had settled back against the pillows. "I'm so sorry," she murmured, brushing her lips across the child's damp head. "So sorry. We're going to be okay, little one. I promise."

Connor folded his arms and leaned against the door frame, knowing that she still needed him to cut the cord, help with the delivery of the placenta and the cleaning of the baby. But for now, it was enough to know that mother and baby were alive . . . and well on the way to falling in love with each other.

∞

After a few minutes of confused fumbling, the baby took Lara's breast and nursed himself to sleep. Wrapped in one of Connor's soft UVA T-shirts, the infant lay in her arms, the perfect image of a healthy baby.

Lara found herself staring at him as if she'd never seen a newborn before. She had delivered more than a hundred babies herself, and yet none of them held any personal fascination for her. She had always counted fingers and toes, checked respiration and heart rate, noted muscle tone, reflex irritability, and color for the Apgar score.

In fact, Lara mused, if it had not been for Helmut Braun and that high dosage of Seconal, this baby would have had scored a perfect ten on the Apgar tests. His heartbeat was strong and steady, he exhibited active motion from the moment of delivery, and his skin had been completely pink. Once she forced breath into his lungs, his cry had been vigorous and strong, but there had been that long moment when he refused to breathe . . .

She had suffered a sharp pang of terror in that moment. And suddenly the only thing that mattered was saving her baby.

She ran her finger over the infant's rounded cheek, knowing that she would never forgive Helmut Braun and Devin Sloane. They had committed an atrocity against her and this innocent child, and she would not let them profit from their obscene manipulations. This baby was her flesh, the fruit of her womb. God had not failed—he had sent a tree of life, a child of promise. And though everything about the child's conception and delivery was bizarre, who was she to question God's methods?

She leaned forward and kissed the baby's nose, then smiled at the sight of downy blond fuzz on the crown of his head. No matter what the origin of his DNA, tonight he had become her son.

She would never give him up.

chapter 21

By midnight, mother and child lay bundled in warm blankets and clean clothes. Certain that Lara would appreciate a change of scenery, Connor gave her his bedroom while he cleaned the guest room and spread fresh sheets on the bed.

Despite his exhaustion, sleep did not come easily.

He woke at eight the next morning, stumbled to the kitchen, and set a pot of coffee on to brew. He had a mountain of sheets and towels to wash and a thousand emotions to fold and put away, but he wasn't ready to tidy up just yet. The experience of the night remained with him, the bond he and Lara had shared was still strong. If he put things back the way they had been, the bond might vanish.

What was he supposed to do with these feelings? Michael Godfrey had certainly never intended for Connor to fall in love with his wife, yet in the act of keeping his promise to look after Lara, he had fallen completely in love with her.

His mind drifted back to his college days, when a professor had once defined love as "a conscious decision to make someone become precious to you." He had decided that Lara Godfrey would become important to him, and she had—as had the child that now slept by her side. He thought—he dared to hope—that he had become important to her as well, but Michael still shadowed her heart.

And now she loved this baby.

Half an hour later, as he stood by the sink sipping his coffee, he felt rather than heard Lara behind him. He closed his eyes as she placed her hand on his shoulder.

"I think," she said, her voice heavy with drowsy contentment, "I forgot to thank you last night."

"It was nothing."

"It was everything." She rose on tiptoe to kiss his cheek, and something in the gesture broke his heart. He would have turned and taken her into his arms, but he knew he'd be lost if he did.

Instead, he folded one arm across his chest and jerked his chin toward the window. "Stay behind me"—he kept his voice low and level—"but look out the window."

She glanced through the curtains, then gasped. "Police? What on earth?"

"They've been coming in and out of your apartment since I got up." Connor's gaze followed one man who walked out with a cardboard box. "I suspect they're looking for you. Someone must have filed a missing person's report, and these are the detectives."

He felt her move closer. "That can't be right. Don't you have to be missing for days before the police will get involved?"

"I would imagine they might make an exception for a pregnant woman." Connor leaned toward the window and looked down the road. Two unmarked cars sat on the far side of the road. "Some of these guys could be plainclothes detectives or private investigators."

"Sloane could hire anyone—"

"But I don't think the police are too keen about PIs trampling through their jurisdiction, especially while a matter is under investigation."

"Come away from the window; this is making me nervous." Lara plucked at his shirt, pulling him away from the sink and into the darkened living room. The baby lay on the couch, still wrapped in Connor's old T-shirt. He sank onto the couch and pressed his hand to the infant's stomach, then grinned when he saw that the baby's bottom was engulfed in one of his dish towels, secured with a large safety pin.

"What are you going to call him?"

"I don't know yet." Lara slowly sat on the other side of the baby, her eyes bathing him in love. "I want to think about it awhile. But I won't call him Michael Junior."

She looked away for a moment, then frowned as she met Connor's gaze. "My house isn't a crime scene. What are they investigating?" She turned sideways on the sofa and propped her head on her hand. "I could really use some things from the house, but I don't dare go over there."

Connor lifted a brow. "I don't know what they're doing, Lara. But if Devin Sloane or one of his puppets makes enough noise, you can bet this is just the beginning." Her face fell, so he paused before asking his next question: "What are you going to do now?"

Tears filled her eyes as she looked down at the sleeping child. "I don't know. What can I do? Devin Sloane is a powerful man. He nearly won—if I hadn't stumbled across that file, he'd have my baby now. I want to fight him, but I don't have the kind of money it'd take to hire lawyers good enough to defeat him."

"You can always tell the truth."

Even in the gloom of the curtained room, Connor saw her face flush. "I don't think so. My dad used to say that a lie could travel around the world while Truth was still putting on his boots. It'd be Sloane's word against mine, and for nearly nine months he's been telling the world that he expects a child in February. All he'd have to do is produce a forged document and I'd be painted as the surrogate who refused to surrender his child."

She closed her eyes. "I was thinking last night, trying to make sense of it all. And I remembered the forms I signed for Dr. Braun. One of them was blank." She turned and pressed her forehead against her palm. "He's got me, Connor. I'll bet he has a surrogate agreement right now, with my actual signature at the bottom of the page. How could I have been so stupid?"

"A paternity test would solve everything. If this child really did come from ancient DNA, the tests would prove Sloane's not the father."

"The tests would show that Michael wasn't the father, either. But more than that, the world would know that my baby was a science experiment, and I won't subject him to that." Her finger ran lightly over the baby's cheek; then her hand gently cradled his head. "Look at him, Connor. He's a miracle. I don't know how or why he came to be, but I asked God for a miracle, so I have to believe God knows what he's doing."

She fell silent for a moment, watching the infant; then her gaze lifted and met Connor's. "I was so upset when I came here—out of my mind with pain and fear and the realization that I've been betrayed. But you've given me time to think. And the simple truth is that this baby is at least half mine. I don't care where the other half comes from. This child needs a mother. He needs me."

Connor listened through a vague sense of unreality. Lara was going to keep this baby, so that could mean only one thing. If she wasn't willing to face Sloane, she would have to take the baby and disappear. Forever.

His hand curled around the armrest of the couch, the only solid reality in a suddenly shifting world. "So what are you going to do?"

She remained silent for a moment, then met his gaze. "I'll need your help. I want an ordinary, safe life. I want this child to have a normal childhood. He's a special gift from God, and I won't let Devin Sloane touch him."

"Then fight! You can get a lawyer; you can go to the police, to the newspapers—"

"No, Connor, I can't. How can I fight the American justice system? I watched the murder trial of the century on TV; I saw a jury look DNA evidence squarely in the face and ignore it. I've seen how money and celebrity and charm can sway justice. Devin Sloane has all those qualities, and I can't win."

Connor struggled to speak through the emotions that clogged his throat. "So how are you going to keep him from finding you?"

"That's where I'll need your help." Her gaze melted into his. "You can help me get lost, can't you? We owe you everything, Connor, and I hate to ask this of you, but you're our only hope."

His breath seemed to have solidified in his throat. He wanted to protest, to point out that she *couldn't* leave without taking his heart with her, but a look of quiet desperation had filled her blue eyes. She would go, with or without his help, but she wouldn't get far.

Unless he taught her how to hide.

Another knock interrupted the quiet. Connor automatically brought his finger to his lips, then looked at Lara and pointed to the bedroom. She gathered the baby in her arms and fled silently down the hall.

Connor stood, wiped his hands on his sweat pants, then opened the door.

A man in a dark trench coat stood on the porch, a notebook in his hand. He peered up at Connor through heavy glasses. "You Connor O'Hara?"

"I am." Connor stepped out onto the porch, then tucked his hands under his arms as a cold wind ripped across the lawn. He jerked his head toward Lara's apartment. "What's going on over there?"

"Your neighbor's missing." The man smiled again, but a sly look filled his eyes. "You know her?"

Connor nodded. "Sure."

"You seen her lately?"

Connor's mind stuttered over the question. Lying went against his principles, but so did telling the truth if it meant a helpless woman and child would be surrendered into the hands of evil men.

He pretended to be fascinated by the police activity next door. "What'd she do? Lara's not the criminal type."

The man's eyes narrowed. "What type is she?"

Connor brought his hand to his chin and rubbed his fingers over the unshaven stubble. "For one thing, she's extremely pregnant. I can't imagine her robbing a store in her condition."

The man sighed heavily. "No one said she robbed a store. Look, she's missing and her friends just want to find her."

Connor thrust his hands back under his arms. "Gee, that's funny. I didn't think she had many friends. Have you talked to her mother-in-law? Maybe she's staying with her."

The man pulled a pen from his pocket. "You know the mother-in-law's name or address?"

Connor lifted one shoulder in a shrug. "Mrs. Godfrey, I guess. I don't know where she lives. In some classy part of town, probably." He shivered. "Look, are we finished? It's cold out here."

The man thrust his pen into one pocket then pulled a card from another. "Look, if you see her, give me a call, okay?"

Connor took the card. "Joe Costello, the Harrington Group." He lifted a brow. "You're not with the police?"

Costello was already down the porch steps and moving away fast. "Just call, okay?" he yelled, pulling his coat tighter around his middle. "Right away."

Connor stepped back into the house, then walked to the bedroom. Lara sat on the floor in a corner, her face pale, her arms sheltering the baby.

"They'll be back," she whispered in a forlorn voice. "I have nowhere to go, Connor, and no way to get away. They'll check Eva's house, and when I'm not there, they'll come back."

Connor sank onto the bed, feeling his heart break even as he whispered the unavoidable truth. "Then we'll get you out of here. I promise."

∞

Rumpled and irritated, Devin Sloane sat behind his desk and glared at Nadine Harrington, whom Lemuel had just ushered into the office. Ms. Harrington had arrived last night and promptly disappeared to begin her investigation while Lemuel sat up with Devin, waiting like a best friend with a nervous expectant father. But though Sloane had called and threatened everyone from the governor to the local police chief, Lara Godfrey had not been located.

That fool Braun had let her slip through his fingers, and by all accounts the birth was imminent.

Devin's own blundering had made matters worse. In a frenzy of fear, he and Braun had gone to Lara Godfrey's house, hoping to catch her before she could flee. When they couldn't find her at home, Braun's frantic calls forced the police to investigate, and as long as the police were involved, Nadine's men couldn't go near Lara Godfrey's townhome. The listening devices they had planted were illegal, and only Nadine's high-tech expertise had prevented the cops from discovering the web of surveillance that had surrounded Lara Godfrey for months.

Nadine walked briskly across Devin's office, her panty hose swishing through the silence, then dropped a hand-held tape recorder on his desk. "The cops finally left, so we were able to get this." Her expression was serious, but one corner of her mouth curled with a secret. "Listen," she said, pressing a button.

Devin froze as the tiny spokes of the recorder began to turn. He heard nothing but an electronic hiss, then a faint meow cut through the white noise.

"What's that?" His gaze moved from the recorder to Nadine's polished face. "So she has a cat—am I missing something significant here?"

"That's no cat." Nadine shut the tape off, then pressed the rewind button. "This tape is from the device we planted in Lara Godfrey's bedroom, which abuts to the bedroom in the town house next door. Listen again."

She pressed play, and again Devin heard a steady and prolonged hiss. Then the mewling sound began, and in a flash of understanding Devin realized what he had heard.

A baby's cry.

"When?" he asked, shock flooding through him. "When—when was this recorded?"

Nadine smiled. "Last night, just after midnight. The sound is muffled because she ran to the librarian, as I knew she would. And he proved incredibly resourceful."

Devin's blood rose in a jet. Standing, he leaned on the desk and gave Lemuel a broad smile. "They're still here! They are in that man's house!" He shifted his gaze to Nadine. "You can get my child today."

"We will retrieve your child, but we have to go through the proper channels." With a boldness he didn't expect, Nadine stepped forward and pressed her hand over his. "Patience, Devin. Lara Godfrey is not going anywhere. I've had people stationed outside the house all night, and I'll keep them there all weekend. If you'll give me a copy of the surrogacy agreement, I'll hand-deliver it to the judge Monday morning. Your lawyer can arrange an immediate hearing, and if all goes well, you'll have custody of your baby Tuesday or Wednesday."

Devin cut a quick glance toward Lemuel, who nodded in silent understanding and moved to close the double doors leading into the study. Nadine Harrington pulled back and frowned. "Did I say something wrong?"

"Have a seat, please." Devin waited until Nadine sat and Lemuel resumed his chair; then he smiled at the bewildered woman. "Several weeks ago, I invited you into a secret circle—do you remember? You are one of five people who know the identity of the mother of my child."

One of her shoulders rose in a barely perceptible shrug. "I've kept your secret. No one in my organization has any reason to suspect that our surveillance of Lara Godfrey has anything to do with you."

"And I appreciate your discretion." He paused and thoughtfully stroked the arm of his chair. "Remember, Nadine, life is a series of circles within circles. Now I must invite you into yet another circle of secrets, one more exclusive and crucial than the first. And I must have your word that you will not repeat what I am about to tell you."

A gleam of interest filled her blue eyes. "As always, I am interested. You have my word."

Devin nodded. "Good. I am about to set another situation before you, one for which you will be generously compensated. But you must understand—this matter lies far beyond the reach of contemporary ethics and law."

Her mouth pursed up in a rosette, then unpuckered enough to ask, "So what you're about to ask is illegal?"

"Strictly speaking, yes."

Lines of concentration deepened along her brows and under her eyes; then she looked at him and the grim line of her mouth relaxed. "Legalities have not stopped us thus far. Please continue."

Devin tried to catch Lemuel's eye, but the assistant's head was bowed over a notepad. "The child is mine," Devin began, transferring his gaze to Nadine, "and I have Lara Godfrey's signature on a legitimate surrogacy contract. But the child born last night is not my biological son— he was created from the DNA of an ancient wise man. I paid for the IVF procedure. I paid the woman's medical expenses. By all legal rights, the product of that conception belongs to me. Ms. Godfrey, however, was not aware of this."

A change came over Nadine's features, a sudden shock of realization. "She didn't know about this"—she spread her hands—"*experiment?*"

"Of course not. She agreed to become a surrogate, not the mother of an improved human race. I didn't think it advisable to heap additional pressure upon her."

Nadine gave him a pale, humorless smile. "I'm assuming that Lara Godfrey suspected something. Do you think she has gone into hiding because she discovered the truth?"

Devin frowned. "I have no way of knowing, but I fear you may be right. We do know that Ms. Godfrey found the computer directory Dr. Braun established for my use, and she may have been clever enough to put pieces of the puzzle together. So you see, Nadine, if your tape is correct, she now holds not only my son, but a creature whose genetic makeup might well hold the key to our survival as a species. That baby is more than a mere child—he is proof of my theory and the culmination of a most radical scientific experiment."

She stared at him, her brows knitting in a frown. "I've read about the Law of Entropy and your theory of devolution. It's an original concept, but if this child is unusual in any way, I would imagine that the child's mother has played a strong role in his development."

"Very little, actually. Conception occurred outside her womb; she did little but carry it to term."

"But it was her egg. This is still her genetic child."

Not willing to concede the point, Devin lifted his hand. "It is *partially* her child, but what will she do with it? Rear it with day-care nurturing? Entertain it with mindless American television? I have planned great things for that child! I will plumb the depths of his capabilities; I will discover the faculties he possesses and we have lost." He gathered his strength as the words began to flow. "Imagine it, Nadine! That child is closer to perfection than you or I could ever be. He is 5,300 years closer to the divine spark!"

She eyed him with a calculating expression. "You surprise me, Devin. I would have guessed that you did not believe in God."

He laughed to cover his irritation. "I believe *we* once were gods, the very deities the ancient Greeks and Romans walked with and worshipped. But time has weakened us until we are but shadows of what we might one day be again. Though my hospital staff is working to eradicate eroded genes in human DNA, that process will take years to complete. But from one hair from this child's head, Nadine"—he leaned across the desk in an effort to make her understand—"we could gather a lifetime of knowledge in an hour."

A deep silence fell over the office; even the moaning wind outside the window seemed to pause and consider the profound implication of his words.

"And so"—Nadine inclined her head—"you are suggesting that we use whatever means are necessary to recover this valuable child."

Devin forced his lips to part in a curved, still smile. "I am not opposed to the proper channels, as long as they are effective. Take the papers, go to the courthouse, and I'll call my lawyer. But if that infant is not safely residing in my house by Wednesday night, I will authorize you to do whatever you must to recover my property."

Nadine gave him a wintry smile. "This could get ugly. Are you willing to risk your public image?"

Devin met her icy gaze straight on. "My image is quite safe. I'm the patron saint of the Ethan Jefferson Pediatric Hospital. No one would dare question my intentions."

∞

At five p.m., while Lara and the baby slept in the bedroom, Connor turned on the television and opened the front curtains in an effort to convince the men outside that this was a typical Saturday afternoon. As World Championship Wrestling blared from the TV, Connor pulled an empty suitcase from the hall closet, filled it with the dirty sheets and towels, then set it on the front porch. Ten minutes later, investigator Joe Costello stood outside his door, a bemused smirk on his face. "Going somewhere, Mr. O'Hara?"

Connor leaned against the door frame. "Yeah. Going skiing at Wintergreen. Is it any business of yours?"

"None at all. Have a good time." The man lifted his hand in a jaunty wave, then walked back down the sidewalk. As Connor watched from the window, Costello slid into the blue sedan parked at the curb, settled in behind the wheel, and tossed his sunglasses onto the dash. He did not drive away.

Connor kept working. By six thirty he had packed another suitcase with his laptop computer, toiletries, and clothes. He set the second suitcase on the porch, too, in full view of anyone who might be interested. He had also spoken with two policemen and hung up on two reporters who called and asked for Lara Godfrey. Somewhere, someone knew she was with him, and they wanted Connor to know they knew. He kept this information to himself, though, and moved silently through the house, preparing for their flight.

Not until sunset stretched glowing fingers across the sky did he knock on the bedroom door. Lara had been up and down with the baby several times during the day, and he knew she needed rest. To his surprise, she was up, dressed in one of his flannel shirts and a pair of overalls.

"I hope you don't mind that I helped myself to your closet," she said, a dark flush coloring her cheeks. "I don't think I could stand to wear that maternity smock another day."

"I don't mind." He stood for a moment, resisting the overwhelming urge to pull her into his arms. Didn't she know she could dress in burlap and still radiate a vitality that drew him like a magnet? Now, with her face fresh-scrubbed and unpainted, she seemed more delicate and ethereal than ever, but that fragility was an illusion. After last night, he knew he'd never meet a woman with more strength.

"I've been watching out the window." He leaned against the wall as she moved toward the kitchen. "There's a guy parked out there, and he isn't with the police. But I figure he's got to eat sometime, so we'll make a run for it when he does. I've left a suitcase on the porch and told him that I'm planning to leave soon, so I think we may be able to give him the slip. We'll only need a few minutes."

She turned in the hallway and smiled at him, her hair shimmering in the light from the kitchen. "I trust you, Connor. Whatever you say, we'll do."

We. Her and the baby. They were a family now.

He shoved the thought away and moved back to the bedroom, then tiptoed to the bed. The baby slept there, his arms thrown out wide, his little face turned toward the light from the window. Gently, Connor eased himself onto the mattress, then slipped his finger beneath the baby's closed fist.

He caught his breath when the tiny hand opened and the pearl-tipped fingers closed around his own. "Hi, little guy," Connor whispered, his heart aching within his chest. "How'd you like your first day?"

The baby's eyes opened then, wide and blue as an October sky. Staring at the ceiling, the baby moved his arms and legs, all the while keeping his fist closed tightly around Connor's.

"Why don't you hold him?"

Lara's voice caught Connor off guard. He looked up, half-embarrassed to be caught tongue-tied before a baby, but she came forward and lifted the child, then nestled him in Connor's arms.

Those wide blue eyes scanned the ceiling, then focused on Connor's face. A delightful shiver ran through Connor at this elemental form of communication; then the baby began his little jig again.

"I think he likes you." Lara moved so close Connor could smell his shampoo in her hair. "I'm sure he'll recognize your voice if you talk to him."

He swallowed tightly as Lara sank next to him. "You think so?"

"Of course." She slipped an arm across Connor's shoulder and tapped the baby's chin with her free hand. "Remember all those nights when you helped me fix dinner? I'll bet the baby enjoyed your goofy jokes more than I did."

Connor answered quickly over his choking, pounding heart. "You didn't care for my jokes? All this time I was thinking I was funnier than Jay Leno."

The touch of her hand was almost unbearable in its tenderness. "I doubt Jay Leno would have stood by me like you did," she said, her head fitting perfectly into the hollow between his shoulder and neck. "I thank God for you, Connor. He sent you to us."

Her hand fell on his, and her touch sent shooting stars up his arm. Connor closed his eyes, breathing in the scents of her and the baby, relishing the warmth of her skin upon his. He had waited a lifetime to feel this, but they could not remain here.

"Lara." He kept his eyes on the wide-eyed baby, not daring to look at her. "I've got to get you away from here. When I call you, I want you to take the baby and slip out the back door. Head straight for my car. Lie down on the floor in the backseat, and don't lift your head until you hear from me again."

"In a minute, Connor."

They sat quite still for a long moment; then she squeezed his arm. "I'll take the baby," she said, opening her hands. "Let me know if I can do anything to help."

Connor gave her the baby and stood, then moved into the hallway, pausing just long enough to turn and imprint her image on his brain. Someday, if God was good, she and her son would find their way back to this house, this room, this place in his heart.

When Connor returned to the kitchen window, the light was fading fast behind the lake, color seeping out of the air. The police cars had long since pulled away from Lara's apartment, but the blue sedan still squatted on the curb with Joe Costello behind the wheel.

Connor crossed his arms and leaned against the kitchen counter, not daring to take his eyes from the scene. When another car pulled up at 6:45, Connor called Lara's name. He heard the quick slap of her shoes on the utility room floor, then the muffled sound of his back door closing.

After passing a bag and soft drink through the window, the driver of the second car hung an elbow out of the car and chatted with Costello, then slowly pulled away. While the investigator contentedly munched on his burger and fries, Connor turned on the porch light and made one last sweep of the house. The guest room was clean and neat, his bedroom restored to its usual condition. He paused when he saw Lara's folded uniform at the edge of his bed. It wouldn't do for them to find *that* here.

He found a bag in a kitchen cupboard, then returned to the bedroom and slipped her uniform into it. Then, in full view of the street, he locked his house, picked up the suitcases on the porch, and moved to his car in the driveway. Conscious of the private investigator's scrutiny, he jingled his keys loud enough to wake the dead, put the suitcases in the trunk, then got in the car and backed out of the drive. As a final coup de grâce, he tapped the horn and waved to Joe Costello.

He glanced in the rearview mirror to be certain the investigator had not followed. "You okay back there?"

"We're fine," Lara whispered from the backseat. The baby made soft gurgling noises, but Lara soothed him.

"I reserved a cabin at Wintergreen in case they check out my story"— he kept his eyes on the road—"but we'll head south and take a motel room somewhere off I-95. There we'll come up with a plan for you and the little guy."

She didn't answer, but he could sense her unspoken doubts.

"Everything's going to be okay. Trust me."

∞

At midnight, Joe Costello eased out of his car and greeted the three men who materialized from the darkness beyond the curb.

One of the men pointed to the town house with a gloved hand. "That the place?"

Joe nodded. "The boyfriend left at 6:45, probably hoping to draw me away. But I've seen no sign of the woman. And his vehicle was here in plain sight the entire time."

One of the men grunted; then the three of them moved away. Joe leaned against his sedan and crossed his arms, watching the house with renewed interest. These guys were pros, and they didn't come cheap. Nadine's client must have given her permission to spend big bucks to find this lady.

Moving silently through the dark, the three men padded up the sidewalk and climbed the steps to the porch. While one of them turned to survey the street, another pulled the glass globe from the porch light, then unscrewed the bulb just enough to break the connection. Joe squinted as darkness swallowed the scene; then through the silvery glow of moonlight he saw two of the men flank the door while the third went to the back of the house. Within the space of ninety seconds, all three had entered the building and a light fringed the edges of the front window.

Joe stopped chewing and listened, half in anticipation, half in dread. Would the woman surrender the child, or would they have to get rough with her? Joe didn't want to think about those three battering a woman, but any gal who'd hide a baby from its father deserved what she got.

He waited. The empty air around him vibrated with the sound of the park's whispering evergreens; then the wind stopped and the silence filled with tension. After a few minutes, the window at the front of the house went dark; then the front door opened and the toughs moved back out onto the porch.

"Nothing there," one of them muttered as he passed. "Call your boss and tell her the house is empty."

Joe nodded silently, then leaned into the car and picked up his cell phone. When he straightened again, the three strangers had vanished into the night.

chapter 22

In a nondescript motel room somewhere south of Richmond, Lara nursed the baby and watched as Connor plugged his laptop into the wall. "I read a book once on how to establish a new identity," he said, glancing at her in the mirror as the computer booted up. "I think I can remember the ground rules. In any case, we've got a few days to get everything together. I e-mailed my boss at the library before we left; no one will expect me back until next week."

Lara cringed as guilt avalanched over her. Connor had done so much, and now he was sacrificing his vacation time, spending money on a cabin at a ski resort he would never see, and literally giving her clothes out of his closet. Before leaving town, he had pulled up in front of an unfamiliar house, gone inside for a few minutes, and returned with more than a thousand dollars in an envelope.

"You're going to need diapers and things for the baby," he had said, tossing the envelope into the backseat where she sat with Junior.

"Did you rob someone?"

Connor grinned as he turned the key. "That was Ethel Jones, my supervisor at the library. I wrote her a check and she cashed it. She also promised not to deposit my check for a week."

Lara stared at the cash in astonishment. She didn't even know anyone who kept this kind of cash around the house, and yet this woman hadn't hesitated to hand Connor a stack of bills, trusting him implicitly.

The money had been useful. Connor explained that they couldn't use credit or ATM cards, neither his nor hers, for a card could be traced only seconds after it passed through a scanner. So as they drove through the little town of Kents Store, Connor pulled into a grocery.

When he returned with a big box of diapers in his arms, Lara had to blink away unexpected tears. Michael had also bought her a box of diapers . . . long ago.

Momentarily safe in the motel, she glanced down at the baby, saw that he had fallen asleep, then put him on her shoulder and began patting his back. "How do we begin?" she asked, meeting Connor's gaze in the mirror behind the desk. She had placed her life and trust in his hands, and she knew he could help. But the hard fist of fear still knotted in her stomach when she remembered that one of the world's most powerful men waited to snatch her baby from her arms.

Connor sent her a smile. "First we get birth certificates for you and the little guy." His gaze fell to the computer screen. "Have you decided on his name?"

"Michael is out," she said, her voice breaking as the name passed her lips. "And nothing else seems right."

"Just make sure it's something you can live with." The quiet click of the computer keys punctuated his words. "Let's hope you won't have to change it."

Lara hid a thick swallow in her throat. She'd only have to change the baby's name if Sloane managed to find them and they had to run again.

She lowered the infant into her lap, then lightly touched his cheek. Instinctively, his mouth turned toward her fingertip, seeking life-giving food. The kid had amazing reflexes. Was that normal—or something he had inherited from his hunter-gatherer father?

In a fit of pique, she grinned at the baby. "I'll call him Hunter. And I'll be Lois Gellis. That way, if you ever get a call from me, you'll at least recognize the initials."

Connor raked his hand through his hair, then looked at her in the mirror. "Sorry, kid, you're too old to start fresh. You've got to become someone already born."

She made a face. "I'm not old. And how can I be someone else?"

"You're going to assume someone else's identity. Tonight I'm going to tap into the library's database, and I'll find someone who was born in"— his mouth curved in a mischievous grin—"what, about 1958?"

She threw him a defiant smile. "I was born in 1974, thank you very much. I'd appreciate it if you didn't age me beyond my years. This experience is already giving me gray hairs."

His roguish expression faded. "I'll start by looking through the 1978 newspaper obits. I'll search for a girl who died at age five or younger; then I'll fax a request for the death certificate. When it comes, that document will tell us the city and state where she was born. Ideally, I'll find someone who was born in one state and died in another—those records are hardly ever cross-referenced. Once I find a good candidate, I'll fax the courthouse where she was born and request a copy of the birth certificate. Once we have that document, you'll be able to get a Social Security number, a passport, whatever you need."

Lara stared at the floor, a little unnerved by the mention of a death certificate. Something in her would die, too, when Lara Godfrey ceased to be. "What about Hunter?"

"He'll be easy to handle. We'll just write up a birth certificate for him, list your new alias as the mother's name, and have Lara Godfrey, physician's assistant, sign it. We'll mail it to the Charlottesville courthouse. They won't be able to tell his record from any other baby you delivered."

"You'd better move his birth date back a couple of weeks. His size is good, so no one will suspect."

Connor nodded, then began typing his letters on the computer. He worked silently for a moment, then stopped and raked his hand through his hair again. In the mirror she could see that the customary expression of good humor was missing from his eyes and the gentle curve of his mouth.

Lara put the baby down, then moved to the end of the bed. "Something wrong?"

"I just can't get comfortable with this." He leaned back in the chair and crossed his arms. "I feel like I'm sending you and the baby off to live a lie when I ought to be encouraging you to honor God. We ought to confront evil, not run from it."

Lara turned and leaned against the desk. "You certainly can't turn us over to Sloane."

"No." He spoke with light bitterness. "I can't do that."

"Then you need to let us go."

Staring at the computer keyboard, Connor pressed his hand to the back of his neck. "Did you ever hear the story about the lying Baptists?"

Lara shook her head.

"In 1804, one simple question divided a Kentucky Baptist church: if a man were captured and tortured by Indians while his family hid in the basement, was the man allowed to lie in order to protect his wife and children? Some church people believed the man had an obligation to protect his family; others felt he should tell the truth even if it meant sacrificing his loved ones. During the debate, the church split into two camps, known for years afterward as the Lying Baptists and the Truthful Baptists."

Lara frowned. "That's my situation exactly. The enemy is at my door, and if I'm going to escape, you've got to help me hide."

Connor's voice softened. "The Bible tells believers to speak the truth to one another. Ministers are commanded to speak truth from the pulpit, and when we take an oath and bear witness in court, we are sworn to speak only the truth. But does God expect us to offer truth to an enemy when lives are at stake? I don't know."

"I wish I never had to know," Lara answered softly. "I wish God had never brought me to this place, but he has. And he brought me *you*, Connor. You're my only hope of escaping Sloane."

A wounded look filled Connor's dark eyes as he went on. "I suppose there are precedents. Look at Rahab, the prostitute—she lied in order to protect the Israelite spies, and she's listed in the New Testament's roll call of faith. When the king of Syria sought to kill Elisha, the prophet prayed that God would strike the Syrians so they wouldn't recognize their surroundings. When they showed up at his door with murder in their hearts, Elisha told them they weren't in the right city."

A flash of bitter humor crossed Connor's face. "There's even a story in 1 Kings about the time God allowed a lying spirit to influence a group of prophets who counseled King Ahab. So something in me wants to tell you that you don't owe truth to the man who is trying to hurt you."

"But something else in you isn't at all comfortable with this."

He nodded in the smallest of movements. "I guess so. I've also read about Corrie Ten Boom, who told the truth even when her family hid Jews from the Nazis. She believed God would honor her commitment to truthfulness, and he did." Connor turned in the chair, his hand reaching out, a visible symbol of the strong, shining bond that had formed between them. "Lara, I can't help but believe God is bigger than Devin Sloane. He can help you fight your enemy. *I'll* help you fight. I'll do whatever I can to make certain the world knows the truth—"

She lowered her fingertips to his lips, cutting him off. He was a good man, full of righteous anger and hope and love, but he had no idea how she had suffered in the last year. Her body had been violated, her trust betrayed, her dreams shattered. Part of her wanted to curl up and cry, but the stronger part wanted to take her baby and leave the state where Devin Sloane lived . . . even if that meant leaving her best friend and everything she possessed.

Tears welled in her eyes as she struggled to speak. "Connor . . . I can't fight right now; I have to think of the baby. You promised you'd help me, so I'm counting on you."

He sat silently for a moment, his eyes dark and unfathomable; then he caught her hand. "All right." He squeezed her fingers and released them, then turned back to the keyboard. "I'll do my best to make sure you are safe."

∞

The week that followed was the strangest of Lara's life. In a strictly platonic relationship, she and Connor lived in the hotel room as Mr. and Mrs. BoJo Jones—the name, Connor confessed, of a popular young adult novel about a teenage couple and their baby. As Lara took care of the baby, a stream of faxes flowed from Connor's computer. When necessary, he went out for diapers and food.

Lara spent most of her time nursing, napping, and trying to sort out the details of her old life. Connor would have to close her bank accounts, sell her furniture, and do something with her car. She agreed to Connor's plan because she could see no alternative; yet still she hoped for some miracle—that Helmut Braun would confess to a reporter, or the evening news would report that Devin Sloane had been lost in a plane crash somewhere over the Pacific.

An urgent news bulletin did interrupt the Monday night movie. A blonde newscaster, her saccharine voice dripping with overly dramatic concern, announced that an Amber Alert had been issued for an unnamed infant boy. Lara Godfrey, an unstable and dangerous personality, had fled the state of Virginia with a stolen infant in her arms.

Ripples of shock spread from an epicenter in her stomach as Lara stared at the television. From his desk, Connor winced as Lara's photograph appeared behind the anchorwoman.

"If you see this woman, call police immediately. The grieving parents are awaiting the safe return of their child."

The screen flickered; the TV movie resumed. Lara turned to Connor, her mind blank. "What was that?" She pushed at the hair that kept falling into her eyes. "Good grief, they're going to have everyone in the country after us."

"No, they won't." Connor wore a grim expression. "That was a clue, Lara—they've hit a dead end. Sloane and his ilk don't make their concerns public unless they have no other choice. They've looked for us and can't find us, so now they're beating the bushes."

Lara grasped at the strand of hope and held it tightly. "They didn't mention you. So we're okay because we're traveling in your car."

Connor's eyes darkened. "They've known about me all along. That news reporter didn't mention me because they want us to be overconfident and make a mistake. No, Lara, from this moment I don't dare go out unless I have to. We'll have things delivered, and as soon as it gets dark I'm going to park the car out back, behind that row of trees." He bit his lip. "I ought to smear the license plates with mud too. But I'm not leaving this hotel again until you're safe."

Lara said nothing, but picked up the baby and cradled him closer. Connor O'Hara had proven himself more resourceful than Michael had ever been. But if this were Michael's baby, she wouldn't be in this situation.

Tuesday came and went. Connor paced in the room, fretting when government offices were slow to respond to his requests. While they waited, they paid for pizza delivery and diapers with their steadily dwindling cash. Lara offered to use her credit card, but Connor flatly refused to allow her to take the chance.

On Wednesday morning, a Federal Express Courier delivered three envelopes, each containing a death certificate for a young girl born in 1973. One of them, Connor told Lara, was ideal. Rose Lynn Shepard died in Lynchburg, Virginia, but had been born in Anniston, Alabama. He immediately faxed a request for Rose's birth certificate to the Anniston Courthouse.

∞

Thursday morning, Helmut Braun drew himself up in his chair and swallowed to bring his heart down from his throat. He had been summoned to Devin Sloane's mansion, escorted into the inner sanctum, and now he sat across from the man himself. To Helmut's right sat a blonde woman Sloane introduced as Nadine Harrington, and to his left, that narrow-faced assistant who buzzed around the office with the persistence of a mosquito.

"Your lawyer cleared everything," the woman was saying, one leg swinging back and forth in a relaxed rhythm. "The judge has issued a pickup order, so any law enforcement official in the state of Virginia has the authority to bring the child back to Charlottesville."

"That will do me no good," Sloane said, splinters of ice in his voice, "if Lara Godfrey has left the state." His eyes, alive with calculation, focused on the woman. "You are an investigator, Nadine. You should have found Lara Godfrey by now."

The woman's eyes glittered with repudiation. "You seem to forget that without our information you wouldn't even know about the child's birth. We have things under control; our safeguards are in place. If Lara Godfrey uses one credit card, if she phones the clinic or her mother-in-law, we'll be able to pinpoint her location. She has been careful thus far, but she's bound to be distracted by the responsibilities of caring for the baby." Her brows rose, graceful wings of scorn. "Women are easy to find because they always look back."

Helmut shifted uneasily in his chair, suspecting that Sloane held him responsible for Lara's disappearance. Sloane had made no direct accusations, of course, but a gleam of resentment filled his eyes every time he looked at Helmut.

"What about the neighbor?" Helmut forced words over the knot in his throat. "What was his name? If they are running together—"

"We're investigating Connor O'Hara as well." The woman's smile tightened as she regarded Helmut. "So far we've turned up nothing unusual other than that odd FBI connection."

Helmut felt sweat bead on his forehead and under his arms. "He works for the FBI?"

"Relax, Doctor." A smile tugged at the assistant's lips. "He's a resource person, not an agent."

"Yes," the woman continued. "O'Hara is skilled and intelligent, but definitely the bookish type. He's supposed to be skiing at Wintergreen, but though he has a cabin reserved, he hasn't checked in. O'Hara is almost certainly the reason Ms. Godfrey has evaded us as long as she has."

Sloane's eyes peered out from deep sockets like caves of bone; he had obviously been losing sleep. "What did your men turn up in O'Hara's apartment?"

Nadine glanced at her hands. "Some very interesting tidbits, actually. We found several long blonde hairs in the master bedroom and bath, but nothing to indicate a woman had given birth in the house. Mr. O'Hara did a good job of cleaning up. When we took the hard drive out of his computer, though, we found a few things that might interest you."

"Such as?"

Her gaze shifted to Sloane, and her eyes thawed slightly. "Internet cookies. We were able to open the cache file and examine the Web sites he'd visited lately. We found a couple of interesting search phrases, including your name, Devin. He's been reading up on you."

Sloane brought his hand to his chin and snorted softly. "Is that all?"

"No." The woman glanced at Helmut, her eyes bright with speculation, her smile half-sly with knowing. "The second interesting search phrase was 'iceman.' I'd say he's onto you, gentlemen."

"Impossible!" Sloane's curt voice lashed at her. "How would he know? There is no connection, no public record to link me with the mummy."

The woman's eyes slid over Helmut, then moved to the seat occupied by Sloane's assistant. Nadine Harrington leaned on the armrest of her chair and winked when she caught the young man's eye. "We didn't find a public link, but a private one." Her eyes widened in accusation. "We found an e-mail message in one of Mr. O'Hara's files—a letter from an unnamed friend containing information about the child Lara Godfrey carried. The message had been sent from an anonymous Web server, but it won't take much to ferret the sender out."

Helmut felt an icy finger touch the base of his spine. He gripped his chair and closed his eyes as Nadine Harrington continued. "Devin, you said only five people knew about Lara Godfrey's child. Since four of those five are present in this room, it stands to reason that Mr. O'Hara's mysterious 'friend' is one of us. And since the letter referred to religious faith"—her voice hardened—"I'd bet my money that Mr. Reis is the one who e-mailed O'Hara about your plans."

"Lemuel?" The suppressed hate in Sloane's voice struck low in the pit of Helmut's stomach. "Did you write O'Hara?"

Falling prey to the drive that compels one man to watch the suffering of another, Helmut lifted his eyelids. Reis had stiffened in his chair, his eyes showing white like a panicked horse. "Sir—I only meant to explain."

Sloane stared at the young man, his eyes hot with resentment. "You brought someone into the circle. Into *my* circle, without my permission."

Reis recoiled from Sloane's burning eyes and tried on a smile that seemed a size too small. "I thought—" he began, flushing. Then, in an admirable act of courage, he lifted his chin. "I thought it was only right that Mrs. Godfrey know the truth. I did not approve of the surrogate arrangement, but you were two consenting adults, so I held my tongue. But I could *not* approve of what you did without her knowledge."

Sloane smiled benignly, as if dealing with a temperamental child. "Go to your room, Lemuel. We will talk later."

Reis's flush receded, leaving two red spots on his white cheeks. He opened his mouth as if he would say something else, then abruptly stood and left the room.

Helmut closed his eyes as everything went silent within him. The situation was worse than he feared. Not only did Lara now know that he'd used her for an experiment, but she also knew he had falsified a surrogacy contract with Devin Sloane. She'd have to be as thick as a plank not to put the pieces together, and Lara was anything but stupid.

Olivia would never forgive him for this . . . if she discovered the truth.

"Will the librarian share Lemuel's letter with Ms. Godfrey?" Sloane asked the question rhetorically, but Nadine didn't hesitate to answer.

"Of course he will. Right now I'd imagine they're both feeling outraged, protective, and isolated. He'll tell her everything."

Sloane's mouth twisted in a cynical smile. "Won't the truth convince her to surrender the child? After all"—his gaze shifted to Helmut—"you assured me she wanted her husband's baby. This is obviously not the child she wanted."

"If she hasn't approached you or the media by now," Nadine said, a warning cloud settling on her features, "she wants to keep the baby. So we wait for her to do something foolish . . . or approach us."

His lips thinning with anger, Sloane glared across his desk. "That infant belongs to me. I don't care how long it takes, I want that child."

The woman lifted her chin, coolly staring in Sloane's direction. "You'll have him. I won't give up."

∞

Apparently the clerk at the courthouse in Anniston, Alabama, had better things to do than answer Connor's request. Thursday morning came and went without a response, and Lara grew alarmed as the television news bulletins became more frequent. News anchors reported that women matching her description had been seen in Washington D.C., New Jersey, and New York, while a three-day-old infant had been found dead in a trash can outside Roanoke, Virginia. Charlottesville police officers had flown to the scene, certain they had found the stolen baby, but medical tests determined that the child could not be the missing infant.

On Thursday afternoon, Devin Sloane entered the media fray and held a press conference outside his mansion. To the clicking and whirring of scores of cameras, he announced that the Amber Alert's missing infant was his son. "In good faith I entered into a surrogacy agreement with Ms. Lara Godfrey," he announced, his normally confident smile dissolving into a bewildered expression of hurt. "Ms. Godfrey was handsomely provided for during the arrangement, and all the proper legal papers are on file. The police believe she has fled with the baby in an attempt to extort money from me, and they have advised me not to pander to kidnappers."

"What about the baby?" a reporter yelled.

"I can only hope that my little son is safe." Sloane's dark eyes seemed to soften as he looked into the camera. "I can't help but think of situations like the Lindbergh baby, but I have to believe Lara Godfrey will keep my son from harm. I pray she will bring him home."

"Will you consider joint custody?" someone else yelled, but one of the dark-suited men next to Sloane pulled the billionaire from the microphone and hustled him away.

"I know that guy!" Connor tapped on the television screen. "He was outside the house right before we left. He even came to the door to question me."

"You're never going to be free of all this." Lara hugged a pillow to her chest. "Even if the baby and I get away, they know too much about you."

"I'm skiing at Wintergreen."

"They're not fools, Connor, they'll know you didn't check in."

He folded his arms and leaned back in his chair. "It doesn't matter. By the time I get back you'll be safely away, so I can tell them the truth. I'll say I changed my mind and decided to vacation in the beautiful"— he gestured toward the barren room—"whatever motel this is. They can even check with the guy at the desk. He'll remember me."

"Oh, no." Lara groaned when Eva appeared on the television screen. Surrounded by a mob of reporters, she was stumbling forward with her head down, struggling to reach her car. When the camera finally caught her in an unguarded instant, Eva's face was a picture of horrified humiliation.

"I don't know anything about Lara Godfrey!" she shouted, trying to keep one hand over her face as she labored to open her car door. "I don't know anything about the baby! I've been in London for weeks!"

The news report abandoned Eva and shifted back to the newsroom, where the anchor gleefully confided other tidbits about Lara—the fact that her patients adored her, that she had been delighted by her pregnancy, and that she'd been distraught with grief after her husband's death. One segment featured an interview with Sharon, Carol, and Gaynel, who confirmed that Lara had known Devin Sloane for several months and that she'd always been fascinated by lifestyles of the rich and famous. "We used to sit in the break room and read the *National Enquirer*," Sharon said, her eyes shining toward the camera. "Lara was *especially* interested in Devin Sloane. She kept insisting that she knew him personally."

The camera zoomed in on Gaynel, who admitted that Lara had been anxious and hysterical on that final day in the office. "She kept saying she was in labor, but we were sure she wasn't." One corner of the nurse's mouth twisted upward as she wound a strand of hair around her finger. "We tried to give her Seconal, but she tricked us. She hit me over the head with this"—Gaynel held up basin—"then ran out the door." Her mouth curved in a wry smile. "That's how I know she tricked us. A sedated woman could never have slipped away from us."

Another news report featured a shot of Sloane's Virginia mansion, where reporters stood outside the gate and shouted at his passing limo with an almost rabid frenzy. Over the next few hours, Lara heard stories of other surrogate arrangements gone bad, watched interviews with two women who had happily carried babies for others, and listened to the results of a random poll about the pros and cons of surrogate arrangements. ABC featured an interview with actors Deidre Hall and Kelsey Grammer, who both received their children from surrogate mothers, and NBC reported that Barbara Walters hoped to find Lara Godfrey and interview her in a special one-hour program.

As the eleven o'clock news ended, Lara sat up in bed. "Connor," she glared at the television screen, "where are the news reports about Sloane? Why isn't anyone prying into *his* life? It's bound to be more interesting than mine."

In the gray gloom of the television's light, Connor snorted softly. "They're respecting his privacy. If they only knew the truth."

Lara studied him—he sat upright in the other bed, his back against a pillow, the white glow of his T-shirt shimmering in the gray light. He looked handsome, capable, and strong, and for an instant her breath caught in her throat. If the situation weren't so desperate, if she hadn't just had a baby, and if she weren't a recent widow . . .

She turned away and waited until the pounding of her heart quieted. When she was certain her eyes were under control, she leaned into the space between the two beds, checked the baby in his dresser drawer bassinet, then curled in her own bed and pulled the blanket closer to her chin.

"Good night," she called, her heart hammering.

She wasn't surprised when he didn't respond. Connor had been a complete gentleman during their time of seclusion, minding his manners with monklike chastity. But he had delivered her baby, given her his own clothes, risked his life and reputation to save her and her son. She felt closer to him than anyone she had ever known—in some ways, he understood her better than Michael—and yet he held himself at arm's length, guarding her like a national treasure.

By Thursday night she was beginning to wonder if she'd done something to offend him.

∞

Rose Lynn Shepard's birth certificate arrived Friday morning. At lunchtime Connor left Lara and the baby asleep in the hotel room and hiked down the highway to Wal-Mart. There he bought a box of cinnamon spice hair color, scissors, a diaper bag, and a few clothes for Lara and the baby. He paid for his purchases with the library's credit card, then carefully pocketed the receipt. Ethel wouldn't report the card's use, and he'd reimburse the next month—as long as Devin Sloane didn't find some way to put him in jail.

The February sun was warm on Connor's shoulders as he trudged back, and he was actually perspiring by the time he returned to the motel. Avoiding a pair of giggling adolescent boys on their way to the snack machine, he cut through the parking lot, then slipped into the tiny office. A trio of blue-haired ladies stood at the counter, protesting a charge on their bill, so Connor pretended to study the headlines in a newspaper vending machine until he found himself alone with the motel manager.

The burly man behind the counter was staring with wide and wary eyes when Connor turned.

"Morning," Connor said, shifting his shopping bag from one hand to the other. He walked to the counter and drummed his fingers on the desk, mentally reevaluating his approach. He'd been dreading this, but he couldn't think of any other solution.

The man straightened, folding his tree trunk arms. "Can I help you?"

"Actually, I was hoping I could do something for you." Connor looked out the window and felt a slow tide of heat begin to creep up his cheeks. "You see"—he nodded toward the parking lot—"I've got a beautiful 1966 Mustang convertible out back, and she's real nice. Only 54,000 miles, AC, automatic, power steering, power disc brakes, the works. I paid almost twenty thousand for her, and she's mine, free and clear."

"So?" The man lifted a bushy brow, and Connor forced himself to look away from the long, stiff hairs that grew out of it.

"Well, my, um, woman and I are a little strapped for cash. I paid the loan off a few weeks ago, so I've got the title with me. You don't need to worry about me pulling some kind of a fast one, but I need to sell this car. You could turn it around and make a profit if you wanted, maybe even double your money. I was wondering . . . would you be interested in buying her?"

The manager frowned, his face settling in upon itself as he considered the question; then the porcupine brows lifted. "I can't afford no fancy car."

Connor leaned against the counter, determination like a rock inside him. "I've got a woman and a baby, and we really need the cash. We're almost completely tapped out. I'll give you the title; I'll sign it over right now for a decent offer."

The man uncrossed his arms, pressed his thumb and forefinger to his closed eyes as if they ached, then crossed his arms again and focused on Connor. "I seen you drive in," he said, his voice flat. "And it was a right pretty car. Guess I could give you five hun'red for her."

Connor's throat seemed to close up. "I was really hoping for a thousand. Haven't you that much cash on hand?"

"Eight hun'red, but that's all the cash I got."

Connor nodded. "Okay."

The man slammed his hand on the counter in an explosion of satisfaction. "Shoot, mister, you drive a hard bargain. You go get the papers, an' I'll get the cash."

Connor turned slowly from the counter, his brain reeling with the realization that he'd just sold his pride and joy for less than his annual car insurance premium.

∞

He gave the hair color to Lara without comment, then chuckled when the corners of her mouth lifted in a wry smile.

"You don't like blondes?" she said, her voice dry. "All right, I'll be a cinnamon spice, whatever that is. But I don't have to stay this color, do I?"

An hour later she came out of the bathroom with reddish brown hair. Connor had been lying on the bed talking to the baby, and the heaviness in his chest seemed to solidify as Lara towel dried her hair and caught his eye in the wide mirror. "One more thing." She held out the scissors. "Cut it for me, will you?"

Without a word, he met her in the center of the room. They stood only inches apart, close enough to exchange each other's breaths, and Connor felt his pulse skitter alarmingly when he breathed in the scent of her clean, warm femininity. His blood coursed through his veins like an awakened river, and his flesh prickled when she placed a pair of scissors in his hand.

"You can do it," she said, her fingertips brushing his palm. "I'm beginning to think you can do anything, Connor."

Except let you go.

He tore his gaze away, then sighed in relief when she sank into the single chair. She held up a comb, but refused to meet his eyes in the mirror.

"I've never done this before," he said, his voice suddenly husky.

"Just cut it like the barber cuts yours." Only the tightening of the muscles in her slender throat betrayed her emotion. "If you make a mistake—well, it'll always grow."

He ran the comb through her wet hair, felt its silky slickness against his fingers.

Come on, bucko, this is important. Cut her hair; finish what you started; help her get away.

The baby whimpered softly and Connor paused, half-hoping she'd jump up to check on him. But she only lowered her head and pressed her hand over her face in a convulsive gesture. "Be brave, Connor; hack away. I need a different look—something short and different."

Steeling himself to the task, he parted off a section of hair and began snipping. When he had finished, hanks of brown hair lay on the carpeted floor like curling question marks. With only the barest glance in the mirror, Lara sprang up, then pulled a pacifier from the diaper bag and slipped it into the fussy baby's mouth.

When he had quieted, she gave Connor a trembling smile. "My little pipsqueak and I had better hit the road," she said, her voice strangely flat. "I guess this is it."

"Just about." Connor knelt on the floor, grateful for the mess. As long as he occupied his hands, he couldn't reach out to her . . . but she knelt, too, her fingers only inches from his as she plucked damp strands from the worn carpet.

"It's not a bad haircut," she said, her voice light. "Kind of cute, don't you think?"

"Sure." He felt his throat constricting. "But I think I'll keep my day job."

"I think you'd better."

When they had finished cleaning up, Connor spread Lara's documents on the dresser. These included a power of attorney, giving Connor the authority to sell her furniture and car, then to transfer her assets into any account he chose. They agreed that he would handle everything and keep the money in a safe place, perhaps for Hunter's future. "Once you decide where you're going to settle"—he stacked the documents in a neat pile—"find the public library and e-mail me from there. Don't identify yourself." He caught her eye. "I'll know it's you."

Next he pulled a certificate from a manila envelope and handed it to her. "This is as precious as gold, so guard it carefully. It's Hunter's birth certificate. All you have to do is sign it."

Her eyes widened. "How'd you get it?"

"It was a long shot, but I called a stationery store and told them I needed a sample certificate to show a physician colleague. They sent one by messenger while you were napping. All you have to do is fill it in and sign it." He pointed to a pair of empty spaces on the form. "I didn't know how you wanted to handle the space for 'father's name'."

Her eyes, large and trusting, moved into his. "What's your middle name?"

Something turned over in his heart. "Allan."

"Then Connor Allan Shepard will be his father." She placed the certificate on the desk, filled in the blank spaces, then signed it as attending physician.

"Mail that to the courthouse in Charlottesville," he said, stammering as he looked into her eyes. She stood so close, barely inches away, and she smelled warm and sweet and clean. "Later, when you get to wherever you're going, you can write the courthouse as Rose Shepard and ask for his birth certificate. They'll send it right out to you, no questions asked."

Her hand floated up to rest on the fabric of his T-shirt, right below his heart. "I can't begin to thank you, Connor. I don't know what we would have done without you."

Almost without meaning to, his hands caught her elbows. "Lara?"

Her gaze flew up to meet his. "Yes?"

"This is killing me."

She smiled at him, joy and wonder and pleasure mingling in her eyes. "I was beginning to think you hated me for putting you through this. You've been keeping to yourself, even after all we've been through together—"

Connor tried to throttle the dizzying current racing through his veins, but her tears undid him. He pulled her into a close embrace, then patted her back and murmured comforting sounds. She clung to him, her hands about his neck, whispering words of regret and sorrow.

"No." His fingertips came to rest on her lips. "There'll be none of that. Can't you see that this has been the greatest thrill I've ever known? I could die tomorrow, knowing that my life accomplished something. I want you and Hunter to be safe."

"But—to leave you! It's not right that you should give so much and then we just walk away."

"I want to give." He pulled her closer, burying his face in her damp hair. The heaviness in his chest felt like a millstone, but he wouldn't pull Lara into despair with him. "I care about you, Lara, and I'll do anything to help you . . . even if it means I have to let you go."

She pulled away then, her eyes shimmering with tears and emotions better left unexpressed. Connor gave her a rueful smile, then sat down before his computer, ready to pack it away. He had purchased her bus ticket to Atlanta online, investigated several smaller cities that might be good towns to settle in, and fretted over every detail. Thanks to the motel clerk, she'd have eight hundred dollars in her Wal-Mart diaper bag when he put her and the baby into the taxi that would take them to the bus station. And he'd have a precious store of memories to keep him company as he hitchhiked his way back to Charlottesville . . .

He stiffened as her arms suddenly tightened around his neck. "I love you, Connor O'Hara." She pressed her cheek to the top of his head. "I'll be grateful to you till the day I die."

Connor closed his eyes as his soul echoed her words. *I love you, too. I'd go with you if you'd only ask . . .*

But then she released him, and Connor felt grief rise like a whip, curling, snapping, sending ribbons of pain in every direction.

∞

Holding the baby against her shoulder, Lara made her way down the aisle of the Greyhound bus, then took a backseat by the window. She dropped the denim diaper bag into the empty seat next to her, intentionally warning away any would-be traveling companions.

As the baby mewed softly, she pulled a thin blanket from the diaper bag, draped it modestly over her shoulder, then set the baby to nursing. A few stragglers were still boarding; the genial bus driver greeting each newcomer with a thin, nasal voice.

Resting her elbow on the armrest, Lara brought her hand to her chin and rigidly held her tears in check. Connor had thought of everything; she had no reason to cry. Somehow he'd come up with eight hundred dollars for her expenses; he had also given her a list of midsized cities where she ought to be able to find work as some sort of medical professional. He'd been so thorough that for a moment she wondered why he was so eager to send her away . . .

Strange, how love felt like grief. She swiped at the hot tear trickling down her cheek. A broad, white-haired woman paused in the aisle, and Lara turned to the window, not wanting to invite company. Babies drew women like honey attracts flies, but Lara was in no mood for conversation.

With a loud sigh, the woman edged into the seat across the aisle, then proceeded to pull a skein of red yarn and a shapeless bit of crocheted something from a carry-all. The bus driver closed the door and the engine grumbled to life.

As the bus backed out of its berth, Lara closed her eyes and relived the pain of that final scene with Connor. He had tried to be casual and caring when he placed her into the taxi, but tears had glistened in the wells of his dark eyes. He closed the door and stepped onto the curb, managed a little wave, then thrust his hands deep into his pockets as his face twisted and his eyes screwed up to trap the sudden rush of tears. His image blurred after the cab pulled away, and tears stung her own eyes.

She had never felt so alone. If not for the baby in her arms, she'd have no one in the world to call her own. She had no parents, no husband, and now no best friend. In one weak moment she had almost begged Connor to come with them, but she had no right to drag him into her mixed-up, crazy, dangerous life.

Oh God, how am I supposed to do this?

She opened her eyes and blinked away more tears as the bus lumbered onto the highway in a gray diesel cloud.

"Are you all right, honey?" The woman across the aisle leaned toward her, a kindly expression on her face.

"Fine." Lara wiped her cheek with the back of her hand and tried to smile. "It's postpartum blues. I don't know why, but I can't seem to stop crying."

The woman's head jerked in an assertive nod. "I remember what that feels like. Right after I had my babies I was goin' crazy with feelings. I had company coming, a colicky baby, and a husband who didn't even know how to change a diaper. I know they say the blues are caused by hormones and such, but there's got to be more to it. A woman's entire world changes when a baby comes along."

Lara nodded slowly, privately doubting a baby had changed any woman's world as much as Hunter's arrival had changed hers.

"Excuse me." She pushed her way out of the seat and reached for her bag. "But I think someone needs his diaper changed."

The ride smoothed out as the bus pulled onto the highway. Lara was grateful for the engine noise as she took Hunter into the small restroom. With the baby on her lap, she sat on the closed commode and yielded to the compulsive sobs that shook her, then wiped her cheeks and changed the squirming baby's diaper.

When Hunter was settled, she pressed her ear to the locked door. All was quiet outside the restroom, so perhaps her talkative neighbor had fallen asleep. She opened the door and made her way back to her seat, then settled the baby in the empty seat at her side. Hunter cried and waved his tiny fists, then found his fingers and slipped them into his mouth.

Only when he had settled did Lara look around. The woman across the aisle had moved, but the bright red garment she'd been crocheting lay in the empty seat. Lara picked it up, then saw the handwritten note beneath it.

O Lord, you know when I sit and when I rise; you perceive my thoughts from afar.
You discern my going out and my lying down; you are familiar with all my ways.
You hem me in—behind and before; you have laid your hand upon me.
Where can I go from your Spirit? Where can I flee from your presence?
If I rise on the wings of the dawn, if I settle on the far side of the sea, even there your hand will guide me, your right hand will hold me fast.
All the days ordained for me were written in your book before one of them came to be.

Lara leaned forward and searched the front of the bus, but saw no trace of the woman's white hair. Confused, she sank back in her seat and smoothed the crocheted garment. It was a baby sweater; warm and soft, the perfect size for Hunter.

"Where can I go?" she whispered, her eyes filling again. "Nowhere without you, Lord."

The woman was likely curled up in a front seat, her head hidden by the tall seat back. She had probably begun this sweater for a grandchild, then felt moved to leave it with Lara. The coincidence that she had finished it exactly while Lara had Hunter in the restroom—well, it could have been exactly that. A coincidence.

But no matter where it had come from, it was miracle enough to comfort Lara's broken heart. She picked it up and laid it over her sleeping angel, then smiled at him through the tears that sparkled on her lashes.

[BOOK TWO]

chapter 23

"Watch me, Mom!"

Lara lifted her hand to shade her eyes as Hunter sprinted to the swings. The quick nap in the car had energized him, and she was glad she had decided to stop at the park before going home. He'd have a chance to run and play, and she'd have a moment to sit and catch her breath after a long day.

Keeping an eye on Hunter, she turned and walked down the trail toward a bench that overlooked the playground, then slowed her step. Another woman sat there, a solitary figure who kept her eyes on the distant horizon as if her thoughts were far away.

Lara thought about following Hunter to the swings, then decided against it. She had spent the entire day on her feet, and her supervisor at the Osceola Oaks nursing home had been in a particularly foul mood. More than once Lara had bit back a protest and obeyed an inane command, knowing full well that the supervisor was not qualified to oversee the staff. But Lara, known to everyone here as Rose Shepard, was a lowly licensed practical nurse, without enough authority to swat a cockroach. She quietly tended her patients, often going above and beyond her job description, because she cared about the people in her wing.

She started to call Hunter back, but the sound of his laughter persuaded her to stay. Sighing, she approached the bench. "Do you mind if I sit down?"

The young woman looked up and gave Lara a distracted smile. "Sure."

"Thanks." Lara sank to the bench and leaned back, then closed her eyes for a moment in blissful relaxation.

"Mom!"

Hunter's cry brought her eyes open again. He stood on a child-sized balance beam six inches above the ground. As she watched, he spread his

251

arms and walked the beam with short, careful steps, an almost perfect imitation of the gymnast he'd watched on television the week before.

"That's good, sweetheart," Lara called. "Very good."

The other woman followed Lara's gaze; then her mouth tipped in a faint smile. "He's cute. How old?"

"Five." Lara turned back to Hunter, hoping the woman would take the hint and stay quiet. Since moving to Florida, she had cultivated few friends. This woman was probably just a tired professional on her way home from work, but even after five years, Lara remained cautious in her dealings with strangers. She'd seen enough to know that money bought power and Devin Sloane had a limitless supply of both.

The woman sighed heavily. "I wish I had a kid. My husband doesn't want them—says they're too expensive. I want a baby more than anything, but he won't listen to reason."

Lara glanced at the woman's hand. A slender gold wedding band shone on her ring finger, a modest piece of jewelry that seemed appropriate for a struggling newlywed. The woman was young, probably not yet thirty, and she wore a denim skirt, a plaid blouse, and brown leather slip-ons. Lara's brow crinkled when she recognized the emblem on the shoes—Manalo Blahnik. If this woman wanted a baby, she'd have to start economizing on footwear.

"Babies may be expensive," she said, her distrust subsiding, "but they're worth it. And if you're careful, you may not feel the expense at all. Baby showers, thrift shops, discount shopping—there are ways to cut costs."

The woman thrust out her hand. "I'm Mary Godfrey."

Lara took a quick, sharp breath at the name, then smiled and shook the woman's hand. "I'm Rose. Nice to meet you."

Mary smiled and released Lara's hand. "I'm really sorry to burden you with all this, but it's nice to talk to somebody. My husband won't even discuss children anymore."

"It's important that he talk." Lara's gaze shifted to follow Hunter, and part of her brain registered the irony that she, a single mother, was dispensing marital advice. Nonetheless, she pressed on. "It's important to have your husband's agreement. A child needs a father."

Mary made a faint moue of distaste. "I don't know about that—a lot of my friends are raising kids alone. And tell me the truth—how much time does your husband spend with your son?"

Lara crossed her arms, feeling a sudden chill. "I don't have a husband." She kept her gaze on Hunter. "That's why I know he needs a father. I try my best to be all Hunter needs, but I can't be everything. I don't have the energy or the time, and I'm not a man." She kept her face blank, trying to hide her misery from Mary's probing stare. "I love my son dearly, but he needs a father. I have no idea how I'm going to provide him with one."

"You could get married." Even wide open, the woman's eyes had a catlike slant to them. "You're an attractive woman. I'll bet the guys would line up if you let them know you were interested."

Lara rubbed a finger over her lip, quelling the sudden urge to laugh. "I don't think so. I don't have time to socialize. Hunter and I get out to church once a week, but other than that, I'm either at work or home with him."

Mary's gaze roved over Lara's navy slacks and white top. "You work in a doctor's office?"

"I'm a nurse."

Mary shrugged and turned toward Hunter. "I'm a preschool teacher. That's how I know I love kids. And that's why I want one."

Hunter's shrill scream broke the heavy stillness of the afternoon, and Lara rose to her feet, her heart pounding. Hunter ran toward her, his hand waving, his face puffy with tears and exertion.

"What's wrong, buddy?"

"Bee!" He turned and pointed toward the playground. "A big bee."

Lara glanced at the glaring red spot on his palm. "You were stung, buddy, that's all. It will hurt, but then the pain will go away."

His sobbing quieted to a soft whimper. "It was a big bee."

A shadow fell over Hunter's face as Mary approached. "He's all right?"

"A bee sting, nothing serious. But I'd better take him home and put some baking soda on it."

"Let me see."

Whimpering, Hunter held up his injured palm for Mary's inspection.

"Poor baby." The woman gave him a soothing smile. "But you'll be all right. I see things like this all the time. I'm a teacher, you know."

Hunter's eyes flew open wide; then he looked at Lara. "She's not, Mom. Why did she lie?"

Lara felt her stomach drop. She grasped Hunter's uninjured hand and pulled him toward the parking lot. "We've got to go," she called, lengthening her stride. "I'd better get him home and put something on this."

"Why are we running? What's wrong, Mom?"

Lara didn't answer until Hunter was safely buckled into his seat. She started the engine, backed out of the parking space, and paused for a moment. Mary Godfrey, if that was truly her name, was still sitting on the park bench, her head down as she pressed a cell phone to her ear.

Hunter followed her gaze. "Who is that lady, Mom? Why did she lie?"

Lara felt a cold hand pass down her spine as she closed her eyes. More important, who was the lady calling?

⚭

From the wide windows in her office, Nadine Harrington watched the setting sun cast the Washington Monument's oblique shadow over the surrounding park. She tented her hands and locked her long nails, congratulating herself for her perseverance and perspicacity. For five years she had sought Lara Godfrey, and she had always known the key to finding the woman lay in Connor O'Hara.

They had questioned him, directly and indirectly, immediately after the woman disappeared. In response to the judge's pickup order, the police had even investigated that silly skiing alibi, but Nadine knew they'd done little more than call the Wintergreen hotel to check O'Hara's registration. Once the police discovered that Connor O'Hara didn't have the woman or the infant, they left him alone. Most cops hated family law cases, and because Lara Godfrey had apparently left the state before the pickup order was issued, technically she had not committed a crime in Virginia.

At Sloane's insistence, the police had picked O'Hara up and administered a lie detector test, which the librarian passed with flying colors. Either the guy had learned how to beat the truth detector, Nadine reasoned, or he honestly didn't know where Lara Godfrey had gone. He admitted helping her leave the city; he admitted seeing the baby—a boy—but he gave them no other useful information.

Sloane had pushed for round-the-clock surveillance on O'Hara's house, but Nadine knew the librarian didn't have the woman. He had sent her somewhere, probably far away, at great personal cost. Watching him one afternoon as he sat in lonely silence on his front porch, Nadine realized just how much it had cost him to help Lara Godfrey. The man had obviously come to love her, and what he had done—well, few men of Nadine's acquaintance would have acted so nobly.

Still, he had to know what had happened to Lara and the child.

When electronic surveillance failed to turn up any sign of Lara Godfrey, Nadine hired private investigators and sent them all over the country, even sending a man to North Pole, Alaska, in case O'Hara had sent the Godfrey woman to his sister. Nadine bought mailing lists from medical associations and physician's assistants' organizations, then hired a team to call every listed name and pretend to conduct a random survey. Because Lara Godfrey had been an avid churchgoer, Nadine hired an innocent-looking elderly woman to visit a different Virginia congregation each week and look for any young mother who matched Lara Godfrey's description. She knew it was a long shot, but Sloane wanted every possible clue checked out.

While her people scoured the countryside, Nadine labored to keep Sloane calm. Unnerved by the Godfrey woman's successful disappearance, he vacillated between believing that O'Hara knew nothing and wanting to send goons to torture the man. Nadine urged Sloane to proceed carefully, remaining within the bounds of the law as much as possible. At some point, she assured him, Connor O'Hara would drop his guard. The child was young; there was still time for Sloane to be a father . . . or at least that's what she kept telling herself.

Her gaze fell upon the faded photo perched on the edge of her desk. Ryan Christopher Harrington was now thirteen, nearly a man. Did he look anything like his baby picture? Did he remember anything about her, or had his stepmother erased all the bad memories?

She gripped the edge of her desk, anchoring herself in reality lest she drown in a sudden wave of guilt. Children were resilient, her therapist assured her. They were like rubber, easily molded, quick to bounce back. Ryan probably didn't even remember her, much less hold a grudge. He wouldn't remember the nights she'd passed out on the kitchen floor, or the time he pulled a pot of boiling water from the stove because she had been careless and left the handle within his reach. The scars on his arm would heal, the doctor had said. Everything healed with time.

The memory edged her teeth.

Abruptly, she swiveled her chair beneath her desk and studied her calendar. December had been a productive month, and the holidays had given her an elegantly simple idea. Beginning on December first, the start of the holiday mailing season, she'd had an agent check Connor O'Hara's mailbox. On Monday of last week they intercepted his neat stack of outgoing Christmas cards; her people spent Tuesday systematically identifying every individual to whom the librarian sent a holiday greeting. Fortunately, Connor O'Hara was a local boy and somewhat reclusive, only three cards were addressed to females outside the state of Virginia. One proved to be the married sister in North Pole, Alaska; another was a sixty-five-year-old coworker who had retired and moved to Florida. The third was addressed to Ms. Rose Shepard in Osceola, Florida.

On Wednesday, December sixteenth, Abby Smith, a young investigator from Nadine's agency, had flown into Clearwater, driven to Osceola, and found a room at a local motel. On Thursday morning Abby found Rose Shepard's home in a crowded trailer park. The subject had changed her hair color and lost a few pounds, but Rose had a preschool child and bore a striking resemblance to Lara Godfrey. Within five days, the investigator had established Ms. Shepard's weekday routine—drive to the preschool, work, back to the preschool, the park, the library, and home again.

This afternoon, Abby Smith made contact.

Rose Shepard, Abby had just told Nadine, reacted strongly to the name Godfrey, had a five-year-old son, had remained unmarried, and worked as a nurse. "And," Abby added, breathless with success, "she left in a hurry."

Anxiety cooled Nadine's racing thoughts. "Did you do something?"

"That's just it," Abby replied, an edge to her voice. "I thought I had completely won her over. I was beginning to win the kid too. Thinking that all little kids love school, I told him I was a teacher, but he looked right at me and caught me in a lie."

Nadine's hand tightened around the phone. "How?"

"I have no idea. But the mother practically yanked him away from me. It was all a little confusing because a bee had just stung the kid, but he seemed completely coherent when he looked at me. It was almost creepy."

Nadine thanked Abby for the report, then told the young woman to return to Washington. After disconnecting the call, she had closed her eyes and felt her stomach sway. She'd had an uneasy feeling about this case ever since Devin Sloane sent that dour young man to invite her to his dark Virginia mansion. If Sloane had let her into his innermost "circle of secrets" on that day, she would never have accepted the case.

What sort of child had Sloane's genetic manipulation created?

A cynical inner voice cut through her anxiety. The boy was probably just like any other kid. Abby was inexperienced and might have slipped somehow. Children could say outlandish things; one never knew what to expect. And if the boy was crying and injured, of course the mother would be eager to take him home. Lara Godfrey hadn't run because she feared exposing her child's unique abilities; she had hurried away because her child was hurt.

But Sloane would not want to hear that he'd spent more than four million dollars to find an ordinary kid.

Nadine picked up the phone and pressed the speed dial button for Sloane, then smiled as she brought the phone to her ear. With any luck, Sloane would have his uniquely talented child home for Christmas.

∞

Lara propped Hunter and his book in an empty chair next to hers, then pressed her finger to her lips. The boy nodded and mimicked the gesture, then promptly defeated the purpose of her little pantomime: "I know, Mom. You gots to be quiet in the li-barry."

Lara smiled ruefully and pointed to the book. Hunter immediately opened the pages and ducked his shining blond head, intent upon another adventure of Curious George.

Knowing that Hunter's attention span was limited, she worked quickly at the computer. She accessed the Internet, logged onto the Web page for Hotmail, then entered her ID and password. She hadn't been able to afford a computer for the trailer, and Connor had insisted she wouldn't be safe with an e-mail account through a local service provider. The Internet was a friendly place, *too* friendly, in Connor's estimation, so he'd asked her to establish seven free e-mail accounts and rotate between them. Tuesday was Hotmail day.

She felt her heart sink when she saw that she had no messages waiting. She had grown accustomed to hearing from Connor nearly every afternoon, but she knew he traveled occasionally and was away from the computer. This must be one of his travel days.

In order to safeguard her privacy, she had allowed an entire year to elapse before she dared send an e-mail to the reference desk of University of Virginia Library. She had sent an innocuous and unsigned query about the book *Mr. and Mrs. BoJo Jones*, and the reference department had responded immediately with another question—"Do you have the book safely stored away?"

For the past four years she had stopped by the library nearly every afternoon. Hunter loved the place and often entertained the librarians by acting out his favorite picture books, particularly relishing the tales of Curious George and Mike Mulligan and his steam shovel.

Now Lara typed in the address for Connor's mailbox, then typed *A Close Encounter* in the subject heading. She tabbed down to the message field.

Dear Mr. O'Hara:
Long time, no hear from you. What's it been, two days? Not like you, my friend, to let me drift so long without a word.

Had a scare today at the park. A bee stung the pipsqueak, and we met a stranger. I thought she was perfectly harmless, but the PS caught her in a lie. I don't know how to explain what he does—I suppose you could call it infallible intuition. But the experience was enough to make me leave the park in a hurry and take the long way as I drove home.

We miss you, my friend. When I saw that woman sitting alone in the park, I couldn't help but remember that five years ago I was just like her.

Now my life is much more full and complete, although I do miss . . . roots. I shall begin to pray for the time and space to put down a few.

As always, I am praying for you. May God hold you tight in the palm of his hand.

Always,

Mrs. BoJo

Lara reread her letter for spelling, then read it again with the detached eye of a reference librarian who might happen to glance over Connor's shoulder as he read the message. She trusted him to be careful, but one careless mistake might bring her fragile world tumbling down.

Satisfied that she had conveyed her heart in the sparest prose possible, she clicked *send*, then smiled at Hunter. "Ready to go home, buddy?"

∞

His attention drifting on a tide of fatigue, Helmut Braun pushed away from his computer, then glanced out his office window at the empty lab beyond. His students had been gone for hours. Only a single light burned over a culture growing in the far corner of the room.

Helmut swiped at a wiry strand of hair that had fallen into his eyes, then sighed heavily. Force of habit urged him to get up and go home, but there was nothing homelike about the bare little apartment he shared with a nameless gray cat.

Wistfully, his mind wandered back to the time when he used to go home to Olivia. At the time he had thought their marriage rather detached and professional, but in the light of his current loneliness their past relationship seemed warm and genuine. How she had made him laugh! Olivia's smile had eased him into relaxation each night; her stories about the practice had carried him through the drudgery of each day. And when she asked him to leave, he had realized, too late, all he had possessed.

With an exhausted sigh, he stood up and patted his pockets, searching for his keys. He ought to lock up his papers before leaving, though it was doubtful anyone would want to look at them. Five years ago, after a few teasing hints from the University's press office, the scientific world had held its breath for news of his great accomplishment, but that announcement had never come. Lara had vanished, taking the results of Helmut's experiment with her.

He had often thought that her disappearance was a good thing. With the child gone, his secrets were safe. Sloane had wanted to try again with another woman, but Helmut had convinced him that until the laws changed, surrogate mothers would cause more problems than benefits. "Concentrate on your phase-one work at the hospital," he had urged Sloane. "You are making progress with the children. And who knows? Perhaps, in time, you will find Lara Godfrey and her son."

But every night before closing his eyes to sleep, Helmut gazed at the ceiling and asked any god who might be listening to keep Lara safely hidden.

He closed the notebook on his desk. The computer was password protected. That security measure wouldn't stop any snoop with more than an elementary knowledge of computers, but it would keep students from prying into his personal thoughts. And if a spy was willing to delve into the past—well, let him have at it. Helmut was past caring.

He stood and slipped into his coat, then halted when the outer door to the lab opened. A tall figure walked through a rectangle of light from the hallway, then merged into the lab's shadows as the door closed. The voice was unmistakable.

"Dr. Braun. I had hoped to find you here."

Helmut stopped dead, his heart beating hard enough to be heard a yard away. "I was just leaving."

"Nonsense, dear professor, you can't leave until you have heard my news." Sloane stepped into the light and leaned in the doorway of Helmut's office. As always, he wore an immaculate and understated suit, but tonight an exuberant quality underlay his posture and expression.

Helmut clasped his hands together. "Devin. How can I help you?"

"The child, Doctor." Sloane's face brightened in a sudden, arresting smile. "We've found him. Nadine's people will pick him up tomorrow."

An anticipatory shiver of dread rippled through Helmut's limbs. "You have found Lara Godfrey?"

"She went to Florida, a logical move for a nurse, considering Florida's geriatric population. She is employed by a convalescent home in Osceola."

Helmut stood there, blank, amazed, and shaken, as Sloane threw back his head and laughed. "It is time to continue, Helmut. The child is nearly six years old, but that is nothing! We can take custody tomorrow and keep him protected until the case comes to trial. By the time Lara Godfrey recovers from Nadine's surprise assault, we'll have so much evidence against her that no judge in his right mind would refuse to grant me permanent custody."

Helmut steadied himself on his chair. "The child—what is he like?"

"We don't know." Sloane's smile faded. "Nadine's contact said he was a perfectly normal-looking boy. But soon we will know more. Nadine, my lawyer, and I are flying to Florida tomorrow to oversee the pickup." Sloane straightened, smoothed the lapel of his suit, then waved his hand at Helmut's cluttered office. "Shelve whatever project you're working on now, Doctor, for the real work is about to begin. Our boy is coming home, and I need you to set up the testing programs. I'll want to harvest a sample of his DNA, and I'll need a team of psychologists at the house to evaluate his IQ, his stamina, his emotional stability. Of course," he frowned, "there's no way to judge what influence the Godfrey woman has had on him, but I trust she's done no irreparable harm."

Helmut stared at the floor, a host of nightmare images rising in his brain—Lara's frightened eyes as he tried to subdue her, the dark, lifeless rooms in Sloane's west wing, and Olivia's wounded expression when she learned that he had tampered with the husband's genetic material.

"I wanted to tell you personally." Devin smiled and gestured toward the door. "I feel like celebrating. Would you care to join me for dinner? The car's waiting outside."

"No, thank you." Helmut tightened his hold on the chair, but managed to look up and meet Sloane's gaze. "I have already made plans."

"Very well, then. I'll keep you informed."

Helmut remained rooted to the floor until Sloane disappeared down the hall. When he had gone, Helmut pulled his keys from his pocket, then stumbled woodenly toward the light outside.

Lara Godfrey was a resourceful woman. Perhaps she would yet escape. She had to.

chapter 24

Nadine stepped off the jet into sunshine so bright it hurt her eyes. Even in December, the cloudless sky above Clearwater shimmered with heat. The asphalt tarmac beneath her heels felt crumbly and soft.

"Let's go," Sloane commanded, leading his contingent forward. "We're due at the courthouse within the hour."

Nadine lifted her briefcase and followed Madison Jarvis, Sloane's high-priced attorney, who shadowed his client like a well-trained dog. Trent Bishop, Sloane's latest assistant, walked behind the lawyer, and Nadine brought up the rear, resenting the fact that she was part of an entourage. She had carved out a career for herself in a male-dominated world, and it galled her to walk ten paces behind a man, even if he was her most lucrative client and one of the most charismatic men in the world.

She lengthened her stride and hurried to catch up with Sloane. She could at least walk *beside* him.

Though he didn't turn to look at her, he must have sensed her presence. "I don't want any press," he said, keeping his gaze fastened to the narrow door that led into the main airport terminal. "Did you take care of that?"

She shifted her briefcase from one hand to the other and leaned toward him. "No one knows about the hearing but us and the Pinellas County judge. I had our judge call him this morning to discuss the pickup order, and we have every reason to expect that the local judge will go along with Judge Weaver's recommendation."

"Why in the world would Lara Godfrey settle here?" Trent Bishop's crooked nose crinkled as he gestured toward the horizon that trembled in the heat haze. "Nothing but bugs and tourists and scraggly palm trees—"

"It worked, didn't it?" Sloane snapped, interrupting his assistant. "We should have thought of Florida. The state has a large number of transients and a huge geriatric population. It makes sense, considering that our girl *is* a medical professional."

"As a matter of fact," Nadine answered, ducking as they walked under the wing of another private jet, "Rose Shepard, as Lara Godfrey is now known, is employed by the Osceola Oaks Nursing Home as a licensed practical nurse. She makes $32,000 a year—a fair wage for a single mother with a small son."

"An LPN?" Trent glanced up, then pulled a handkerchief from his pocket and mopped his brow. "I thought she was a physician's assistant. That's practically a doctor—"

"She's not a fool," Sloane interrupted. They had reached the terminal entrance, and Sloane stood back, waiting for Trent or Jarvis—or maybe Nadine—to open the door.

Nadine gripped her briefcase with both hands. "We've been searching through medical professional organizations and databases for months, hoping she'd show up," she told Trent. "We found a midwife named Lara Jefferson out in Milwaukee, so I sent two agents to check her out. We spent a week investigating, but it wasn't our girl."

Trent regarded the door with a puzzled expression. "Is it locked?"

Sloane closed his eyes in an attitude of exasperation. "Why don't you try it and see?"

The assistant opened the door, and Sloane passed through, his bearing imperious. Nadine gave the young man a brief smile of thanks, then sighed in relief when a blast of cool air ruffled her hair. She drank deeply of the air conditioning and wished she'd worn a lighter suit. If all went well they'd be back in Virginia tonight, but one could never be certain about child custody cases.

Sloane stopped abruptly and turned. "What's the plan?" His face had gone pale, and faint droplets of sweat shone like pearls on his upper lip. "I want to be apprised of everything that happens."

"Mr. Jarvis and I"—Nadine gestured toward the lawyer—"are going to the Pinellas County courthouse to confirm the pickup order. You and

Trent will go to a hotel and wait for us. Once we have confirmed the local sheriff's department's support, we will go to Lara Godfrey's residence and conceal ourselves. The moment after she comes home, we'll surround the trailer. We'll take the child into protective custody, then bring him to you at the hotel."

A shade of uncertainty crept into Sloane's expression, and Nadine smiled at the sight of it. In her wildest moments she would never have imagined Sloane capable of insecurity or uncertainty.

"Don't worry." She placed her hand on his arm and gave him a confident smile. "Little boys are just like big boys. Play with him if he's restless, feed him if he's hungry, and comfort him if he cries. As soon as we get the all clear from the judge, you can take him home."

Sloane's shoulders slumped in what looked like relief while eagerness and anxiety mingled in his expression. Nadine watched, amazed at this unusual display of emotion. He behaved as though he felt something for this little boy, though she couldn't imagine how he could love a child he had never known. Then again, she no longer knew her own son, yet something stirred in her heart every time she thought of him . . .

Jarvis cleared his throat and glanced pointedly at his watch. "Nearly eleven thirty. If we're going to get to the courthouse before lunch, we'd better hurry."

"Go." Sloane waved Nadine away. "Trent and I will take a hotel room near the airport. You have my number if you need me."

"Got it," Nadine said, moving away. With the lawyer at her side, she stepped into the flow of arriving tourists and headed toward the exit. Christmas carols spilled from overhead speakers, covering the murmur of welcoming voices with a joyous holiday sound.

Nadine walked silently and studied the crowd, imagining Lara Godfrey's face upon every passing thirty-something woman. Soon she'd no longer have to engage in this habitual ritual; she'd be face-to-face with the real McCoy in only a few hours.

She stepped through the sliding doors and moved toward a taxi that would take her and Jarvis to the Pinellas County sheriff and Devin Sloane's son.

❧

Lara stepped into the carpeted hallway that dissected the church's educational building and smiled as she followed the sound of a boisterous chorus of "We Three Kings." Hunter's preschool classroom lay around the corner from the school's security desk, and she waved at the gray-haired officer on duty before turning the corner. The spirited carol originated in Hunter's classroom, and she leaned on the shelf of the half door and grinned at the students' happy enthusiasm. Hunter's teacher, Rachel Williams, saw Lara and flashed a smile.

As the teacher's aide continued the song, Rachel pulled Hunter's backpack from a row of hooks along the wall, then walked toward Lara. "Merry Christmas, Mrs. Shepard," she said, placing the backpack on the shelf in front of Lara. "You're early today."

"Yes, my boss let me go," Lara said, her eyes following her son. "We Three Kings" had ended and now the children were choosing parts for "The Twelve Days of Christmas." Hunter, apparently, was struggling to imitate one of the lords a-leaping.

"Actually, I'm glad you're early." Rachel's blue eyes softened. "I wanted to talk to you a moment about Hunter."

Lara tensed immediately, but forced herself to remain calm. "Oh? Did he misbehave in class?"

"Oh, no, not that. Hunter's a little angel." The teacher stopped suddenly. "I feel a bit disloyal for bringing this up because I don't want to contradict anything you're teaching him at home. But something happened today, and I'm a little concerned that you may be limiting Hunter's full potential."

Lara shook her head. "What on earth do you mean?"

The woman bit her lip, then answered in a rush of words. "Hunter has trouble . . . with his imagination. We played a pretending game today, and I asked Hunter to be the donkey in the manger where Jesus was born. You can imagine my surprise when he stood and said he wasn't a donkey and he could never be one." A look of discomfort crossed the teacher's face. "Honestly, Mrs. Shepard, in that moment I felt like I was teaching the children to *lie*, but we were only pretending."

Lara sighed as a wave of relief and frustration swept over her. "You're right, he's very matter-of-fact about things, but I can assure you that I've never told him imagination is wrong. I suppose he hasn't yet learned to tell the difference between fancy and fact."

"That leads me to another matter." The teacher placed her arms on the shelf and leaned closer. "Actually, most of my kids have no trouble with lying. With a perfectly straight face some will tell me their daddy is the president or their mama is flying to the moon next week. I usually spend a lot of time teaching kids *not* to use their imaginations so freely. But Hunter—"

Lara lifted a brow when the teacher hesitated. "What does Hunter do?"

"Well—" Lara saw a look pass across the teacher's face, a look she had worn herself. She had reacted the same way the first time Hunter displayed his remarkable gift.

"Tommy stole some cookies from Lauren's lunch box, but no one saw him, not even Hunter. He couldn't have seen Tommy, because Hunter was on the playground with me when Tommy was here in the room. But later, when Lauren noticed that her cookies were missing, I went around and asked each child if they had taken Lauren's snack. When I asked Tommy, he said no, he hadn't taken them, and that's when Hunter spoke up." Rachel shot Lara a half-frightened look. "Without any prodding, Hunter said, 'He's lying, Miss Williams.' Well, I thought Hunter had seen the theft, so I looked in Tommy's pockets and sure enough, I found a handful of cookie crumbs. But when I asked Hunter if he saw Tommy take the cookies, he said no. When I asked how he knew Tommy was lying, Hunter couldn't answer. He said he just knew." The teacher's gaze moved into Lara's. "How does he know?"

Lara's heart had slowed when Rachel first broached the subject. It now resumed beating much faster than usual, as though to make up for lost time. "I—I don't know," she stammered, resisting the troubling thoughts rising in her brain. "Perhaps Tommy mentioned something to him. Maybe he gave Hunter a cookie."

Doubt shone in Rachel's eyes, but she pulled away and turned toward the children. "Hunter, your mother's here," she called, pausing to unhook a construction paper Christmas stocking from a string along the wall. As Hunter pulled out of the circle and sprang forward like a leaping lord gone amuck, Rachel pressed the stocking into his hands and stooped for a quick hug. "You have a merry Christmas. We'll see you after the holidays, okay?"

"Okay!" Hunter yelled, straining to be heard over the music. Rachel opened the door, and Lara wrapped her hand around her son's, then smiled her thanks and waved as they walked away.

∞

"Mom, can I get a book?"

"Not today, buddy; this is a quick visit. Mom just wants to check her e-mail." Lara sat Hunter in the spare chair with his construction-paper stocking, then logged onto Juno.com with her ID and password. She smiled as a message from Connor flashed on the screen.

Dear Secondhand R:

What do you mean, long time, no hear from me? I was only away for two days. The conference was nice, but boring. Couldn't wait to get back and check in with you.

By the way, you haven't mentioned my Christmas card. I sent a check for the Squeaker and my very best wishes for a blessed Christmas. I hope they arrived safe and sound. If not, let me know. I'm praying for you every day and night. I'll write more later, but things are bustling around here.

Love and blessings to you.

C.

Lara frowned as she read the message again. Connor didn't say when he'd sent the Christmas card, but he obviously thought enough time had passed for her to receive it. It could have been lost in the Christmas deluge, of course, or misdirected in her crowded trailer park. Many of her neighbors had headed north for the holidays, so the card could be languishing in any one of their mailboxes.

Her gaze fell upon Hunter, who was lumbering silently around her cubicle, his arms dangling loosely from his shoulders as if he were a chimpanzee. He walked with an awkward gait, turning one foot outward. No telling what *that* was supposed to represent.

She frowned as his teacher's words came back to her. Why would her son love to pretend in private and refuse to play a pretend role in front of his classmates?

She clicked her tongue and smiled when his wide blue gaze lifted to meet hers. His eyes were clear and trusting like Michael's—and yet they were nothing like Michael's. Her son was unlike any child she had ever known.

She held out her hand. "Let's go, buddy."

Hunter slipped his damp fingers into her palm, then stooped to pick up his crumpled Christmas stocking from the floor. That bit of construction paper art probably wouldn't last until they got home, but at least she could say Hunter had enjoyed it to death.

As they left the library, Hunter lifted his knees and marched beside her, humming a slightly off-key version of "We Three Kings." Lara gave the librarian a rueful grin as she led her noisy little boy out. She half-expected the woman to cast her a warning glance, but the white-haired lady only waved and winked as they walked away.

∽

In the penthouse suite of the Airport Marriott, Devin Sloane thrust his hands behind his back and paced before the window, trying to corral his unproductive, rebellious thoughts. He and Trent had been waiting at the hotel for five hours without a word from Nadine. Madison Jarvis had called shortly after two to report that the Pinellas County judge had approved the pickup order and Nadine was en route to the sheriff's office to enlist the aid of several deputies.

Devin glanced at his watch again. Five fifteen, yet no news was probably good news. What did another hour or two matter? He had lost five years, but he had to admit the child may not have been harmed while in his mother's care. He had selected Lara Godfrey because she was a warm, nurturing person. She had probably done an excellent job of caring for the boy through infancy and the toddler years. Nadine's investigator had said the boy seemed charming and bright, so even if the boy's genes had been slightly damaged by exposure, they'd still be of far greater quality than anything else on the planet.

He turned to Trent, who sat on the couch, his eyes fastened to the television. "Pull out that report again, please. What is she calling my son?"

Trent opened his briefcase and fumbled with the pages that had arrived an hour ago. The report, faxed from the Harrington Group in Washington, contained every scrap of information available—legally and illegally—on Rose Shepard of Osceola, Florida.

Trent flipped through the stapled pages. "On her tax returns for the last four years, she listed one son, Hunter, as a dependent. His Social Security number is 267-08-3945."

Devin smacked his fist into his palm. "She's amazingly good! I never would have suspected that Lara was capable of such thoroughness."

Trent's mouth twisted in a grudging smile. "She thought of everything. This report lists credit card numbers, her address, even her Social Security earnings. But the earliest record of her reported earnings is dated February 1999."

Sloane turned back to the window. "Of course. For all intents and purposes, our Rose Shepard was born that month. But she is finished now."

He jerked his chin toward the laptop on the coffee table. "Read the media list back to me. Who have I forgotten?"

Trent dropped the report back into the briefcase, then leaned forward to scroll through the computer list. "The list looks complete, sir. You've included Katie Couric, Tom Brokaw, Barbara Walters, Oprah Winfrey, the four major networks, Fox News, CNN, the *Washington Post*, the *New York Times*, and the *Los Angeles Times*. I think we've covered the major media."

"Good." Sloane thrust his hands behind his back. "As soon as the child arrives, I want a press release faxed to everyone on that list. 'Devin Sloane wishes to announce the safe return of his son'—" He paused. "What do you think? I had planned to call him Adam, but perhaps it's not wise to change a child's name right away. I wouldn't want to traumatize him."

Trent quirked his brow. "Do you like the name Hunter?"

Laughter floated up from Sloane's throat. "I think it marvelously apt. I've spent almost six years searching for the boy, and our missing mother names the child 'Hunter.' I adore the irony."

Trent turned back to his keyboard. "Keep the name," he said, his voice flat. "Spare the child and retain the name. It'll be good PR."

Sloane nodded, satisfaction pursing his mouth. "I'll leave the particulars of the announcement to you, Trent; just make certain it's dignified and restrained. We'll hold a press conference one week—no, we'd better give the doctors more time—two weeks from today. Mention that all questions will be answered, the truth revealed, etc. List Madison Jarvis as the contact person."

Trent's fingers flew over the keyboard; then his hands stilled. "Anything else?"

"No." Devin's gaze moved toward the wide windows, where the blazing Florida sun had already begun to dip toward the western horizon. Surely by now Lara Godfrey had left work and was driving home.

Keeping his eyes upon the narrow ribbon of highway that ran beside the hotel, Devin leaned on the back of a chair in a vain attempt to control the spasmodic trembling within him. His phase-two project, for which he had nearly abandoned all hope, would soon be in full development, paving the way for phase three and his own immortality.

"Excuse me, ma'am, but can I get you a cup of coffee?"

Nadine turned from the window of the bland little community building and gave the fresh-faced deputy a distracted smile. "No, thank you. I'm keyed up enough as it is."

She looked back to the window, but the man would not be dissuaded. "If you're nervous about Bob, ma'am, you can rest assured he knows what he's doing. Bob's a good guy under pressure; he won't let anything slip."

Nadine craned her neck, searching the street for Lara Godfrey's white vehicle. "I'm not worried about Bob."

The Pinellas County sheriff had sent her out with four deputies, three men and a female officer, and three of the four were waiting with her in the clubhouse. The fourth, a square-faced, taciturn fellow named Bob Andrews, had parked his vehicle off the entrance road. The mobile home park manager had agreed to cooperate with what would appear to be a random check of vehicles entering and exiting the community, but Nadine cared only about one car—a white Altima, Florida license number GYZ 395, registered to Rose Shepard.

It was risky to place a cop where Lara Godfrey could see him, but Nadine wanted to be certain the child was in the car before they approached the trailer. If Lara had chanced to drop the boy at a friend's house, their surprise raid would do more harm than good. She'd know they'd found her and would have time to convince a friend to hide Hunter.

The female deputy sat down at the ramshackle piano and proceeded to plink out the opening notes of "Heart and Soul." Nadine grimaced, then glanced over at Madison Jarvis, who sat at a table with a sheaf of documents spread before him. He seemed oblivious to the chatter and the tinny music; the man seemed to care for little but the law. Nadine doubted she'd heard him speak more than two dozen words since he boarded the jet in Washington. She certainly hoped his tongue would loosen once they brought their civil case to trial.

"Heads up." The deputy nearest her spoke in a low and vibrant voice. Nadine turned to the window and automatically took a half step back as a white Altima pulled into the mobile home park.

"They can't see you," the deputy said, a cocky smile in his voice. "No need to jump back."

Nadine flexed her fingers until the urge to strangle the deputy had passed. She'd like to have them all fired, beginning with the wannabe concert artist on the piano.

"All right, people," the deputy called, turning from the window. "It's show time. Ready your weapons, show them if she resists, but don't fire unless you absolutely must."

"Good grief." Nadine ripped out the words, then turned to face Mr. Machismo. "Don't forget—this is a pickup order for a civil case and you'll be dealing with a five-year-old child. We don't want to frighten the boy."

"Thank you for reminding me, ma'am," the deputy drawled with distinct mockery.

The piano stopped tinkling and a chilly silence enveloped the room. All three deputies were staring at her; even Jarvis looked up from his legal papers.

"Sorry," Nadine said, glancing sharply at the lawyer. "Just remember you're not after Bonnie and Clyde. Just a mother and her kid."

Nadine turned back to the window, then heard the soft leather brush of holsters as guns were drawn and checked. "All right, we'll wait until she goes into the trailer; then surround it," the deputy said, moving toward the door. "Let's hope Bob doesn't do anything to spook her."

❧

"Something wrong, officer?" Lara lowered her window and gave the sheriff's deputy her most innocent smile. "Trouble in the park?"

"No, ma'am." The sheriff touched the brim of his hat as he came closer, then smiled as he glanced at Hunter. Placing one hand on her window, he leaned forward and spoke in a confidential tone. "Just a routine traffic stop. Somebody's reported a couple of skateboarders, and the manager asked us to see if someone's driving 'em in."

Lara leaned back against the seat and smiled. "Yes, I've heard them. They go up and down the road at all hours."

"We'll try to find them, ma'am." In a polite salute, the deputy touched the brim of his hat again, then straightened and waved Lara through.

As she drove away, Hunter's voice cut through her thoughts like a knife. "He told you a lie, Mom."

"What, buddy?"

Hunter pressed his hands together and squeezed, his worried gesture. "That policeman. He lied. That wasn't the truth." His velvet eyes had widened. "Policemen aren't supposed to lie, Mom. My teacher says the policeman is my friend."

Lara clutched the steering wheel and felt her heart leap into the back of her throat. The woman at the park. The sheriff. They had both lied. The woman wasn't a schoolteacher, and this deputy wasn't here to check out a complaint about skateboarders—

He'd come for her.

Instinctively, her foot moved to the brake; then she forced it back to the gas pedal. She couldn't stop in front of the cop, but she couldn't back up and pull out with tires squealing, either. There were probably others waiting somewhere, and they'd stop her in an instant if they saw her try to run. Plus, there was Hunter to consider. One small boy could be hurt in a car crash . . .

But they would not take her son.

Her adrenal glands dumped such a dose of adrenaline into her bloodstream that her fingers trembled. "Hunter, buddy, listen to me." She kept her eyes on the road, allowing the car to idle down the narrow lane. The speed limit was ten miles per hour, so the cop wouldn't think it odd that she was moving slowly. She needed time to think, to put her plans in action.

For she had always known this day would come.

"Hunter, buddy, you know that little suitcase under your bed? When I stop the car, I need you to run to your bedroom and get it. I'm going to get out and unlock the front door for you, then I'm going to come back to the car. I want you to run and get your suitcase; then run back to the car as fast as you can, just like we practiced. Okay?"

For an instant Hunter's flushed face seemed to open. She saw bewilderment there, a fast flicker of fear, then complete and unquestioning trust.

"Bad people lie, don't they, Mom?"

Lara nosed the car into the driveway, shoved the gearshift into park, and cut the engine. "I don't know if that deputy is a bad person," she whispered, her fingers fluttering helplessly over the seat-belt buckle. She drew a deep breath, then met her son's gaze and tried to smile. "Sometimes people lie when they're hiding something. And when they are, sometimes we have to hide too. This is one of those times."

"Like when you use your pretend name?"

Laura took a quick, sharp breath. Hunter had never called her anything but "Mommy" or "Mom," and he'd never heard her called anything but Rose. But apparently not even her *name* rang true with him.

"Yes," she whispered. "This is why I use a pretend name."

Hunter nodded gravely and remained silent as she got out of the car and glanced toward the clubhouse. The deputy still stood at the edge of the parking lot; now he was bent toward Mr. and Mrs. Adams's blue Lincoln, probably assuring them there was no cause for alarm. She waited, not moving, while Hunter clambered out of the car and walked toward the rusting wrought-iron steps that led to the front door. Lara left her purse in the car and followed, the keys jangling against her hand with a sharp metallic sound.

She would leave her photographs, her clothes, her papers. Every single remnant of Rose Shepard would remain in this trailer. After tomorrow, Lara wouldn't care what happened to Rose. By six o'clock tonight she would be someone else and, if necessary, someone else next week. Connor had taught her to be prepared, and in the last five years she'd had time to plan for this day.

She brought her key to the door. As she unlocked it, she looked in the small window and studied the reflected street behind her. The deputy was moving toward the clubhouse with his head down.

"Okay, buddy." She took Hunter's hand and urged him through the door. "Run into your bedroom, grab the suitcase, and come right back out. Don't worry about anything; just run back as quickly as you can."

She patted him on the fanny as he scooted past; then she returned to the car, slid into the driver's seat, and started the engine. As the air conditioner poured cool air over her fevered face, she checked the gas gauge.

Less than a quarter of a tank. Well, that voided several options. She didn't have enough gas to get far, so she wouldn't try to leave town. But in Hunter's little suitcase she had a half dozen credit cards in two new names, two sets of new birth certificates for herself and Hunter, and five thousand dollars cash.

She heard the metallic slam of the front door and looked up. Hunter was running toward her, both hands clutching the bright plastic suitcase, the picture of a grinning purple dinosaur knocking against his knees with every step. From her open door, Lara pulled him into the car and over the gearshift, then slammed the door and threw the car into reverse. She pounded the gas pedal, sending gravel and sand flying as the Altima spun back onto the street.

"Buckle up, buddy." Galvanized by the iron in her voice, Hunter rushed to obey. Holding her body in rigid check, Lara eased down the road at a careful pace. A bead of perspiration traced a cold path down her back as she neared the clubhouse, then her breath exploded in a gasp. Through the open door a stream of uniformed officers moved into the sunshine, two of them with weapons drawn.

They weren't expecting to see her, but one of the deputies pointed and yelled. Lara stomped the gas pedal, leaving her pursuers to scramble for their vehicles.

She had to get away. "Father God," she whispered, her car rattling and bounding over the shoulder as she tried to weave her way into the highway traffic, "help us now."

Behind her, above the sound of Hunter's frightened whimper and the blare of horns, she heard the loud whoop of a siren.

∞

The deputies sprinted for their vehicles, but Nadine remained rooted to the concrete sidewalk like a witness to a fatal accident. Her well-laid plans had just gone awry, and she had no idea why. Did Lara Godfrey have some kind of sixth sense? Abby reported that the woman was a creature of habit, the trailer park manager confirmed that she rarely went out after coming home from work. Yet the woman had just pulled away, and from the way she took that corner, any fool could see she wasn't popping back to the grocery store to pick up something she'd forgotten.

What had tipped her off?

She heard the clubhouse door click, then Jarvis's deep voice broke her concentration. "I take it the woman ran."

"Like the hounds of hell were giving chase." Nadine crossed her arms. She'd let the deputies handle the pursuit; they'd probably enjoy the excitement. With any luck, they'd pull Godfrey over within the hour and she'd still be able to tell Sloane that the boy had been taken into custody.

Jarvis thrust his hands in his pockets and gave her a sly grin. "You going to call Sloane?"

Nadine returned his smile. "No, I'm going to see him. I can call the sheriff from the hotel, and if they pull her over in the next few minutes, we'll be able to give Sloane good news."

As she moved away, she kept that smile on her lips like a label on a bottle, hiding her humiliation. She had been so certain, so sure of herself, and yet Lara Godfrey had managed to slip away. How? The woman was a glorified nurse, for heaven's sake, not a brain surgeon . . .

"I'm glad I'm not in your shoes," Jarvis said, following her inside the clubhouse. "I'd hate to be the one to tell the boss that he came all the way to Florida for nothing."

"You couldn't wear my shoes," Nadine snapped, her irritation rising as high as the temperature outside. She yanked her briefcase from the table, then threw the lawyer a defiant glance. "And the day is not over yet, Mr. Jarvis. By now every cop in this county has Lara Godfrey's license plate number. It'll be a miracle if she makes it another ten miles."

∞

Nadine sat on a sofa in Sloane's suite, a cigarette dangling from her fingers. She'd given up the habit months before, but a few minutes ago Madison Jarvis pulled a pack from his pocket and Nadine extended her hand. Smoking was a nasty business, bad for her health and her budget, but neither seemed to matter now that she had lost Devin Sloane's son.

The county sheriff had called a few minutes after eleven. He spoke to directly to Sloane, who hung up and relayed the information in a clipped voice. He did not, Nadine noticed, look in her direction.

The sheriff had put out an all points bulletin on the white Altima, Sloane told them, but the last hour of daylight passed without any reports of the vehicle. Finally, after dark, they began a search of public areas. At ten thirty a deputy reported finding the car abandoned at Clearwater Beach, its tag facing the Gulf and smeared with wet sand. "Clever girl," Sloane concluded, his mouth twisting in something not quite a smile.

"Where could she have gone from the beach?" Trent asked, his ruddy brows rising. "This is not Manhattan. Surely there aren't too many places she could have gone."

Sloane glared at his assistant. "Clearwater Beach is a haven for tourists. There are a dozen hotels within walking distance, and each hotel would have a taxi stand. She could have gone anywhere."

"I've already spoken to a sheriff's deputy about checking the car rental agencies and the bus station." Nadine tasted her cigarette, but only barely; she was anxious to make her point. "They said they'd also fax her description to the airports. She won't get away without someone seeing her."

Trent looked at her with an insincere apology in his eyes. "Excuse me, Ms. Harrington, but don't you think Lara Godfrey will slip away long before the sheriff's department gets the word out? This is a densely populated area. The people working airport security are frazzled enough; they're not going to do your work."

Nadine felt her lower lip tremble as she returned the assistant's glare. This arrogant brat knew nothing about security, yet here he was, lecturing her.

She drew a ragged breath and struggled for self-control. "I didn't know she'd slip away. We had her *cornered* in that trailer park—"

Trent cut her off with an uplifted hand. "You still haven't explained how she gave you the slip. What tipped her off?"

"I don't know." She brought the cigarette to her lips and drew deeply, rattled by the arrogant assistant's attitude. She despised this red-haired braggart, and her antipathy grew with each passing hour. Lemuel Reis had been mournful and melancholy on occasion, but at least he had never tried to upstage her in front of Sloane.

She flicked her ashes onto the floor and narrowed her eyes at Trent Bishop. Did he know what happened to Lemuel Reis? Someday when *he* made a mistake, she'd take pleasure in explaining how shocked and horrified Sloane had been to find Reis's body hanging from an oak tree on the mansion grounds. It had happened on a cold night in '99, not more than a few hours after Lemuel confessed to sending a message intended to warn Lara Godfrey.

The body had been stiff and blue and dusted with snow when servants found it. Snow was convenient that way—any incriminating footprints had been covered over by morning. The medical examiner never did figure out how Reis managed to string himself up in that tree.

But Nadine knew. And she knew the blame for Reis's death belonged on her head. If she hadn't told Sloane about the e-mail they'd found on Connor O'Hara's hard drive, Lemuel Reis might still be alive.

Another sin on her conscience. Sometimes she hoped Sloane was right about God being corrupted by time. She hated to think she would be judged by a being who had managed to remain pure and truthful while her own standards had been eroded by convenience and the pursuit of success.

She drew on her cigarette and felt Sloane's eyes boring into her. "Nadine, do you think she went to Tampa?"

"I don't know. But that's where I'd go."

Tampa lay on the other side of the bay; on the map it seemed a world away. But if a suspect wanted to fly in a hurry, she wouldn't run to a small commuter airport like the one at Clearwater. She'd go to the largest and busiest, from which she could fly to any one of the four corners of the earth.

Nadine leaned back in her chair and let the hand with the smoking cigarette fall to her side. How could she be defeated again? She had set a trap for one of the most wanted women in America, and in the space of a heartbeat had lost the woman and the child.

She hadn't even managed to *see* the kid. Aside from a few blurry Polaroids Abby had taken during her day of surveillance, none of them had a clear idea of what the boy looked like.

"I would understand," she said slowly, her voice trembling, "if you wanted to dismiss me. Perhaps you should."

Gathering her courage, she looked at Sloane. He had perched on the arm of Trent's chair, a lofty location from which to radiate his disapproval.

A thunderous scowl darkened his brow. "I wouldn't think of dismissing you," he said, rancor sharpening his voice. "You have failed me, Nadine, but I learned long ago that most people tend to learn from their mistakes. You will have one more chance to find my son—and I doubt you'll fail next time."

"Did Lemuel Reis get a second chance?" The question slipped from her tongue before she could stop it.

Sloane flinched, then met her gaze. "Lemuel Reis was a troubled young man. I was deeply disturbed when he took his own life."

Nadine leaned back and lifted her cigarette. She drew heavily on it, then let a thin plume of smoke drift from the side of her mouth. "Of course you were, Devin. Forgive me for bringing it up."

When her employer stood and moved with oiled grace into the privacy of his bedroom, Nadine turned her stare upon Trent, who lifted one shoulder in a shrug. "He's upset," the assistant said, stating the obvious. "Give him time and he'll come around. I know he still believes in you. We all do."

She brought the cigarette to her lips again, but couldn't stop her fingers from trembling. If only Lara Godfrey had money. It wouldn't take much to convince Nadine to switch sides.

chapter 25

The twenty-fourth of December dawned clear and crisp. Connor dressed in jeans and the red sweater Lara had given him, then slipped out of the house and headed to the library. A quiet stillness reigned over the UVA campus; most of the dorms had emptied out a week before, at the beginning of Christmas break. The only students remaining on campus were those too far from home or too poor to travel, and Connor knew they would soon be arriving at the library in search of a morning newspaper and a fresh cup of coffee.

In honor of Christmas Eve, the library would close at lunchtime, but Connor wouldn't have minded working a full day. Christmas was as lonely for him as for the dorm-bound students. His parents had died in the years since Lara left, his mother in the winter of 2001, and his father the following spring. His sister had invited him to spend Christmas with her family in Alaska, but something in him wanted to remain close to the library in case Lara e-mailed him. He had warned her not to contact him through his personal account on AOL, but to send all messages through the library. The UVA reference desk received inquiries from all over the world; even Sloane's people would have a hard time recognizing her messages in the flood of electronic mail.

The library was quiet when he arrived, with most of the staff out on vacation, and Connor imagined that half of his coworkers were milling around in the mall. The other half were probably at home, happily decorating Christmas trees and baking Christmas cookies—things he might have been doing if God had set his feet on a different path. But though sometimes the air in his little house felt thick with the dullness of despair, he did not regret his decision to send Lara and Hunter away. They were safe in Florida, safe even from Devin Sloane.

Though his Sloane project for the FBI had ended three months after Lara disappeared, Connor had continued to collect articles, information, and gossip about Charlottesville's resident billionaire. While the other librarians' computers powered down at night, Connor's combed the Web for new mentions of Sloane's name. Every morning an updated list of Web pages and news reports flashed on Connor's screen.

He poured a cup of coffee, smiled his thanks at Ethel, who had been thoughtful enough to start the antiquated machine, then moved to his computer and tapped the touch pad, waking the machine. The screen flickered as the monitor powered on, and he glimpsed his watchdog screen saver before the password query appeared. He typed in the password, then picked up his coffee and sipped it as the hard drive whirred to life.

The Web spyder had plucked nearly thirty articles from the Web, many of which Connor had seen before. He clicked on the first link, then settled back and frowned at his coffee as the page loaded.

"Ethel, don't we have sugar?" he called over his shoulder, keeping one eye on the monitor.

"We're out of everything," the librarian cheerfully answered. "Martha usually stocks the coffee cabinet, and Martha's—"

"Out for the holidays." Connor finished the thought and leaned toward the screen. The link had taken him to a PR release from the Ethan Jefferson Pediatric Hospital for Genetic Research. According to the report, Dr. Gene Wilkerson, one of the hospital's leading doctors, had successfully cured a child with cystic fibrosis. "We were able to inculcate the patient's lungs with a new gene, one that effectively 'turned off' the defective gene which causes CF," the doctor said. "We have every hope this treatment will soon become available to hospitals across the country. None of our work would have been possible without the generous support of Devin Sloane."

"Three cheers for Saint Devin," Connor murmured, moving to the next article. "What else has the man been up to?"

The next article was about Sloane support for angiogenesis, a treatment in which genetically altered cells were injected into diseased heart muscle. *Doctors at the Ethan Jefferson Pediatric Hospital for Genetic Research have discovered that new cells cause the damaged heart tissue to repair itself, leading some researchers to predict that immortality—or at least longer life—might become a possibility within the next fifty years.*

Intrigued by the prospect, Connor propped his elbow on the desk and studied the screen. Immortality? Sloane had voiced some bizarre opinions in the past, but this was a new wrinkle.

"Excuse me?" A pretty coed stepped up to his desk, a microfilm cassette in her hand. She gave Connor a slanted brow and a pouting smile. "I'm all thumbs when it comes to these things. Can you help me?"

"Sure." Connor left his desk and led the way to the microfilm player. He remembered this girl—she had been hanging around the library for at least a month, asking him to help her find books hidden in plain sight and begging for computer help. Any literate six-year-old could have figured out the computer system by reading the printed instructions, but Connor held his tongue. Even foolish and flirtatious young women had a right to assistance—especially at Christmas.

"Connor?" Ethel Jones waved for his attention, then pointed at the telephone on the reference desk. "Call for you."

"Be right there." Connor took another moment to make certain the coed understood how to thread the microfilm cassette properly; then he moved toward the desk. Telephone callers didn't usually ask for librarians by name, but occasionally a patron he'd helped before made an effort to single him out.

Connor picked up his extension. "Reference desk."

"Connor? It's me." The voice on the other end set his nerves to jangling. He hadn't heard that voice in five years.

"Lara?" Wave after wave of shock slapped at him. This couldn't be good. Lara wouldn't call unless the risk of *not* calling outweighed the risk of contacting him.

He sank into his chair and braced himself for the worst. "What's wrong?"

"They found us yesterday. Hunter and I barely got away."

"Where are you?"

"Roanoke. We flew out last night and I took a hotel room. I figured Sloane would never dream I'd run back to the one state where I could be arrested on sight."

Connor lowered his head as a wave of sheer black fright swept through him. "How did you pay?"

"It's okay—I'm Mary Tobias now. I have set of credit cards in her name, and I used them to pay for the flight and the hotel." She laughed. "You taught me well, Connor. The bills go to a mail drop in Los Angeles. I used the cards a couple of times to establish a pattern."

He took a deep breath. "Okay—how can I help?"

"Can you come here?" Her voice was low and controlled, but Connor heard an undertone of desolation in it. "I hate to ask, but I really need a backup. E-mail won't cut it this time."

He glanced at his watch. Ten o'clock; so he had plenty of time to get to the airport. He could swing by the house and pick up a bag, and get to the hotel before nightfall . . . unless they were watching. He'd have to drive by the house and make sure before going in.

"I'll take the next available flight," he whispered, surveying the reference area. Every person in the library had suddenly taken on a sinister aspect, and he wondered if Sloane's people had thought to cover his movements. They had certainly tailed him the last time they lost Lara.

"We're at the downtown Hilton." Her voice broke with huskiness. "Thank you, Connor. I—we—we can't wait to see you."

"I'll be there tonight."

He hung up the phone, then pulled his jacket from the back of his chair. He could probably drive to Roanoke before he would be able to find a flight, but Sloane's people might be looking for his car. And though the airport was bound to be jammed with holiday travelers, he might be able to fly standby . . .

He leaned into the doorway of the head librarian's office. "Ethel? I'm sorry, but you know those fifty vacation days I've accumulated? I'm taking them all."

Ethel looked up, too surprised to do more than gape at him.

Connor rapped the door frame. "If anyone calls for me, tell them I'll be back in ten weeks or so."

Ethel pressed her hand to her ample chest, her face a study in concern. "Is everything okay?"

Connor gave her an apologetic smile. "It's a family emergency. I'll explain when I return."

Before she could protest, he strode out of the reference area, pushed his way through the glass doors, and braced himself against the blustering wind.

∞

The young man at the hotel registration desk gave Connor a plastic smile. "May I help you, sir?"

"I'm here to meet my wife, Mary Tobias. I believe she's already checked in."

"Certainly, sir." The clerk glanced down at his keyboard, then paused. "I'll need some identification."

Connor automatically reached for his wallet, then froze. He had nothing to indicate he was related in any way to a woman calling herself Mary Tobias.

Act like you know what you're doing.

He opened his wallet, fished out his license, and flipped it over the counter. The clerk eyed the photo, looked up at Connor's face, then frowned as he peered at the name.

"Mr. O'Hara?"

Connor leaned casually against the counter. "My wife is a very modern woman."

The clerk's mouth pulled into a thin-lipped smile. "That's fine, sir. Would you mind if I called to confirm that she expects you?"

"Not at all."

The clerk picked up the phone, punched in a number, and murmured something in a low voice. Connor turned, trying to appear bored and disinterested, though a creeping uneasiness stirred at the bottom of his heart. Had Sloane's people followed Lara? Had they followed him from Charlottesville?

His gaze drifted over the people gathering, greeting, and waiting in the large lobby. A group of businessmen in dark suits huddled over drinks at a corner table; a grandmotherly woman struggled under the weight of Christmas packages while next to her a younger woman tried to restrain a squirming toddler. Across the tiled lobby, a dripping teenage girl darted by in bare feet and a towel under the concierge's disapproving eye—

"Connor?"

Electrified by the sound of her voice, he turned. Lara stood by the door, brunette and beautiful, her brows raised. A blue-eyed boy clung to her hand, his head crowned with a cap of shining blond hair.

Within a moment she was in his arms, one hand warming his neck, her cheek soft against his. He rubbed her back, conscious of the clerk's eyes upon them, then pulled away and gave her a quick kiss.

"Thanks, but I don't think I'll be needing your help," he called to the clerk as he slipped his arm around Lara's waist. They must have looked like any other happy couple, an ordinary husband and wife catching up after a brief separation.

The clerk smiled and hung up the phone, then turned his attention to the next guest.

Connor saw the question in Lara's eyes. "I told him I was your husband."

"That's not true." Hunter's voice rang through the lobby, cutting through the noise of passing guests and noisy luggage carts.

Connor looked at Lara, but she only took his hand and pulled him toward the parking lot.

"I've already rented a car," she said, reaching out to Hunter with her free hand. "I'll explain everything as we drive. We have a lot to tell you."

∞

Hunter slept on a faded couch while Lara and Connor feasted on fried chicken in a country cabin well off the main roads. She had been afraid of late-breaking news reports, Lara explained, and the hotel was too crowded and too public a place. So she'd searched a local phone directory and called a real estate agent about renting a cabin for a week. The owner of this little place had been happy to rent it over the holiday, and he had taken Mary Tobias's credit card number without hesitation.

"I arranged the whole thing over the phone," she said, wiping her hands on a towelette, "so he doesn't even know what I look like."

Delighted by how well she'd done, Connor grinned at her. "You're getting good at this," he mumbled around a chicken leg.

"I had a good teacher."

A fire burned in the blackened fireplace while carols played from the old black-and-white television in the corner. With a shock Connor remembered the date—Christmas Eve. Despite the tense circumstances, he couldn't think of a better way to spend the holiday. Lara seemed to have relaxed since they entered the cabin, and Hunter had promptly fallen asleep on the sofa. Lara sat next to her son, one hand occasionally brushing his hair as if to reassure herself he was safe.

On the floor, Connor sat on an orange shag carpet that had probably been installed at the peak of the Monkees' popularity. "Do you remember that other Christmas?" he asked, wrapping his hand around his cup of diet soda. He felt a subterranean quiver go through him when she smiled. What was wrong with him? He was as nervous as a sixteen-year-old on a first date, yet he had delivered this woman's baby!

"The Christmas before Hunter was born?" Laughing softly, she leaned her elbow on the arm of the couch, then rested her cheek against her palm. "How could I forget? You decorated that entire tree in booties and rattles. It was the most creative tree I'd ever seen in my life."

"Yet none of those things did you any good." Connor lowered his cup, then rubbed his damp hand against his jeans. "I felt so bad about sending you away with so little. I can only imagine how difficult those first few weeks must have been."

"The experience was good for me. I learned how unimportant *things* really are." She looked down, her lashes hiding her eyes. "Those first weeks were tough, but God helped us through those times. He seemed to guide my steps, and I was more fortunate than a lot of women who might have been in the same situation. I had skills, and you had given me the tools I needed to make a fresh start. Any guilt I felt about my false identity paled in comparison to my fear that Sloane might find us."

"But he didn't."

"No, but I was still scared. I used to run from the craziest things. Once when I was standing in line at K-Mart waiting for a baby photographer, I realized that the setup was an ideal way to search for kids of Hunter's age. So I pulled him out of the line and ran through the parking lot like a madwoman. I worked in five different hospitals or nursing homes while I lived in Pinellas County, and I moved us to a different trailer park every year so we wouldn't get attached. It meant less money, because I never stayed in any place long enough to build seniority, but I had already learned that *things* don't matter. People do."

Connor set his cup on the floor and reached for the suitcase he had packed in a hurry. He withdrew a brown paper bag and handed it to Lara.

A smile crinkled the corner of her eyes. "A Christmas present?"

"Something like that." He thrust his hands in his pockets. "When the landlady insisted I empty your apartment, I couldn't stand the thought of not keeping anything for you. So I kept this, because it was one of my favorites. I hope it was one of yours."

She reached into the bag and pulled out one of Michael's better watercolors. The framed picture depicted the sunlit park as brilliant with spangled foliage, accented by the pond shimmering against the distant horizon.

Her blue eyes softened. "Mirror Lake in Summer."

"I donated most of your things to your church thrift store." He sank back to the floor. "I gave the other paintings to Michael's mother. She was thrilled, and who knows? Maybe Michael will still be famous some day."

"I doubt it." Lara's mouth curved with tenderness as she set the painting on the wooden end table. "Michael was a good artist, but I don't think he would have ever been *great*. All the great ones seem to be troubled, dark souls, and Michael was too happy. Too content. And with Eva's money behind him, he never had to worry about actually *selling* any of his work." She shifted her position and tucked her feet under the crocheted afghan on the sofa, then looked down at her sleeping son. "But thank you,

Connor, I appreciate the gift. Hunter likes to draw pictures, too, and some of them are about as good as Michael's. Not that Hunter is terribly artistic—but I've come to realize Michael really wasn't."

Connor ran his fingers through the stiff carpet, not sure how to broach the subject of the boy's genetic manipulation. Hunter seemed like a normal little boy, but from the guarded look in Lara's eye, Connor suspected there was something . . .

"What about Hunter? Is he . . . what you expected?"

She looked down at her son, the fringe of her lashes hiding her eyes. "Hunter is unique."

"Of course. He's your son."

"No—he's *really* special. I don't know what Devin Sloane and Dr. Braun expected from their bizarre experiment, but I'm not sure if they'd appreciate what I've discovered. Hunter's gift isn't great strength or knowledge or health, though he is a bright kid and a fairly healthy one." She looked up, and the look in her eyes pierced Connor's soul. "He judges truth."

He stared at her, baffled. "I don't understand."

She grimaced in good humor. "I can't explain it, either, but I noticed it when he first began to talk. If I ever told him something that wasn't quite true—you know, something like 'Hunter, be a good boy or Mommy will never buy cookies again,' he'd look at me in dead seriousness and say 'no.'" At first I thought he was just bent on saying 'no' to everything, then one afternoon I realized he wasn't rebelling—he was *disagreeing*."

A trace of unguarded tenderness shone in her eyes as she looked toward her sleeping child. "When he became a little more verbal, he'd say, 'That's not the truth, Mommy.' One afternoon he was watching a television preacher who said God wanted everyone to be rich. Hunter looked right at the television and yelled, 'That's not true!' and I—well, I nearly fell off the couch."

A smile nudged itself into a corner of her mouth. "You probably think I'm crazy, but others have seen it too. His kindergarten teacher noticed it, and the manager of our trailer park. Hunter can tell when people are lying—and that's the only reason we escaped yesterday. A deputy sheriff was checking cars that entered our trailer park, and by the time I saw him it was too late to turn back. I asked him what the trouble was and he said something about skateboarders. He lied, and Hunter knew it."

Connor experienced a blank moment as a swarm of thoughts buzzed in his brain; then he scratched his chin. "But truth is sometimes subjective, Lara. This ability can't be infallible. If I *believe* something, I'm likely to sound sincere, and my beliefs become truth to me. That's why lie detectors aren't admissible in court. They can't judge between subjective and observed truth."

Lara shook her head. "What you believe doesn't matter. Hunter seems to be clued in on some universal truth, and sincerity doesn't sway him. Last summer we ran into a group of Buddhists at the beach. One young man stopped to give Hunter a flower and he said something like, 'All paths lead to God, little boy.' I don't doubt that he was sincere, but Hunter stared at him and very politely said, 'That's a great big lie.'"

Connor stared at her, then burst out laughing.

Lara tilted her brow. "You think I'm kidding? I remember his words exactly because that was such an unusual thing for a kid to say. I've never talked to him about Buddhism, yet he seemed to know what God himself would say in that moment."

She shivered slightly and rubbed her hands over her arms. "Sometimes his ability frightens me a little. I'm not afraid of *him*, for he's a sweet and obedient boy—not perfect by any means, but completely truthful. I'm more afraid of what might happen to him if Sloane finds us."

Connor leaned back against a chair and rested his arms on his bent knees. His thoughts darkened as ideas he dared not verbalize whirled within. Lara had every right to be frightened, but the world posed more danger than Devin Sloane. If she was correct about Hunter's unique gift, what would the world do with such a child? A human truth detector— the concept was staggering. Some would disbelieve and seek to discredit Hunter; others might want to worship and elevate him as some sort of evolved human being. Bald truth, unadorned and uncompromising, was politically incorrect. Diplomacy was the language of this century and inoffensiveness its creed. People who feared truth the most were those who held the most dangerous secrets . . . and the means to protect them.

Those thoughts had barely crossed his mind before another followed. If Hunter was somehow tapped into the source of truth, how had the connection been made? Was genetics solely responsible . . . or something else?

Outside, the sun had begun to set, sending streamers of blue-veiled twilight into the room. Connor stretched out on the floor, then looked at Lara through the fire-tinted darkness. "Do you remember what we talked about that last Christmas we were together? We wondered when Jesus understood his mission and how much he realized as a child."

A melancholy frown flitted across her features. "I can't tell you how many times I've thought of that conversation. But Hunter is not the Son of God. He's fully human and he's not perfect. He disobeys sometimes, he loses his temper, and he can't seem to learn the difference between an inside voice and an outside voice. But I can honestly say he's never told me a lie. And I have never, ever known him to be wrong when he says someone else is lying."

Connor opened his mouth to protest, then suddenly clamped it shut. Lara was one of the most sensible women he knew, and if she said Hunter was never wrong, he had to believe her. After all, just yesterday she had staked her life on Hunter's gift.

"We'll take some time to think about this." He turned and rested his arm on the seat of the chair behind him. "Why don't you come over here. You look like you could use a shoulder to lean on."

She came without hesitation, taking her place beneath his arm and resting her head on his chest. He cradled her gently, stroking her hair while he prayed for wisdom and the words to ease her burden. "Lara, honey, you've come so incredibly far. For some reason, God has given you this boy, unique though he may be. I suppose the best thing to do is trust God to show you what to do next."

Her body shook in a dry, choked way, but she did not weep. "I'm so tired. So tired of running. And I can't help but see the irony in my situation—I have a son who tells the truth, and I'm forcing him to live a lie."

Connor's spinning thoughts came to an abrupt halt. "What have you told him about his father? If he can tell when you're hiding the truth—"

"I told him that God is a father to the fatherless." She turned the catch in her voice into a soft cough and went on. "That is the truth, and he's never questioned it."

Connor settled back, enjoying the feel of her in his arms. The television's gray light blended with the orange glow of the fire, and Lara's breathing relaxed and deepened as the local news came on. Silence, calm and peaceful, filled the room as the news anchors bantered with each other and wished their audience a merry Christmas.

The news reports were brief and mostly nonviolent. A traffic accident had snarled I-75 through downtown Atlanta; a snowstorm over Chicago had stalled twelve hundred holiday travelers departing from O'Hare. The president and first lady had tucked themselves away at Camp David to observe the holiday with their children, and the mayor of Roanoke used the occasion of his community Christmas concert to call for peace and racial harmony.

Connor was beginning to think Lara had fallen asleep until Devin Sloane's face flashed on the screen. "This just in from Florida," the news anchor said, her eyes wide as she read the teleprompter. "Financier Devin Sloane nearly brought his son home for Christmas, but the woman formerly known as Lara Godfrey slipped away from police yesterday. Living in Osceola as Rose Shepard, the woman and her five-year-old son led police on a four-hour chase before disappearing into the throngs of holiday tourists."

"That's certainly not the truth." Lara's voice cracked the silence. "I drove to the beach and took a taxi to the Tampa airport. I was out of Pinellas County in less than thirty minutes."

A photo of Lara appeared next. It was an old photograph from her Charlottesville days, when she wore her hair long and blonde. She must have been pregnant in the picture, for her face was rounder.

"Is it true that blondes have more fun?" he quipped, not taking his eyes from the screen.

"The jury's still out on that one," she answered, sitting upright. "Being a redhead wasn't bad, though. I tried that for about a year."

"If you have seen this woman," the reporter said, "please call the National Center for Missing and Exploited Children at 800-555-3957."

Lara's photo disappeared, replaced immediately by a shot of Hunter.

Alarm rippled over Lara's face. "No! How'd they get his picture? I was so careful!"

The news report continued: "The woman will be traveling with this child. The boy is blond, blue-eyed, and approximately three feet, nine inches tall."

"The kindergarten." Lara groaned and dropped her head to her hands. "School picture day—why didn't I think?"

Connor ran his hand over her back. "It's okay. We're safe here and we'll think of something."

She lifted her head but remained upright and tense as the news broke for a commercial. "Hunter deserves better than this," she muttered. "Children need security and stability. This isn't good for him."

"He seems happy."

"He is—but you wouldn't notice the things I've seen. He has begun to walk on the outside of one foot, so I need to take him to the pediatrician to see if he needs orthopedic shoes. And I think the stress is getting to him—sometimes I see him grimace for no reason. It's like a nervous tic. He doesn't even know he's doing it."

Connor searched for soothing words and found none. The television news anchors lit up the corner of the room again, and this time the screen filled with images of children milling around a smiling Santa who wore the traditional red suit minus the white beard. This Santa's beard was short-clipped and silver.

The news reporter explained why. "I'm here with Roanoke attorney Franklin Blythe," she told the camera, her eyes sparkling, "who, when he's not practicing law, devotes his time to the city's less fortunate children. Attorney Blythe collects contributions from his clients during the year and distributes those gifts each Christmas Eve."

The camera zoomed in on Santa, whose dark eyes twinkled above a gentle smile. Moving through a group of youngsters, he pulled gaily wrapped packages from a huge black bag and placed them in the hands of grateful youngsters.

"Did you ever tell Hunter about Santa Claus?" Connor asked, hoping to distract Lara from the news.

She lifted one shoulder in a shrug. "How could I? I tried to once, but he wouldn't even consider a story about a man coming down the chimney." Her smile deepened as she glanced toward her son. "Not that we had a chimney, living in a mobile home. When I realized he would never accept the myth, I told him the truth about Saint Nicholas. He accepted that story, but he never wanted to visit the Santas we saw at the mall."

She turned back to the television and sighed. "Although," she whispered, her voice softening, "I think *that* Santa is the kind of man Hunter could believe in. Look at him, Connor—what drives a man to spend his Christmas Eve with children he doesn't even know?" She turned, her steady gaze boring into him. "What brought you here to help us, when we haven't seen you in years? You should have gone on with your life; you should have told me you had other plans. I didn't want to drag you away on Christmas Eve when you could have gone to visit your parents—"

"Hush." Entranced by the sadness in her eyes, he brushed the back of his fingers along her cheek. "Don't you know life stopped for me when you left? I struggled, too, just to get through the day, until you sent me that first e-mail. Then life had meaning again, because I could help you. Because you needed me."

"I always will." She leaned back, nestling beneath his arm again. "I'm tired of running and I'm tired of living without you." She chuckled with a dry and cynical sound. "I think I'm tired of being a lying Baptist. It's time to tell the truth."

A pulse beat and swelled at the base of her throat, as though her heart had risen from its usual place. Connor pressed his fingertip to that pulse point, luxuriating in the texture of her satin skin. The touch of her breath sent an involuntary chill through him, and his heart thudded in response.

His lips brushed her cheek. "It's time to stop running." Lifting his head, he gazed into her eyes and found the answer he'd sought for years.

Lara Godfrey had come home.

chapter 26

Franklin Blythe closed the door of his BMW, then tugged on his jacket and studied the slanting cabin. A rusting mailbox gaped openmouthed at the edge of the drive, and the space that passed for a front lawn was black and heavy with sodden leaves.

He'd driven all the way out here for only one reason—the desperate woman on the phone had claimed to be Lara Godfrey, the surrogate mother running from Devin Sloane. Ordinarily he would have told her to return to Charlottesville and find a lawyer practicing family law there, but as they spoke he heard something. So, on the day after Christmas, he stood outside an apparently deserted cabin and wondered why in the world he had agreed to this meeting.

A curtain moved near the front window. He was being watched. The woman had insisted he come alone, and he wondered what he would do if she proved to be some crazy who saw Devin Sloane as an opportunity to cash in an unwanted kid. The news reports had said that Lara Godfrey was a medical professional, but Franklin couldn't imagine any professional living in a dump like this.

He hunched forward against the chilly wind and moved toward the sagging front door, the brown-black leaves slippery beneath his feet. A beige sedan sat in the graveled sludge that passed for a driveway, the Hertz bumper sticker revealing that the car was a rental. He glanced around the yard. No sign of toys, tricycles, or tree houses. That was good. If Lara Godfrey was inside, she wouldn't have had time to accumulate the typical amount of kiddy debris.

He mounted the concrete steps to the porch, then rapped on the door. In an instant, a man opened it, his handsome face splitting into a smile.

"Well, I'll be." He stepped back so Franklin could enter. "I didn't think you'd come."

Franklin stepped inside and removed his gloves, trying not to be obvious as he scanned his surroundings. Perhaps these people had seen him on TV and decided to hold him for ransom. Not that they'd get any great reward for his return, but Harriet would have a stroke if Franklin didn't return in time to take her to the mall to exchange the too-small dress he'd given her for Christmas.

The man at the door laughed. "Don't worry, Lara's not Ma Barker. We're not armed and we're not dangerous. But we are in danger."

Franklin flushed. "You've roused my curiosity, Mr.—?"

"Connor O'Hara." The man extended his hand and shook Franklin's. "It's nice to meet you. I'm a friend of Lara Godfrey's."

Franklin nodded as he surveyed the living space. A few K-Mart bags littered one corner of the room, and a child-sized pair of jeans lay on the couch alongside two bright sweaters. A fire crackled noisily in a stone fireplace against the wall, and a newspaper had been neatly folded by the side of an easy chair. A small box of Fruit Loops sat on the kitchen table, and Franklin smiled at the ordinariness of it. Years ago his own son had loved Fruit Loops.

"We arrived here on Christmas Eve," O'Hara said, gesturing for Franklin to take a seat on the couch. "Lara flew straight from Tampa and brought nothing with her. I came in from Charlottesville and went out this morning for a few things. But we don't intend to stay here long."

Franklin eased onto the sofa, then felt the poke of springs through his wool trousers. Shifting his weight, he asked, "What do you intend to do next?"

"That, Mr. Blythe, depends entirely upon you."

The woman's voice startled him, and Franklin jerked toward the sound as a door opened from the dark hallway. He noted the heart-shaped face, the tilted eyes, the pointed chin—no matter what the hair color or style, he would have recognized this woman as the notorious Lara Godfrey. Behind her stood a small blond boy, his face half-hidden by his mother's denim skirt.

Franklin stood and offered his hand, which she accepted with a gentle smile. "Thank you for coming. I'm so grateful we saw you on TV the other night. That's when I knew we were supposed to contact you."

"I'm still a little confused as to why you called me. My practice is in Roanoke, and I don't deal with high-profile cases. If you're looking for someone to represent you, I really don't think I'm the best choice."

"I think you are," she answered, her voice calm, her gaze steady. "But before we talk further, I'd like you to meet Hunter."

She turned slightly and prodded the little boy forward. He stepped into the open space between Franklin and his mother and for a moment Franklin had the eerie feeling he was gazing into the wary eyes of a much older child.

"'Lo," he said, twisting his hands at his waist.

Franklin clasped his hands, too. "Hello, Hunter. My name is Mr. Blythe." Despite his reluctance to involve himself, his heart flowed toward the child. "You can call me Mr. Franklin."

The boy nodded soberly, a sheaf of wheat-blond hair falling across his forehead. "Okay." His blue eyes darted toward O'Hara, who had taken a seat in a battered easy chair by the fireplace. "Do you like Connor?"

Franklin glanced toward O'Hara, then laughed. "I suppose I do. But we've just met. It takes time to really know a person."

The boy nodded again, gravely considering this information. "Do you like my mom?"

Franklin kept his eyes on the boy. "Yes, I do. She seems like a very nice lady."

The boy returned his smile in full measure. "She was praying for you to come, and you did. She says God sent you to us."

"Does she?" Franklin glanced up at the woman, expecting to see a blush or some sign of denial, but she merely removed the jeans and sweaters from the couch and gestured for Franklin to have a seat.

"Mom tells the truth," Hunter said, moving closer. "And so do you."

"I try." Franklin sank to the couch and tilted his head, trying to analyze the quality that drew him to this boy. He had worked with charming children before, adorable and verbal preschoolers who won his heart along with his compassion, but none had ever fascinated him like this boy. There was something in the child's eyes . . .

"Mr. Blythe," Lara Godfrey sat at the sofa's opposite end, "Hunter and I would like you to represent us in our case against Devin Sloane. I need you to agree before I begin, though, because the story I'm about to tell you cannot leave this room . . . for Hunter's sake."

Still watching the boy, Franklin exhaled slowly. He didn't need a surrogacy case; he had absolutely no experience in such matters. Sloane probably had an entire firm of legal experts working for him. Franklin would be blown out of the water before he even presented his opening statement.

But if the woman had prayed . . .

"I'd like to hear your story." He extended his palm to the boy, who grinned and slapped it with the exuberance of an NBA player after a three-point shot.

"That's my cue." Connor O'Hara rose, then scooped the boy into his arms. "Come on, buddy, let's take a walk so your mother can talk to Mr. Blythe. Do you think we can spot a redheaded woodpecker? I thought I heard one knocking last night."

"That's not true!" Connor yelled, his voice fading into a cascade of giggles as Connor rubbed his stubbled chin across the boy's belly. "Ouch! That tickles!"

Lara Godfrey waited until her friend and her son had left the cabin; then she shifted on the couch and ran her hand over the faded upholstery. "It all began because I wanted to have my husband's child," she said, managing a tentative smile. "My late husband and I had often spoken of children, and we were quite sure a baby was part of God's plan for us . . ."

She talked for an hour, and Franklin listened, amazed, as her story filled his head with a series of images and bizarre possibilities. She ended by telling him of the boy's special gift, and Franklin sat for a long time in stunned silence, realizing that he'd been on trial since the moment he crossed the threshold. The child had judged him and found him truthful.

When he finally found his voice, he met Lara Godfrey's direct gaze. "Do you mind if I talk to the boy? If we're going to court with this story, I'd like to know the full extent of his abilities."

"We'll go to court with you, Mr. Blythe, but we will not expose my son." She smiled, but a silken thread of warning lined her voice. "I won't have people prodding, testing, or manipulating him. He is a five-year-old boy, not a science experiment. That's why we must defeat Devin Sloane on *his* evidence. He says that a surrogate arrangement existed between us, but that's not true. If he produces a contract to prove his contention, the contract was created after Hunter was conceived. If he produces witnesses, they'll be liars."

"Let me play devil's advocate for a moment." Franklin's gaze settled on her, analyzing her reaction. "What do we have to *disprove* Sloane's assertions?"

"We have Hunter." She spoke in a firm, final voice. "And we have the truth."

"If you return to Charlottesville," Franklin clasped his hands, "you will be subject to the judge's pickup order, so you will be immediately taken into custody. I can go to the judge before you arrive and try to arrange some sort of surrender, but I'm certain Sloane's people will want you in custody or at least under some kind of bond. You've proven you're a flight risk, so the judge may not allow you to retain custody if Sloane convinces him you will run again."

"I won't run, but I will not let that monster have my son!" Her voice rose, but, thankfully, the front door creaked and broke the rising tension in the room. O'Hara and Hunter stamped their way into the house, their faces flushed with cold.

O'Hara's gaze swept over the woman's face. "Everything all right?"

Lara Godfrey took a deep breath. "Everything's fine and we're glad you're back." She gave O'Hara a quick smile, then touched Franklin's arm. "I'm sorry, Mr. Blythe, but this is frustrating." She spoke slowly now, measuring each word, and Franklin realized she was mindful of the listening boy. Hunter seemed to pay no attention, however. He plopped down on the rug by the fire and pulled a pair of rocks from his pocket. As O'Hara tossed a fresh log onto the crackling fire, the little boy pushed the rocks through the long shag carpeting and made low, vrooming sounds.

"Tell us what would happen," Lara continued, her voice low, "if we *willingly* went back to Charlottesville to face Sloane's lawsuit."

Franklin opened his hands. "It's nearly impossible to say, but I can hazard a guess. Since it's a civil suit, if we go to the court before they act on the pickup order, you won't be arrested unless they can prove you broke a law in the state of Virginia."

Her face remained impassive. "And then?"

"Sloane's lawyer will want to be certain you don't run again, so the judge will probably require you to post bond. I expect the amount will be about $50,000, but it could be higher if Sloane's lawyers force the issue."

She caught her breath. "And if I can't afford that?"

Franklin looked down at the boy. "If you can't post bond, they may ask you to surrender the child. Custody could be granted to a foster home, the plaintiff, or a guardian ad litem." He heard her gasp, then rushed to assure her. "I don't think they'd grant custody to Sloane if we tell the judge what you've told me. I don't see how any compassionate person could do that."

Her expression twisted in the desperate lines of a hunted animal. "But Sloane has power and money. If we go to trial, I risk losing Hunter, and I can't let Sloane have him."

Franklin heard a dull clang as O'Hara dropped the poker he'd been using to adjust the logs. "I may know an answer," he said, looking at Franklin.

"I'd love to hear your thoughts."

The line of Connor's mouth clamped tight for a moment; then his throat bobbed as he moved toward Lara Godfrey. "Lara"—his eyes shone with apprehension and concern—"I have roots in the community, and the court will know I'm not a flight risk. This may not be the most romantic proposal in the world, but I'd love it if you'd marry me. Let me be your husband and let Hunter become my son. Marry me, and I promise I'll love you both forever."

Franklin lifted both brows and turned to Lara, who stared at O'Hara with her lips parted. Her eyes, which a moment ago had been direct and focused, were now as soft and dreamy as a summer sky.

Franklin smiled, recognizing the look of a woman in love. He slapped his hands on his knees. "I believe that is a remarkably creative solution."

"But if we get married now, here"—Lara's eyes clouded with confusion—"won't that lead Sloane to us? If I marry under my real name, there'll be a public record."

"You'll have a few days lead time," Franklin answered. "And you're going to face Sloane anyway, so there's no risk. Beat them at their own game, Lara. Stand up to them." He shifted and smiled down at the boy, who was staring at his mother with wide eyes. "Hunter, would you like to walk with me out to my car? I believe I may have a special Christmas gift for you in the trunk."

The boy's blue eyes widened further, then cut a quick glance to his mother. "Can I go, Mom?"

Lara turned slightly, a blush staining her cheek. "Yes, buddy." She stood with Franklin and squeezed his arm before smiling at her son. "Be sure to thank Mr. Franklin, okay?"

The boy stood and trotted happily toward Franklin, who took his hand and led him out onto the slanting wooden porch. A soft whispering echoed from the room behind him, and Franklin closed the door, leaving the two lovers alone.

"Well." He looked at the boy by his side. "I believe we're going to be seeing quite a bit of each other. I'm going to help your Mom and Mr. O'Hara so you can live in one place for a long, long time."

Hunter grinned, happiness sticking out all over him like porcupine quills. "I'd like that," he said, pulling Franklin toward the car.

"You know," Franklin said, following the boy, "I do believe you're telling the truth."

∞

Inside the cabin, Lara tried to force her confused emotions into order. "Connor"—her hand rose to his face and caressed it gently—"do you know what you've just done?"

"I asked you and Hunter to marry me." His brown eyes melted into hers. "And you didn't say no. So I guess that means you agree."

"I just want to be sure that *you're* sure." She lowered her hand to his shoulder. "I'm not the usual girl next door. And Hunter's not exactly the average kid."

His hand reached up and caught hers. "I love you, Lara. I let you go once, but I won't go through that kind of torment again. I want to be with you and Hunter, all the way, no matter what happens. We'll confront Sloane and, God willing, we'll settle this thing and get on with our lives."

She listened to him as her heart swelled with a feeling she had thought long dead. How could she have walked away five years ago? Connor had been every bit as brave, courageous, and noble when Hunter was born, but she had been so focused on the baby that she hadn't had the insight to realize that the most incredible man in the world was spending his heart and life for *her*.

How could she not love this man? He loved her, and he would protect Hunter with his life.

"Of course I'll marry you, Mr. O'Hara," she whispered, stepping forward to bury her face against his throat. "As soon as possible; you name the day."

And then, as her arms slipped around his neck, he lifted her from the floor, his hands tight under her knees and shoulders, as solid as his promise he would never let her go.

chapter 27

Nadine Harrington swallowed hard, trying not to reveal her frustration as yet another Tampa airline clerk handed her a report. "We had thirty standby passengers December twenty-fourth," the clerk said, tapping the printout with a manicured fingernail. "Eighteen male passengers, fourteen women, two children under twelve." She snapped her gum. "Most of them were college kids or businesspeople trying to get home for Christmas."

"I'm interested in a woman traveling with a child." Nadine scanned the list. "She would have flown out sometime after five o'clock."

"We only have three flights out after five." The young woman shifted her weight and pulled on her earlobe as if she were bored. "One to Winston-Salem, one to Dallas, one to Miami."

"This one." Nadine tapped the list. "Mary Tobias, traveling with a child, Taylor." She frowned at the string of ticket codes. "I see she went to Winston-Salem, but where after that?"

The clerk craned her neck to look at the passenger manifest, then nodded. "Yeah. That's Roanoke, Virginia. She woulda got in at 9:05 that night."

"Thanks." Nadine tossed the printout back, then turned and left the office. The pieces fit, but Lara Godfrey's chutzpah surprised her. What in the world would drive her back to Virginia?

She considered the question for a moment, then laughed. There were two things, Nadine had decided, that motivated every human being—love and money. Lara Godfrey had gone back to Virginia to find one or both.

❦

On Sunday morning, after church services at the Roanoke Community Chapel had concluded, Connor took Lara's hand and led her to the front of the church. Standing before God, Hunter, Franklin and Harriet Blythe, and a few stragglers, he listened to the minister explain the mystery and meaning of marriage.

The minister lifted his gaze above the spectacles on the end of his nose. "Do you, Connor O'Hara"—he blinked in the lights—"take this woman to be your lawfully wedded wife?"

"I do." Connor squeezed Lara's hand and turned to face her. Her soft, earnest eyes sought his as if to ask again, *Are you sure about this?* He squeezed her hand again. They'd stayed awake half the night discussing strategy with Mr. Blythe; then the lawyer left and Connor spent the rest of the night convincing Lara that his proposal was based upon more than concern for Hunter. He loved her. He confessed that he had loved her since the day she first asked him if he thought she'd make a good mother. He had known even then that she'd make a wonderful wife.

"Do you, Lara Godfrey"—the minister paused, his brow wrinkling as if the name rang a distant bell—"take this man to be your lawfully wedded husband?"

Her wet eyes glistened. "I do."

"Do you have a ring?"

Caught unaware, Connor stared at the minister for a moment, then remembered. Hunter stood at his side, the delicate Black Hills Gold band taped to a white satin pillow. Connor pressed his hand to Hunter's back as he pulled the ring free of the tape, then slipped the circle of gold onto Lara's finger, grateful that she hadn't minded using his former Christmas gift as a wedding band.

The minister nodded in approval. "By the powers vested in me by the commonwealth of Virginia and this county, I pronounce you man and wife." The minister stepped back, clasped his hands, and smiled at Connor. "You may now kiss your bride."

Connor dropped Lara's hands and lifted the edge of her veil, then smiled as Harriet Blythe sniffed from the front pew. The lawyer's wife had been miffed that her husband missed their shopping appointment, but after learning about the wedding, she had graciously offered to loan her wedding dress and veil so Lara could be married in something other than a denim skirt or her nurse's uniform.

Connor pushed the cloud of veiling away, then took Lara in his arms and kissed away the loneliness of five long years. For a moment he forgot everything but the feel of her lips against his, and then Hunter's voice rang through the nearly empty sanctuary. "Oh my goodness, they're kissing!"

Laughter pulled them apart, and then Connor extended his hand to Hunter. "Come on, buddy." He paused to thank the minister, then turned to Mr. and Mrs. Blythe. "We're all yours." He gripped Lara's hand. "Tell us what to do. We're ready."

Franklin linked his wife's arm through his. "My wife and I want to take Hunter with us tonight so you and Lara can have a honeymoon. Hunter will be safe with us. I'll leave for Charlottesville tomorrow morning and make an appointment with the judge appointed to Devin Sloane's case."

"We'll go with you to Charlottesville," Lara said. "I don't want Sloane to think I'm afraid of him."

A grin overtook the lawyer's features as his eyes met Lara's. "All right. Enjoy tonight with your husband, let Harriet take care of Hunter, and leave the legal work to me. I'll call the cabin when I have news; then you can pick up your boy and drive to Charlottesville."

Connor felt Lara grip his arm with her free hand; then she reached down to ruffle Hunter's hair. "Mrs. Blythe is going to take good care of you," she told her son, her voice brimming with love. "You don't have to worry about anything, buddy."

For an instant the boy's face clouded as if he doubted her words, then his pink mouth curled in a one-sided smile. "Okay, Mom."

Mrs. Blythe chuckled as Hunter stepped forward to take her hand. "What fun!" she trilled, patting her ample bosom as she bent to meet

Hunter's gaze. "Did you know I have a grandson about your age? I love him so much, but he lives far away. We have a closet, though, stuffed with toys for a little boy like you."

Connor held his breath, half-expecting Hunter to weigh Mrs. Blythe's words and pronounce the woman guilty of gross exaggeration, but apparently the woman spoke the truth. Hunter's brows lifted; then he moved toward the door, tugging the lawyer's wife behind him.

"He'll be fine." Franklin met Connor's gaze. "Harriet understands this is a sensitive situation. She'll keep him inside the house, safe and out of sight."

Lara dropped Connor's arm, then stepped forward and kissed the lawyer on the cheek. "We thank God for you."

As a tide of dusky red crept up the lawyer's throat, Connor placed his hands on Lara's shoulders. "We'll be at the cabin if you need us."

The lawyer grinned broadly, then winked at Connor. "Congratulations, son. You'll make a fine family."

Connor wrapped his arms around Lara's shoulders, holding her tight as she bit her lip and waved at Hunter with a false show of bravado. He felt a trembling from deep inside her and realized she had probably never been separated from her son. When you've risked your life to keep someone safe, it isn't easy to let that someone walk away . . .

He knew how much it hurt to let go. But God had brought Lara back and this time Connor wouldn't let go no matter what Sloane threatened.

With Hunter walking between Harriet and Franklin, the Blythes passed through the sanctuary doors and stepped out of sight. The stragglers and the minister had disappeared too, leaving Lara and Connor alone in the quiet sanctuary.

Connor gently turned her to face him. "There you go"—he stepped back and smoothed the billowing veil at the crown of her head—"changing your name again."

Tears sparkled in her lashes, but a sweet smile trembled on her lips. "Lara O'Hara," she whispered, moving closer. She placed her hand on the front of his shirt and lifted her gaze to meet his. "It's about time I made that name change, wouldn't you agree?"

When Connor kissed her, it again seemed to him that he, too, had finally come home.

§§

On Monday afternoon, Nadine, Trent Bishop, and Devin Sloane booked a suite at the Roanoke Hilton. Through interviews with a cabdriver and hotel personnel, Nadine had traced Lara Godfrey to this hotel, but apparently she had fled after meeting her "husband" in the lobby.

"The so-called husband has to be Connor O'Hara," Nadine insisted, crossing her legs as she shifted on the sofa to face Sloane. "We talked to a woman in the UVA library who says O'Hara left abruptly on December twenty-fourth, two hours before closing time. He said something about taking his accumulated vacation days for a family emergency, then took off without giving her any idea where he was going."

"The child has to be in the area." Sloane walked to the bar, one hand in his pocket, his brow furrowed. "But why would Lara come here? Why not go to Richmond or Charlottesville or Lynchburg?" He looked at Nadine. "Does she have family in Roanoke?"

"No." Nadine looked at Trent. "But Connor O'Hara's parents used to live in Lynchburg, and that's only an hour's drive from here. She might have hoped to distract us by coming here when she intended to rendezvous with O'Hara in Lynchburg. I'll drive over there this afternoon and check out the old homestead—"

"Listen!" Lifting his hand in an abrupt gesture, Trent raised the television remote and jacked up the volume. Nadine felt her blood chill when Lara Godfrey's image filled the screen.

"This just in," the CNN reporter was saying. "Authorities in Charlottesville, Virginia, are reporting that Lara Godfrey, the surrogate mother who allegedly fled with billionaire Devin Sloane's child, has made an appearance at the Charlottesville District Court with her attorney, Franklin Blythe. With Ms. Godfrey this afternoon was her new husband, Connor O'Hara, a Charlottesville librarian who previously denied having any knowledge of Ms. Godfrey's whereabouts."

Sloane cursed softly. "How does she manage to stay one step ahead of us?"

"Not to worry," Trent said, his eyes fixed to the television. "Jarvis is in Charlottesville; he'll take care of this. He'll have things well in hand by the time we fly back."

The news cut to a video clip of Lara Godfrey—brunette, short-haired, and thin—as she climbed the courthouse steps flanked by two men. Nadine recognized Connor O'Hara immediately—the intervening years had done nothing to diminish that man's rugged appeal. His arm was securely wrapped around Lara's waist, his body language warning away anyone who would threaten her. The other man was a cherubic-looking gentleman with rosy cheeks above a manicured silver beard.

Sloane let out an audible hiss. "Why doesn't she just give up? She told Braun she didn't want any child but her husband's, so why has she put me through this?"

"She probably came to love him—" Trent began, but Sloane silenced him with a snap of his fingers. "She wants money."

Nadine bit the inside of her lip, amazed at the man's blindness. If Lara Godfrey had wanted money, she would have dangled the boy like bait for a hungry fish. She would not have dropped off the face of the planet.

"All right, then." Sloane straightened and gave the image on the television a hostile glare. "She's turned herself in, so at last the battle will begin. We're ready. We have our witnesses." He glanced at Nadine. "You'll contact them all for me, of course. Dr. Braun, the nurses at the clinic, even the mother-in-law. I want you to find anyone and everyone who can testify that Lara Godfrey was unbalanced, thrilled with the pregnancy, whatever. We'll subpoena the lot of them and let Jarvis sort them out."

Nadine reached for her briefcase. "I'll get on the particulars."

An inexplicable look of withdrawal fell over Sloane's face. "Trent, will you excuse us?"

The assistant looked up, surprised; then his face colored. "Certainly," he said, fumbling for his notepad and pen. He rose and retreated to one of the bedrooms without a backward glance.

Nadine lifted a brow. She knew something unpleasant was bound to be forthcoming.

Sloane sank to the wing chair adjacent to the couch, then took a moment to smooth the crease in his trousers. "I'm sure you're aware"—a frown puckered the skin between his dark eyes—"that one potential witness might severely injure our case."

Nadine kept her face smooth and expressionless as her brain raced through the names she'd come to know as well as her own. The nurses, the neighbors, the doctors could all be guided to give testimony helpful to Sloane's cause—then, in a barely comprehensible flash, she remembered. Five years ago Sloane had struck Dr. Olivia Densen-Braun from the witness list, stating that her friendship with Lara Godfrey might negatively influence her testimony. Nadine had thought little of the omission, especially since Sloane assured her that Dr. Helmut Braun, Olivia's husband, would be a supportive witness. The woman certainly would not contradict her spouse in a court of law.

But four years ago Olivia Densen had divorced her husband.

Nadine chose her words carefully. "Are you thinking about Dr. Olivia Densen?"

Sloane gave her a tense nod. "I'm concerned about animosity between her and Dr. Braun. If she feels duty-bound to antagonize her husband, she might come out against us on the witness stand."

"She seems a rational, intelligent woman. Surely she is above that sort of pettiness."

Sloane rubbed the bridge of his nose. "She and Lara Godfrey were strong friends." His voice, low and passionate, chilled the room. "She will be a hostile witness. She must not testify."

He spoke softly, but the venom in his voice was unmistakable . . . as was his meaning. He had asked Trent to leave because he wanted Nadine to make certain Olivia Densen would not testify on Lara Godfrey's behalf.

An odd coldness settled upon Nadine, an awful and darkly textured sensation like a gust of fetid wind. She had broken the law before—engaged in illegal wiretapping and surveillance, pried into records she had no business seeing, and paid out large sums in bribery and burglary—but she had never asked anyone to commit murder.

Sloane was watching her, his eyes glittering like a snake slithering toward a paralyzed bird. He owned her; she'd been bought with a princely retainer and a generous expense account. Her agency had come to depend upon the prestige and support of her affiliation with Devin Sloane . . . but she could not conscience murder.

"Circles within circles?" Her mouth twisted in bitter amusement. "If you're inviting me into yet another secret circle, Devin, I have to refuse. I'm not an assassin."

"I would never ask you to do anything unpleasant," he said, his voice as smooth as quicksilver, "but surely you know people who could take care of this situation? I'll provide whatever funds are needed. I only require thoroughness and discretion."

Nadine felt a plastic smile creep across her face. "You're on your own now." She placed one hand on top of the other, and noted with some surprise that her flesh had gone as cold as ice. "Why don't you call the people who took care of poor Lemuel Reis?"

"There's an idea." Sloane's black eyes sank into nets of wrinkles as he smiled. "I'd nearly forgotten about those fellows. Thanks for the reminder."

She felt her lips curve in an expression that hardly deserved to be called a smile, but it sufficed.

chapter 28

On Thursday, December thirty-first, Devin adjusted his tie and smoothed his jacket, then crossed his legs and glanced across the windowless courtroom to his adversaries at the opposite table. Lara and Connor O'Hara sat beside their lawyer, Franklin Blythe.

Devin smiled as he lowered his gaze. He could not understand why a woman as clever as Lara Godfrey had selected a semiretired nobody from Roanoke to represent her, but apparently they had religion in common. Nadine's background report stated that Blythe was a deacon in his Baptist church and well-known for philanthropy in the Roanoke area. Do-gooders, Devin knew, tended to flock together.

His lawyer, Madison Jarvis, had moved heaven and earth to schedule this pretrial hearing before the start of the new year. He and Sloane hoped to use this opportunity to petition for custody and establish a high bond for the flighty Mrs. O'Hara. In Jarvis's best-case scenario, Devin would gain full and immediate custody of the child; in the worst-case script Sloane would be allowed to visit the boy in foster care and establish a relationship. Jarvis had warned Devin that anything could happen in Judge Harold Weaver's courtroom, but Devin couldn't help but feel certain that the judge would see things his way.

A polished brass railing transected the courtroom, dividing the noisy spectators from the participants. The bailiff called the unruly crowd to order, and Devin stood with the others as the judge entered and took a seat behind a high mahogany bench that must have cost the taxpayers a pretty penny. Weaver was a good-sized man, wide through the torso, with a neck so thick that his head appeared to rest directly on his shoulders. His face, though, was serious and dedicated.

He looked at the uncommon scene before him with eyes as hard as dried leather.

Devin coolly met Weaver's steady gaze. After making subtle inquiries about the judge's aspirations and tastes, he had learned that Harold Weaver was an unambitious man, as content to serve this court as he was to live in the modest house he and his wife had purchased as newlyweds. Rumor had it that Weaver was immune to bribery and only a fool would try to buy him. But every man had his price.

"Ladies and gentlemen of the media," the judge began with no preamble, "let me assure you that this is a court of law, not a soap opera. You will remain silent in my courtroom and you will mind your manners. Any reporter causing a disturbance during this hearing will be dismissed and barred from attending any further proceedings."

The threat blanketed the spectator's gallery with an immediate stillness. Devin smiled in a silence that felt like the holding of a hundred breaths.

As the courtroom ritual began in earnest, he crossed his legs and made a note on his legal pad. Nadine had completed a background check on Weaver, but he'd have Trent prod her to see if anything had changed in the last few days. By the time the trial began, he wanted to know Harold Weaver's darkest secrets.

"We are here"—the judge folded his hands—"to resolve two particular issues before this case can go to trial. First is the matter of the child's immediate custody, and second is the matter of bond for Mrs. O'Hara." He shifted his gaze toward Devin's table. "I'll hear from the plaintiff's attorney first."

Jarvis stood and buttoned his jacket, then moved out from behind the desk to make his statement. "This case, Your Honor," he said, looking up at the judge over his reading glasses, "is a simple matter of broken faith. We have a contract between these two parties, an agreement entered into in mutual good faith, which the second party, Ms. Lara Godfrey O'Hara, has chosen to ignore. Under the terms of the surrogate agreement, Mrs. O'Hara agreed to bear a child for Mr. Devin Sloane. When the child was born, not only did she refuse to honor a legal contract, but she took the child—*Mr. Sloane's* son—and ran to Florida."

Madison pulled a copy of the surrogate contract from his portfolio and handed it to the judge. "The laws of this state, Your Honor, are clear. Payment can be made to a surrogate for living expenses, and genetic parents are recognized as biological parents. Mrs. O'Hara's lawyer may try to tell you she believed the child to be the result of insemination with her late husband's sperm, but we will provide testimony to prove she knew the child was not her husband's. She knowingly, willingly, *flagrantly* took the infant and fled the jurisdiction of this commonwealth, fully intending to keep Mr. Sloane from his own son."

The judge frowned as he flipped through the contract. "What compensation did Mrs. O'Hara receive for carrying the child?"

Madison clasped his hands. "She received full medical care, as well as access to one of the best genetic laboratories in the country. More important, she knew full well that the Muriel Foundation, headed by Mr. Sloane, had agreed to contribute in excess of one million dollars to the genetics research program at the University of Virginia. In accordance with the laws of this commonwealth, she was not paid for her role, but we can provide witnesses to prove she knew about and appreciated Sloane's contribution in exchange for her participation in the surrogate arrangement."

Jarvis shifted his weight. "In summary, Your Honor, we would like to ask that the child's custody be immediately awarded to Mr. Sloane until the trial resolves this matter permanently. Mr. Sloane has missed the first five years of his son's life. He does not deserve to miss another day."

The judge transferred his gaze to the defendant's table. "Are you ready with your statement, Mr. Blythe?"

The portly lawyer rose. "Yes, Your Honor. I would first like to say that Lara Godfrey O'Hara is not the guilty party here; she is a victim of the most flagrant kind of injustice. There was no surrogate agreement, and until the day the child was born she believed the child was her husband's. The document in your hand was written *after* the insemination and over Mrs. O'Hara's signature. There is no evidence to suggest that the child in question is the legitimate offspring of Devin Sloane, thus my client never intended to deliver her child to him. She did, however, discover a plot to deprive her of her son, so she fled for her own safety. In the five years she lived in Florida she has established a solid reputation as a loving and nurturing mother."

The lawyer glanced at Sloane for a moment, then returned his gaze to the judge. "Sir, we would ask that during this pretrial period the child remain with the mother he has always known and loved."

The judge skimmed the surrogate agreement again, his face darkening with unreadable emotions. Finally he set the document aside and looked to the defendant's table. "Your fault, Mrs. O'Hara, lies in not approaching the authorities five years ago. Because you have proven yourself a flight risk, the court shall require you to report to an officer of the court every morning until the trial. You must not leave the city until after this case is resolved."

A cold knot formed in Devin's stomach as the judge turned to him. "Mr. Sloane, if this document is genuine, I can sympathize with your desire to have custody of your son. Children, however, are not property, and they cannot be treated as such. At five years old, this boy will not benefit by being taken from the only parent he has ever known. I am therefore denying your motion for temporary custody."

Devin settled back, disappointed, but his spirits lifted when the judge looked again to the defendant's table. "Mrs. O'Hara, in family law, the judicial system must not only consider the rights of the two opposing parties, but also of the child. I am therefore appointing a guardian ad litem to represent the best interests of the boy who shall be known simply as 'Hunter.' Someone will be contacting you within a few days, and I must remind you that he or she will represent the full authority of this court. You must offer your full cooperation and allow the guardian ad litem to visit."

From the corner of his eye, Devin saw Lara O'Hara nod slowly.

"I will not require a bond for you, Mrs. O'Hara," the judge continued, folding his hands. "But if you leave the city for any reason you will be considered in contempt of this court. In other words"—he lowered his voice—"if we have to come looking for you, you'll be arrested when we find you. If you take the boy beyond the city limits, you'll face criminal charges for kidnapping. Do you understand?"

"Yes, Your Honor." Her voice was a thin whisper in the cavernous room.

"Then I wish you all a good day." The judge banged the desk once with his gavel, then stood and exited through the oak door through which he'd come.

The courtroom erupted into sound as Devin turned to his lawyer. "Not exactly what we had hoped for," he said, struggling to maintain an even, pleasant tone, "but not bad. And now we have time to work."

Jarvis frowned as he shoved a portfolio into his briefcase. "I had hoped he'd see things our way. The situation would be much improved if we had access to the boy. We could show familial affection and demonstrate how you've provided for him."

"I'm not worried." Devin crossed his arms and gave the lawyer a small smile. "I'll set Nadine on the matter of the guardian."

Jarvis's eyes hardened. "The guardian ad litem is supposed to be an impartial third party."

Devin stood and grasped his lawyer's arm, then smiled at a waving photographer. "We'll make sure this guardian is as impartial as the grave."

❦

In the silence of his bedroom, Helmut Braun lay curled in a ball, watching the glowing red numerals on his digital clock. The minutes passed, one indistinguishable from another as they slipped into eternity. He had been lying on his bed since the six o'clock news ended, his thoughts too loud and turbulent to allow any measure of rest.

The red numerals shifted and Helmut closed his eyes, a shiver spreading over him as he remembered the newscast. The mannequinlike anchorwoman had announced that Devin Sloane had suffered a major setback in his civil trial against Lara Godfrey O'Hara. The judge had ruled that the child would remain with the mother until the trial's conclusion.

The newscast had switched to footage of the mob outside the courthouse, where the camera zoomed in on Lara's face. She had changed in the last five years; her hair was dark now, and shorter, but Helmut would know those direct, honest eyes anywhere. Two men walked by her side, probably her lawyer and her new husband.

A confusing rush of anticipation and dread whirled inside Helmut as a news reporter shouted a question at Lara.

"We are not giving up," she said, her voice unsteady and thick. "We are confident the truth will come out. My son belongs to me, not to Devin Sloane."

The truth will come out. And when it did, the world would know Helmut Braun as a fiend and a fraud.

He listened to the rest of the report with rising dismay. Lara Godfrey O'Hara had won a battle today, but experts were already predicting a victory for Devin Sloane. Judge Weaver had a solid record of deciding in the best material interest of the child, ruling for the parent with the greatest means of financial support in 95 percent of his cases. The court would appoint a guardian ad litem for the boy, and any questions of what was best for the child would be settled by negotiations between the guardian and the judge. The trial was scheduled to begin in two months.

The camera drew in for a tight shot of a young woman with shoulder-length brown hair. "The court has just appointed Karyn Gower as guardian ad litem for the child," the reporter explained in a voice-over. "Ms. Gower is a social worker employed by the city of Charlottesville. Over the next eight weeks, she will evaluate the child and his current living conditions, then present a recommendation to the judge. Though no one doubts that Mrs. O'Hara loves her son, neither can anyone deny that he would enjoy an exceptional lifestyle if permitted to reside with Mr. Sloane."

Helmut closed his eyes and clicked the television off. The burning rock of guilt in the pit of his gut would not go away. The fates of Lara Godfrey and her son would rest with the courts, but Sloane would call on Helmut to testify, to repeat the lies that had burdened his soul for more than six years.

He brought his knees closer to his chest, his vision gloomily colored with the memory of Lara in his office, her eyes bright with hope and longing for her husband's child. He had taken her trust and twisted it;

he had allowed his own desire for knowledge, reputation, and success to subvert his ideals. Distracted and tempted by Devin Sloane, he had sold Lara's son for a research grant. Since then, he had deceived and dissembled in every area of his life, losing his wife, his friends, and his self-respect. He had spoken his lies so often and so convincingly that the world accepted them as truth.

He pressed his hand to his face as grief welled in him, black and cold. What a failure! He had not even managed to be a very good liar. He had failed even in his deception, and soon Sloane would realize how completely Helmut had deceived him. Once he did, Helmut's life would be worthless.

He realized he was crying only when he tasted salt at the corners of his mouth. He sat up, dashed the useless tears away, and opened the drawer of his nightstand. The .357 Magnum lay on top of a pile of assorted papers, and he gently placed the gun on the table, then rummaged through envelopes and ads and note pads until he found the small tape recorder.

He had bought both the gun and the recorder for unexpected revelations. He had never had an occasion to use the revolver, but several times he had pulled out the recorder as ideas came to him in that fertile time of half sleep. Unfortunately, all too often the ideas he thought brilliant at two a.m. seemed inconsequential and trite in the stark morning light.

He pressed the eject button, checked the microcassette, then inserted it again, closing the mechanism with an emphatic click. He knew the batteries were good; he'd replaced them last week.

While outside his neighbors celebrated the dawning of a new year with bottle rockets and firecrackers, Helmut pressed the record button and recited the story of his fruitless life—true and unabridged, beginning with the moment he met Devin Sloane and continuing until the present hour. When he had finished, he told Olivia he loved her, then pressed the stop button.

He pulled himself from the bed, then moved to his desk and slid an envelope from a drawer. After writing Olivia's name and the clinic address in block letters, he affixed a stamp, then sealed the microcassette inside.

He moved to his closet and shoved his weary feet into a pair of loafers. Moving with a quiet tread, he opened the front door and walked to the mailbox. The letter wouldn't be picked up until Saturday, but that would be soon enough.

When he returned, Helmut locked the front door, kicked his shoes off in the foyer, and made his way back to the bedroom.

He looked again at the clock, ready to mark the moment of completion. He had come into the world at 6:15 a.m. on a January 15, and at some moment around 11:39 p.m., on December 31, he would leave it. He couldn't say he had lived well or honorably, but in this last hour he had done what he could to set things right. Perhaps, like everything else in his life, it would not be enough.

He lay down on the bed, felt the familiar touch of his pillow, then turned and saw the Smith and Wesson gleaming in the moonlight. He picked up the gun and rubbed its cold body against his cheek. The gun was a favorite of highway patrolmen who liked to blow holes in fleeing vehicles.

Helmut settled the gun in his right hand, then pressed its body against a throat that ached with regret.

So many lies. So much promise, wasted. So sorry.

He swallowed, felt the muzzle move against the soft skin under his chin, then pulled the trigger.

∞

"Hold my calls, will you, Gaynel?" Olivia Densen glanced at the envelope in her hand with dismay. The handwriting was Helmut's, and through the paper she could feel the edges of a microcassette. It could contain anything from another weepy apology to a copy of his latest lecture, but she didn't want to be interrupted while she listened.

She checked her watch. Ten o'clock. She had only an hour to get to the hospital, where she had a biopsy scheduled for eleven thirty. Dr. Stock and Maria Kremkau, the physician's assistant, were handling patient appointments, so she could let the tape play while she cleared her desk.

She sank into her leather office chair, pulled her recorder from a desk drawer, and popped the cassette into the machine. She picked up another letter as the tape began to play, but something in Helmut's tone alarmed her. His usually robust voice seemed weary and fragile, as if he had suffered through hours of weeping.

What had happened?

She parked her chin in her hand and felt the nauseated sinking of despair as Helmut clarified and explained the events of the past years. At the end of his soliloquy, when he whispered that he loved her, Olivia closed her eyes.

Helmut was not the monster she had imagined. He had been too weak to resist Devin Sloane, but perhaps she could support him now . . . if it wasn't too late.

She dialed Helmut's lab and twisted the cord as the phone rang. A research assistant answered and said that Dr. Braun had not yet arrived.

Olivia disconnected the call and dialed Helmut's apartment. Again the phone rang. For no reason she could name, the sound of the persistent ringing raised the hairs on the back of her neck.

She hung up, then dialed 911 and spoke with the professional sense of detachment that always accompanied her awareness of impending disaster. "This is Dr. Olivia Densen. Will you please send paramedics to 397 Court Street?"

"What is the nature of the emergency, Doctor?"

"I'm not certain." Her voice drifted into a hushed whisper. "But please hurry."

She dropped the phone back into its cradle, then pressed her fingertips to her lips, afraid of what the paramedics would find. Helmut had never been strong, and Lara's reappearance had flushed old sins and secrets to the surface.

Helmut, she knew, had called it quits.

Cold, clear reality swept over her in a wave so powerful it stole her breath. She had heard the popping sounds of firecrackers on the tape; he must have recorded it on New Year's Eve, right after Lara's pretrial hearing. Three and a half days ago.

A suffocating sensation tightened her throat. If he had taken pills or cut his wrists she might have been able to save him . . . but not now.

Trembling, she picked up her purse and stood; then her gaze fell upon the tape in the recorder. Lara would need that tape. It was priceless, for it had been wrung from the life of a dear man with more heart than strength.

Olivia pulled the cassette from the recorder and tapped it against her fingers. Once Helmut's death was made public, Devin Sloane might search for a last letter or some other form of communication. He might check Lara's mail—or her attorney's.

So who could she entrust with this tape? The neighbor was now Lara's husband, so he was no longer an option. Lara had no other family, except for the mother-in-law . . .

She pulled out a phone book and copied Eva Godfrey's name and address onto a padded manila envelope. After jotting a quick note on a clinic memo pad, she dropped the note and the tape into the package. Before leaving the office, she asked Carol to mail the envelope and cancel her afternoon appointments.

Carol nodded, her eyes wide and curious, but Olivia pushed through the double doors and strode into the rising wind, knowing full well what she'd find when she reached Helmut's apartment.

∞

Olivia bid farewell to her last patient, recorded her notes for the transcriptionist, and nodded at Gaynel as the nurse locked the front doors. An almost tangible pall had hung over the office ever since the news of Helmut's suicide, but in her work Olivia found a mindless routine that helped camouflage the despair of grief. If she paused to dwell on what might have been, she'd drown in a tide of regret and loss.

She moved into her office and slumped into her chair, then swiveled to face a mound of reports and patient files. Her eyes burned from sleeplessness; her muscles screamed from the strain of unrelenting tension. She had spent Monday evening poring over Helmut's personal records, searching for some indication of his funeral wishes; she'd spent Tuesday with her lawyer, a police investigator, and a funeral director. She had said nothing to the cop about Helmut's taped confession—according to Helmut, Sloane's influence extended far and wide, and she didn't want the tape to end up in his hands. Carol had mailed the tape on Monday; with any luck, Eva Godfrey would receive it Tuesday or Wednesday and deliver it to Lara.

Olivia picked up a patient file and skimmed it, then dropped it back to the stack, her concentration dissipating in a mist of fatigue. She'd spent a full day in the office, grateful for the opportunity to think about something besides her own misery. Today she had sealed off all thoughts of Helmut, his anguish, and their failed marriage, but those thoughts were banging on her brain now, demanding an audience.

She stood and swiped her hand through her hair, then picked up her purse and moved toward the front desk. Carol and Maria had gone home, but Gaynel, Sharon, and Rita were pulling the files of patients scheduled for the next morning. They'd understand if she left early. The entire office staff had tiptoed around her all day, scarcely mentioning Helmut but telegraphing their compassion with every guarded glance and sad smile.

Olivia stopped at the desk and leaned over the front counter. "I'm going home. If anything comes up, Dr. Stock has agreed to take my cases." She closed her eyes, mentally running through her list of OB patients near delivery. "It should be a quiet night—"

An odd flapping sound broke her concentration. She turned as a big man, tall and wide-shouldered, walked in from the back hallway. His black trench coat slapped against his jeans as he strode into the lobby.

"Excuse me?" Olivia asked, irritated by the current of anxiety racing through her. "Can we help you?" She frowned as a particular realization struck her—how had he come in? The back door was always locked.

Gaynel recovered next. "This office is closed," she snapped, her voice sharp with disbelief.

The man lifted his head and met Olivia's gaze. Ignoring the note of disapproval in Gaynel's voice, he gave Olivia a dry smile.

"Good evening, ladies," he drawled, reaching into his coat pocket. With one hand he pulled out a stack of brochures. "I was wonderin' if you'd let me leave a few of these papers in your lobby."

Olivia glanced at the brochures and recognized the logo of a radical antiabortion organization. "I'm sorry, but we have a policy against political literature in the lobby."

"That's too bad." The man stopped six feet from the desk, then flung the brochures across the circle of seats in the waiting room. They fluttered like frightened birds, lighting on chairs and carpet and the photograph album filled with Polaroids of Olivia posing with newly delivered babies.

Terror lodged in Olivia's throat as the smile vanished from the stranger's face, leaving him ghostly and grim under the fluorescent lights. Without another word, he pulled a gun from a slit in his raincoat and trained it on the women.

One corner of his mouth pulled into a slight smile. "Sorry about this."

Olivia opened her mouth to scream, but the man shifted his stance, pulled the gun into both hands, and began firing. She suddenly thought of a firefighter spraying the room with a water hose, but there was no fire, only pain that seared her chest and arms and throat as the scent of acrid gunpowder filled her nostrils.

Olivia reached out, felt carpeting under her fingertips, and wondered who would feed her cats.

Then the world went soft and black.

∞

Franklin Blythe stopped by the town house Thursday morning to see how Lara was taking the news. She had risen early and switched on the television, only to hear that the bodies of four women—Dr. Olivia Densen, Gaynel Sheridan, Sharon Swensen, and Rita Gordon—had been discovered at the Women's Medical Clinic at ten p.m. the previous evening. According to police, Sharon's husband had gone out searching for his wife, peered through the locked glass doors, and discovered the grisly scene.

When Franklin arrived, Lara was still in her pajamas, sitting on the floor before the TV with a cold cup of coffee in her hand. Connor answered the door and let the lawyer in.

Lara heard the soft whoosh of the couch cushions as Franklin sat down, but she couldn't tear her gaze from the television.

"They say," she began, her voice trembling, "that they were cut down by a radical antiabortionist because the cops found pro-life leaflets scattered around the room. But that's impossible, because Olivia didn't perform elective abortions, and neither did Dr. Stock. All the pro-life people in town knew her position."

"That theory is going up in smoke even now." Franklin spoke in a hushed voice. "This morning I talked to a detective who said the scene looks too clean for an amateur. The front doors were locked tight, and there was no sign of forced entry. So someone either allowed this guy into the building, or he opened the door electronically—and that would require high-tech equipment."

Beset by a tumble of confused thoughts and feelings, Lara turned. "Someone could do that?"

"Professionals can do nearly anything these days." Connor came into the living room, and Franklin waved away the cup of coffee that he offered. "Coming so soon after Helmut Braun's death, I can't help but think the two events are related."

Lara stared at the lawyer. "You think this horrible thing had something to do with me?"

He nodded, a faint line between his brows. "Unfortunately, I do. This terrible event has wiped out four witnesses who might have testified on your behalf."

Lara stared at Franklin in a paralysis of astonishment. She did not doubt that Devin Sloane was capable of evil, but would he murder four people in order to take her child? A chill struck deep in the pit of her stomach as that thought brought another in its wake. "Merciful heavens. What's to prevent him from killing *me*?"

"You're too obvious a target." Franklin squeezed Lara's shoulder. "Don't worry, my dear, we're going to get your family through this. Sloane may think he has the upper hand, but his sins will find him out."

Lara drew her knees to her chest as a flash of wild grief ripped through her heart. She closed her eyes, resisting the flood of tears that burned the back of her eyelids, then felt Connor's strong arms pulling her toward him. She curled tighter, letting him shelter her, and wept.

After a long moment, she heard Connor's voice, deep and husky. "We'll be okay, Franklin. Keep us informed, will you? I'm still on vacation, so I'll be here to keep an eye on things."

"A good idea, son." Lara heard Franklin stand and make his way to the door, but Connor stayed beside her, his arms around her shoulders, one hand resting protectively on her head. Surrendering to the pull of grief, she threw her arms around his neck and freely vented her fear and sorrow.

∞

For Lara, the next week passed in a blur of tears. Hunter seemed confused by her mournful mood, so he spent most of his time with Connor, diving into his new role as "Daddy's boy" with a glee that ordinarily would have made Lara jealous. She could find no place for jealousy, however, when her heart had been consumed by fear.

To make matters worse, several members of the media set up camp in front of the house. When they crowded the front porch and tried to peer through the bedroom windows, Connor called the police, who warned the nosy reporters to stay off private property. The reporters pulled away from the town house, but since the park across the street was public property, they loitered there at all hours in hopes of catching a glimpse of Hunter or Lara.

And so Lara's small family remained housebound and tried to keep from getting on each other's nerves. Lara felt the most sorry for her son, who could not go outside and play. Connor and Hunter spent hours playing educational games and creating computer art, but the time of isolation was beginning to fray Lara's nerves.

On Thursday morning she received a call from Judge Weaver's law clerk. Karyn Gower, the court-appointed guardian ad litem, planned to stop by the house that morning for an interview with Hunter. Lara's nerves tensed immediately, but Connor assured her he'd remain in the kitchen while Ms. Gower conducted the interview. If the woman made a move toward the door with Hunter, he'd stop her.

The doorbell chimed precisely at eleven. Lara rose from the couch, smoothed her slacks, and tried to fix a smile on her face. For Hunter's sake, she had to appear confident, competent, and rational, as perfect a mother as she could be without seeming false.

Gathering her courage, she opened the door. A young woman stood on the porch, a pouchlike purse hanging from her shoulder and a friendly smile on her lips. A bandanna-print headband held back the wealth of long, dark hair that spilled over her peasant blouse.

Peering through dark granny glasses, she extended her hand to Lara, introduced herself as Karyn Gower, then looked down. Hunter had wedged himself into the space between Lara's leg and the door frame. He eyed their visitor with a critical squint.

"Hello, Hunter." Karyn grinned. "I'm so glad to meet you."

Hunter ducked and clung to Lara's leg.

"Sorry." Lara smiled an apology. "He's not always comfortable around strangers."

"I can imagine." The woman gave Lara an understanding look, then lifted her chin. "Can I come in? Hunter can remain with us if he'd like."

Lara opened the door and let the woman in, her anxiety easing somewhat. Karyn Gower was nothing like the stiff, formal social worker of her imagination. She had expected someone with hair twisted in a schoolmarm's bun, perhaps with a clipboard under her arm, ready to record every infraction of a parenting rule. Karyn Gower, however, seemed completely at ease in her role, even slipping out of her low pumps as she settled into the couch.

Lara took the opposite end of the sofa and turned to face the woman. "How can I help you, Ms. Gower?"

"Call me Karyn. I don't believe in formality."

"All right." Hunter came to stand by Lara's side, then leaned into the couch. Lara slipped her arm around her son and lovingly patted his belly. "Hunter may seem a little shy at first. I suppose he's like any other five-year-old, quiet one minute and a wild man the next."

Leaning toward Hunter, Karyn rested her elbows on her knees, then propped her chin on her hand. "I like kids; that's why I signed on to be a guardian ad litem. I have a little brother myself."

Hunter blinked, his features hardening in a stare of disapproval. "No, you don't."

Lara felt a cold panic creep between her shoulder blades and prickle down her spine. What was Hunter *doing*? This wasn't the time to expose his gift. She couldn't let this woman think Hunter anything but an ordinary little boy who needed to be with his mother.

Karyn laughed. "How do you know I don't have a brother?"

"I just know." Hunter thrust his hands in his pockets and nestled closer to Lara. "You're lying."

"He's, ah, quite a little prophet." Lara stumbled over the words. "You know how some parents are embarrassed when their children tell lies? I'm sometimes embarrassed when my son tells the truth. He's always catching people in little white lies—you know, about Santa Claus and the Easter Bunny. Hunter doesn't much like to play games."

"That's not true, Mom." Hunter's lower lip edged forward in a pout. "I like Chutes and Ladders and Candyland and playing with Connor."

"I know you do, buddy." She turned her son toward the kitchen and patted his fanny. "Why don't you go see if Connor will play with you now?"

She held her breath, afraid either Hunter or Karyn would protest, but Hunter canted away with the peculiar bent-foot gait he'd adopted ever since leaving Florida.

Lara shifted her gaze to find Karyn studying her with a curious intensity.

"I don't want you to think we don't allow Hunter to pretend or play games." Words sprang to her lips in a mad rush. "We do. In fact, his preschool teacher in Florida always commented on Hunter's sweet nature. He plays well with us and other children; he's really a happy child."

"Relax, Mrs. O'Hara." Karyn set her lips in a straight line. "Was he limping? Has he hurt himself?"

"No, no, nothing like that. He's been limping for a while, but I don't think it's anything serious. I took him to the pediatrician, who recommended a specialist, but the specialist is in Richmond, and I'm not allowed—" She broke off, suddenly aware that Karyn might recommend that Hunter be removed from Lara's custody in order to receive medical treatment.

She gave the woman a confident smile. "I'm planning to take him to Richmond as soon as the trial is over. Our pediatrician seems to think it's only a phase. Sometimes Hunter walks hunched over like Curious George, the chimpanzee. There's nothing wrong; it's just something he wants to do."

Karyn nodded, then picked up her bulky purse and slipped the strap onto her shoulder. "Thanks very much for your time, Mrs. O'Hara. Hunter is a darling boy, and I'll enjoy visiting with him for the next few weeks. Maybe next time he'll be a little more willing to talk to me."

Lara stood with the guardian, then accompanied her to the door. As Karyn stepped onto the porch, Lara lingered in the doorway. "You won't recommend that he be taken from me, will you?" she asked, aware of how pitiful she sounded. "He's never known any parent but me, and you can see how attached he is."

"I think he's in the perfect place right now." Karyn gave Lara a lovely, wide smile, more warming than the feeble winter sun. "And if you don't mind, I'd like to visit with him alone next week. Perhaps, in time, he'll even allow me to take him to McDonalds for a treat."

Lara nodded, too overcome with relief to object. She waved as Karyn turned and left; then she closed the door and rested her forehead against the cool wood.

Another test, apparently passed. Karyn Gower could either be Lara's best friend or her worst enemy, but so far, all signs were good.

Lara pulled herself off the door, then gasped to see Connor standing in the hallway. "Goodness! You startled me."

He didn't answer, but moved into the living room and stood behind the sheer curtains, his eyes following Karyn Gower as she got into her car. As the car pulled away, he turned to Lara with a shadow in his eyes. "Hunter said she told a lie," he said, with a warning look that put an immediate damper on Lara's rising spirits. "What kind of social worker tells lies?"

Lara pushed her hair back from her forehead. "I'm sure it was no big deal. I don't even remember what it was, some little something she probably said just to make Hunter feel comfortable."

"You don't win a kid by lying to him. Anybody should know that."

"Connor, it was nothing. She *likes* us. That means she'll tell the judge to let him stay with me."

Her words seemed to hang in the air as if for inspection. Too late, she realized what she'd said.

"With *us*, Connor. I want him to stay with *us*."

"I don't trust her, Lara, so don't play up to her. You've got to keep being careful."

She lifted her hands in exasperation. "I've been careful for six years. It's time I learned to trust somebody!"

"Trust your son. Trust Franklin and Harriet. And trust me."

"That's not fair." She crossed her arms, irked by his cool, aloof manner. Why was he trying to antagonize her? For the last five years she had looked out for Hunter's interests *alone*, and she'd done a darn good job of keeping him safe and secure. Connor had been back in her life for just three weeks, yet here he was, trying to tell her what to do—

She had no intention of surrendering her role as Hunter's protector, not even to the man she loved.

She lowered her voice to a reasonable tone. "I like Karyn Gower, and I think she likes me. I'm going to do everything I can to help her see us in a positive light. If I resist her in any way, she could tell the judge that I'm not a good mother. If I view her as the enemy like *you* obviously do, she'll give Hunter to Devin Sloane!"

He flinched as though she had struck him, but he showed no sign of relenting. "I'm only trying to point out a rather obvious fact—Karyn Gower lied to Hunter. How will you know if she lies to you? And she's certainly no fool. She'll discover sooner or later that Hunter is a special child—"

"Connor?"

Lara turned at the sound of Hunter's voice. He stood in the bedroom doorway, one hand pressed to his eye, the silver track of tears marking his cheek. Lara reached for her son, her blood running thick with guilt, but Hunter climbed into Connor's arms.

Lara stood still and heard her heart break. "You okay, buddy?"

Connor straightened, cradling Hunter's head against his chest. "I think he's tired," he said, unspoken pain alive and glowing in his eyes. "Let me convince him it's time for a nap; then we'll talk."

Lara moved forward and blocked Connor's path. As her heart brimmed with regret and fear, she drew her loved ones into her arms, then rested her head on her husband's shoulder.

He had done so much for them. He had waited for her through five long years. In a way, he had sacrificed more and received far less than she had.

"Why don't we all lie down together?" She searched Connor's face. "Tomorrow, after we've had some time to pray and rest, we'll know what we should do."

Connor lifted his hand to stroke her cheek, then slipped his arm around her shoulders and guided her toward the bedroom where he'd brought Hunter into the world.

∽

"You say the mother seemed pleased to have you involved?"

Nadine asked the question, since Sloane had done little but smile since Karyn Gower reported that she'd visited with the boy that afternoon. The three of them sat now in Sloane's monstrously plush library. Nadine and Karyn occupied the sofa while Sloane sat in a wing chair, his eyes focused on thoughts Nadine couldn't even imagine.

"Yes." Karyn looked at Nadine and lifted a brow, asking in feminine shorthand if she should wait for Mr. Sloane to snap out of his reverie.

Nadine shook her head in an almost imperceptible gesture. "Tell me everything. Is the boy well? Healthy?"

Karyn cast a quick glance at Sloane, who stared out the window; then she shrugged. "He seems as healthy as any other kid, but the mother did mention that she thought he ought to see a doctor. She didn't seem worried, though. And the kid talked to me for a few minutes; then Lara sort of hustled him out of the room." The young woman's mouth quirked with humor. "He's a funny little guy. I was trying to put the boy at ease, so I said I had a brother about his age. From out of the blue, the kid looks at me and says, 'You're lying.'"

Nadine reached for her purse; she needed a cigarette. Sloane didn't know how much this little recital of information was costing him, and he probably wouldn't care that he had effectively doubled Karyn Gower's yearly salary. But he could at least *listen* to the girl.

"You say the child knew you lied?" Sloane shifted, and beneath the polished veneer of his face Nadine saw a suggestion of activity, as though an idea were trying to surface. "How did he know?"

Karyn shrugged again. "I have no idea. The mother said something about him being a little prophet."

"A prophet." A thin smile rose to Sloane's lips as he looked at Nadine. "Can you imagine? What an intellect he must possess! Perhaps he saw the contraction of her pupils; perhaps he knew enough to intuitively read the way she tugged on her ear or scratched her nose—"

"I didn't do anything like that." Karyn drew back. "We were only talking."

Sloane leaned forward. "The scientific study of body language has proven that humans routinely transmit telltale clues when they indulge in prevarication. But perhaps this boy has inherited some sort of intuitive knowledge." Sloane's forehead creased in thought; then his brows rose. "An ancient hunter would have needed to know how to read his surroundings. His life would have depended upon being able to interpret the tensing of a panther about to spring. He would have known how to judge whether an enemy spoke the truth or lied about danger outside the camp." A livid hue overspread his face as he smiled at Nadine. "A prophet! How wonderful! No wonder Lara was so anxious to shoo the boy away!"

"Really, Mr. Sloane, it was a little thing." Karyn gazed at him with a bland half smile, but the social worker had no idea of the boy's heritage. She probably thought Sloane a raging eccentric.

"A prophet speaks through divine inspiration." He sat up and ran his hands over his knees, then gave Nadine a smile of pure rapture. "I told you he would be closer to the divine spark!"

The social worker frowned in confusion, but Sloane reached out and patted her knee. "My dear, you have outdone yourself. I salute you." His smile deepened to laughter. "How eagerly we will await your next report!"

Nadine knocked a cigarette from the package, then held it between her fingers. "I'd counsel against too many visits. We don't want to alarm Lara."

"Lara O'Hara would never suspect this charming girl." Sloane's eyes smoldered as he turned to Karyn. "Keep visiting my son, Ms. Gower, and gently push for private moments with the boy. When you are alone, you might begin to tell him about the man who has been waiting a lifetime to see him."

Karyn accepted the assistance that Sloane offered and let him pull her to her feet. As Nadine lowered her head to light her cigarette, she heard the girl twitter as Sloane bent over her hand for a fervent kiss.

She brought her head up, breathed deeply through the contrivance that would most likely put her in an early grave, then blew an elegant stream of smoke toward the happy twosome.

chapter 29

Sloane paused outside the hospital room, studying the information on the card clipped to the door. This particular Ethan Jefferson Pediatric patient was Jenna Rand, a seventeen-year-old suffering from myasthenia gravis . . . and ten weeks pregnant.

He lifted a brow in Dr. Johnson's direction. "Does she know?"

Johnson frowned, his eyes level under dark brows. "She thinks she's getting better. I overheard her speaking to her parents on the telephone. They were discussing the pregnancy, and she seemed happy about it. I don't think they told her of our requirement."

Sloane snorted softly. "What is with parents today? They allow their damaged children to have children and happily pass on the problems of the race. When will they learn?"

Dr. Johnson pushed the door open and led the way into the room. At the sight of her visitors, the blonde girl in the bed struggled to push herself upright. Her head bobbed in greeting, presenting the men with a thin, sallow face in which frightened blue eyes occupied most of the available space. The disease had weakened her muscles so much that closing her eyelids would soon be a struggle.

"Good morning, Jenna." Johnson moved to the foot of the bed. "You remember Mr. Sloane, don't you?"

"Of course." One corner of her mouth twitched in what must have been a smile. "I couldn't have come to this hospital without Mr. Sloane's help."

"We do what we can." Devin thrust his hands behind his back and looked around the room. There were no flowers on the nightstand, not a single card taped to the wall. Most of the girls brought at least a family photo, but Jenna Rand had brought nothing from the pitiful West Virginia trailer she and her parents called home.

"I was talking to my mom," Jenna said, her gaze moving to the doctor's face. "An' she wants to know if I can come home soon. Since I'm feelin' better an' all—"

"We're not quite finished with your treatment." Johnson lowered his clipboard and gave the girl a fixed smile. "There's still the matter of your baby. Even if we could eradicate the bad genes from your body, there's always a chance your baby will have this disease too."

"But if he doesn't?"

"He could still be a carrier. And that would be bad for the rest of the world, don't you see? One little stone tossed into the lake creates an infinite number of rings."

Devin lowered himself to the edge of the girl's bed. "I wanted to stop by and tell you that it's been a pleasure to have you as our guest. We've learned a lot from your DNA, Jenna. I expect we'll learn a lot from your fetus's, too."

The girl's smile twitched again. "But my baby's not born yet."

"It can't be born." Devin patted her hand. "That's one of our rules, sweetheart. In exchange for free treatment, all genetic disease patients must agree to sterilization. Unfortunately, you came here already pregnant."

The girl's gaze darted around the room. "But—I want my baby."

"It's already been decided, Jenna; it's in the contract. Sometimes the things we want aren't right for us. It's not right to bring a deformed child into the world. If you want something to love, go home and get yourself a nice puppy."

Dr. Johnson cleared his throat. "I'm afraid I have another bit of bad news. You see, Jenna, sometimes a person gets a disease because they have only one nucleotide in the wrong chemical form. We can cure it by changing the abnormal nucleotide back to its original form, but when a person is already born"—he shrugged—"the job is a lot harder. We can't change millions of cells; the task is simply too big."

In Jenna's wide eyes Devin saw ignorance and confusion. They had learned all they could from her; it was time to move on.

He gave her hand a squeeze, then stood. "Thank you, Jenna, for being such a wonderful patient. I'm sure your parents will be happy to have you home."

She tilted her head and looked at Johnson. "I don't want a puppy."

He leaned on the bed frame and met Devin's eye. "We'll do a complete hysterectomy. She won't be aware of anything."

Devin turned to leave. "Thank you, Doctor."

∞

"Here." His nostrils flaring with distaste, Stuart dropped an envelope on Nadine's desk. "Another set of applications from Sloane."

She smiled at him, obscurely comforted by the knowledge that someone else shared her growing antipathy toward Devin Sloane. "I don't need to see them." She used the tip of her pen to push the envelope away. "Have Simon do the usual background checks—history of frivolous lawsuits, appropriate income limits, that sort of thing. Sloane wants his hospital patients poor and serious."

Eyeing the package as if it were a bad smell, Stuart picked up the envelope and gingerly held it between two fingers. "By the way, Nadine, we had to order a new set of filing cabinets just to handle the Sloane hospital paperwork."

Nadine looked up from the report she'd been reading. "We've been doing that many intake packages?"

"Yes and no." Stuart paused, the envelope dangling from his hand like a dead animal. "Yes, we've been doing a lot of background checks. But it's the dead files that take up so much space. I wanted to put them all on computer disk, but Simon says we need to keep the actual documents."

Nadine tapped her pen on the desk, trying to comprehend what she was hearing. "Dead files—you mean applicants who are rejected?"

"I mean the files of dead *patients*." Stuart's mouth thinned with distaste. "Bodies are piling up like cord wood."

"Cut the sarcasm, Stu. Sometimes patients die." She reached for her diet soda, then smiled. "You just don't like Sloane."

"You're right, I don't." He dropped the envelope into a chair and moved closer to her desk, a dim flush racing across his clean-cut features. "I know he's one of our biggest clients, but honestly, Nadine, something's out of whack with his hospital."

Nadine sipped her soda, then lifted a warning brow. "Don't you think Sloane has all kinds of people watching over his shoulder? He's had his critics, but they've never been able to prove a single allegation against him."

"I think he's killing people, but he covers himself. And people like us help him do it."

She put down her soda and looked her assistant in the eye. "I may have done some things I'm not proud of, but murder would be crossing the line. So don't come to me with exaggerations and suspicions about Sloane unless you can back them up."

Stuart matched her intensity, look for look. "Give me ten minutes at my computer and I'll show you what I mean."

Convinced the young man was wasting her time, Nadine waved him out the door. He returned five minutes later, a computer printout trailing behind him.

"Most hospitals," he began with no preamble, "lose between 10 and 15 percent of their patients per year. The mortality rate at Sloane's pediatric hospital last year was 18 percent, not terribly unusual. But the mortality rate of the hospital's *discharged* patients jumps to 78 percent."

Nadine leaned forward, her heart going into sudden shock. She pulled the pages toward her, read the statistics, saw the long list of patients who had been transferred into Stuart's "dead files."

"You're comparing apples and oranges." She frowned. "Sloane's patients are terminally ill. His is the hospital of last resort."

"He's *supposed* to be curing them. But despite all the hype, the statistics suggest Sloane is sending these kids home to die."

The thought was so absurd that Nadine couldn't stop a smile, though she felt a long way from genuine humor. "If something were wrong, these people would be suing for medical malpractice. Instead, they're heaping praise on Sloane's head."

"Think about his patients' families, Nadine." Stuart dropped into the empty chair before her desk, his face a study in exasperation. "His admissions policy virtually guarantees they're all poor and relatively uneducated."

"It's a charity hospital; it's *designed* to aid the poor."

"It's *designed* to cure genetic diseases. The media creates so much hoopla over Sloane's few successes that these parents send their kids to Sloane and hope for a miracle. When they don't get their miracle, they're stuck. They can't criticize Sloane, because at least he cared enough to take in their kid. Which brings me to another point—if he's not curing these kids, what *is* he doing with them?"

The question snapped like a whip, making Nadine flinch. "What do you mean?"

"I mean"—Stuart lowered his voice—"it's a research hospital. What if he's only using these kids . . . as guinea pigs?"

She shook her head. "Not even Sloane is that low." She skimmed the list in her hand, then stabbed her pen at a name. "Look here. Tommy Brown, age ten. Sickle cell anemia. He was accepted into the program, but died before he was ever admitted." She leaned back and met Stu's gaze. "There goes your theory about Sloane being a merchant of menace. These kids are dying because they're sick, not because they've spent time in his hospital."

Stuart shrugged. "I don't know, but I find the figures terrifying. If my kid ever developed a genetic disease, the Ethan Jefferson Pediatric Hospital for Genetic Research is the *last* place on earth I'd send him."

"You don't have a kid."

Stuart gave her a grim smile. "Neither do 78 percent of the families who send their children to Sloane's hospital."

∞

Nadine managed to shove Stuart's accusations to the back of her mind, but she couldn't help feeling trapped in an ever-shrinking space between the weight of her suspicions and her knowledge of Sloane's temperament. His exploitation of hapless Lara Godfrey had already proven that he'd do virtually anything for science.

Had he been using sick children to further his own knowledge?

Her need for answers impelled her onto a jet; by sunset she was being ushered into Sloane's paneled office. He greeted her with a warm smile, finished dictating a thought into his tape recorder, then came forward to greet her, his hands outstretched.

"Nadine! What brings you to Charlottesville?" When she didn't step into his embrace, he looked at her with a speculative gaze. "Not bad news about Ms. O'Hara, I hope? Madison says the trial is proceeding as planned."

"This has nothing to do with Lara or the boy." Nadine took the seat he offered, then crossed her legs and fixed him in a steady gaze. "Devin . . . my assistant came to me this afternoon with some serious concerns."

"Really?" He sank into a chair across from her, then pressed his fingertips together. "We are a team, Nadine. Ask what you will and I'll try my best to answer."

She glanced at the floor and tried to rein in her scattered thoughts. "An inordinate number of your hospital patients are dying once they return home." She met his direct gaze. "Seventy-eight percent last year. Doesn't that number seem high to you?"

Devin tilted his head. "That's probably correct. Our patients are seriously ill, you know. We do what we can to help them, but we are only beginning to research some of the rarer diseases."

"That's what I thought, but records indicate that some of your patients are dying from diseases for which you have already found a cure. Three of your cystic fibrosis patients have died in the last six months, but you've had a breakthrough with CF."

Devin scratched his ear. "I can't comment without looking at the case files, but I suspect the patients came to us after we solved that problem. We're not taking any more CF cases."

Nadine gaped at him. "You could cure these children and yet you're not willing—"

"I'm not interested in curing children. I'm interested in repairing human DNA." Devin spoke in a calm voice completely at odds with the dreadful truth he'd just expressed. "I'm not going to paint a rosy picture for you, Nadine; you know me too well. If we happen to stumble across a cure in our work, fine, we'll make millions as we sell our research to other hospitals. Yet financial gain is not our ultimate goal. These children are valuable because in studying what went wrong in their genetic makeup, we can learn how to make things right again."

A tremor of terror shot through her. "You're using children as lab rats."

He smiled. "Actually, we're helping mankind. We've sterilized every last one of our patients, so we are sparing a future generation from similar suffering. Best of all, we give worth and meaning to our patients' stunted lives. Before they leave us, we take samples of their DNA to help chart our progress back up the genetic staircase. We have devolved, Nadine, but step by step, gene by gene, my researchers are rebuilding the potential of the human race."

She stared at him, unable to speak.

"Now," Sloane said, his voice cold and exact, "we find ourselves at the edge of another set of circles. Congratulations, Nadine, I had not thought to bring you this far. But you are a most persistent woman."

"More circles?" Her voice, like her nerves, was in shreds.

"Three more—my threefold plan. The first phase of my plan was the hospital, of course. Lara Godfrey O'Hara confounded phase two when she took off with the boy, but soon I'll have access to a human being with a 5,300-year head start on the work we're currently doing."

Outside, the sun had set and only a single lamp lit Devin's office. The encroaching darkness felt heavy and threatening. Nadine shifted in her chair. "What will you do with the boy?"

"Rear him, of course, with all my love and attention. Use his DNA as a model. And occasionally take a tissue sample for my work with phase three."

Nadine closed her eyes. Resisting the urge to clap her hands over her ears, she gripped the armrests of her chair. "Go on."

Sloane chuckled softly. "I see I've upset you, and that's a pity. Have you ever considered what makes one man old at age sixty while another is strong and vibrant at seventy? The mechanism that controls human aging is tied up in our genetics. With Hunter's DNA, I will be able to rejuvenate my own genes. I'm fifty-two, but once we find the boy, the implementation of phase three will begin. From our initial research, I believe I will be able to live at least another hundred years . . . in relatively robust health."

His voice was as low as a lover's, but his next words were sharp and tinged with poison. "I trust you with this information, Nadine, because I know you value our association. Those of us in the circle must protect each other, for if the ring breaks, all are equally vulnerable."

She sat without speaking as his threat reverberated through the room and knew he wouldn't hesitate to act against her. If she went to the authorities, Sloane would know—and he'd get to her long before anyone managed to pierce the wall of security around him.

She uncrossed her legs and stood, feeling as hollow as her voice sounded. "Just remember this, Devin." She lowered her gaze into his. "By seeking to transcend human nature, you may fall far below it."

chapter 30

Alternating between optimism and despair, Lara marked off the weeks on the kitchen calendar and tried to help Franklin prepare their case. The trial, the lawyer explained, would be a bench trial, so the final decision would rest in the judge's hands. "We could have elected to have a jury," Franklin said, "but I don't think it's wise to complicate things. Sloane wants to avoid a jury because he fears facing a group of mothers. I'm happy to waive the jury because I'm worried about facing a panel of folks who are too easily impressed with Sloane's money."

"There is one thing that concerns me," he told Lara one afternoon. "Since Sloane's claim rests upon this supposed surrogacy contract, is it possible he is the biological father?"

Lara resisted a sudden wave of nausea. "No. Not according to what Connor and I have learned. But Sloane knows I won't allow DNA testing because there's no telling what it might reveal."

While Franklin prepared interrogatories and subpoenaed records, Lara tried to concentrate on impressing the guardian ad litem. On some days, particularly after Karyn Gower had visited, Lara felt buoyed with a sense of rising confidence. She felt certain that Karyn would support her claim for custody. If the judge agreed with Karyn's assessment, Devin Sloane could never bother their little family again.

On other days, however, particularly if Hunter reported that he'd caught "Miss Karyn" in a lie, Connor would retreat into offended silence. In those moments Lara was certain they were doomed to divorce. Sloane would bribe the judge and take her son; Connor would stare at her with the light of love extinguished from his eyes. He would truthfully say he had tried to warn her, yet she had stubbornly refused to listen.

Standing at the kitchen sink on a Sunday morning, Lara looked out the window, frowned at the horde of reporters loitering across the street, and thanked God for sending Franklin and Harriet Blythe to see her through the most intense trial of her life. The Blythes had unselfishly given of themselves, going so far as to sublet a small apartment so Franklin could prepare for the trial in Charlottesville. Harriet enjoyed taking care of Hunter while Lara and Connor met with her husband, and Franklin seemed to thrive on the work he did for others.

Lara smiled as she remembered the first time she'd seen the lawyer. The generous spirit that drove him to play Santa for poor children was her only defense against Sloane.

The Blythes had been the only guests at Hunter's sixth birthday party. Harriet baked a cake and Franklin bought Hunter a baseball cap and glove. Lara blew up balloons until black spots danced before her eyes, but Connor offered the best gift—an hour in the park tossing the baseball, free from interruptions and reporters. Somehow—Lara didn't quite understand how he arranged it—he called in a favor to his contact at the FBI. An hour later, a swarm of men in dark blue jackets showed up and cleared the park of every news crew and photographer. Lara managed to get some good pictures with her own camera—shots of Connor and Hunter, Harriet and Hunter, Hunter on Franklin's broad shoulder.

Their birthday merriment faded as the days of February slipped by. The news on the investigative front, Franklin reported Friday, was not good. He had found an FBI handwriting expert who would testify that Lara's signature on the surrogacy document *may* have been forged, but with one look at a copy of the contract Lara knew it was authentic. She had signed that paper, but it had been blank at the time. And the witness to her signature, Helmut Braun, carried the truth to his grave.

"Everything we can do," Franklin explained, "Sloane can do better. Our only hope to win this case lies in the judge and how he perceives what's best for Hunter. That's why your relationship with the guardian ad litem is crucial."

Franklin explained that the surrogacy contract was practically a moot point. The Commonwealth of Virginia had taken the halfhearted position of not appearing to endorse surrogacy while not discouraging it, either, so the legal issues involving surrogacy would scarcely bear upon the judge's ruling. More distressing was the knowledge that Judge Harold Weaver had single-handedly raised his six children after his wife abandoned the family in 1990. He fully believed in a father's ability to parent. Franklin feared Weaver might even exhibit an anti-mother bias, particularly if he thought a mother had attempted to flee from her obligations.

As the chime of the doorbell broke into Lara's thoughts, she turned from the kitchen sink and wiped her hands on a towel. She paused by the entrance to the living room to look at her son. Though it was scarcely midday, Hunter had fallen asleep on the couch. One hand lay curled under his chin, bent in what looked like an uncomfortable position.

She resisted the urge to straighten him out, then moved to the door and looked through the peephole. She half-expected Karyn to drop by for an unannounced visit, but Franklin and Harriet stood outside, both of them hunched into their overcoats as a bitter wind blew over the porch.

Lara hurried to open the door. "Hello!" She stepped forward to embrace Harriet. "It's so good to see you."

"I'm sorry for coming by without calling," Franklin said, taking his hat from his head. "But we were on our way back from church, and I thought it might be a good time to go over a few things before the hearing tomorrow. There's something particular I want to discuss with you."

"And," Harriet twinkled with grandmotherly concern, "I wanted to see how my darling boy is doing."

"Come in. Connor's gone to the grocery store, but he'll be back before long." Lara stepped aside, then helped Harriet with her coat as Franklin moved into the living room. She felt a tinge of guilt at the mention of church, but she and Connor had decided that worship attendance would have to wait until after the trial's end. Too many reporters might follow them into the sanctuary.

When Lara and Harriet joined Franklin, the lawyer stood by the side of the couch, his eyes large and liquid as he stared at Lara's sleeping son.

"He's tired." Lara struggled to speak over the lump in her throat. "I don't know why; maybe he senses the strain we've been under these past weeks." She lowered her voice and gestured toward the ottoman and wing chair, inviting the Blythes to sit down. "Lately Connor and I have not exactly been agreeing about what's best. I think Karyn is going to give us a good recommendation, but Connor doesn't trust her because Hunter caught her in a lie."

"One lie?" Harriet pulled her mouth in at the corners. "Goodness, that's not so bad. The little darling has caught me in more than that, even catching my little exaggerations."

Lara felt the corner of her mouth droop as she sank to the end of the couch. "Actually, he's caught her in several fibs. I keep telling Connor it's no big deal. The girl probably *has* to cover up certain things to preserve her own privacy, but Hunter sees through everything."

Franklin pulled an envelope from the inner pocket of his suit coat. "I did a little checking up on Karyn Gower."

Lara felt her mouth go dry. "Don't tell me she's not legit."

"Oh, she's a legitimate guardian ad litem, and she is employed by the city of Charlottesville as a social worker." His face locked with anxiety as he looked at the sleeping boy. "I was more concerned about what she's been doing since taking Hunter's case. I hired a private investigator, expressed my concerns, and he did a little scouting around. I'm not sure exactly how he managed it, but he was able to get a copy of Ms. Gower's bank account records."

Lara fought down the momentary doubt that wrenched her stomach.

"What I found curious," Franklin went on, "is that Ms. Gower earns approximately two thousand dollars per month in her role as a social worker. Last year's bank records show that she deposited nineteen hundred dollars every two weeks, like clockwork, but her pattern changed on January first of this year."

Lara's hands were damp with sweat, yet her mind had gone cold and sharp, focused to a needle's point. "She got a raise?"

"If so, it's news to the city of Charlottesville. They list her salary as $28,000 per year, plus use of a city vehicle for her work. But on January fifteenth, Ms. Gower paid cash for a $15,000 car and made a cash deposit of an additional $13,000. The check she deposited was issued by the Harrington Group and signed by Nadine Harrington."

The lawyer's words didn't register on Lara's dizzied senses. "Is that supposed to mean something to me? I've never heard of them."

"I didn't think you had. They are a private investigation agency in Washington, D.C. Though they'd never admit it, rumor has it that Devin Sloane is at the top of their client list. Nadine Harrington spends so much time in Charlottesville that she has taken an apartment only two miles from Sloane's mansion. And Nadine Harrington has apparently hired Karyn Gower."

Lara stared at the carpet, the muscles of her throat moving in a convulsive swallow. The woman who had smiled at her and held Hunter's hand was Devin Sloane's proxy? Through Karyn Gower's youthful fingers, *Sloane* had run his fingers through Hunter's blond hair, smiled into his blue eyes, caressed his round cheek—

She leaned forward as a nauseous geyser threatened her throat. "How do you know this Harrington woman works for Sloane?"

Franklin pulled a photograph from the envelope, then handed it to Lara. The photo featured a striking blonde woman, and Lara's hand trembled as she ran her fingertips over the image.

"Our investigator flashed that picture around the airport, and one of the pilots confirmed that he'd seen Harrington on Sloane's private jet."

Lara stared at the picture, an image focusing in her memory. She closed her eyes and saw the woman with a different hairdo, in a different outfit. She had come to the clinic complaining of a headache.

Her face burned as the memory came flooding back. "I think I know this woman. She came to the clinic when I was pregnant."

"The pilot said she's been involved with Sloane for years. I think it's safe to assume he brought her in about the time Hunter was born."

"*Before* Hunter was born." Lara's hand flew to her stomach, as if Hunter still lay safely hidden there. "She asked questions about my pregnancy and said she was a widow herself. That's why I remember her—we seemed to have so much in common." She shook her head. "I really liked her."

She handed the picture back, then raised her eyes to find Franklin watching her with a serious expression. "So—isn't this good news for us? If we can prove that Sloane is pulling Karyn Gower's strings, the judge will have to admit we're the innocent party."

Franklin shook his head. "That's just it, I can't prove anything. The pilot our investigator talked to works for Sloane. Though we could subpoena him, there's no way he's going to risk his job by testifying against his boss. And no investigative agency is going to reveal the names of its clients, particularly as wealthy a client as Devin Sloane. Secrecy is their business. If word gets out that Nadine Harrington can't protect her clients' privacy, she'll be finished."

"But—the bank records!"

"I can't prove the connection. Nadine could say she hired Karyn Gower for some other job."

"But we can't let them win!"

"We won't. We have another weapon."

His eyes drifted again to the couch and Lara bit down hard on her lower lip as Franklin said the words she'd been dreading: "Hunter can validate your story."

She shook her head, afraid to speak.

"He tells the truth, Lara. With a small demonstration, we can prove Sloane is lying. Even if Weaver doesn't believe Hunter, Sloane may be rattled enough to slip up. There's something terribly powerful about that little boy's eyes when he pronounces you a liar."

"I won't use him like that."

"It could save your case."

"It could destroy him." Her voice went hoarse with frustration. "Don't you see? The media will be there. If we let Hunter demonstrate his gift, they'll pick up on his story no matter how we try to shield him. Within two hours the *National Enquirer* will be saying he's the child of aliens, and we won't ever be able to live a normal life. I can just imagine what the world will to do to him—"

"We could ask that the interview be held in the judge's chambers. Hunter is so young; I can't imagine the judge interviewing him publicly."

"I won't use him. He's a child, and lately he hasn't been feeling well. He needs a normal, stable life, a life where I can take him to the park and to the doctor's office without a horde of reporters hounding our every step."

"We need the truth, Lara. And that's what Hunter is."

She fell silent, unable to argue. She looked toward her sleeping angel and saw a helpless boy, a sweet cherub who walked with a limp, hated peas, and loved to deepen his voice to mimic Connor's baritone growl . . .

She closed her eyes, wishing Connor were home. Though lately they had been arguing about little things, they did agree that Hunter's gift should remain a secret. If the world learned the story of Hunter's parentage, he'd become another proof of science's miraculous advance, a one-boy freak show. She couldn't subject Hunter to that sort of scrutiny.

Their lives had never been normal . . . but, for a time, at least they had known quiet. And Hunter had known peace.

She smoothed her damp hands on her jeans and clenched her jaw to kill the sob in her throat. "I appreciate what you're saying, really, I do." She looked up at the lawyer and smiled. "I know you love Hunter, and I know you want what's best for him. I'll think about what you've said, but I've got to trust God to make everything all right. I don't think God would have given Hunter to me if he didn't want me to protect him."

Harriet's chin quivered up. "Have you ever thought that God gave Hunter to you in order to reveal his gift of truth?"

Lara answered as gently as she could. "I don't think God expects a five-year-old to teach the world. I do believe God sent Hunter to me for a reason, but I haven't quite figured it out yet. But I will . . . in time."

"I understand why you don't want the world to know about Hunter's gift." Harriet's eyes filled with distress. "But won't you let us tell the court about the Iceman? The world thinks Hunter is Sloane's biological son, but if you let us explain how you were used in that obscene experiment—"

Disconcerted, Lara crossed her arms and pointedly looked away. "I see your point, and I know it may come to that. But that story is nearly as fantastic as Hunter's gift, and I don't want him to go through life as the Iceman's baby." She looked Franklin in the eye. "If you have to tell that part of the truth, you may. But use it only if you absolutely must."

"There's one more thing." Franklin patted his jacket pocket. "I received a call yesterday from a woman who claims to be your mother-in-law."

Lara laughed. "It had to be a reporter. Connor's mother is deceased."

Franklin pulled a pink slip from his pocket and stared at it intently. "Her name is Eva Godfrey. She discovered that your new number was unlisted, but she says she would like to speak to you."

The corner of Lara's mouth twisted. "So Eva finally decided to call," she said, taking the message. "A reporter probably made the connection between us and parked on her doorstep. I'll bet she wants me to call off the hounds . . . as if I could."

"Nothing like that," Franklin said softly. "She said she'd spent the holidays at her flat in London and only returned last week. She has read the paper, of course, and her apology for not contacting you sooner seemed quite sincere."

Lara dropped the message to the coffee table. "She doesn't have to get involved in this. She hates publicity, and she'll really hate it once the trial starts. She was a part of my life a long time ago, but not anymore."

Franklin pushed the message toward Lara. "She wants to help. And at a time like this, one can never have too many friends."

Lara hesitated, then picked up the paper again. "All right. I'll call her."

"I think you'll be glad you did." The lawyer and his wife stood. "If you need anything, don't hesitate to call us."

Lara stood too. "Thanks for coming by. I love you both and appreciate all you've said, but I need to talk to Conner about using Hunter in the trial. We'll tell you what we've decided when we see you in court tomorrow."

She forced a smile when Harriet took her arm. "I'll come here to babysit," she said, her brows a brooding knot over her eyes. "That way, if you need Hunter, I can run him right over to the courthouse."

Lara drew a breath, about to say Hunter wouldn't be going to the courtroom at all, then remembered that she'd promised to at least discuss the idea with Connor.

She patted Harriet's hand, then walked the couple to the door.

∞

Lara stood by the phone and studied Eva's message. Hunter had awakened right after the Blythes left, and Lara welcomed the chance to prepare lunch and talk to her husband and son. But after only a few minutes of play, Hunter grew tired again. Now he lay in her bed with Connor, his arm tucked around the stuffed monkey Connor bought him, his head on Connor's chest. Connor had stretched out with a book, and Lara knew he'd lie there, quiet and still, for as long as Hunter napped.

If she was going to call, she might as well do it while the house was quiet. Eva was probably afraid Lara might mention her name in the trial or that some tawdry bit of testimony would tarnish the Godfrey family lineage.

"No need to worry," Lara murmured as she dialed. "My son is no relation to you."

The phone had scarcely completed its first ring when she heard Eva's voice, breathless and husky. "Hello?"

"Eva." Lara forced a smile into her voice. "Mr. Blythe gave me your number. I hear you've been in London."

"Of course, dear; you know I always winter there. I wanted to apologize for not reaching you sooner, but I had no idea you'd come back until I landed at La Guardia and happened to see a newspaper."

Lara hesitated. Was she supposed to apologize for disappearing to save her child's life? Or perhaps Eva was upset because there were no messages from Lara on her telephone answering machine. Lara *could* have tried to call after returning to Charlottesville, but she could see no purpose in it. Eva had been against Lara's pregnancy from the beginning, she had disapproved of Connor, and she would pass out in a genuine aristocratic faint if she ever learned the full truth behind Hunter's conception.

Still, the woman had been Michael's mother, and the two of them had once been close. Perhaps she deserved an explanation she could palm off on her fellow Women's Clubbers.

"Eva," Lara began, "Hunter is not your grandson. So don't feel obligated to call or visit or check up on us. We're going to get through this."

"Lara." Eva's tone was coolly disapproving. "I know everything. When I came back, I found a package from Olivia Densen in my mail. I'm not sure why the poor woman sent it to me, but her note said the tape was recorded by Helmut Braun."

Lara felt a shock run through her. "A tape?"

"That's what I said, isn't it? I listened to it, and on this tape Braun confessed what he did to you. I know all about the Iceman and Sloane's involvement. I know how he tried to create a superhuman from ancient DNA—"

"That's great, Eva, I'm sure my lawyer will want to know all about it." Unwilling to hear another word, Lara glanced toward the bedroom. The secret she wanted to keep buried had just reared its head from an unexpected source. "Send Mr. Blythe the tape, will you? It will help convince the judge I'm telling the truth."

"Lara, I'd really like to see the boy."

"I don't think that's a good idea. He's not well; I think the stress is getting to him. So pray for us and send the tape to my lawyer."

"Lara, I'd—"

"I've gotta run, Eva, before Hunter wakes up. Thanks for calling."

Lara hung up before Eva could speak again; then she leaned against the refrigerator and slowly slid down it until she sat on the floor.

So Helmut had made a tape before he died. In a fit of conscience, probably, he spilled the secrets of his soul, mailed the tape to Olivia, then pulled the trigger.

Olivia, bless her heart, hadn't known how to reach Lara. So she mailed the tape to Eva Godfrey, knowing Eva would deliver it.

And though Lara had been shocked to hear that her mother-in-law knew the truth, Eva would be the last woman in the world to reveal that her supposed grandson had been begotten by an Iceman. Women like Eva still went pale at the thought of visiting a gynecologist.

Lara pressed her hands over her face and sighed. If things began to look bleak during the trial, at least the tape could prove there had never been a surrogacy agreement.

chapter 31

Lara shifted uneasily in the wooden chair and wished she owned a more comfortable suit. She had sent Connor to the mall to buy something suitable for the trial, and the size 10 he brought home was cut for a younger, less sedentary woman. The waistband insisted on creeping toward Lara's ribs, making it nearly impossible for her to draw a deep breath.

After arriving at the courthouse she had turned, just once, to survey the mob behind her. The resulting strobic blaze of camera flashes was enough to make her resolve never to turn around again. As Franklin led her and Connor into the courtroom, she saw that people were wedged into the long rows of the spectator's gallery like church members on pack-a-pew night. More reporters stood at the back of the room, camera bags dangling from their shoulders and steno pads in their hands.

Only two rows back, almost directly behind Lara, Eva Godfrey held her purse on her lap as though she feared one of the rabid mob might try to snatch it.

Lara shifted and tried to find a comfortable position. Connor sat at her left hand and Franklin Blythe at her right. Immediately across the aisle from Franklin, Devin Sloane sat with an entire battery of lawyers, his demeanor as cool as an undertaker at a hanging.

Lara averted her eyes, wishing a more friendly metaphor had come to mind. She had lain awake half the night praying for Franklin, for Hunter, and for the judge. Connor roused himself at three a.m. and joined her by the side of the bed. Together, on their knees, they prayed and wept, then greeted the sunrise with a prayer of thanksgiving. "I will praise you, Father, and I will trust you with whatever tomorrow brings," Lara whispered as dawn glowed sullen and gray around the edges of the curtains. "I will praise you, even if you take all I hold dear. For if you take Hunter from me, you will have taken everything."

Connor sat silently beside her now, his expression impassive. He reached out, his fingertips brushing her back. "You okay? Do you want a glass of water?"

Lara shook her head. "Don't look now, but Eva is sitting behind us."

Connor folded his hands, but he didn't turn around. "Is that good?"

"I don't think so. I'm surprised she came at all, but I asked her to give that tape to Franklin. I'm sure that's the only reason she's here."

"You should say hello." A spark of some indefinable emotion flashed in his eyes. "I'm sure she's trying to be supportive."

"Supportive?" Lara's voice coagulated with sarcasm. "If she wouldn't support me when she thought I was carrying her grandson, what makes you think she'd support me now?"

"All rise," the clerk interrupted. The courtroom fell silent as Judge Weaver entered and took his seat behind the imposing bench. As Weaver pulled out his glasses, the clerk officially began the proceeding. "This court is now in session. Civil Action 993-2957, Sloane versus Godfrey."

Lara straightened and tried to compose her features into smooth, pleasant lines.

The judge opened by asking all those without a seat to leave immediately. "This is a court of law, not a circus," he said simply, surveying his domain. "If order is not maintained in this courtroom, I will not hesitate to clear the gallery. And I see cameras—though I can't deny the press its right to take pictures, I do have the power to limit that right in my courtroom. Tomorrow I will ask the guards to confiscate any cameras at the security checkpoint. Is that understood?"

Silence, thick as wool, wrapped itself around Lara, and for an instant she wondered if the crowd had slipped out of the chamber. But a screech of a chair cut through the stillness as Madison Jarvis, Sloane's lawyer, stood and tucked his fingertips into his vest pockets. With all the thunder and righteousness of a revival preacher, in his opening statement he accused Lara Godfrey O'Hara of selling the child in her womb, then changing her mind and fleeing with the baby in the hope of further extortion.

"For five long years, that woman kept *my* client, Devin Sloane"—Jarvis gestured toward the billionaire—"from enjoying a relationship with his *own* son. We would ask the court, Your Honor, to honor the terms of the surrogacy contract and require Mrs. O'Hara to surrender the child she has *willfully* and *spitefully* abducted."

A long, brittle silence followed, broken only by a few nervous coughs from the gallery; then Franklin rose to make his opening statement. "My client, Lara Godfrey O'Hara"—he gestured respectfully toward Lara—"has done nothing to Mr. Sloane, as the evidence will prove. This woman wanted nothing more than to bear a child, and she *believed* she was carrying the child of her late husband. The surrogacy document is not genuine, and Mr. Sloane cannot produce a shred of proof to indicate that my client either attempted or intended to commit extortion. *We* shall prove that my client has not only been harassed and maligned, but is a victim of the most heinous sort of battery imaginable. We will show, Your Honor, that Lara Godfrey was impregnated with an embryo conceived from a stranger's DNA, not her husband's. Being the sort of woman she is, she loves the child regardless of his paternity, and she has sacrificed five years of her life to be sure the boy lay beyond Mr. Sloane's considerable reach. At this moment, the child is happy and well cared for in her home. She and Mr. O'Hara are loving, nurturing parents."

The judge scratched his nose. "Because this case involves a minor, I would like to hear from the guardian ad litem at this point." He peered over his reading glasses and searched the courtroom. "Is Ms. Gower present?"

Lara closed her eyes, knowing that Karyn Gower sat on the first row behind Devin Sloane's counsel table. Lara had tried to catch the young woman's eye as they entered the courtroom, but Karyn had steadfastly refused to look in her direction. Not a good sign.

"Your honor." Karyn's clear voice rang through the chamber. "In eight supervised visits with the child, Hunter Godfrey, I saw signs of indisputable neglect. Not only has the boy been deprived of stability, but he has few belongings, toys, and not nearly enough clothing. Most important, he suffers from a limp and extreme weariness, but the mother has refused to seek medical treatment."

Lara leaned over to whisper in Franklin's ear. "Not true! We saw a doctor, but we weren't allowed to leave town to see the specialist!"

"I have also had occasion to visit in Mr. Sloane's home," Karyn went on. "And I can attest to the preparations Mr. Sloane has made for his son. The boy will benefit from every material comfort as well as the attention of a well-adjusted, stable parent. My preliminary recommendation is that the boy be consigned to the care of his biological father."

"Thank you, Ms. Gower. The plaintiff and defendant will, of course, reserve the right to call you to the witness stand." The judge glanced at his notes, then folded his hands and stared at Sloane's entourage. "We'll let the plaintiffs call their first witness."

The parade of witnesses began. Sloane's lawyer produced a psychologist who stated that over the past few years Sloane had spoken to him several times about his son, always with worried concern. "Devin Sloane is a loving and concerned father," the doctor concluded. "And I hope he will be able to care for the child he loves."

Lara gave Connor a sidelong glance of utter disbelief when the bailiff called Carol Bartlett to the stand. Lara had not seen the medical transcriptionist since leaving Charlottesville six years before. She had always considered Carol a friend, but six years could put considerable distance between people . . .

After Carol had been sworn to tell the truth, Madison Jarvis paced before her in a dignified, stately gait. "Did Mrs. O'Hara, who was then Lara Godfrey, ever mention Devin Sloane in your hearing?"

"Oh yes, quite frequently." Carol smiled at Sloane, her eyes creasing in an expression of admiration. "We had these little coffee klatches, you see, and we were always talking about celebrities. I particularly remember one day when someone mentioned that Devin Sloane was expecting a child from a surrogate mother. Right away, Lara piped up and said she'd recently met Sloane herself."

Jarvis turned and stared at Lara. "Did Lara Godfrey seem at all upset by her encounter with Mr. Sloane?"

Carol twittered at the question. "Oh, no. She was really quite excited. She said she'd met Mr. Sloane at the cryogenics lab, which we all thought was a little strange. Only later did I realize that it was only logical—if she was Mr. Sloane's surrogate, of course they'd meet there."

"Objection!" Franklin leapt to his feet. "The witness is speculating, not reporting the facts."

"Objection sustained." The judge rested his chin in his hand and glanced down at Carol. "Please tell us only what you saw, Ms. Bartlett. I'm afraid you must leave the conclusions to me."

"We'll move on." Jarvis's brow lifted. "What did Lara Godfrey tell you about the baby she carried?"

"She said it was her husband's." For the first time, Carol's gaze darted toward Lara. "But we all knew there'd been problems. Olivia—Dr. Braun's wife—said her husband was concerned about Lara's husband's genes. He'd died of bone cancer, you see. We knew Lara didn't want a baby that might develop cancer. She once told me that she'd suffered so terribly with her husband, there was no way she wanted to go through that again."

"But she led you to believe the baby was her late husband's?"

Carol smiled and fingered a loose tendril of hair on her neck. "That's what she said, sure."

"Did she say or do anything that would cause you to doubt her word?"

The transcriptionist leaned forward, regarding the lawyer with an intense but secret expression. "Well, we all remarked on the coincidence of her baby being due at the same time as Mr. Sloane's. There was a lot of press about Sloane's surrogate arrangement, and whenever we talked about it, Lara turned away or left the room. Then, late in her pregnancy, Sloane began to visit the office, and Lara told us that he made her uncomfortable—she said he made her feel like an egg about to hatch. Now I can see why she said that. He was waiting on his baby, so of course he wanted to know how Lara's pregnancy was progressing."

Franklin sprang to his feet. "Objection, speculative! Your Honor, that remark is highly presumptive. The witness cannot know what Devin Sloane was thinking."

"Objection sustained." The judge frowned. "Again, Ms. Bartlett, I ask you to confine your remarks to things you actually observed."

"Yes sir."

Madison Jarvis moved to the counsel table, consulted his notes, then turned again to his witness. "I'm sorry, Ms. Bartlett, about the recent tragedy that claimed the lives of four of your colleagues. Such a random act of senseless violence is difficult to comprehend."

Carol's brows drew together. "Thank you, sir. Yes. Dr. Densen, Gaynel, Rita, and Sharon were good friends as well as coworkers."

"If they had not been so cruelly murdered, could they have offered testimony to substantiate your recollections?"

Carol nodded. "Definitely. It was a small office, so we all knew everything the others were going through. The other ladies heard everything I heard."

"Objection." Franklin stood again, his face a mask of weary exasperation. "Your honor, the witness cannot speak for the deceased."

"I'm only establishing the fact that Carol Bartlett is not the only one who heard these comments made by Lara Godfrey." Jarvis turned toward the judge. "She is not putting words into their mouths."

The judge folded one arm on the desk and pointed at the plaintiff's counsel pen. "I'll allow it, but tread carefully, Mr. Jarvis."

Madison Jarvis paused to stroke his chin. "Tell me about January 29, 1999. You were working at the clinic office, correct?"

The transcriptionist nodded, then sent a superior smile winging Lara's way. "Yes. Dr. Densen had been called to the hospital to deliver a baby, but Gaynel, Sharon, Rita, and I were working. Lara was in the office too, though we all knew she was due to deliver."

"What happened that morning?"

"Lara thought she might be in labor, so she had Olivia examine her." A half smile crossed the transcriptionist's face. "It was false labor. So Olivia went on to the hospital and Lara stayed at the office. I found her at my desk, working at the computer. She had opened her patient file and was staring at the computer monitor with this really strange expression on her face. Then she became hysterical."

"Hysterical?" Jarvis lifted one eyebrow and pointed at Lara. "That professional, rational woman became hysterical?"

Carol nodded. "It happens sometimes when women go into labor. They think they know what to expect, and then—wow. So when she got rattled, I called Dr. Braun."

"Dr. *Helmut* Braun?"

"Yes."

"Why would you call him? He's not an obstetrician."

"No, but he was involved with Lara's case. I knew from the chart that he'd been receiving updates of her patient file."

"Was that unusual?""

Carol shrugged. "A little. But Dr. Braun had handled the IVF and embryo transfer. He came around the office a lot, and I knew Lara trusted him. So he came over and gave her something to calm her down so he could drive her to the hospital. He asked Gaynel to keep an eye on Lara while he went to get his car."

"What happened next?"

The line of Carol's mouth tightened. "When I came into the hall, I saw Gaynel standing there, rubbing her head. She said Lara hit her, then ran out the back door. I was so shocked, I didn't know what to think."

"Would it be logical to assume that Lara Godfrey knew her labor had begun?"

Carol glanced at Franklin Blythe. "She was a physician's assistant, so she certainly knew the signs."

"In your experience, Ms. Bartlett, have you encountered women who made adoption or surrogacy plans and then experienced a change of heart?"

"Yes." Carol surveyed the courtroom with a prim and forbidding expression. "I couldn't begin to count the number of women in our practice who planned to surrender their babies but panicked at the last moment."

"That morning, when you found Lara Godfrey staring at her own chart on the computer—is it possible that the expression on her face was one of *panic*?"

"That's exactly the word I'd use, so yes, it's certainly possible."

"Perhaps she'd had a change of heart?"

"Perhaps."

Madison Jarvis turned and looked at the crowd of spectators. He spoke to his witness again without facing her. "Ms. Bartlett, when did you next see Lara Godfrey?"

"This morning, sir, in this courtroom. She disappeared in January '99, and I haven't seen a trace of her till today."

A churchlike stillness reigned in the courtroom, with nothing but a muffled cough from the gallery to disturb it. Madison Jarvis turned to Franklin Blythe. "Your witness."

Franklin stood, tapped his fingertips on the notepad on the table, then smiled at the woman on the witness stand. "Ms. Bartlett, you have just testified that you called Dr. Braun the morning of January 29, 1999. Do you remember what you told him on the telephone?"

Carol looked at the lawyer with a suggestion of annoyance in her eyes. "Word for word? No, I don't recall."

Franklin moved toward her. "But you are certain you called."

"Yes. Dr. Densen was in surgery, and Dr. Stock was somewhere—I don't remember where."

"I checked the records. Dr. Stock was enjoying a day off, though she was on call."

Carol lifted one shoulder in a shrug. "Whatever."

"I also checked the phone records, Ms. Bartlett, and there was no record of any call from the Women's Medical Center to the cryogenics lab. You did not call Dr. Braun—so can you tell me how he knew to come rushing over?"

The woman's brows rose; then a cold, congested expression settled on her face. "I'm certain *someone* called. That's why Dr. Braun came to the clinic."

"But *you* don't specifically remember calling."

She glared at the lawyer. "It was a long time ago. I have trouble remembering what I did last week."

Franklin shrugged as if to say her poor memory didn't matter. "Ms.

Bartlett, would you say that you and Lara Godfrey were good friends before her disappearance?"

She answered with an impersonal nod. "We were friends."

"*Good* friends?"

"Just friends. We didn't socialize, but Lara didn't socialize with anyone outside the office. She was sort of reclusive."

"Really? Isn't it likely that she didn't have much time for socializing? After all, the woman had spent three years nursing her husband through cancer. At the time of her pregnancy, she was still mourning his loss."

Carol stroked the hair at the back of her neck. "I suppose that's possible. She didn't talk much about her life outside the office."

"But at least twice today you have attempted to tell the court what Lara Godfrey was thinking. Did you know her well enough to read her thoughts?"

"I knew her well enough in the office," Carol said, her mouth set in annoyance. "We were close enough."

"That's fine. Knowing her as you did, in the first few months of Lara's pregnancy did you have any reason to doubt her contention that she was carrying her husband's baby?"

"I've already said," Carol answered, a hint of censure in her tone, "that I began to notice things—like the coincidence of her baby and Sloane's being due at the same time. And Sloane kept coming around, and Lara would get all weird when he showed up. So, yes, I had reason to doubt her contention."

"Did Lara Godfrey ever speak of her plans for the child?"

Carol blinked. "Pardon?"

"Her plans—you know, how she was decorating the nursery, what sort of crib she wanted. Did she buy baby clothes? Did you and the other women ever discuss giving her a baby shower?"

"Olivia mentioned it once." Carol's gaze kept flicking away from Franklin, as though afraid to rest very long on the saintly countenance before her. "But Lara said she wanted to wait until after the baby was born. She said she had everything she would need in the beginning."

"Did she mention that she and her late husband had already decorated a nursery?"

Carol's eyelids lowered. "She might have said that."

Franklin turned and looked at Lara. "Ms. Bartlett, does a woman who plans to surrender a child decorate a nursery and buy baby clothes?"

Silence filled the space between the lawyer and the witness stand.

"Does she, Ms. Bartlett?"

"She does if she's thinking about changing her mind!"

"But she decorated the nursery while her husband was still living, long before she became pregnant. So Mrs. Godfrey did not change her mind and *then* decorate the nursery. She planned and prepared for her husband's baby because she fully intended to keep it."

Lara felt her tense nerves relax when her lawyer smiled at Carol. "Thank you very much, Ms. Bartlett. You've shed light on some important issues."

The judge looked back to Madison Jarvis. "Do you wish to cross?"

Jarvis cast a glance of well-mannered dislike in Franklin's direction, then stood. "No, Your Honor. We'd like to call our next witness."

Franklin returned to the defense table as Carol exited the witness stand. The judge glanced at his watch. "This court will take a short recess," he said, rapping the bench with his gavel. "We will convene in ten minutes with the plaintiff's next witness."

"That will be Devin Sloane," Franklin whispered, leaning toward Lara. "If you want a minute to yourself, there's a private ladies' room through that doorway." He nodded toward a door near the front of the courtroom. "Don't go into the main hall or the media will eat you alive."

The solemn quiet of the courtroom dissolved into noise as the judge slipped away from the bench. Lara stood and squeezed Connor's shoulder. "I'll be back," she whispered in his ear. "I need a breath of air."

He squeezed her hand. "Go ahead. I'll be waiting."

∞

Lara had just left the courtroom when Connor felt someone tug on his jacket sleeve. He turned and saw Eva Godfrey standing behind him, as polished and porcelain as when he had last seen her over six years before. Her hair gleamed with more silver than it had then, but the steel in those blue eyes had not diminished.

"Mr. O'Hara." Her powerful gaze, which could intimidate most men even from a good distance, seemed to shine with a beaten sadness, and her voice was husky. "May I have a word with you?"

"Certainly, Mrs. Godfrey." He stood, then tapped Franklin's shoulder. "Mr. Blythe, I'd like you to meet Eva Godfrey."

In a sweeping gesture of gallantry, Franklin stood and clasped Eva's hand. "Mrs. Godfrey, it is good to finally meet you." One of his brows lifted. "Did Lara return your call?"

"She did." The lady took a deep breath and reinforced her wavering smile. "I'm afraid things didn't go very well between us, but she did ask me to give you this." She pulled her hand from the lawyer's grip, then reached into the leather handbag that hung from her shoulder. From it she took an envelope and gave it to the lawyer. Connor recognized the Women's Clinic logo next to the return address.

"I believe that tape is Helmut Braun's final confession." Eva laced her fingertips together and paused. "Dr. Braun speaks quite candidly—he certainly explains a great deal more than I ever wanted to know. I tried to tell Lara that I knew the truth, but she asked that I give the tape to you. I'm sure you can use it to clear up this ridiculous notion that she agreed to be a surrogate mother for Devin Sloane."

The lawyer seemed to weigh the packet in his palm. "I'll listen to it tonight, Mrs. Godfrey. If it really is Braun's dying confession, we can get it admitted as evidence tomorrow morning . . . if Lara will allow it. I'd like to make this case go away as soon as possible, for Lara's sake and Hunter's."

A flash of longing illuminated the lady's blue eyes. "I'd love to see the boy, Mr. O'Hara. I know that with just one look I could clear up so much confusion—"

"I'll have to ask Lara." Connor would have said more, but the judge had returned to the bench, and spectators were surging forward to reclaim their seats. "I'll do what I can."

Eva smiled, then returned to her place on the second row. For a long moment Connor and Franklin stared at the envelope on the table; then Franklin opened it. Inside was a single microcassette and a slip of paper. A feminine hand had written, "Lara—this is from Helmut. Use it. All my best, Olivia."

The sharp crack of the gavel jolted Connor as Lara slipped into her place between the two men. Connor glanced at Franklin, wondering if he would tell Lara about the tape, but the lawyer had already whisked the envelope, tape, and note out of sight.

Connor sat back, quite willing to keep quiet until the proper time.

∞

Buoyed by an indefatigable sense of certainty, Devin Sloane obeyed the summons and moved to the front of the courtroom.

"Do you, Devin Sloane, swear to tell the truth, the whole truth, and nothing but the truth, so help you God?"

"I do."

Devin removed his hand from the Bible, then stepped onto the dais and sat in the witness chair. Madison Jarvis stood before him, his eyes shining.

"Mr. Sloane, do you recognize the woman seated at the defendant's counsel table?"

"I do."

"For the record, would you tell us where you first met her?"

"Certainly." Devin flashed a smile toward the sketch artist. "I first met her in a laboratory outside Helmut Braun's office in the spring of 1998. We spoke briefly. During the conversation she impressed me as a warm, giving, nurturing person."

"The sort of person who would make a good mother?"

"As a matter of fact, yes." Sloane leaned back and crossed his legs. "The very next day, I visited Dr. Braun again and told him I had met Lara Godfrey. As it happened, I had provided certain genetic material to Dr. Braun and he had been searching for a suitable candidate to bear my child. None of the other candidates had proved as appropriate as Lara."

Jarvis pulled a document from his litigation case and carried it to the judge's bench. "Here, Your Honor, are affidavits from twenty women, all of whom have sworn that in the winter of 1997–98 they submitted biographical material to Mr. Sloane's representative, Bill Masters. The affidavits state that each woman *clearly* understood that her biographical information would be used to gauge her suitability as a surrogate mother."

The judge lifted the document, thumbed through it briefly, then dropped it onto his desk. "Continue."

The lawyer turned back to Sloane. "Did Lara Godfrey discuss this surrogate arrangement with you?"

"Not directly, no." Sloane shifted in his chair, then looked across the courtroom to Lara. "I didn't think it wise to approach her before the pregnancy was established. I didn't want any complications to arise between us if for some reason the IVF procedure failed."

"Did Ms. Godfrey make any demands of her own?"

"As a matter of fact, she did. Mrs. Godfrey was quite explicit in her request that we not fertilize several embryos at once. The disposal of unneeded embryos went against her religious convictions, so Dr. Braun was forced to do a separate IVF procedure prior to each attempt at implantation."

"Wouldn't that involve a great deal of expense?" The lawyer frowned. "She demanded that you perform in vitro fertilization for only one embryo when you could have fertilized half a dozen?"

"Expense was no object; I wanted to her to be happy." Devin folded his hands in a tranquil pose. "I respected her religious convictions, in fact, I was grateful for them. I wanted my son to have a capacity for spiritual interest and thought it highly significant that Lara Godfrey was a deeply religious person."

Jarvis leaned toward him in a gentle, inquiring fashion. "Did you speak to Mrs. Godfrey while Dr. Braun was performing the IVF procedure?"

"I did not." Devin's gaze slid across the gallery, noting the quick movement of pens over notepads. "For the sake of avoiding future entanglements, I did not want to become too close to Mrs. Godfrey. I didn't want her to become attached to me, either. Fortunately, though, the first implantation was successful. Lara confirmed her pregnancy with Dr. Braun on May 22, 1998."

Jarvis nodded. "During the pregnancy, did you make any effort to contact Mrs. Godfrey?"

Devin spread his hands. "I'll confess, I didn't think it prudent to remain in close contact with her. So I kept to myself and began to prepare for the baby. I arranged for a nanny and remodeled a wing of the house for his nursery and the nanny's quarters. I even asked my administrative assistant to clear my calendar for an entire year after the baby's due date." He looked away, grateful that a flush heated his face. "I'm afraid I made quite a fool of myself. The tabloids and entertainment programs gathered all sorts of footage of me buying toys and whatnot. I know I should have been more restrained, but I couldn't help it. I was thrilled with the idea of having a son."

"Mr. Sloane"—Jarvis stepped back to allow the gallery an unobstructed view—"why did you want a child? You are not a young man. Why would you want to invest your time and energy in a *baby*?"

Sloane lowered his eyes, allowing the silence to stretch. "I had a wife and a son," he finally whispered, his voice breaking, "until an unfortunate accident snatched my loved ones from me. For several months after the tragedy, I poured myself into my work. But I soon discovered that work is meaningless unless you are performing it for the benefit of others. That is why I established the Ethan Jefferson Pediatric Hospital for Genetic Research and named it after my son. Every patient we treat is needy, and no patient is ever charged a penny for treatment."

He lifted his head and looked straight into the judge's eyes. "My son did not suffer from a genetic illness, but many other parents are not as fortunate. No one wants to pass lethal genes on to their children if they can help it, and our work at the pediatric hospital is slowly changing the face of the future. The Human Genome Project spent ten years decoding the three billion chemical letters that spell out more than seventy thousand genes; my researchers are now determining which combinations of those chemicals result in a corrupt gene, which will in turn lead to illness or premature death."

Shifting in his chair, Devin looked at Lara and saw a flash of cold in her eyes. "I met Lara Godfrey and knew she was an extraordinary woman. I thought it propitious that we should meet at Braun's lab, a place where life could be created. So I selected her to bear my son, an extraordinary boy with spiritual depth and unique gifts."

Devin smiled at the reporters in the gallery. "I have always been honest about the surrogate arrangement and how my son came to be."

"Objection!" Wearing a weary expression, Franklin Blythe stood. "The witness is supposed to be speaking to the court, not grandstanding for the media."

"Objection overruled." The judge looked down at Devin. "I appreciate your candor, Mr. Sloane, and I'll allow your comments in the record, but I must ask you to confine your remarks to me and the lawyers. Let the members of the media earn their pay; don't spoon-feed them."

Jarvis turned back to the counsel table, ostensibly to study his notes, but Devin noted the flurry of activity in the gallery and knew the lawyer was giving the reporters time to catch up. That last speech would make a perfect sound bite . . . if the judge had allowed video cameras into the courtroom.

Turning to face his client, Jarvis leaned on the oak counsel table. "We've heard testimony from Carol Bartlett that you often visited the Women's Clinic in the winter of 1998–99. Why did you go there?"

"I couldn't help it." Devin gave the judge a tentative smile. "I tried to discipline myself, but I was like a kid who can't wait for Christmas. I wanted to see Lara Godfrey, to make sure things were okay. I know how wonderful it is to *share* a pregnancy, and I was beginning to feel a little left out. So I asked Dr. Braun if I could accompany him to the clinic, just once a week or so."

"Did you ever say anything to Mrs. Godfrey about the arrangement?"

"Never. I didn't want to make her feel uncomfortable in front of her coworkers."

"Did you ever mention the surrogacy agreement to any of the other clinic staff?"

"No. I didn't know if she had confided in any of them."

Jarvis turned and pulled a copy of the contract from a folder. "Is this the surrogacy contract, Mr. Sloane?"

Devin gave the document a cursory glance. "Yes, but I believe that's a copy. Ms. Godfrey signed the original in blue ink."

"Is that your signature?"

"Yes."

"Were you present when Mrs. Godfrey signed the agreement?""

"No, Dr. Braun had her sign it at the lab. He witnessed both signatures, but at different times."

Jarvis pulled another document from his case and walked it to the judge's bench. "Your Honor, I'd like to submit the original contract between these two parties and an affidavit from Jules Bergen, a handwriting expert from the FBI. Mr. Bergen has studied signatures from Mrs. Godfrey and Mr. Sloane. He attests that both signatures on the contract are original."

"Your Honor, I object."

Devin sank back as Lara's lawyer stood.

"The issue at hand is not whether the signatures are original—the issue is whether the document is binding. My client does not dispute that she signed several papers while at Dr. Braun's lab."

The judge shot the opposing lawyer a withering glance. "Objection overruled. Save it, Mr. Blythe, for your cross-examination."

"Thank you, Your Honor." Jarvis left the affidavit and contract on the judge's desk, then tugged on his coat as he turned to Devin. "What was the exact arrangement between you and Mrs. Godfrey?"

Devin scratched his chin. "It was actually quite simple. She agreed to bear my child and surrender him immediately after birth; in return, I agreed to cover all expenses related to the cyropreservation, IVF, embryo transfer, and prenatal care. In addition, because Mrs. Godfrey held a vital interest in cancer research, I agreed to donate one million dollars to the cancer research program at the University of Virginia Medical School." He glanced at the judge. "That money was donated in the name of the Muriel Foundation, a philanthropic organization dedicated to the memory of my late wife."

Devin suppressed a smile when a flutter of surprise rippled through the gallery. He could play this crowd like a piano.

The judge rapped on his desk and called for order.

When quiet had been restored, Jarvis turned to the defendant's table and pointed toward Lara Godfrey. "Did you at any time offer that woman a lump sum payment for carrying your child?"

"No." Devin clipped the word. "Such an act would be illegal."

"Did she demand money from you?"

"No." Devin's gaze lowered, as did his voice. "She behaved with perfect honor until the moment she fled and took my child with her."

"Did you try to find Mrs. Godfrey and the baby?"

"Of course. I called the police; I had a judge issue a pickup order for the child. When those efforts proved fruitless, I hired a private investigator. But we found nothing, not a trace, until three months ago. One of the investigators found a nurse in Florida who matched Lara Godfrey's description. After that, we were able to confirm her identity."

"What happened next?"

"She ran again."

"Do you believe she has stopped running now?"

"I certainly hope so, but I'm afraid she came here only because she had no other options."

Jarvis came forward and tapped his fingers on the witness box railing in a meditative rhythm. "Mr. Sloane, do you hate this woman? Do you resent her for all the sorrow and grief she has caused you?"

"I could never hate my son's mother."

Jarvis gazed at Lara Godfrey with chilling intentness for a long moment, then gripped the rail of the witness box. "Have you any words for Lara Godfrey?"

From the corner of his eye Devin saw Franklin Blythe begin to rise, but Lara's pale hand caught his elbow. The old lawyer sank back into his chair, a weight of sadness on his lined face.

"I would like Mrs. Godfrey—excuse me, Mrs. O'Hara—to know that I love my son. I have planned for him, prepared for him, and I will protect him with my life." Devin's gaze met Lara's and for once she did not pull away. "What can you give him that I cannot? I see him as the beginning of the future, a bright hope for mankind. I will bequeath all that I am and have to him, and he will be the one to lead future generations into a world of light and truth."

Lara's eyes widened; then she hunched forward, her hand rising to smother a choking sound that sprang from laughter or sorrow, he couldn't tell which. Connor O'Hara embraced his wife while the lawyer's face brightened to a tomato shade.

The reporters, Devin realized, hadn't noticed Lara's reaction. Their eyes were intent upon their notebooks, their pencils dutifully recording his prophecy.

"That's all, Mr. Sloane." Jarvis stepped back and glanced at the defense lawyer, then smiled. "Mr. Blythe, you may cross-examine the witness."

chapter 32

Lara felt her stomach twist as she considered the irony in Sloane's words. Lead future generations into a world of *truth*? Sloane had no idea how right he was. Hunter was capable of leading the world all right, but Sloane and others like him wouldn't recognize Hunter's truth. Hunter recognized *absolute* truth, not the sort of half-truth Sloane had indulged in today.

She looked down and studied the whorls in the wooden table as Franklin began to question Sloane about the contract and their supposed arrangement. Franklin was right; she saw that clearly now. Sloane was a liar and a manipulator, but he had leavened his lies with enough truth that the judge might find them palatable. That *was* her handwriting on the contract, and nearly everything he said on the stand today could be proven or supported by other witnesses. She could protest until the dawn of eternity, but nothing would change the fact that she had signed a blank document and might pay a severe penalty for her foolishness. She had trusted a friend who had proven himself open to temptation.

She rested her elbow on the table and covered her mouth as her mind burned with the memory of Eva's call. There remained a tape. Eva said Helmut had left a confession that would resolve the case; surely that meant he had confessed to creating the surrogacy contract *after* she signed a blank page. But apparently Dr. Braun had also confessed to using the Iceman's DNA for her son's conception.

A sense of foreboding descended over her with a shiver. Did she want the world to know the full truth about her son? If Franklin submitted the tape as evidence, her life and Hunter's would be an open book for every eye in the courtroom to read. As much as it pained her to admit it, Hunter might be better off living in disguise than to be so exposed. The world would call him a freak; political cartoonists would sketch him with a sloping forehead and hairy arms. Scientists would think of him as some kind of bizarre evolutionary throwback. If the world pressed for more information about her son, it would only be a matter of time before they discovered his gift . . . and tried to abuse it.

Her heart thumped against her rib cage. *Dear God, what am I supposed to do? Why did you bring us to this place? I want to settle this matter, but I can't give my son to Sloane. If it means taking Hunter and running again, I'll do it, but how can we leave Connor?*

The sound of Franklin saying, "I have nothing else for this witness" snapped her back to the present. Had he already finished with Sloane? Lara searched Connor's face, hoping for some clue to indicate how Franklin had fared in the cross-examination, but her husband's eyes were flat and dark under the fluorescent lights, unreadable.

Madison Jarvis stood and addressed the judge. "We would like to call Lara Godfrey O'Hara to the stand."

Scarcely aware of what she was doing, Lara pushed back her chair, then moved toward the bailiff. She placed her hand on the Bible and felt comforted by the touch of soft leather beneath her skin. "Do you swear to tell the truth, the whole truth, and nothing but the truth?" the bailiff intoned, his eyes not meeting Lara's.

If only he knew! She'd been speaking truth for nearly six years. Hunter would accept no less.

"I do." She lifted her hand and stepped into the witness box, then sat and adjusted her skirt, suddenly aware of the pressure of myriad pairs of eyes.

"State your name for the record," the bailiff instructed.

"Lara Godfrey O'Hara."

Madison Jarvis stepped forward with brittle dignity. "Mrs. O'Hara, do you have a son called Hunter?"

"Yes."

"His age?"

"His sixth birthday was January twenty-ninth."

"You are his biological mother?"

"Yes."

"Where was he born?"

"Charlottesville, Virginia."

Her answer seemed to amuse him. "Let me rephrase the question. Where—*precisely*—was your son born?"

Lara glanced at Connor, then lowered her gaze. "He was born in my neighbor's apartment."

The lawyer retreated a step, his face contorting in an expression of mock horror. "Not in a hospital? Surely you, a medical professional, understand the importance of being prepared for childbirth!"

"I couldn't go to the hospital." Lara fastened her gaze to the lawyer's face. "I was afraid they would take my son. I knew by then, you see, that Devin Sloane wanted my baby. I also knew he had the resources to take him."

"Are you saying my client is above the law?"

"Your client is quite powerful." Despite her intention to remain calm, she felt heat stealing into her face. "I did not feel safe at the hospital, but I felt safe with Mr. O'Hara. I am a physician's assistant, so I know how to deliver babies. I didn't expect any problems during my delivery."

"But you did experience a problem. The child nearly died because of your decision to avoid a hospital, didn't he?"

Lara stared, speechless. No one but she and Connor knew about Hunter's condition at birth. She had never told that story to anyone but . . . She sank back, remembering. One afternoon, in a burst of earnestness, she had told the story to Karyn Gower. She'd been trying to illustrate that she and Connor made a good team, but the little snitch had gone straight to Sloane.

"My son," she began, each word a splinter of ice, "would not have experienced respiratory distress if Dr. Helmut Braun had not given me a sedative prior to labor. The drug affected the baby, but he pinkened right after we helped him begin to breathe."

"How many other medical mistakes have you made with the boy?"

"None."

"Isn't it true the child is suffering at this moment? I have here a report from the court's appointed guardian ad litem. It states that your son suffers from a limp, a pronounced facial tic, exhaustion, depression, and paranoia."

Lara grasped the arms of the chair and struggled to control her temper. "That's not true!"

"Is he limping, or not?"

"Sometimes." Lara could feel rage boiling under her skin. "He limps when he's tired. The pediatrician thought it was nothing, but said I should take him to a specialist to be sure."

"But you haven't done that."

"I can't." She spat the words in contempt. "The court has ordered us to remain in Charlottesville. When this trial is over, I will do whatever I must to protect my son."

"Will you run again?"

"Objection!" Franklin roared.

"I'll withdraw the question."

As Jarvis turned to peruse his notes, Lara cast a withering stare at his broad back. He *knew* she couldn't leave the city, yet he seemed determined to paint her as an irresponsible mother. And where had that nonsense about depression and paranoia come from? Hunter *was* often tired and perhaps stressed from all they had endured in the last few weeks, but who wouldn't be?

"Mrs. O'Hara," Jarvis whirled to stare at her, his voice cold and lashing. "Who is your son's biological father?"

Lara clung to the chair, frozen in a limbo where all answers and options seemed impossible. How could she answer? Michael wasn't Hunter's father, but neither was Devin Sloane. The truth lay somewhere in Dr. Braun's lab, perhaps even on that tape, but she couldn't announce *that* truth . . .

She looked around the courtroom; saw the reporters' expectant faces and the sketch artist with her uplifted pencil. Then her gaze fell upon Eva, who sat stiff and pale, her hand at her throat.

Telling the truth would destroy Eva. She might know about the

Iceman, but if the story became public knowledge she'd never be able to hold up her head in town.

"Shall I repeat the question?" Jarvis captured her eyes with his. "You heard Mr. Sloane testify under oath that he provided the genetic material for your child's conception. Since you will not agree to let us perform a genetic test to establish Mr. Sloane's paternity, the court needs to know—*who is your son's biological father?*"

Through the veil of her hair, Lara heard the judge's voice. "Mrs. O'Hara, I must ask you to answer the question.

She grasped the edge of the witness box, then raised her gaze to meet the lawyer's. "I don't know."

Jarvis lifted a brow, then turned to the crowd. "Is it possible that some other man fathered your child while you were preparing to be implanted with the embryo? Have you refused to allow DNA testing because you're afraid the world will discover you are not only guilty of kidnapping, but of fraud and immorality as well?"

She pressed her hand to her chest, amazed at the accusation. "What are you suggesting?"

"Is it possible, Mrs. O'Hara, that you became pregnant with another man's child and neglected to tell Mr. Sloane because you feared the loss of the benefits he had promised?"

"No."

"Weren't you dating another man at the time?"

"I was not."

"Isn't it true that you and Mr. O'Hara were close? Didn't you visit him often?"

"Before the baby, no. I scarcely knew him."

"You weren't seeing him?"

"No more than I'd see any neighbor. I was still mourning my husband; I wasn't interested in other men."

"How do you feel about Mr. O'Hara now?"

Lara looked across the room and met Connor's gaze. His eyes were large and soft with pain, but his mouth lifted in a small smile of encouragement.

"He is my husband and the only father Hunter has ever known." She looked at the judge. "But we were mere acquaintances when I first became pregnant. I grew to love him later. When the baby was born, Connor held my world together while I was falling apart. It took every bit of strength I possessed to leave this town . . . to leave Connor."

The reporters scribbled as Jarvis pressed on. "Would you mind explaining why you will not allow genetic testing upon your son? Mr. Sloane has requested it. He is most eager to prove that the boy is his."

"No, he's not." Lara looked past the lawyer toward Sloane, whose mercurial black eyes sharpened at the touch of her gaze. "Dr. Braun performed the in vitro fertilization in his lab, and I can't say whose DNA he used during the procedure. I may not know who fathered my son, but I can virtually guarantee Devin Sloane is not my child's father. I know my boy and there is nothing of Sloane in him. Nothing at all."

"Appearances can be deceiving, Mrs. O'Hara."

"I'm not talking about physical appearances. I'm talking about character."

Jarvis flinched at this unexpected retort, and Lara flushed when Sloane narrowed his eyes. She looked at the lawyer. "Is there anything else, Mr. Jarvis? I'd like to have my lawyer tell the truth about what happened, and I suspect it's nearly time for our lunch break."

Jarvis snapped his mouth shut, then turned to the counsel table and leafed through his notes. Lara crossed her legs, relieved that he had been rendered momentarily speechless. The judge had promised this would be a quick trial—the sooner it was finished, the less chance she'd have to directly involve Hunter.

Jarvis leaned over the counsel table and whispered something to Sloane. A look of malignant satisfaction crept over the man's handsome features as he inclined his head in a barely noticeable nod.

The lawyer whirled to face Lara. "Mrs. O'Hara, you say there is nothing of Devin Sloane in your son, but by your own admission you don't know Mr. Sloane very well. He is a most intelligent and resourceful man."

"So I've heard."

The grooves beside Jarvis's mouth deepened into a smug smile. "Perhaps your son has inherited something from Mr. Sloane after all— isn't it true that he has exhibited a most remarkable ability?"

Lara felt terror brush past her, stirring the air and lifting the hair on her forearms. Of course they knew about Hunter's gift; Karyn Gower had told them everything. But if Sloane cared for Hunter at all, surely he wouldn't expose the secret in a public courtroom . . .

Jarvis stared at her until her heart raced. "We're waiting for your answer, Mrs. O'Hara. Does your son have an unusual ability?"

She took a deep breath, looked at Connor, and somehow found her voice. "He's a bright child."

"*Very* bright, wouldn't you say? Isn't it true you told his guardian ad litem that he was a *prophet*?"

Lara pressed her fingers to her lap in an effort to keep them from trembling. "I didn't mean it literally."

"No? A prophet foretells the future; he solves riddles; he can see into the minds of others. Isn't it true that your son has exhibited these traits on more than one occasion?"

A murmur rose from the gallery, a flutter of horrified excitement. The judge slammed his gavel and Lara lowered her head, desperately seeking a way out. *Lord, what do I say?*

"Mrs. O'Hara, we await your answer."

Lara lifted her head and gripped the railing in front of her. "He doesn't foretell the future, and he doesn't read minds. Yes, he can solve riddles, but so can any other five-year-old if he hears them repeated often enough. If you ask him why the man threw the clock out the window, he'll tell you it's because he wanted to see time fly."

The gallery rocked with laughter, and Lara sighed with relief when Judge Weaver lifted his hand to cover a smile.

Jarvis's face went brick red. "Have you ever had your son's IQ tested?"

"No."

"Isn't that because you're afraid of what you'll find? Mr. Sloane has an IQ of one hundred forty. Aren't you afraid you'll discover that your son has inherited something from his biological father?"

"Objection!" Franklin Blythe stood from behind the counsel table. "Your Honor, Mr. Jarvis is leading the witness."

"Objection overruled." The judge nodded at Lara. "Answer the question, please."

Lara's mood veered sharply to anger. "I repeat, Mr. Jarvis, my son has inherited *nothing* from Devin Sloane—and Sloane knows it."

Jarvis stared at her across a sudden ringing silence; then his dignified mask settled back into place. "I have nothing else for this witness, Your Honor."

On cue, Franklin rose and walked toward the witness stand. He gave Lara a bland smile, with only a wary twitch of the eye to show he knew she had been treading on risky ground.

"Mrs. O'Hara"—he propped his arms on the witness box as if they were neighbors gathering for a casual conversation over the backyard fence—"tell me, in your own words, how your signature came to be on that surrogacy contract."

Lara straightened, took a deep breath, and began to tell her story.

From his place at the counsel table, Connor watched Lara progress surefootedly through her testimony. Franklin had done a good job of coaching and helping her stick to the pertinent facts. She told the court about the blank paper, her trust in Dr. Braun, and his promises that the baby she carried was Michael's. She told the judge about her fears that the child might carry a cancer gene and how Dr. Braun had reinforced, then soothed those fears. "That's why he said we had to do IVF and embryo transfer instead of a straight insemination," she explained, undoubtedly aware that the judge probably knew far less about such procedures than she did. "Dr. Braun said he altered Michael's DNA—he removed the cancer-causing gene."

"You believed him?" Franklin asked.

"Of course." Lara's lips twisted in a frayed smile. "He was a professional geneticist and my best friend's husband. I thought he was doing me a tremendous favor."

"And your medical expenses? Did you know Sloane was paying them?"

"Dr. Braun said there were lots of foundations who were eager to support cancer research, so I assumed he arranged for one of them to support my case. I didn't think it odd—after all, I worked for a clinic affiliated with the university hospital, so I assumed the hospital brass would be eager to help me." Her brow furrowed as she looked down at her hands. "I should have known better, but I thought such arrangements were routine."

"Did you know about the million-dollar bequest Sloane made through the Muriel Foundation?"

"I knew the Muriel Foundation was covering my expenses, but I had no idea Devin Sloane was affiliated with that organization."

"Mrs. O'Hara"—the lawyer moved to the side of the witness stand—"we've heard a lot today about biology and genetics. But, if the truth be told, is the issue of your son's paternity a matter of crucial importance?"

"Not to me." Lara swallowed hard and boldly met the judge's gaze. "I am Hunter's mother—biologically and emotionally. I have loved him, protected him, and provided for him as best I could. I came back to Charlottesville because I do not want my son to spend the rest of his life hiding from Devin Sloane."

"What about those who say—with some justification, I might add— that a boy needs a father figure?"

"Hunter has my husband, Connor O'Hara. Connor helped bring Hunter into this world, and I know he loves my son"—Connor smiled when her gaze met his—"as much as I do."

Connor felt his heart turn over the way it always did when she looked at him, but he couldn't help but wonder if she realized the irony in her words. She called him a father, and she knew he loved Connor. Why, then, did she refuse to give him an equal stake in her son?

Franklin turned and clasped his arms behind his back. "Several times the opposition has stressed that you will not agree to have your son's DNA tested. Why are you opposed to a procedure that could refute Mr. Sloane's paternity?"

She answered with easy defiance. "Because this case isn't about Hunter's father; it's about Mr. Sloane's fraud. I will not allow Hunter to be exploited. I will not allow him to be offered up like a piece of real estate to be divided by whoever owns property rights. He is a little boy, and he needs stability. That's why I came back to Charlottesville, and that's why I'll protect him with my last breath. I am his mother; I love him. Connor loves him. We have established a home, and Hunter is happy with us."

"Mrs. O'Hara," the judge interrupted, frowning, "this home you've established is only two months old. Surely you can't expect this court to see you as a model of stability."

"We may have been married for only two months, but we've been in love far longer than that." A blush stained her cheeks. "While I was living in Florida, Connor faithfully kept in touch with us. We came to depend upon him, and Hunter has known who Connor is for several years. He is not my son's biological father, but he is a psychological father in every sense of the word."

Connor wiped his face with his hand, struck again by the incongruity in her answer. If he was Hunter's psychological father, why did she insist on carrying Hunter's burdens alone? Last night as they knelt by the bed, she had prayed "I will praise you, even if you take all I hold dear. For if you take Hunter from me, you will have taken everything."

Everything? Connor knew she loved him, but he could not deny that she loved her son far more.

∞

After taking her seat at the counsel table, Lara exhaled in relief, then grasped Connor's hand, relishing the strength of his grip. She would have been lost without him; she would have dissolved into tears or a fit of temper if his calming gaze hadn't worked its magic on her.

The lawyers at the opposing table huddled; then Jarvis whispered something to Devin Sloane. Lara saw Sloane's head jerk in an emphatic nod, then Jarvis straightened and approached the judge's bench.

"Your Honor, for our next witness, we'd like to call the child to the stand. We realize he is not present in the courtroom, but would like to ask for a recess until he can be brought to court."

Judge Weaver glared at the plaintiff's lawyer. "You want a five-year-old to testify in this case?"

"Yes, Your Honor."

"Perhaps you should explain why I should consider something so irregular."

One of the other lawyers passed a document to the end of the counsel table, but Jarvis didn't look back. "His name was on the witness list and there is legal precedent, Your Honor. Several children of preschool age have testified in criminal proceedings against day-care operators—"

"And those cases have been lost on appeal. The testimony of children is easily manipulated."

"With all due respect, Your Honor, this child won't be coerced in any way. He will not be rehearsed by plaintiff *or* plaintiff's counsel, since we have not been allowed access to the boy. My client, however, wishes to see the child. It is our understanding that the child is exceptional, but we have been unable to arrange even a single visit with him."

The judge's brow wrinkled. "You're not seriously suggesting the boy is a prophet."

"No, sir, but he is unique. My client believes we will be able to demonstrate this uniqueness if the child is allowed to appear."

As Madison Jarvis accepted a folder from one of his associates, the serpent of anxiety wrapped around Lara's throat slithered lower to writhe in her stomach. Jarvis pulled several documents from the folder, then walked toward the judge. "I have here several affidavits, Your Honor, ranging from the child's preschool teacher in Florida to the guardian ad litem this court appointed." He handed the documents over and continued as Judge Weaver flipped through the pages. "As you can see, sir, in each case, sworn testimony indicates that the boy has demonstrated unusual gifts and atypical behaviors. Because the boy has never been formally tested or evaluated by a psychologist, we are eager to ascertain whether or not his developmental maturity is on par with his peers. My client is concerned that his vagabond life with Mrs. O'Hara has significantly affected his development."

Judge Weaver pushed his glasses higher on his nose, studied a page before him, then lowered the paper. "You are confusing me, Mr. Jarvis. You say your client is concerned that the child is developmentally delayed, but when you questioned Mrs. O'Hara, you intimated the child is a budding genius." He glared down his nose at the lawyer. "Which is it?"

"We believe the child may be a genius but has been stifled by the restricted lifestyle Mrs. O'Hara has forced upon him." Jarvis rested his hands on his belt. "Because Mrs. O'Hara lives in an irrational state of paranoia, the child cannot go outside to play; he has no friends, no relatives, no playmates. We believe he is exceptionally gifted, but his gifts will be wasted as long as he continues to live with Mrs. O'Hara. At the very least, Your Honor, we would like to be able to interview the boy, to gain a sense of how content he is in his present environment—"

The judge cut the lawyer off with an uplifted hand. "I've been given many things to consider today," he said, his gaze strafing the documents stacked on his desk. "I am going to call a recess until tomorrow morning."

As he crossed his arms, his gaze shifted to Lara. "At nine a.m. tomorrow, Mrs. O'Hara, you will bring your son to my chambers for an informal interview. You, your husband, and Mr. Blythe may attend, as may Mr. Sloane and Mr. Jarvis." His eyes narrowed as he surveyed the crew clustered around Sloane's table. "Aside from my court reporter and bailiff, no one else will be permitted in the room. At the conclusion of that meeting, I will decide if the boy should be allowed to testify."

He lifted his gavel, brought it down with a solid whack, then stood and exited the room. Lara sank back in her chair, her nerves throbbing with weariness.

Connor picked up her hand and massaged it as though he could push energy back into her body. "It'll be okay."

"I hope it will." Franklin shifted and looked at Lara with compassion in his eyes. "But I have no idea what Weaver will do. Remember, in a bench trial, the judge makes the final decision. He could spend five minutes with Hunter and decide that Sloane could never have fathered that child. He could order a DNA test. He could also consider you a flight risk and decide that Hunter would be better off in foster care."

Franklin's bluntness shattered Lara. "Foster care? It's bad enough to think of my baby in the same room with Sloane, but Hunter would die in foster care. He'd be lost without me—" Her voice braked to a halt as her mind floundered.

The lawyer nodded. "I can't promise anything, but I'll do the best I can. And let's not underestimate Hunter. He may surprise us all."

Something moved at the corner of Lara's eye. She turned, then closed her eyes to the sight of Eva standing behind the rail.

"Mr. Blythe," Eva said, her voice like velvet-edged steel, "might I have a word with you?"

Franklin grasped Lara's shoulder. "Why don't you and Connor go on home and get some rest?"

The suggestion filled Lara with relief. She didn't have the strength to deal with the trial and Eva, too.

Connor helped Lara to her feet. As he led her away, he wished Franklin a good day, then paused. "Good day to you, too, Mrs. Godfrey," he called over his shoulder. "I hope we'll see you tomorrow."

Irritated by her husband's unfailing good manners, Lara walked away without waiting for Eva's reply.

chapter 33

Lara greeted Harriet Blythe with an embrace and a weary hello. After a moment of meaningless chitchat, the older woman slipped away, leaving the little family alone. Hunter jabbered a few moments about the stories "Miss Harriet" had told him, but he grew quiet as Connor spread their dinner of hamburgers and French fries on the table. Lara knew her perceptive son had noticed the shadows behind her smile.

Connor and Hunter finished eating, then moved into the living room to gather the latest sports scores from ESPN. From the kitchen table Lara could see them on the couch, one dark head and one blond, both sitting with an ankle propped across a knee, both clutching a sofa pillow.

Hunter had lived with Connor for little more than two months, yet he had already begun to mirror the man. How long would it take him to become a miniature Devin Sloane if the judge ruled in that fiend's favor?

She could not live in this city or this house while Sloane imprisoned her son in that walled mansion only a few miles away. She could not walk past that bedroom, knowing her son had been born there; she would not be able to look at Connor without thinking of the boy who had been stolen from her.

She would never let Sloane have her son. If the trial went badly tomorrow, she would snatch Hunter up and run. On the pretext of taking Hunter to the restroom, she could walk out of the judge's chambers and make her way out of the building. With a ten-minute head start she could take a cab to the bus station, and from there she could go almost anywhere. She'd just have to make sure that she carried her collection of credit cards and birth certificates with her; they were all she'd need to leave town and begin again.

She dunked a limp French fry into a pool of ketchup. Karyn Gower would describe this meal as junk food. If she had witnessed this dinner, she would undoubtedly tell the judge that Sloane's cook would offer Hunter a dinner of baked fish, steamed vegetables, fresh-baked bread, and carrots. Brain food. Nutritious food. Three-hundred sixty-five days a year.

Lara swallowed the French fry, then lowered her head into her hand. Despite her resolve to hide her fear in Hunter's presence, she couldn't stanch the swell of pain rising in her chest. She felt as though a tumor had blossomed between her lungs, pushing them aside, taking up the space she needed to breathe. She gasped to fill her lungs with air, then heard Hunter's alarmed cry from the living room: "Mom?"

"It's all right, buddy." She closed her eyes, her voice sounding shrill and false in her own ears. "Mom's just tired."

She heard the muffled creak of the couch springs as Conner stood; then the television went silent. "Hunter, your mom and I need to talk to you," Conner said. His creditable attempt at naturalness was marred only by the thickness in his voice. "We spent the day in court, and the judge there—a nice man named Mr. Weaver—has asked that you come with us tomorrow. He'd like to talk to you."

Lara shifted and peered at her son through her fingers. She saw the clean profile of his face and noticed that his eyes had gone serious. He said nothing, but waited with the patience of a child who trusts the one who leads him.

She looked at Connor, then fought down the small sprout of jealousy stirring in her breast. Connor had entered this marriage with an open heart for each of them, but he hadn't spent six years checking his rear-view mirror and yanking Hunter inside the house every time an unfamiliar vehicle passed on the street. He was a shiny new hero in Hunter's eyes, and it wasn't fair that her son knew her as the one who had to say no a dozen times a day.

Connor held out his palm and grinned at Hunter. "Can you give me five? We'll be with you tomorrow, right beside you all the time. I think you'll like the judge."

Hunter held his hand over Connor's for an instant, his face aglow with a wide smile. Lara smiled too, warmed by the sight of his joy, but her smile froze when she noticed the way his hand trembled over Connor's. He wasn't shaking his arm voluntarily; this was a shiver, almost a spasm.

Anger beat a bitter rhythm in her heart as she clenched her fist. Devin Sloane was responsible for this. If her son was ill, it was because of the stress Sloane had put on all of them.

She stood and began to clear the table, turning her back on the living room so neither Connor nor Hunter could see her eyes blazing with anger.

∞

Lara heard the hall clock strike nine, then covered her mouth and pretended to yawn. "If you don't mind, Con, I think I'm going to bed. I'm exhausted." She spoke lightly, hoping he wouldn't be offended. Usually they stayed up and talked during the quiet hours after Hunter's bedtime, but she had to search for her false credit cards and the birth certificates. She wanted to be sure they were safely tucked into her purse before morning.

She pushed herself up, then tossed her magazine into the basket by the couch. She hadn't been reading it anyway; she'd only stared at the pages while her mind raced over all the possibilities tomorrow could bring. The judge could see that Hunter was better off with her, or he could be swayed by Sloane's false concern. But tomorrow would definitely be the day of decision; Franklin had made that clear. Judge Weaver was not the type to draw out a trial when the fate of a child was at stake.

Connor picked up the remote and clicked off the television. "I'll come to bed, too. Tomorrow's a big day."

Lara held up her hand. "Don't let me stop you from watching TV."

"There's nothing on."

"There's sports on ESPN."

"Lara." His penetrating gaze fixed on her. "The truth may hurt, honey, but it's the lie that leaves a scar. I'm not blind. I know when you're hiding things from me."

Sighing, she gave up the charade. "Honestly, Connor, I'd like a few minutes alone."

Connor moved to block her path, his gaze lifting to her face in an oddly keen, perceptive look. "Don't you think I know what you're planning?" He spoke in a hoarse whisper, as though the words were too terrible to utter in a normal voice. "I know you want to run. I know you'd run without me. That's okay, but it won't be good for Hunter if you do."

Stunned by his appraisal, Lara took a half step back. She opened her mouth to deny it all but shock caused the words to wedge in her throat.

Connor guided her to the sofa. "Lara, we need to talk about this."

She sat down but couldn't look at him. "I don't want to talk."

"I know you don't, and that's the problem. Lara, we're married. We took vows—for better or worse, remember? And though I included Hunter in those vows, you won't let me into his life. You won't even let me into *your* life. Oh, you've let me dance around the fringes, hold you in my arms, and we've shared a few secrets. But Lara, I'm your husband and I love you. I need you to trust me."

Lara lifted her head to look at him. For the first time she noticed that his strong face bore the marks of anxiety and grief, while loss shadowed his eyes. She sat silently, absorbing the reality of his suffering, then slowly shook her head.

"Connor, he's my son. I've had him—by myself—for six years. I am responsible for him, and I can't let Sloane have him. You could follow us after we leave, but if you come there's a greater chance Sloane will find us."

"Can't you hear what you're saying?" His eyes were wild with pain and despair. "I want to love you. I want to help Hunter, but you won't let me! You won't let anyone help. Poor Eva Godfrey wants desperately to see Hunter, but you won't give her the time of day—"

"God gave him to *me*! It's my job to take care of him!"

"God gave *both* of you to me. I want to take care of you, but it's not easy when you keep pulling away. It's always 'Hunter and me,' with you, Lara; it's never 'us.' Last night you told God that if you lost Hunter you'd be losing everything"—his voice broke—"and I know you meant it."

Something in her shriveled at his expression. She'd hurt him, and she never meant to. She loved him, but that love lived in a tidy little compartment while her love for Hunter overshadowed every crevice of her life.

She'd been wrong to marry Connor. She had accepted the proposal of a dear, wonderful man who deserved more than what she brought to the marriage. She loved him as much as she could love any man, but Hunter *needed* her . . .

She clenched her hands. "I don't know what you expect of me. I have to take care of my son."

"Then let's take care of him together. We have to be a united team, especially tomorrow. Let me be the leader of this family; let me protect you. You've fought your own battles for so long; let me pick up the sword for a while. God will give me the courage I need to face whatever comes our way."

She nearly choked on a desperate laugh. At that moment, with his hair askew and his eyes blazing, Connor looked more like a warrior than a librarian. If this were a medieval love story, he would leave her by the fire and race out to saddle his warhorse, then gallop off to fight Devin Sloane in a duel . . .

But this was reality, and Devin Sloane was more powerful than Connor or Lara could ever hope to be. You couldn't outduel Sloane. The field of competition would never be level. If he hadn't already bought Judge Weaver's decision, he soon would.

"I love you, Connor," she said, her anguish almost overcoming her control, "but I can't let you throw your life away on us. You were happy before we came back; you were content, but we've turned your life upside down." Unable to look at him, she lowered her gaze. "If things start to go badly tomorrow, I'm taking Hunter and we're disappearing. I'll contact you through the library e-mail when I know it's safe."

She stood up and evaded his quick reach.

"Lara!"

"I'm going out." She ran to the front hall and plucked her coat from the wall hook; then she slipped into it.

Connor stood behind her in the hallway, his eyes gleaming in the dim light. "Don't go."

Swallowing the sob that rose in her throat, she looked up. "I'll be back soon. I just need . . . to get out."

Before he could protest again, she slipped out the front door. She knew he wouldn't follow. He wouldn't leave Hunter alone.

Pulling her jacket hood over her head, she hurried away in the darkness.

∞

Hunched in her coat, Lara ran through a neighbor's lawn, then cut across to the sidewalk, hoping to avoid the attention of the reporters encamped across the street. Fortunately, the night was black and starless, the March wind bitingly cold. She exhaled deeply, watched her breath mist before her face, then realized that she'd left in such a hurry that she hadn't even picked up her purse.

She searched her pockets and felt cold metal. Shivering, she pulled out a dozen quarters—all that remained from Hunter's last visit to the video arcade. Great. Enough for a cup of coffee, should she be lucky enough to find a place that sheltered frantic mothers who enjoyed running away from home.

She came to a quiet intersection, hesitated on the corner, then jogged across the street. A major road lay ahead, and Lara knew she'd find an open convenience store, a gas station, and a Barnes and Noble within a few blocks. If the bookstore was open, she'd be able to order a cup of coffee and pretend to skim a magazine.

After maintaining a quick pace for a half mile, she pushed through the glass doors of the bookstore, then pulled her frozen hands from her pockets and rubbed them together. The shop hummed with the quiet, librarylike hush she always associated with books. Pushing the jacket hood from her head, she moved toward the coffee bar.

She ordered a plain cup of coffee, strong and black, then moved to a table against the wall. A pair of teenagers huddled at a table in the center of the cafe, and Lara sat with her back to them, not wanting to be drawn into idle conversation. She needed time to think, to be alone. She couldn't think clearly with Connor's wounded eyes flashing before her.

She wrapped her chilled hands around the foam cup, wishing she had one of Connor's ceramic mugs—at least glass conducted heat. Just last night she had sipped from one of those mugs in the living room while Connor pulled out a Bible to read something to encourage them for their court appearance. He chose the story of Gideon, and Lara identified with the Israelite when he lifted his voice and said, "If the Lord is with us, why has all this happened? Where are all the miracles our ancestors told us about? The Lord has abandoned us now."

Connor's voice deepened when he read the Lord's answer: "I will be with you."

Connor smiled, terribly encouraged, but the Lord's promise hadn't been enough to persuade either Gideon *or* Lara. Gideon had insisted that God prove his presence by showing him a wet fleece on dry ground and, the next morning, a dry fleece on wet ground. Lara thought it wouldn't take anything so dramatic to convince her of God's promise— a simple case of spontaneous human combustion involving Devin Sloane would have done the trick.

Connor's lips parted in surprise when she said as much, but he didn't chide her. He had only pulled her closer, lowered his sheltering hand to her head, and prayed aloud for the trial to come.

Lara lifted her coffee cup and took a scalding sip. She had hurt him; she could see that now. She had hurt him with her indifference, with the limits she placed on her love, with her own half-truths. In the court-room today she told the judge that Connor was Hunter's psychological father, but wasn't that a lie? So far she hadn't given him the right to discipline, guide, or make plans for her son. Though she'd said all the right words, in reality she had only given him the right to be Hunter's friend.

She sipped her coffee again, then set the drink on the table and watched her reflection shimmer in the cup. When she prayed for a child, she had no idea that the tree of life she'd receive would cause so much pain. What was God doing? She had always tried to trust him with little things . . . could she trust him tomorrow when Hunter's fate rested in the balance?

Another woman came in from the cold and moved to the coffee counter. Lara lowered her head and sipped from her coffee cup, hunching forward on the table. She should have picked up a magazine; no one would interrupt her if she pretended to read.

"Whew!" blustered the woman, an indistinct form moving toward Lara. She stamped her feet and held her coffee cup in both hands. "It's so cold I'd go to church just to hear about fire and brimstone!"

Lara turned, easing into a polite smile; then her facial muscles froze. The woman's face was familiar, the voice an echo of some distant memory. Was she a reporter? An old neighbor?

The woman sat down at the next table, then nodded. "It's good to see you again, Lara."

The memory opened as if a curtain had been ripped aside; then a surge of rage struck Lara like a bolt of lightning. "You're the investigator! You work for Sloane!"

"Not anymore." The woman boldly met Lara's gaze. "In fact, I wanted to thank you for coming home; your surrender freed me from my agreement with Devin. I'd been wanting to quit for years, but he hired me to find you . . ." She shrugged as her voice faded away. "That's old news. I know this is a difficult time, but if you don't mind, I'd like to talk to you."

Lara stared, too startled by the woman's audacity to offer any objection.

Interpreting Lara's silence as assent, the woman leaned forward. "Let me begin with a proper introduction. I'm Nadine Harrington. And I've been desperately hoping for a chance to meet you."

Lara finally found her tongue. "I seem to recall that you *have* talked to me. You lied to me."

"I was working then, but not now. And this isn't business; it's . . . personal."

"What makes you think I'd want to talk about personal things to a stranger?"

"No reason . . . except we're both mothers. And we love our sons."

Lara lifted her cup and drank, grateful for a chance to look away from the woman's penetrating gaze. She could be lying even now, but her eyes were clear and direct.

Lara lowered her cup, then laced her fingers together. "How'd you find me?"

Nadine shrugged. "I sweet-talked one of the reporters who's been following the trial. When he saw you leave the house tonight, he called me." She smiled. "Actually, you should be grateful because I paid the man a hundred bucks not to follow you himself. If I hadn't paid him off, you'd be the headline of tomorrow's local paper. You know—'Distraught Mom Runs Out in the Middle of the Night.'" She shuddered slightly. "Those reporters can be nasty."

"And investigators aren't?"

Nadine lifted both brows. "Very good, my dear. It's good to know you haven't lost your spunk."

Lara inhaled deeply, then lifted her coffee cup and drained it. "I'd like to say it's been nice to meet you, but I'll just say good-bye."

"Please don't go." Nadine Harrington gripped her arm, all traces of flippancy vanishing from her eyes. "I really need to talk to you."

Lara hesitated, torn between curiosity and her dislike for anyone affiliated with Sloane. She ought to jerk her arm free and go, but if Nadine Harrington could offer any information that might be useful in tomorrow's hearing . . .

Slowly, she eased back into her chair. "What's so important?"

Nadine's eyes remained serious, and a muscle quivered in her cheek. "Your son. You've worked very hard to keep him."

"Of course I have. I love him."

"But you and I both know what Sloane did to you in Braun's lab. Replacing your husband's DNA was an atrocious, despicable deed."

Lara stiffened. "*You* know about the Iceman?"

Nadine stretched her hand over the table, then traced a circle with a manicured fingernail. "See? This represents the first circle of Sloane's secrets. Over the years, he allowed me access into ever-smaller circles. On the way I learned everything he did to you." Her eyes became dark holes in the woman's pale face. "I learned more than I wanted to know. The man is corrupt, Lara, but there's a genius to his madness. Evil sounds reasonable when he justifies it. He has seduced more people . . ."

Hope rose in Lara's heart like a startled bird. "Please, you've got to come to court tomorrow! If you tell the judge what you know, he'll believe you!"

Nadine recoiled. "Lara, I am many things, but I'm not a fool. I wouldn't testify against Devin Sloane if my life depended on it—because it would."

"Has he threatened you?"

"Sloane never threatens. He *acts*." Her tone went dry. "And no one is ever able to prove anything."

Lara stared at the woman, her mind filling with sour thoughts. If Nadine Harrington feared Sloane, then she and Hunter didn't stand a chance of defeating him.

"About your son," Nadine continued, her finger tracing the tabletop again, "have you ever made a mistake with him?"

Lara laughed bitterly. "According to Sloane, I've made nothing *but* mistakes."

"I don't care what Devin says. Seriously—do you regret anything you've done?"

Lara fell silent as she considered her motherhood. Perhaps she had made mistakes from the beginning. She begged God for a miracle child, then ran away the first time disaster struck. She'd acted in blind panic, but she could have come home to face Sloane at any time. She had put Hunter through a gypsylike life when he could have known stability.

"Sure," she whispered, "I've made mistakes. Every mother makes mistakes. But we ask forgiveness and we go on."

"That's the part I don't understand." Nadine's finger abruptly stopped circling. "I have a little boy, you see—well, actually he's not so little anymore. He's thirteen and he lives with his dad in Maryland. I haven't seen him in eleven years."

Lara blinked, stunned by the confession. "Why don't you visit him?"

"I'm afraid to." Nadine rested her elbow on the back of the chair, then propped her head on her hand. "I was a drunk, you see, when he lived with me, so my husband left and took my son. I finally got sober, but now I'm afraid my son hates me—not for being a drunk, but for staying away. With every day that passes, it's harder to even *think* about facing him."

Her voice faded to a hushed stillness. "When Sloane hired me, he said he knew I'd understand how he felt because I surrendered my child to a parent who could take better care of my son. What he didn't know was that I began to wonder why you fought so hard to keep your boy. Even now, I wonder what makes you continue fighting . . . and lately I've begun to think I should try again."

"Maybe . . . maybe you should."

She gave Lara an abashed smile. "Once I told Devin that you'd be easy to find because women always look back. Now I find that *I'm* the one who can't stop thinking about who I left behind."

"Then go back." Lara dredged the advice from a place beyond logic and reason. She didn't know why she felt led to encourage this woman, but the thought of an abandoned teenager tore at her heart. "It's not too late. Apologize for the past, ask his forgiveness, and let him tell you what he's thinking."

Nadine looked away, her expression softening into one of fond reminiscence. "He was such a cute baby. I imagine he's a very handsome boy."

"You'll never know unless you go to him."

"I suppose not." Nadine sighed; then her gaze settled on Lara. "You've been an inspiration. You were more clever than I expected, and far more steadfast."

A smile found its way through Lara's uncertainty. "I wasn't the clever one. That was Connor. I would have been lost without him."

Nadine pushed back her chair. "A good man. You should keep him too." She stood, then placed her hand on Lara's shoulder. "I don't know how I can help you openly, but I'll see what I can do quietly. If you lose the case tomorrow, I'll see that your lawyer receives a packet of materials that might help you convince another judge to overturn the decision. I won't sign it, but you can tell your lawyer it's trustworthy information." She hesitated, her vivid blue eyes distant and still. "I warn you— it's going to be tough for me to expose Sloane without implicating myself in serious trouble. He pulled me into the circles, you see."

"I hope you break free."

"Me too. Maybe I'll have my people check into the witness protection program. It might be a little tricky to run my business from some town in Wyoming or Iowa, but anything is possible these days. And staying alive is a big plus." Nadine bit on her lower lip, then squeezed Lara's shoulder and left the cafe. As Lara watched her cross the foyer and disappear into the night, she lifted a prayer: *Father God, bring peace to that woman . . . and to her son.*

She sat in silence for a few moments, the brooding sorrow over her heart seeming to spread until it mingled with Nadine's and Connor's and a hundred thousand other griefs and sighs of despair. The entire world ached tonight and, like Gideon, its people wondered, *If the Lord is with us, why has all this happened? Where are all the miracles our ancestors told us about? The Lord has abandoned us now.*

But God said, "I will be with you." Jesus amplified that promise: "I am with you always, even to the end of the age."

She was not alone. God had not left her. Her tree of life was sleeping peacefully in his bed, guarded by a loving father and husband. She had been through dark days, but God had never left her comfortless. He was her heavenly Father; he loved her; he would never let her face any trial he had not allowed.

A wry smile crossed her face. *Lord, I won't even ask for the miracle of the fleece. Just fight for us tomorrow, and strengthen us to face whatever will come.*

As she slipped out of the bookstore and began to walk home, snatches of her conversation with Nadine rose in her memory.

Don't give up.

A good man. You should keep him too.

It's not too late if you'll go back and find him. Apologize for the past, ask his forgiveness, and let him tell you what he's thinking.

Two blocks from the town house, Lara broke into a jog. Connor would still be up, and she had a lot to confess. But he was a good man, and he would forgive.

He wanted to be her warrior, and Lara was finally ready to lay down her arms.

chapter 34

The next morning, Lara suppressed a smile as Connor stepped off the elevator with Hunter's hand in his. She had dressed her son in his favorite outfit, a Miami Dolphins T-shirt and jeans, caring more for his comfort than about what Sloane and his cronies might consider proper attire. Six-year-olds, she and Connor had decided, did not belong in court, so Hunter could wear anything he wanted.

Once they were out of the elevator, Lara took Hunter's other hand, and together the threesome turned a corner and walked through a wide corridor. The mere thought of her son facing Devin Sloane gave Lara a cold chill, but Connor had spent half the night assuring her they had nothing to fear. "The night Hunter was born, you told me you had to believe God knew what he was doing," he reminded her. "If he knew then, he certainly knows now. God loves Hunter, too, even more than you and I do. We have to trust him."

She could believe everything would be okay—if God would send her a letter of confirmation.

They turned another corner and Lara's heart congealed into a lump when she recognized Sloane's angular form at the end of the corridor. He stood with his lawyer outside the judge's door, his head turned toward them, his dark eyes focused on Hunter with predatory intensity.

Lara steeled herself against the impulse to snatch her son and run. In an act of blind faith, she had left her collection of credit cards and birth certificates on the bed, where Connor would be sure to see them. She had promised him that she wouldn't run, and she had made a bargain with God. She would stay put and stand strong if the Almighty would consign Sloane to some faraway pit—Alcatraz, maybe, or San Quentin.

She slowed her step, pulling Hunter back, and Connor stopped too. He turned and knelt in front of Hunter, effectively blocking Sloane's view. "Now, Son"—Connor pressed his hand to Hunter's round belly— "remember what your mother and I told you. This is going to be easy, a piece of cake. We're going to go in and talk to the judge; then we'll take you out to lunch. Anywhere you want to go, buddy, you name the place."

Hunter's face brightened. "Pizza Town?"

Connor caught Lara's eye and grinned. "Pizza Town it is. And you can order whatever you want."

Lara looked away, wishing the judge would step out and get things started. She heard the rapid click of footsteps; then Franklin flew around the corner, flushed and breathless.

"Sorry I didn't get here sooner." He glanced toward the end of the hall where Sloane and his lawyer waited. "Everything okay?"

Lara managed a small, tight smile. "Everything's fine, but we're glad you made it."

"So am I." Franklin transferred his heavy leather bag from one hand to the other, then bent to gently poke Hunter's tummy. "Hey, little buddy, how are you? Are you excited?"

"I'm going to talk to the judge," Hunter said, his tone strangely matter-of-fact. "I'm going to tell him I lost my tooth."

"You lost a tooth?" Lara pulled his lower lip down. "My heavens, you did! Where is it?"

"I ate it." Hunter grinned as if this were an accomplishment worthy of high praise.

"Why didn't you tell Mom?"

"I told Daddy."

Lara looked at Connor. "You told Daddy," she whispered, her hand falling on Hunter's head. A blush rose to Connor's cheeks, and Lara felt a slow smile spread across her face. "That's great, bud."

"Congratulations." Franklin paused as the door to the judge's chambers opened and the bailiff nodded at them. "I think that means they're ready for us, but I've something to tell you."

Lara flinched at the tone of his voice. "Bad news?"

Franklin scratched his brow. "Interesting news. I can't go into it now, but at some point during the morning I'll need to bring it up. Just trust me, Lara."

Again someone had asked for blind trust.

Still clutching Hunter's hand, Lara walked forward on legs that suddenly seemed as insubstantial as air. Franklin led the way, guiding them through an outer office where a secretary watched beneath a silver mound of sternly coifed hair.

The judge's expansive chambers were richly paneled in dark wood and dominated by a carved wooden desk beneath a wide window. Someone had placed two groups of chairs before the desk, one to the left side and one to the right, while two single chairs sat in an intimate grouping at the center of the room. Without being told Lara knew that those chairs were for Hunter and the judge.

There were only three chairs on the left side of the room, so Lara pulled Hunter onto her lap and kept him within the circle of her arms. As Connor and Franklin seated themselves on her left and right, she let her gaze rove over the desk, the bookshelves, and the pattern in the oriental carpeting. The court reporter took her place in an out-of-the-way corner, so Lara watched her a few moments, wondering if the woman enjoyed hearing the details of other people's lives.

Lara would not, *could not*, look at Devin Sloane. She felt the burning pressure of his eyes without glancing in his direction. He was feasting upon the image of her son, and she was powerless to stop him.

After a few moments of an almost palpable silence, the judge entered. Without his robe he seemed smaller and more vulnerable. Lara felt her spirits droop. Could this little man stand up to Sloane?

Judge Weaver walked to the center of the room and turned, his gaze falling upon Hunter. His thin lips spread into a narrow smile. "So this is the young man I've heard so much about."

Hunter broke into a wide grin.

The judge clapped his hands on his legs and jerked his head toward the two empty chairs. "Would you like to sit in a chair of your own while we talk? Or would you rather stay with your mother?"

Lara's arms tensed, but Hunter had already begun to slide from her lap. "It's not my chair," Hunter remarked as his sneakers hit the carpet. "It's not yours, either."

A smile ruffled the judge's mouth. "Well—that's absolutely right, young man. Can you tell me who the chair does belong to?"

Hunter walked to the chair and began to climb up, head and arms first. "No," he said, turning around in the seat. He propped both arms on the right armrest. "But you can tell me."

Judge Weaver sat in his own chair. "The chair belongs to the taxpayers. Nearly everything in this office does—except for my personal belongings, of course."

"I don't belong to the sax players." Hunter dropped his arms and crossed them over his stomach.

"Who do you belong to, then?"

Hunter tilted his head and gazed at the judge through the thin veil of his bangs. "To God."

"Ah. Let's talk about that." The judge crossed his legs and brought his hand to his chin. "Who is your mother?"

Hunter grinned and pointed to Lara.

"Of course. You're a smart boy and that was an easy question. Can you tell me who your father is?"

With a concentrated effort, Hunter lifted one blue-jeaned leg until it crossed the other, then brought his hand to his chin in a perfect imitation of the judge's posture. "That's *not* an easy question." He deepened his voice in a playful growl. "I have two daddies."

Weaver's eyes widened in pretend surprise. "Two?"

"One over there"—Hunter pointed to Connor—"and one in heaven." He slapped his hands together and grinned at Franklin. "One plus one equals two. Miss Harriet taught me that."

Lara cleared her throat, anxious to explain Hunter's answer. "He's not being sassy. I've always taught him that God is a father to the fatherless. For a long time, Hunter didn't have a daddy."

"I had one in heaven." Hunter put both hands on one arm of the big chair and pulled himself up to peer at Lara. "I still do."

"I know, buddy." She smiled, hating the fact that Sloane was hearing this intimate exchange.

The judge rubbed his chin. "Hunter, do you know the difference between telling the truth and telling a lie?"

Hunter sank back into his seat and stopped squirming. "Yea-es," he said slowly, drawing the word out into two syllables. "The truth is. A lie is not."

"Amazing," Sloane murmured, his voice carrying from the other side of the room. "Absolutely amazing."

The judge lifted his hand in silent rebuke.

"That's a good answer," the judge continued, not taking his attention from Hunter. "Can you tell me something true?"

Hunter nodded, then reached out to grasp the toes of his sneakers. Grinning, his gaze rose toward the ceiling, then dropped back to the judge. "God loves me and God loves you. That is true."

A beatific smile creased the judge's lined face. "Yes, that is true. Now can you tell me something that is not true?"

Hunter tilted his head and rolled his eyes as if listening to an inward voice, but after a moment he shook his head. "I can't find a lie in me."

"In Hunter's entire life," Lara kept her voice low, "I can't remember a single time when he told me a lie. He's not perfect—he can be mischievous and disobedient—but he does not lie."

"Surely you're not serious." The judge shot her a twisted smile. "I'll admit that the boy seems a bit precocious for his years, but I've never heard of a child who doesn't fib on occasion. Just last week, my two-year-old granddaughter climbed up in a chair and knocked over a plate of cookies. When we asked her who did it, she pointed to the dog!" He shook his head. "Children are barely verbal at that age, but they have a firm grasp on the art of prevarication."

"Not this child." Devin Sloane's voice grated on Lara's nerves, and for the first time she looked over at him. His narrow face was set in lines of concentration, his dark eyes trained on Hunter like gun barrels. "Your Honor, I have not been entirely truthful with you myself. I did provide genetic material for this child, but it did not originate with me . . . biologically." His voice, so flat an instant before, filled with vibrant wonder. "Helmut Braun and I set out to produce a better, less-degenerated example of human life, and now I see that we succeeded far beyond our expectations."

"You what?" Disbelief echoed in the judge's voice.

Conscious of Hunter's listening ears, Lara's heart rose to her throat. "That's enough!"

Sloane ignored her strangled cry. "We provided an improved DNA strand," he continued, ignoring Lara's distress. "We weren't sure what the results of our germline therapy would be, but the chromosomes we injected had to be far superior to any contemporary human's."

Lara stood, ready to carry Hunter from the room, but Connor's iron grip closed around her arm. "You admit performing an experiment upon Lara without her knowledge?" he asked.

The judge's eyes went thin. "Is this true, Mr. Sloane?"

Sloane's lawyer rose to his feet, his face purpling in affronted rage. "Your Honor, this is irrelevant. Lara Godfrey signed every document in the possession of this court! She freely gave permission for Dr. Braun to alter the genetic strand. She has testified that she wanted her husband's baby, but she most assuredly did *not* want his flaws and weaknesses. She instructed Braun to alter the DNA, to eradicate a gene that might have led to cancer."

"We took her request one step further," Sloane added as his lawyer took his seat. "We gave the fertilized egg a completely refined DNA strand. In short, we financed the experiment and she agreed to surrender the child. In fact, I had the distinct impression that Dr. Braun offered to perform another embryo transfer after this boy's birth. If she wanted a baby, we were willing to give her one—but not *this* child."

Choking on Sloane's half-truths, Lara caught her breath, then remembered her son. During Sloane's speech Hunter had squirmed in the huge chair; now he stared at the enemy from behind the armrest like a soldier peering out from behind a bunker. How much had he understood?

Sloane laughed softly. "Your Honor, I am known throughout the world for my philanthropy. I care about children. Through my work at the Ethan Jefferson Pediatric Hospital, I am working to improve the lot of children who would otherwise be a burden on their families and society in general."

Lara reached toward her son. "Buddy, come sit in Mom's lap." She'd clap her hands over Hunter's ears if the judge let this continue.

"Really, Your Honor," Franklin interrupted, "this interview was supposed to center upon the child. The discussion has veered into areas that are likely to alarm him."

"Mr. Judge?" Hunter's voice cut through the confusion like a thrown knife. He still crouched inside the chair, his eyes fixed upon Sloane. He lifted one stubby finger and pointed at the man who had haunted Lara's days and nights for six years. "That man is lying."

Sloane's eyes had been abstracted, but they cleared and sharpened as Hunter's verdict echoed in the room. His brows lifted. "I beg your pardon?"

"You told lies." Hunter straightened in his chair. With the righteous indignation of an old-time preacher, he thrust out his chin and wagged an accusing finger. "You shouldn't tell lies."

Connor leaned forward. "What lies, Hunter? Can you tell us?"

Hunter looked at Connor, then nodded. "Uh-huh. He said 'she agreed to sur-sur—'"

"Surrender?"

"Yes." Hunter inclined his head in an assertive nod. "That part was a lie. And he doesn't care about children." He crinkled his nose. "That was a *big* lie."

"Now, wait a minute," Jarvis began, but he was drowned out in a rising chorus of voices—Lara's, Franklin's, and Sloane's.

After a moment of confusion, the judge stood and held up his hands for silence. "It's obvious to me that none of you have been completely honest with this court," he said with a look that suggested his mind was now working hard at an entirely new set of problems. "I'm going to step behind my desk and go through the evidence, piece by piece, and then I'm going to address the issues before us." He took a deep breath, then glanced at his watch. "I've asked Karyn Gower to join us in the courtroom at one o'clock, since she is the child's guardian ad litem. And you might find it interesting to know that this morning before you arrived, I received another motion on behalf of this child."

Jarvis flicked a basilisk glance at Lara's lawyer. "Who else has an interest in this case?"

The judge crossed his arms. "The petitioner seeks visitation rights with this boy. The motion was filed this morning by a lawyer representing Mrs. Eva Godfrey."

Lara gasped. "My mother-in-law?"

Light glittered in the rims of the judge's eyeglasses as he turned to her. "The woman has made an interesting point. If, as you say, the child was *not* conceived in order to fulfill a surrogate agreement with Devin Sloane, then he must be your late husband's son and Mrs. Godfrey's grandchild. She says you have forbidden her to see him since you returned to Charlottesville. So she is suing for the right to spend time with the boy."

Lara stared wordlessly, her heart pounding. Had she been caught in a web of her own weaving? To protect Hunter, she had wanted the court to believe Hunter was not Sloane's son. But Hunter had nothing in common with Eva, nothing at all. Eva had no reason for wanting to visit the boy unless this was some ill-considered attempt to punish Lara for trying to have Michael's child in the first place.

"Your Honor," Franklin said, "may we address one issue at a time? And may we send the boy out of the room while we continue? I can call my wife; she'd be happy to watch him."

"There's no need," the judge said, moving toward the door to the outer office. "My secretary has four grandchildren and knows how to occupy little ones. She'd be happy to keep an eye on Hunter."

Weaver opened the door and gestured to Lara. She stood and took Hunter's hand. "You're going to talk to that nice lady in there," she said, trying to keep her voice light. "Maybe she will have some crayons. You can draw some pictures; then we'll go for pizza."

She released Hunter's hand at the doorway, then froze. Eva stood in the outer office, her blue eyes widening. Before Lara or the judge could move, Eva dropped to one knee and flung out her arms. "Hunter, baby! I'm your grandma!"

Never in a thousand years could Lara have predicted how Hunter would handle this obvious untruth. She expected him to either laugh or rebuke Eva, but he tilted his head, hesitated for an instant, then ran toward her with his limping gait and threw himself into her arms.

"Oh, Hunter." Eva's voice broke with huskiness as she smoothed his silky hair. "Oh, darling, I'm so sorry. I'm so very sorry."

Momentarily speechless, Lara stood in the doorway until she felt a hand on her shoulder. "Come back to your seat, Lara," Franklin whispered, a note of pleading in his voice. "I've something to tell you—something I couldn't mention in front of the boy."

Lara moved stiffly back to her chair, then watched as Franklin removed a small cassette tape and two sets of documents from his briefcase. "Your Honor," he said, handing the tape and documents across the judge's desk, "yesterday Eva Godfrey gave me new information I'd like to introduce into evidence. The information is contained on this tape, so I've taken the liberty of having the contents transcribed and several copies made. The evidence is a confession, the final declaration of Helmut Braun, recorded in the hour before his death. I believe this tape holds most of the answers we seek today." His eyes softened as his gaze moved to meet Lara's. "Attached to the transcript is an affidavit from one of Dr. Braun's lab assistants, attesting to the fact that the voice is Dr. Braun's."

The judge pushed his reading glasses up the bridge of his nose and studied the first page of the transcript. After a moment, he looked at Devin Sloane, then handed the second copy to Madison Jarvis. Lara saw that Sloane's face had gone dead-white, sheened with a sweat that shone in the soft lamplight.

The judge dropped the pages to his desk, then folded his hands. "We're going to take a three-hour recess so the plaintiff and his counsel can familiarize themselves with this tape's contents. I'll read it as well. We'll reconvene in the courtroom at one o'clock. Anyone not present will be held in contempt of court." Weaver shifted his gaze to Franklin. "Mr. Blythe, has your client been informed as to the contents of this tape?"

"Not all of it, Your Honor."

"Then I suggest you enlighten her as well."

chapter 35

Eva took a wincing breath as the door opened and everyone but the judge exited the room. Sloane and his lawyer strode immediately to the hallway, but Lara knelt next to the coffee table where Hunter was drawing a picture of his house and family members.

"Lara," Eva whispered, not knowing how to begin. She had to explain that her suit for visitation rights was only a ruse, a desperate act intended to press for the truth. But she'd discovered the truth today; she'd seen it the instant the child ran toward her.

"Mrs. Godfrey, why don't you join our discussion?" The lawyer sat on the sofa next to her, a friendly and open smile on his face. Lara had not yet looked up to meet Eva's eyes—she was undoubtedly furious.

"If you all will excuse me," the secretary said, standing. "I believe I'll let you have this room. I've forwarded the judge's calls to the office down the hall, so you all just go on about what you're doing. Take care of my little friend here."

She paused to ruffle Connor's hair before leaving, then bent and impulsively kissed him on the cheek. Touched by the gesture, Eva blinked away sudden tears.

"First, Mr. Blythe"—Eva put her hand on the lawyer's arm—"let me assure you that I'm withdrawing my suit for visitation rights. I would not press myself where I am not wanted. But now I know Hunter is my grandson."

"You don't know that." Lara spoke with quiet, desperate firmness. "You *can't* know that."

"But I do know it! I have only to look at the boy—"

"You're seeing only what you want to see." Lara's gaze, as remote as the ocean depths, moved to meet Eva's. "I've played that game before, and it doesn't work."

"I am his grandmother."

Lara opened her mouth to protest, but Connor was quicker. "Ladies," he said, sinking onto the floor next to Hunter, "let's hear what Mr. Blythe has to say."

Lara sat in a chair next to Hunter and Eva bit her lip and turned to the lawyer. She knew everything Helmut Braun had done, but Lara didn't. She couldn't behave like this if she knew the entire truth.

Franklin Blythe plucked a group of stapled pages from his battered leather case. "This tape was apparently recorded right before Braun, um, expired." He glanced up at Lara.

Connor rapped on the coffee table to get the lawyer's attention. "Should you read this in front of Hunter?"

Mr. Blythe nodded. "It's mostly technical. I don't think it will do any harm."

The lawyer awkwardly cleared his throat and began to read: "'I, Helmut Braun, would like to set the record straight before I die. I have done many things of which I am not proud, but one thing is worse than all the others. It concerns my wife, whom I lost; an innocent woman, Lara Godfrey; and an innocent child. I pray God will forgive me for what I did to all three of them.'"

Eva let her gaze fall to the boy contentedly drawing his pictures. He was such a gift. Helmut Braun may have committed a terrible injustice, but at least something precious had come out of it.

"'In the spring of 1998,'" the lawyer continued, "'Devin Sloane approached me with an idea to create a new sort of man—*Homo Tyrolensis*, he called it. He planned to extract DNA from the 5,300-year-old Iceman found in an Italian glacier. I was instructed to find a suitable candidate to bear a child conceived from this ancient DNA in the hope that the resulting human's genetic makeup would be far less debased than ours . . . a child fresher from the hand of the Creator.'"

Blythe looked up, glanced around the room, and met Eva's gaze. She nodded, urging him to continue reading.

"'Before Sloane approached me, I had agreed to help one of my wife's coworkers, Lara Godfrey, who wanted to have the child of her late husband through AIH, artificial insemination by husband. Mrs. Godfrey, however, had expressed concern that her husband's DNA might carry the gene for bone cancer—and in fact, I found this to be true. But before I could work on eradicating the faulty genes, Sloane met the young woman and was impressed with her intelligence and sincerity. By the force of his personality and the promise of financial gain, he convinced me that she would not be harmed by a substitution and that mankind would greatly benefit from this experiment, should we prove successful. The arrangement itself was easily accomplished—I convinced Lara Godfrey that the DNA strand I spliced was her husband's, while we intended to override the husband's genetic material with artificial human chromosomes containing the Iceman's DNA. She signed all the usual papers for cyropreservation, in vitro fertilization, and embryo implantation. To cover our deception, I had her sign additional documents, including a blank form which Sloane agreed to fill in later. Legally, Sloane told me, this would appear to be a surrogacy agreement. When the time came for the birth, we would arrange for complete sedation and take the child at delivery. We would tell Mrs. Godfrey that there had been an accident and the baby had died, and I would encourage her to conceive another child. Sloane promised that Lara would not be harmed, the child would be well provided for, and we would render mankind a great service.'"

Blythe stopped reading as Lara hiccupped a sob. Connor slipped his arm around her shoulders and Hunter looked up for a moment, his eyes wide. Lara smoothed her features and gave him a watery smile. After a moment, Hunter went back to his drawing, and the lawyer resumed his reading.

"'My first attempt to manipulate the ancient DNA resulted in utter failure. The fertilized egg would not divide. And time was a factor—Lara was at the appropriate point in her cycle and Sloane was furiously impatient. And so, hoping that I could at least buy myself a measure of time, I went to work on a second procedure—I withdrew another egg;

I fertilized it in a petri dish; I watched it divide into the blastocyst stage. My wife implanted it within the woman, who confirmed her pregnancy within a week. But I did not tell Sloane the entire truth. Fearful of failing again, I tried a different approach. Instead of germline therapy, I mixed sperm infused with the ancient DNA with unaltered sperm from the late husband's donation. When the woman became pregnant, I alone knew the truth—it was entirely possible that her fetus sprang from contemporary genetic material.'"

Shock flickered over Lara's face like summer lightning. "Does that mean—Michael?"

Eva nodded. "That's what I was trying to tell you. After I got the tape, I knew there was a chance. I thought if I could just see the boy, I'd know if he was Michael's son." Her smile wobbled as her gaze lowered to that silken head. "I knew it the moment he ran to me."

Franklin cleared his throat. "I think you'll be especially interested in Braun's last statement: 'Devin Sloane, who places his confidence in his wealth and his knowledge, is completely dangerous. Auschwitz is gone, but the criminal indifference to life remains embodied in men like Sloane. May God have mercy on my soul. May God have mercy on us all.'"

A heavy silence filled the air; then Franklin rolled up the transcript and thumped it against his palm. "There's more, but I can summarize the rest. Braun figured he'd have at least nine months to solve the problem while you carried the baby, Lara. He thought that if he could get the ancient DNA to fertilize an egg that would survive to the sixteen- or thirty-two cell stage, he'd be able to persuade Sloane to leave you alone and focus on another candidate. But Braun never convinced the ancient DNA to cooperate—and then you discovered the truth. He says he was glad when you disappeared. But when you came back, he knew his secret would come out. Frankly, he feared for his life."

Blythe lifted one brow and looked at Connor. "There's enough on this tape to keep the police and FBI busy for several months. Braun states that Lara's apartment was illegally bugged during her pregnancy. Worse yet, he implicates Sloane in the murders of two Austrian scientists and suggests that Sloane's work at the Ethan Jefferson Pediatric Hospital might bear close investigation. According to Braun, Sloane is a Nazi in contemporary clothing. You were right to run, Lara. The man is evil."

Connor's arm tightened around Lara's shoulders. "Is she safe now?"

"I don't think she's the one who needs to worry." Franklin leaned forward and rested his hands on his knees. "Frankly, if I were Sloane, I wouldn't return after this recess. He'll be in contempt of court if he skips out, but his lawyer is slick." He glanced at his watch. "I sent a copy of this transcript to the FBI's Washington headquarters this morning in case Sloane thinks he can leave the country. He'll be lucky if he gets across the border. Deathbed confessions carry great weight with criminal investigators."

Franklin turned to Lara. "As soon as this is settled, I'd advise you to file a civil suit against Sloane. He has committed fraud and personal battery against you, not to mention slander and libel. He'll go to jail for the criminal charges, but you might be able to recover something for the grief he's put you through."

Lara's hand fell on her son's head. "I don't care about money," she said, her expression as soft as her voice. "It's funny—all this time, I thought Hunter was special because he sprang from a unique source. Now it's clear Hunter is special simply because he's Hunter."

Connor patted the boy's leg. "Hey, buddy, you weren't kidding, were you? You really do have a daddy in heaven."

"Of course I do." Hunter stopped coloring and turned his picture so the adults could see. He pointed to a series of stick figures in the house. "Look. There's Mom and Connor and me and Mr. Franklin and Miss Harriet." He pressed his finger to another stick man, this one drawn next to a cloud. "That's my daddy in heaven."

Lara drew closer. "I thought that was Jesus."

He brought his hand to his mouth to stifle a quick giggle. "Jesus is with God and God's indivisible."

"Invisible," Connor corrected.

"Yeah." Hunter went back to coloring.

"Hunter—" Eva slid forward on the couch. "Who told you about your daddy in heaven?"

"God."

She looked up and caught the quick exchange of glances between Lara and Connor. "Does God talk to you often?"

Hunter nodded. "Sometimes."

"What else does he tell you?"

He tilted his head, then exchanged the blue crayon for a green one. "He told me I'll see my daddy soon."

Staring at the picture, Eva chose her words carefully. "Did he mean your daddy Connor?"

"No." Hunter paused to scratch his nose. "He meant my daddy in heaven. He's waiting for me."

Eva placed her hand on the boy's head as a weary sense of déjà vu swept over her.

"I don't understand," Lara whispered, her voice fainter than air. Her eyes blazed into Eva's with an extraordinary expression of alarm. "Tell me how you knew he was Michael's. Do you have the gift too?"

"I don't have a gift." Eva threaded her fingernails through the boy's shining hair. "But I do have a secret. Something tucked so neatly away that not even Michael knew it. It's the reason I didn't want you to have his child. I didn't want Michael to risk having children at all." She looked up, gave Connor a brief, distracted glance, and tried to smile. "I would have aborted Michael if abortion had been legal in those days."

"Good heavens, why?"

"Because I lost a son from dystonia." The words came slowly, dredged up from a place deep and dark. Her emotions barely dammed, Eva pressed her lips together. The fountain of sorrow welled and overflowed, and she felt the first tears, heavy and warm, roll down her cheeks.

"Ricky was born before Michael, and he was the only child I ever wanted. He was such a delight! Beautiful and blond, with eyes the color of a turquoise sea. He was six when I noticed the first sign. He started walking on his tiptoes, then sometimes on the outside of his shoes. The doctor said he'd grow out of it, but then Ricky started twitching at odd times, though he'd scarcely be aware of it. The pediatrician laughed at me until Ricky's arm drew up in something like a permanent spasm;

then he sent us to a specialist. The diagnosis was dystonia . . . . and there was no cure."

Connor put a protective arm around Hunter, who seemed oblivious to Eva's story. "That's awful, Mrs. Godfrey, but you can't be thinking our boy will go through the same thing."

Eva pulled a tissue from her purse, then dabbed at her eyes. "I don't know much about what they're doing today. I do know dystonia is a muscle disorder most adults manage to live with. But when Ricky fell ill, the doctor couldn't tell me of a single child with inherited dystonia who had survived past the age of fourteen."

She sighed, wrapped her fingers around the wadded tissue, and stared at her fist. "Ricky died thirteen months after the day I noticed him walking in that funny way. The muscles spasm repeatedly, until they wear out. When the muscles supporting the heart and lungs deteriorate, there's not much you can do."

Eva closed her eyes and wished she were a thousand miles away from this sorrow. Despair was seeping through the room like a fog; the only one unaffected was Hunter himself. When she lifted her gaze, he was still coloring, but Mr. Blythe, Lara, and Connor stared at her with ashen faces.

"It was the most miserable way to lose a child I can imagine," she whispered, dabbing at her streaming eyes. "That's why I didn't want you to have a baby, Lara. That's why I couldn't bring myself to come around when you were pregnant. I thought I couldn't bear to endure the pain again, that I couldn't lose another person I loved. I lost Ricky; I lost Michael; I lost my husband. I didn't want to fall in love with another child and face the possibility of losing him."

"Hunter?" Eva scarcely recognized Lara's ragged voice.

The boy didn't look up from his picture. "Yes, Mom?"

"Can you tell me if your grandma is telling the truth?"

He stopped coloring and smiled up at his mother. "Yeah. She is."

Lara crumpled like a wax figure tossed into a flame. Connor rose and drew her into his arms. Franklin Blythe's eyes filled with water as he mindlessly thumped his palm with the rolled-up transcript.

Eva stood and extended her hand to her grandson. "Hunter, why don't you and I see if we can find a candy machine. Does that sound like fun?"

"Sure!" The boy unfolded his legs and stood slowly, then placed his hand in hers. Eva rubbed her thumb over his soft skin, unable to prevent another memory from rising—Ricky had held her hand just this way, trusting her completely, yet she could do nothing to save him.

Eva caught Connor's gaze. "We'll be back in a few minutes."

He nodded silently, then turned toward his wife as his own tears began to flow.

Eva opened the door and left them to comfort each other.

∞

The click of the closing door unleashed a torrent in Lara's soul. She clung to Connor, unable to stem her tears, her rage, the utter feeling of hopelessness. "Why?" she cried when she could finally push words past the clot of emotion in her throat. "Why would God do this to us? He promised that Hunter would be a tree of life. I *know* he wanted me to have Hunter. I came here today ready to trust God, I *was* trusting God, but what did I do to deserve this? Just when I think there's a chance we can be a normal family, why would God want to take my son?"

She pulled out of Connor's embrace to better see his face. Lines of heartsickness and weariness had descended on his countenance, or had they been there all along? A muscle flicked at his jaw, but his eyes blazed with an inner fire.

"I don't know why God does the things he does." Connor leaned toward her until his forehead rested on hers and his voice filled the space between them. "But I trust him. Look what he's done! You prayed for your husband's child and you *received* your husband's child. You prayed for safety, and God kept you safe. You prayed for courage, and God granted it. You prayed for justice, and we're about to see Devin Sloane receive everything he deserves. You say God promised you a tree of life—how can you look at Hunter and think he is anything else?"

"I wanted a normal, healthy baby!"

"The perfect child?" Connor's voice held a note of gentle reproach. "Lara, there are no perfect children, no perfect moms, no perfect dads. We live in a fallen world. Heaven is the only place we'll find perfection."

She brought her hand to her mouth as truth crashed into her consciousness like surf hurling against a rocky cliff. Why, she'd been nearly as manipulative as Sloane and Braun! She had wanted Michael's baby, but she hadn't wanted to deal with the threat of cancer. She wanted perfection—the same thing Sloane wanted. She wanted the child without the risk, the silver lining without the cloud. Michael, without the cancer that had refined and strengthened his character as he prepared himself for eternity.

"Lara," Franklin's voice broke into her thoughts, "do not lose sight of the most important thing. Hunter is unlike any child I've ever met. He loves the Lord and seems to understand the heart of God. Surely he was sent here for a reason, and he was given to *you* for a purpose. God would not have allowed you to suffer all this"—he waved his hand, indicating their surroundings—"unless he wanted to use this situation to teach us something. How do we know that God's reasons—that *Hunter's* reasons for being—are not tied up in this trial?"

He hesitated, then looked at her with eyes that shone with peace. "The world has beaten a path to your doorstep over the last few weeks. I know you haven't enjoyed the media attention, but why not use it? Let Hunter attend the trial this afternoon. Perhaps the world needs to meet him."

Lara turned the thought over in her mind and considered everything that had happened. She had seen enough death to know it held no fear for those who believed in Jesus. She had seen enough pain to appreciate peace, and she had seen enough hate to cherish the love she felt from the men sitting with her.

After a long pause, she clutched Connor's hand and nodded at Franklin. "All right."

"Wait a minute"—Connor pushed his hair back from his forehead—"maybe we're jumping to conclusions. The things that happened to Ricky Godfrey don't have to happen to Hunter. That was two decades ago; maybe medicine has found a cure. And we don't know for sure that Eva is seeing this dystonia disease in Hunter; maybe it's nothing."

Lara shook her head, knowing that time was too precious to be distracted by false hope. "You heard Hunter yourself. He said Eva spoke the truth . . . and he said he was soon going to be with his daddy in heaven."

She laced Connor's fingers between her own. "Franklin is right. Tomorrow we can take Hunter to the specialist and do whatever we have to do, but today will never come again. We need to ask God about what we should do . . . and when Hunter comes back, I suppose we ought to ask him."

Franklin stroked his chin and studied the door leading to the judge's chambers. "I've never heard of a young child doing what I'm about to suggest to the judge, but little about this case has been routine. And, given the way Judge Weaver was impressed with our boy this morning, I have a feeling he just might allow it."

∞

They ate lunch at Pizza Town as Connor had promised, and then the small group ran the gauntlet of reporters to reenter the courthouse. At one o'clock, Lara couldn't help noticing that Franklin had guessed correctly—though Madison Jarvis and his team had grouped around the plaintiff's counsel table, Devin Sloane had not returned.

The door leading to the judge's chambers opened and the bailiff called, "All rise! This court is now in session, the Honorable Judge Harold Weaver presiding."

As she stood, Lara glanced over her shoulder for an instant—Franklin was right about something else, too. Smelling a decision, members of the media had crowded this room even more densely than yesterday. Several reporters were practically sitting in each other's laps.

Lara closed her eyes and breathed another prayer. They had left Eva and Hunter in the judge's office, knowing the bailiff could fetch them in a moment if the judge allowed Hunter to testify.

The judge took his seat, and the spectators jostled for positions. There were no preliminaries. The court reporter began tapping at her machine the instant Judge Weaver began to speak.

"Ladies and gentlemen, we've passed an interesting morning in my chambers. The most crucial development has been the admission of new evidence produced by the defendant's counsel. This evidence not only appears to clear Lara Godfrey O'Hara of any wrongdoing or breach of contract, but it thoroughly implicates the plaintiff, Mr. Sloane, in criminal charges."

"Your Honor!" Jarvis snapped to his feet. "We must object. We have no proof that this transcript is a verbatim record of the tape, and we cannot be certain the tape in evidence is Dr. Braun's deathbed confession."

"I listened to the tape during the break; I can vouch for the verbatim record." Judge Weaver nodded decisively. "And I'm going to let the police investigate its validity." He leaned forward, his brows lifting. "Mr. Jarvis, you seem to have lost your client. Did I not specifically state that I expected all parties to be present this afternoon?"

"You did, Your Honor, but Mr. Sloane had to handle an emergency. I'd like to ask for a postponement."

"Denied." The judge folded his hands. "Your client is hereby found in contempt of this court. I cannot imagine any emergency important enough to pull a loving, sincere parent away from a hearing to decide the fate of a child."

"Your Honor." From the defendant's table, Franklin Blythe stood. "In light of the new evidence, I'd like to file a motion for nonsuit. The plaintiff has failed to establish a prima-facie case because the evidence clearly shows that no contract existed between my client and Mr. Sloane. The plaintiff's case has no merit."

The judge's stern features softened as he turned his attention to the courtroom. "Ladies and gentlemen, I have found myself feeling a bit like Solomon as I have listened to the testimony in this case. Devin Sloane, the plaintiff, claims the child as his own, yet I have seen no evidence to indicate that he feels any sort of paternal love or affection for the boy. Lara Godfrey O'Hara, on the other hand, has demonstrated great sacrifice, love, and compassion. I am hereby granting the defendant's motion for nonsuit and awarding full custody of the child to Mrs. O'Hara and her husband."

A cry of relief broke from Lara's lips. Connor wrapped his arms around her as the gallery buzzed, but the judge slammed his gavel on the desk and regarded the spectators with a steely gaze.

When the gallery quieted, he folded his hands. "This case has been particularly disturbing, for not only has Mr. Sloane made a false accusation, but the defendant's counsel has uncovered proof of a criminal conspiracy. I am therefore turning over all evidence and the transcripts of this trial to the district attorney for his full investigation." Judge Weaver looked down at Sloane's lawyer with eyes from which the film of impartiality had been peeled away. "Mr. Jarvis, I know your client has great resources, but you should warn him not to leave the country. If he does, he may find himself unable to return."

This comment triggered more buzzing in the gallery. The judge rapped his desk, but Franklin's uplifted voice quieted the crowd.

"Your Honor!"

The judge looked down. "You have a problem with my decision, counselor?"

"No, Your Honor. But my client and I have discussed the child's welfare and we know there has been considerable public speculation about his unusual gifts. In order to safeguard the family's privacy from this day forward, we would like to broker a trade under the auspices of this court."

The judge sat back. "I don't follow you, Mr. Blythe."

"May I approach the bench?"

"Please do."

Franklin stepped out from behind the counsel table and walked toward the judge. "Considering the rumors and speculation that have surrounded this case," Franklin said in a lower voice that still carried to where Lara sat, "Hunter and his parents may never know a moment's peace. If you'll recall, sir, in sworn testimony the child was labeled a *prophet*."

The lawyer glanced back at the assembled reporters, most of whom regarded him with frank curiosity. "But, Your Honor," Franklin turned back to the bench, "if we could allow the boy to respond to a few questions in this controlled environment, perhaps the media's inquisitiveness could be satisfied. In exchange for the boy's participation, we'd like you to issue an injunction to all the media representatives assembled here. They are not to follow this family or contact them for a period of not less than two years."

The judge's gaze shifted and Lara flushed when his eyes met hers. "You would agree to this, Mrs. O'Hara?" he asked.

Lara gripped Connor's hand. The judge would never know how intensely she and Connor had agonized over Franklin's suggestion at lunch, but she had finally recognized the wisdom in it. If Hunter had been given to them to be a witness for Truth, he might never have a larger audience than the one crowded into this courtroom. The gesture would buy them two years of privacy, enough to see that Hunter lived the rest of his life in peace.

"Yes, Your Honor." Lara heard her voice ring clear and strong. "My husband and I have agreed. And Hunter is prepared."

The judged exhaled heavily into the microphone, then drummed his fingers on the desk. Finally, he nodded to his bailiff. "Bring the boy in," he ordered. As the bailiff exited, Weaver lifted an admonishing finger toward the assembled reporters. "No cameras, no intrusive questions, no queries designed to embarrass the boy or his parents. I'll take three questions from three different media outlets and that's it. And if a single reporter or photographer approaches this family within the next two years, you and your employers will find yourselves cited for being in contempt of this court's ruling. Someone will spend time in jail."

As the silence grew taut with anticipation, Lara could almost hear the reporters' brains humming. After hearing the testimony and rumors, they probably thought Hunter could pick winning lottery numbers or answer the profound mysteries of the universe. How would they react when they discovered that his gift was so simple . . . and so profound?

Poor things. They'd expose their own secrets if they weren't careful.

The door opened and the bailiff appeared, followed by Eva. Because of the tall bench, Lara couldn't see Hunter until Eva led him to the front of the courtroom. Limping slightly, he walked confidently into the room with his hand wrapped in his grandmother's.

When they paused before the tall bench, Judge Weaver stood and leaned forward so Hunter could see him. "Hello, Hunter. Do you remember me?"

Hunter nodded, his hair shining in the overhead lights.

"Would you like to sit up here on my desk? A few of these folks would like to ask you some questions."

Hunter's face brightened. "Okay."

A ripple of laughter moved through the crowd as Eva retreated and the bailiff lifted Hunter up. Lara looked away, feeling as if she'd abandoned her son to drowning. For six years she had done her best to hide Hunter's talents, but in the last hour her world had turned upside down.

What good could come out of this? Only God knew.

"That's good; you sit right there." The judge settled Hunter atop the bench, his blue-jeaned legs dangling over the edge. With his hands firmly on Hunter's belt, Weaver nodded toward the bailiff. "John, I'm going to hang on to this boy. Why don't you choose three well-behaved journalists and let them line up to ask their questions."

The frenzy that had threatened to erupt subsided as the reporters vied for the title of most polite. Grinning like a man holding four aces, the bailiff stalked forward. With one hand on his belt, he counted out three reporters. This trio, one woman and two men, scrambled toward the rail that separated the gallery from the front of the courtroom.

"All right, then." The judge cocked his head to look at Hunter. "You okay, sport?"

"I'm okay." Hunter clapped his hands and grinned—probably, Lara realized, at the fuss the adults were making over him.

"One more thing." The judge looked at the three reporters with a warning in his eyes. "You've probably heard stories about this child being some sort of psychic guru. I talked with the boy this morning and found him to be an ordinary but delightful child. His talent—if you can call it that—is discerning the truth. So watch your step."

Weaver nodded at the first reporter, a petite and fluffy blonde. The woman stepped forward and gave Hunter a sweet smile. "Hello. I'd like to know how you feel about Devin Sloane. What do you know about him?"

Lara closed her eyes. Aside from whatever information he'd picked up this morning, Hunter knew practically *nothing* about Sloane. Still, he'd heard a lot in the judge's chambers, so he could say anything . . .

Hunter looked down at his hands.

"Do you know Mr. Sloane?" the woman asked helpfully.

"I saw him this morning." Hunter lifted his elbows as he twisted his hands. "He told a lie to the judge."

The reporters began to scribble. "Anything else?" the blonde asked.

Hunter nodded. "God loves Devin Sloane very much."

The blonde opened her mouth as if she would ask a follow-up question, but the judge waved her away. "Next?"

The second reporter, a mustached fellow with a shock of woolly brown hair, lifted his pen in Hunter's direction. "Jeff Thomas, ABC News," he recited offhandedly. He looked at Hunter and smiled. "Hi, kiddo. If a tree falls in the woods with nobody there to hear it, does it make a sound?"

Hunter's eyes went wide, and then he held his tummy and giggled. "You're silly," he crowed, bringing a smile to the judge's face. "Of course it does. God is always there. He hears *everything*."

Lara let the sound of Hunter's delight wash through her, his happiness shivering her skin like the caress of a spirit. The world was so hungry for simple truth. Thousands of people would be happy to set their problems and confusion aside to hear Hunter assure them that God loved, he heard, and he cared.

Unfortunately, as many thousands would line up to debunk or destroy him. Evil would resist truth as long as God allowed the world to continue in its fallen condition.

The third reporter stepped forward, his hands clasped at his waist. He tilted his head and looked at Hunter with narrowed eyes. "Good afternoon, young man. Can you tell me my name?"

Hunter shook his head, an uncertain smile on his face.

"All right. My name is Randy Higgs."

Hunter's mouth twitched with the need to smile. "No, it's not." The reporter laughed. "Okay. My name is Ed Munger."

Hunter nodded. "Yeah."

"What I want to know is—how do you do it? How can you tell when people are lying? Do you see something in their faces? Hear something in their voices?"

Lara tensed when Hunter's face emptied of expression for an instant. She'd often wondered the same thing, but never considered asking Hunter how he did it. She might as well ask a bird how he flew . . .

"I just know," Hunter finally answered, his eyes roving over the courtroom. "Like the sun knows to go down at night and the stars know to come out. God made things the way they are. He doesn't know how to lie, and it hurts him when people do." His gaze fell upon Lara, and her heart melted when he smiled. "God loves everyone; he made everyone; he understands everyone. He wants everyone to know him, but they don't listen to the truth. There are too many lies."

He halted and bit his lip.

"Is that all you want to say?" the judge asked.

Hunter nodded.

"Then you can go sit with your mom and dad."

The bailiff helped Hunter down from the bench, and then Lara held out her arms. Hunter ran to her and buried his head in the curve of her neck. She held him as the judge shared his final thoughts.

"Ladies and gentlemen," the judge said, his voice ringing with depth and authority, "in considering various aspects of this case, I am reminded that humankind has always sought to explain the inexplicable. We can command what we can understand, so we attempt to find answers for things that have sprung from the hand of heaven. Do not speculate about this child; do not search for answers in science or psychology. This boy is a gift from God, and he deserves to live with his parents in peace."

Lara closed her eyes and heard the sharp report of the judge's gavel.

The trial was over.

chapter 36

Ten months later, Lara sat beside Hunter's hospital bed and waited for her son's body to stop spasming. He usually twitched and trembled until he dozed, but his muscles often spasmed for hours before they would relax to the point of sleep.

The act of watching him exhausted Lara.

Eva had indeed told the truth. At first the doctors tried to tell Lara that her son suffered from mitochondrial disease or muscular dystrophy, but a DNA test confirmed Eva's diagnosis. On chromosome nine, the doctor found the markers indicating the presence of a gene known as DYT1, associated with childhood-onset dystonia. Further tests indicated that Michael's DNA had contained the same markers.

Lara accepted this news in silence, knowing that anger and despair were hurtful, wasteful emotions. If Helmut Braun had completed his genetic screening of Michael's DNA before Sloane tempted him, would her life have been better? No. If she had known about the cancer and the dystonia, she might have decided not to have a baby, and Hunter would never have been born. But God wanted Hunter to manifest his unique gift in her life, and Lara could not trade her pain for emptiness.

As the weeks passed she silently listened to the doctors' hope-filled speeches, then closed her eyes when Hunter grunted his disagreement of the physician's prognoses. She could not hide the truth from him, for he could discern between a painted promise and honest truth. None of the doctors wanted to admit that dystonia, a disease with which adults could survive, seemed intent upon taking her son's life.

Last week the doctors had to put Hunter on a respirator for a while, and Lara knew it was only a matter of time. When the muscles supporting the heart and lungs gave out, Hunter would go home.

He had lost 50 percent of his body weight, then gained nearly thirty pounds of water weight as the doctors tried various drugs to stop the seizures that caught him every five or ten minutes. Eva was right about another thing—this was a terrible way to die, yet Hunter never complained. He spoke nearly every day of going to see his other daddy; lately he had begun to add that Jesus waited for him.

Lara believed it.

Last month, a new hospice worker had stopped by the house to visit. The woman glanced through Hunter's scrapbook, read the headlines that had appeared right after the trial (*Truth-Telling Boy Says God Loves Everyone, Devin Sloane Implicated in Hospital Malpractice*), and professed amazement at the stack of letters that had arrived after Hunter's impromptu press conference.

"So many letters," she murmured, studying the bundles stacked in Hunter's room. "What did all those people want?"

Lara shrugged. "Some wanted Hunter to foretell the future; others wanted him to clear up some misunderstanding from the past. We got several from convicts who wanted him to go to court and clear their names—we actually considered letting Hunter participate in one of those interviews, but by that time he was suffering." She pushed her hair out of her eyes and smiled. "Amazing, isn't it? So many people seek the truth, not because *it* is lost, but because they are. Hunter can't help them, but God can. That's what we've been trying to tell people."

After making polite, forced conversation for a few more moments, the hospice volunteer left a basket of puzzles and stood. After stepping onto the front porch, she turned: "So—was it worth it? All the trouble you went through?"

Lara understood the curiosity behind the question. She had jeopardized her life and her future in that mad rush to Florida; even now she couldn't return to that state because she had technically committed fraud each time she signed a false name to a document. She had risked everything to save Hunter, and now, despite her best efforts, she was losing him.

"You're not a mother, are you?"

The girl dropped her eyes before Lara's steady gaze. "No."

"If and when you become one, you'll understand."

Lara reached up and fingered the gold necklace around her neck. A package with no return address had arrived in the mail a few weeks after the trial. Lara had opened the box and lifted out a chain from which six gold rings dangled. Hanging from the chain, the rings created a jumble of golden hoops, but one afternoon Lara discovered that she could slide the rings off the chain and lay them flat, one inside the other. Like a puzzle they fit together, rings within rings.

That's when the enclosed note made sense. A feminine hand had written, *Circles within circles, remember? I've found my way free to forgiveness. Thank you, Lara, for my son.*

Those words came back to her now as she reached through the bed rail for Hunter's hand. His fingers, which had once been so pliable, were now fixed and rigid, bound by corded muscles that would not relax. Yet Hunter's eyes were still his own, and when she looked up, they were fixed on her.

"Mom?"

"Yes?"

"Jesus is waiting for me."

"Hang on, buddy." Holding tight to his hand, Lara bent and smoothed his cheek. "I called Daddy and Grandma; they're on their way. I know they'll want to say good-bye."

Hunter couldn't answer. As his eyes rolled back in his head, Lara braced herself for another seizure. She reached for the gauze-coated mouth blade, placed it between his jaws, then turned him on his side as his muscles revolted.

Hurry, Connor and Eva, please. We need to let him go.

epilogue

On Hunter's birthday, Lara gripped the bouquet and waited for Connor to open her door. She had begun to gain weight much earlier in this pregnancy, and, at seven months, she felt clumsy and immobile. Were it not for the pediatric patients who needed her, she doubted if she could have summoned the energy to pull herself out of bed.

Connor opened the door and stepped toward her, gallantly offering both hands. Squinting into the bright winter sun, Lara grinned and allowed him to pull her up and out of the car.

A brisk wind breathed through the trees that canopied the cemetery, and Lara shivered in the heavy warmth of her coat. Walking briskly, she lengthened her stride to match Connor's, and allowed him to take her hand as they negotiated the brick walkway that led to the oak.

They had chosen this spot because it overlooked Mirror Lake, the park, and the townhouse. Though it was a winding half hour's drive from their new home, Lara felt that Hunter belonged here, next to Michael and the lake he had loved to paint. Whenever she thought she might drown in a fresh wave of grief, she thought of Hunter and Michael and found comfort in the knowledge that they were together.

There was no headstone on Hunter's grave, only a dignified bronze marker and a two-foot statue of a boy in a baseball cap. Lara stopped by the statue for an instant, summoned up the image of Hunter before the disease had gripped him, then knelt to place the bouquet beside the marker.

She tried to get up, but rocked forward instead, her hand hitting the ground. Connor knelt beside her in an instant, a rueful smile on his face. "Sorry," he said. "I should have been quicker."

"No. Pregnant women shouldn't kneel on uneven ground. I should have known better."

They stood in silence for a moment, their hands intertwined, then Connor cleared his throat. "He would have been eight today. Do you ever think what would have happened if he had—"

She lifted her free hand to his lips. "Of course I do. And I think God was merciful to take him when he did. Hunter would be an oddity, and not even Judge Weaver could keep the press from him forever. We would have no chance at a normal life . . . and neither would our baby."

He slipped his arm around her and held her close. The shadows under the bare forsythia were already cold and blue; sunset was not far away.

Strange, how grief felt like love. She smiled as unbidden memories poured into her thoughts, jostling each other like rowdy little boys. Hunter at play, Hunter asleep, Hunter speaking simple truths the world longed to hear . . .

She would never stop missing him, nor would Connor, but her memories would never lose their luster. Her sense of loss now went far beyond tears, but occasionally, when one of the rowdy little memories slipped into her thoughts, water would spring to her eyes in an over-flow of feeling.

"You know," she whispered, verbalizing thoughts she'd been formulating for months, "I've been thinking about those poems people always read at children's funerals—you know, those stories that imply heaven needed another angel, so God took a child to fill that spot. I've always thought those stories were overly sentimental, at other times I thought they were simply silly. Humans aren't angels and never will be, and God certainly wouldn't take a child just to populate heaven."

Connor squeezed her shoulder. "I've heard those things too."

"But lately I've been thinking about God and kids—do you remember when we talked about Jesus as a child? I realized John the Baptist was special too. The Holy Spirit touched him even before he was born, and God had a unique purpose for his life. That's when I began to understand that the purpose of living—no matter how short or long life is—is to find and follow God's will. Hunter understood that from the moment I told him about Jesus. His faith was always stronger than mine."

"You've always been strong, Lara."

"Strong-willed, maybe. Not always strong in faith." She reached up to stroke her husband's cheek. "I thought God gave me Hunter so I could protect him. My motherhood became everything to me—I valued it even above you, Con, and I'm sorry for the pain I caused you. But in that courtroom, when Franklin asked the judge if Hunter could testify, I realized God didn't want me to hide my son; he wanted me to *share* him. If I wanted him to be what God intended him to be, I had to let go."

She looked away and caressed the little boy's statue with her eyes. "That was harder than saying good-bye in the hospital."

Connor held her for a long moment, then caught her hand and pressed it to his lips. "At least other children won't have to suffer like he did. The judgment will help with the research. Maybe they'll find a cure soon."

Lara smiled in the calm strength of hope. After Sloane had been found guilty of arranging the murders at the Women's Clinic and committing fraud and malpractice at his hospital, Franklin Blythe had filed a civil suit on behalf of Lara and the families of every pediatric patient. The jury sent back a verdict for the plaintiffs, awarding more than forty million dollars from Sloane's estate. Several of the grief-stricken parents turned their portions of the settlement over to Lara after they learned of the O'Haras' plans to invest in Sloane's defunct hospital. The Hunter Godfrey Center for Children would work not only to improve the future, but to enrich the life of every parent and child who passed through its doors.

After the trial, Eva Godfrey gave up her club activities and threw her energies into raising money for legitimate research. As she traveled to educate others about dystonia and other genetic diseases, she continued to spread Hunter's simple message of truth: God loves everyone . . . and wants them to know him.

Connor pressed his lips to Lara's hair. "Are you cold? The wind is picking up, and the forecast calls for snow."

Lara lifted her eyes to the tiny bit of remaining blue sky and sent a smile winging toward heaven. "Let's go home."

acknowledgments

No book is ever completed without contributions from others, and I found that the library just couldn't provide the real-life experience I gleaned from professionals. To that end, I'd like to thank attorney Chuck Holloway and physician Jack Lipps for plowing through the manuscript, Dr. Barry Leber for allowing me to buttonhole him in the church gymnasium, and nurse Gaynel Wilt, who never failed to find an answer to my bizarre queries.

I owe these folks a debt of gratitude for letting me pepper them with questions at odd hours. Any errors of legal or medical procedure are mine, not theirs.

I would also like to express my appreciation to Lind and Pam Krenzke, who freely shared the story of their dear sons, Bobby and Eric. Without their help, I would never have heard of dystonia.

Blessings to you, my friends.

Discussion Questions for Readers' Groups

1. Angela Hunt originally wrote this book in 1998 and updated it in 2005. Are the issues as timely today as they were in the late nineties? What, if anything, has changed?

2. Given the story of the "Lying Baptists" and the "Truthful Baptists," which camp would you belong to? Do you think there is a proper time and/or place for lying?

3. Can you think of a famous lie that has changed or influenced history? (Consider politicians, religious leaders, and examples from your own history.) How would things be different if truth had prevailed?

4. Devin Sloane held a theory of "devolution," i.e., that mankind is regressing, not progressing. Do you agree with his theory? What might be the cause of this regression?

5. Do you think the characters of Lara, Connor, Eva, Hunter, and Devin were believable? How could you relate (or not relate) to them? Who was your favorite character?

6. Even though Lara loves Connor, after they are married she finds it difficult to completely trust him with Hunter. Have you seen this attitude in other blended families or remarriages? How does it help or hinder the new family?

7. What themes do you think Hunt meant to stress through the story? What will you remember most about it?

8. Hunt has also dealt with the clash between science and ethics in her book *The Pearl*. If you have read that book, how is it similar to *The Truth Teller*? How do the stories and themes differ?

9. Often a reader will be impressed by passages or snatches of dialogue that come to mean more than the author intended. Did any particular passages mean something special to you?